R. Gupta's®

POPULAR MASTER GUIDE

BSF

Border Security Force

CONSTABLE

TRADESMAN

- Cobbler • Tailor • Carpenter • Cook • Water Carrier
- Washer man • Barber • Sweeper • Waiter

Recruitment Exam

2020 EDITION

Ramesh Publishing House, New Delhi

Published by
O.P. Gupta *for* Ramesh Publishing House

Admin. Office
12-H, New Daryaganj Road, Opp. Officers' Mess
New Delhi-110002 ℐ 23261567, 23275224, 23275124

E-mail: info@rameshpublishinghouse.com
Website: www.rameshpublishinghouse.com

Showroom
● Balaji Market, Nai Sarak, Delhi-6 ℐ 23253720, 23282525
● 4457, Nai Sarak, Delhi-6, ℐ 23918938

Book Code: R-2035

ISBN: 978-93-88642-30-9

HSN Code: 49011010

SELECTION PROCEDURE

- The Written Test for 100 marks containing 100 questions (qualifying marks 35% for Gen Category & Ex-Servicemen and 33% for SC/ST/OBC) will consist of only OMR based objective type multiple choice questions to be answered using a Blue or Black ball point pen only.

- The question paper will consist of one objective type paper containing 100 questions carrying 100 marks with the following composition:

S. No.	Subject	Number of Questions	Maximum Marks	Duration Time allowed
1.	General Awareness/ General Knowledge	25	25	
2.	Knowledge of Elementary Mathematics	25	25	2 hours
3.	Analytical Aptitude and Ability to observe the Distinguished Patterns	25	25	
4.	Basic Knowledge of the candidates in English/Hindi	25	25	

CONTENTS

Model Paper 1-16

● **GENERAL AWARENESS/ GENERAL KNOWLEDGE** 1-72
Indian History and Culture; Indian Polity and Constitution; Geography of India and World; Indian Economy; Science; Science and Technology; Awards and Honours; Games and Sports; Miscellaneous.

● **ELEMENTARY MATHEMATICS** 1-112
Arithmetic—Number System; HCF and LCM; Simplification; Surds and Indices; Ratio, Proportion & Partnership; Average; Percentage; Profit & Loss; Simple & Compound Interest; Time & Work; Time & Distance; Mensuration.
Algebra—Set Theory; Simplification & Factorization; Linear & Quadratic equation; Logarithm; Geometry; Trigonometry.

● **ANALYTICAL APTITUDE AND ABILITY TO** 1-72
OBSERVE THE DISTINGUISHED PATTERNS
Series; Finding the Wrong or Superfluous Number; Analogy; Finding the Odd One Out; Questions Relating to Clocks and Calendars; Coding and Decoding; Questions Based on Relationship; Questions Related to Directions; Arranging the Letters to make Meaningful Words; Arranging Words in their Natural Order; Miscellaneous; Place Arrangement; Diagrammatic Puzzles; Cubes and Dices; Rows and Ranks.

● **ENGLISH** 1-96
Test of English Language; Spotting The Errors; Some Fundamental Rules for Correction; Fill in the Blanks; Comprehension; Arrangement of Parts of Sentences; Synonyms and Antonyms Words; Close Test; Practice Paper; Previous Test Papers.

● ● ●

BSF—Constable (Tradesman)

• Cobbler • Tailor • Carpenter • Cook • Water Carrier • Washer man • Barber • Sweeper • Waiter

Recruitment Exam

1. The President of India holds office for a period of:
   A. 6 years
   B. 5 years
   C. 4 years
   D. 7 years

2. The judges of the Supreme Court are appointed by the:
   A. Prime Minister of India
   B. Speaker of the Lok Sabha
   C. President of India
   D. Ministry of Law & Justice

3. Currency notes in India are printed and supplied by the:
   A. SEBI
   B. FICCI
   C. IFCI
   D. Reserve Bank of India

4. The smallest planets is:
   A. Venus
   B. Mercury
   C. Jupiter
   D. Earth

5. Which planet is known as a blue planet?
   A. Mercury
   B. Venus
   C. Jupiter
   D. Earth

6. Which is the crop of the longest duration?
   A. Gram
   B. Millet
   C. Barley
   D. Sugarcane

7. About .... of the earth's surface is covered by water.
   A. 60%
   B. 70%
   C. 79%
   D. 55%

8. Capital of which of the following states of India is not situated on the Bank of river?
   A. Bihar
   B. Jammu & Kashmir
   C. Uttar Pradesh
   D. Madhya Pradesh

9. Who was the first Muslim President of India?
   A. Dr. A.P.J. Abdul Kalam
   B. Fakhruddin Ali Ahmad
   C. Dr. Zakir Hussain
   D. None of these

10. Which state enjoys a special status Under Article 370 of the constitution?
    A. Jammu & Kashmir
    B. Himachal Pradesh
    C. Andhra Pradesh
    D. Arunachal Pradesh

11. The Konark temple in Odisha is dedicated to:
    A. Lord Indra
    B. Lord Rama

C. The Sun God
D. None of these

12. The Kanha National Park, tiger reserve, is located in:
A. Uttar Pradesh
B. Madhya Pradesh
C. Rajasthan
D. Punjab

13. Supreme Command of all the three wings of the armed forces is vested in the:
A. Prime Minister of India
B. President of India
C. Chief of Army Staff
D. Defence Minister

14. In size, India is .... largest country in the world.
A. seventh   B. second
C. third   D. tenth

15. Telegraph was invented by:
A. Enhorse   B. Morse
C. Graham Bell   D. Rontgen

16. Famous Leaning Tower of Pisa is in:
A. Italy   B. Greece
C. Cyprus   D. Turkey

17. China's sorrow is:
A. Hwang Ho
B. Tigris
C. Irewadi
D. Cantaon

18. Jojila pass is in:
A. Rajasthan
B. Jammu & Kashmir
C. Uttar Pradesh
D. Punjab

19. Bangladesh came into existence in December 1971. Formerly it was known as:
A. East Bengal
B. Banga
C. Brahmadesh
D. East Pakistan

20. The largest in the world in respect of Area is:
A. China   B. India
C. Russia   D. USA

21. 'Silly point' word is connected with:
A. Tennis   B. Cricket
C. Hockey   D. Football

22. In which game the term 'Tee' is used?
A. Chess   B. Golf
C. Billiards   D. Snooker

23. Charak was a renowned:
A. Historian
B. Physician
C. Minister
D. Astronomer

24. Who founded the Indian National Congress?
A. W.C. Bannerjee
B. A.O. Hume
C. Sardar Patel
D. Subhash Chandra Bose

25. Olympic Games are held every ....
A. 2 years
B. 4 years
C. 5 years
D. 6 years

26. The ratio of 25 cm to 3 m is:
A. 25 : 3
B. 3 : 25
C. 1 : 12
D. 12 : 1

27. The sum of two numbers is 70 and their difference is 16. The value of greater number is:
A. 27 B. 43
C. 86 D. 54

28. If 76 is divided in to the ratios of 7, 5, 3 and 4 then the smallest part will be:
A. 14 B. 18
C. 32 D. 12

29. Two numbers are in the ratio of 12 and 19. The sum of these two numbers is 217, the value of smaller number is:
A. 81 B. 64
C. 70 D. 84

30. If $\dfrac{x}{y} = \dfrac{5}{2}$, then find the value of
$$\dfrac{8x + 9y}{8x + 2y}.$$

A. $\dfrac{29}{22}$ B. $\dfrac{17}{16}$

C. $\dfrac{22}{29}$ D. $\dfrac{16}{17}$

31. The value of $(100)^\circ$ is equal to:
A. 0 B. 10
C. 1 D. 100

32. Third power of 4 is equivalent to:
A. 64 B. 81
C. 12 D. 49

33. What is the difference between the third power of 2 and the second power of 3?
A. 2 B. 5
C. 3 D. 1

34. Find $12\dfrac{1}{2}\%$ of ₹ 400.
A. ₹ 25 B. ₹ 50
C. ₹ 75 D. ₹ 100

35. The value of 10% of 250 – 5% of 280 is:
A. 8 B. 10
C. 11 D. 12

36. If 75% of a number is 15, then the number is:
A. 20 B. 25
C. 40 D. 35

37. Ram bought an old Car for ₹ 5200 and spent ₹ 1700 on its repairs. He sold the Car for ₹ 8200. State how much profit did he make?
A. ₹ 1500 B. ₹ 1300
C. ₹ 1200 D. ₹ 3000

38. A rectangular garden is 8 hectometres long and 6 decametres broad. How long will a man take to go round it once, if he walk 4 decametres in one minute?
A. 28 minutes B. 33 minutes
C. 43 minutes D. 34 minutes

39. A train runs at a speed of 36 km/hr. How many metres will it run in 36 seconds?
A. 220 m B. 300 m
C. 440 m D. 360 m

40. A contractor built a tank on a piece of land 45 m long and 34 m broad. He got paid at the rate of ₹ 625 per square metre. How much money did he receive for the whole work?
A. ₹ 9,56,250   B. ₹ 9,23,560
C. ₹ 9,56,320   D. ₹ 9,30,562

41. A bus makes seven rounds of a certain place. 52 persons can sit in it and 8 can stand. Bus is full in every round. Find out the total number of persons who travel in the all seven rounds.
A. 220   B. 320
C. 420   D. 240

42. The cost of 5 tables is equal to the cost of 7 chairs. If the cost of 1 table is ₹ 210. Find the cost of one chair.
A. ₹ 150   B. ₹ 140
C. ₹ 160   D. ₹ 145

43. A family consists of 8 members. Their total income is ₹ 900 per month. What is the average monthly income of each person?
A. ₹ 120.50   B. ₹ 112.50
C. ₹ 122.50   D. ₹ 102.50

44. 40 boys can do a piece of work in 6 days. In how many days can 10 boys do the same work?
A. 36 days   B. 18 days
C. 24 days   D. 30 days

45. A train is running at the speed of 72 km/hr and passes an electric pole in 15 seconds. Find the length of the train.
A. 250 km   B. 300 km
C. 350 km   D. 275 km

46. A train 300 m long is running at a speed of 54 km/hr. If it takes 40 seconds to cross a bridge, then find the length of the bridge.
A. 250 m   B. 300 m
C. 325 m   D. 350 m

47. The perimeter of a rectangle is 28 cm. If one side of the rectangle is 8 cm, then find its area.
A. 48 cm²   B. 40 cm²
C. 58 cm²   D. 50 cm²

48. A room is in the form of square whose each side is 14 metres is to be paved with marbles. If the total cost of paving is ₹ 5880, then find the cost of marble per square metre.
A. ₹ 50   B. ₹ 40
C. ₹ 30   D. ₹ 25

49. A boy cycles from home to school and back every day except on Sundays. If his school is 6 km away from his home, how many miles does he cycles in a week?
A. 80 miles   B. 45 miles
C. 60 miles   D. 77 miles

50. An Isosceles triangle has two sides with length x. The third side is half of x. What is its perimeter?
A. $2\frac{1}{2}x$ B. $5x$
C. $3x$ D. $4\frac{1}{2}x$

Directions (Qs. 51 and 52): *For each of the following questions, four words have been given of which three are alike in someway and one is different. Find the odd word.*

51. A. Cow   B. Buffalo
     C. Goat   D. Hen

52. A. Coffee   B. Curd
     C. Milk   D. Tea

Directions (Qs. 53 and 54): *In each of the questions below, find out the correct answer from the given alternatives.*

53. If in a certain language EXIST is coded as ESIXT, how is PLUTO coded in that code?
     A. OLUTP   B. PTUOL
     C. PULTO   D. PTULO

54. If in a certain language CURTAIN is coded as CAITURN, how is HILLOCK coded in that code?
     A. HOCLILK   B. HCOLLIK
     C. HKLIOC   D. HOLLICK

Directions (Qs. 55 and 56): *Complete the following series.*

55. 4, 8, 16, ?, ?, 128
     A. 30, 38   B. 64, 32
     C. 32, 64   D. 40, 48

56. 24, 22, 20, ?, ?
     A. 16, 14   B. 18, 16
     C. 20, 18   D. 20, 19

57. 'Bank' is related to 'Money' in the same way as 'Transport' is related to:
     A. Goods   B. Road
     C. Movement   D. Speed

58. 'Tree' is related to 'Root' in the same way as Smoke is related to:
     A. Cigarette
     B. Fire
     C. Heat
     D. Chimney

59. If "+" means "÷"; "÷" means "–"; "–"means "×" and "×" means "+", what will be the value of $8 + 2 \div 3 - 4 \times 6 = ?$
     A. -2
     B. $-15\dfrac{1}{3}$
     C. 12
     D. 15

60. If "+" means "÷"; "×" means "–"; "÷"means "×" and "–" means "+", what will be the value of the following expression?
$9 + 3 \div 4 - 8 \times 2 = ?$
     A. $6\dfrac{3}{4}$ B. $-1\dfrac{3}{4}$
     C. $-6\dfrac{1}{4}$ D. 18

Directions (Qs. 61 and 62): *Select odd one out.*

61.

     A.   B.   C.   D.

62.

     A.   B.   C.   D.

Directions (Qs. 63 and 64): *Second figure in the first unit of problem figure bear a certain relationship to the first figure. Locate the answer figure bears the same relationship to the first figure of second unit.*

63. Problem Figures

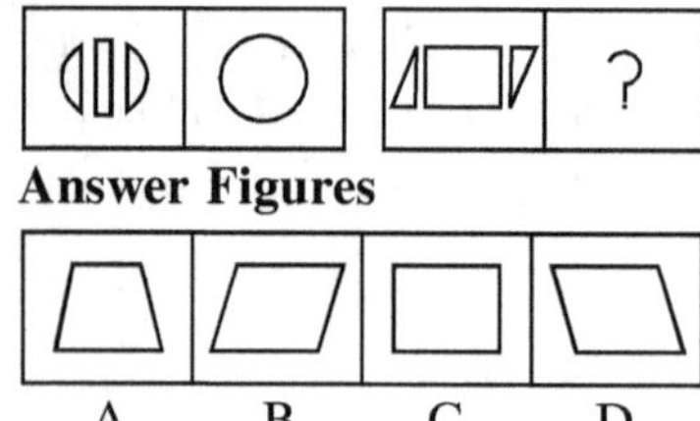

Answer Figures

A.   B.   C.   D.

64. Problem Figures

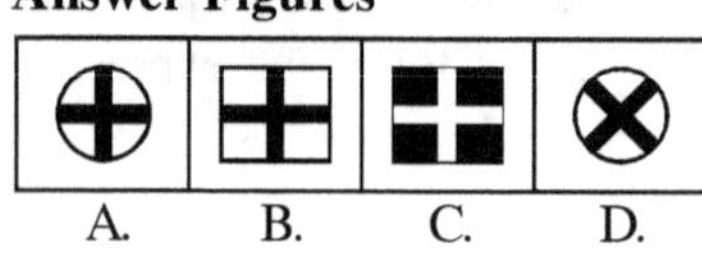

Answer Figures

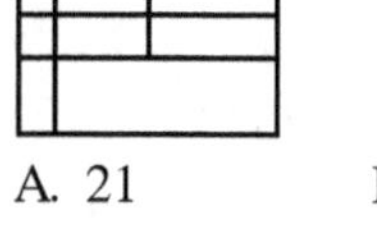

A.   B.   C.   D.

65. The number of rectangles in this figure are.

A. 21   B. 24
C. 23   D. 25

66. Mini is to the right of Rajni but to the left of Ananta. Saya is to the right of Mini but to the left of Jaya. Who is on the extreme left if all the girls are facing North?
A. Jaya   B. Mini
C. Rajni   D. Saya

67. Dingi runs 40 km towards North then turns right and runs 50 km. He turns right and runs 30 km, and once again turns right and runs 50 km. How far is he from his starting point?
A. 90 km   B. 50 km
C. 10 km   D. 5 km

68. A lady said, "The person standing there is my grandfather's only son's daughter". How is the lady related to the standing person?
A. Sister   B. Mother
C. Aunt   D. Cousin

69. 1.12.91 is the first Sunday. Which is the fourth Tuesday of December 91?
A. 31.12.91   B. 24.12.91
C. 17.12.91   D. 26.12.91

70. Jaya ranks 5th in a class of 53. What is her rank from the bottom in the class?
A. 49th   B. 48th
C. 47th   D. 50th

71. In a chess tournament each of six players will play every other player exactly once. How many matches will be played during the tournament?
A. 12   B. 15
C. 30   D. 36

Directions (Qs. 72): *Which set of letters will come in the place of question mark?*

72. MEQI : JUOD : : ANIW : ?
A. RUKE   B. URIA
C. EUIO   D. PTRE

73. Which letter is midway between G and S?
A. L   B. N
C. M   D. No letter

74. If 15 horses eat 15 bags of gram in 15 days, in how many days will one horse eat one bag of grain?
A. 15 days
B. 1/15 days
C. 1 day
D. 30 days

75. Mamuni went to the movies nine days ago. She goes to the movies only on Thursday. What day of the week is today?
A. Sunday
B. Tuesday
C. Thursday
D. Saturday

Directions (Qs. 76 to 78) : *Spell the word correctly.*

76. Gram ....
A. mor   B. mar
C. mer   D. mre

77. Indivi ....
A. dual   B. duel
C. dull   D. dule

78. Emba ....
A. rrass   B. rass
C. rras   D. rase

Directions (Qs. 79 to 81) : *Choose the correct option.*

79. .... I was twelve I left my village.
A. Where   B. When
C. Why   D. How

80. Don't talk on a mobile phone .... driving.
A. while   B. why
C. where   D. what

81. I opened the window .... it was very hot.
A. but   B. so
C. or   D. because

Directions (Qs. 82 to 84) : *Fill in the blanks with the suitable alternatives.*

82. I don't have .... money in my pocket.
A. any   B. some
C. little   D. a little

83. I want to read .... more books.
A. the little   B. some
C. a little   D. any

84. Raj is .... intelligent than Rohan.
A. much   B. very
C. more   D. most

Directions (Qs. 85 to 87) : *Choose the correct answer.*

85. He's .... doctor of law.
A. an   B. the
C. a   D. one

86. .... she like chocolates?
A. Does   B. Has
C. Is   D. Do

87. The student is .... papers.
A. writing
B. writes
C. write
D. is wrote

Directions (Qs. 88 to 92) : *Read the passage and answer the questions that follow:*

There are two types of camels in the world. One has a single hump, and the other has two. The dromedary camel has a single hump, and has domesticated in Arabia over 4,000 years ago. They are also found in North Africa, India, Pakistan and Australia. The size of the hump varies, becoming smaller and leaning to one side during times of starvation.

The lips of dromedary camels are thick to allow them to eat coarse and thorny desert plants. Their legs keep their bodies high off the ground to avoid the baking heat of the desert's surface.

Bactrian camels have two humps, and are found in the deserts of Central Asia. They are extremely adept at withstanding wide variations in temperature–from freezing cold to blistering heat. They can survive without water for months at a time, but when water is available, they may drink up to 57 litres at once. When well fed, the humps are plump and erect.

88. What types of camel are there in the world?
A. Dromedary
B. Bactrian
C. Both (A) and (B)
D. None of the above

89. Single hump camels are found in ....
A. India and Pakistan
B. India and Sri Lanka
C. Pakistan and Nepal
D. Australia and Nepal

90. One unique characteristics of Dromedary camel to avoid the baking heat of the desert's surface is
A. thick lips
B. thick hump
C. long neck
D. long legs

91. Bactrian camels have .... humps.
A. one
B. two
C. three
D. four

92. The feature that make Bactrian camels unique is
A. Adept at various temperatures
B. Adept only at freezing temperature
C. Adept only at hot temperature
D. None of the above

Directions (Qs. 93 to 96) : *Select correct meaning of the following sentences.*

93. A person who plays the piano.
A. cellist
B. flautist
C. organist
D. pianist

94. One who writes dramas.
A. drama queen
B. artist
C. playwright
D. actor

95. One who is trained in the art of cooking.
 A. cook
 B. kitchen king
 C. chef
 D. cooker

96. A medicine given for building immunity against diseases.
 A. injection
 B. medicine
 C. therapy
 D. vaccination

Directions (Qs. 97 to 100) : *Choose the correct tense form from the options given below.*

97. Oily food is not good for health.
 A. Simple present tense
 B. Simple past tense
 C. Simple future tense
 D. Past perfect tense

98. I have just reached office.
 A. Present perfect tense
 B. Past perfect tense
 C. Simple past tense
 D. Past perfect continuous tense

99. The carnival will last for 10 days.
 A. Simple present tense
 B. Simple past tense
 C. Simple future tense
 D. Past perfect tense

100. When he stepped inside, he was crying.
 A. Past continuous tense
 B. Simple past tense
 C. Both (A) and (B)
 D. None of them

ANSWERS

1	2	3	4	5	6	7	8	9	10
B	C	D	B	D	D	B	D	C	A

11	12	13	14	15	16	17	18	19	20
C	B	B	A	B	A	A	B	D	C

21	22	23	24	25	26	27	28	29	30
B	B	B	B	B	C	B	D	D	A

31	32	33	34	35	36	37	38	39	40
C	A	D	B	C	A	B	C	D	A

41	42	43	44	45	46	47	48	49	50
C	A	B	C	B	B	A	C	B	A

51	52	53	54	55	56	57	58	59	60
D	B	D	A	C	B	A	B	A	D

61	62	63	64	65	66	67	68	69	70
D	C	B	A	C	C	C	A	B	A

71	72	73	74	75	76	77	78	79	80
B	B	C	A	D	B	A	A	B	A
81	82	83	84	85	86	87	88	89	90
D	A	B	C	C	A	A	C	A	D
91	92	93	94	95	96	97	98	99	100
B	A	D	C	C	D	A	A	C	A

EXPLANATORY ANSWERS

26. Ratio of 25 cm : 3 m

$$= \frac{25}{300} = \frac{1}{12}$$

$$= 1 : 12.$$

27. Let numbers are x and y

$\because$ $x + y = 70$ ...(i)

and $x - y = 16$ ...(ii)

Adding equations (i) and (ii), we get

$$2x = 86$$

$\Rightarrow$ $x = 43$

$\therefore$ $y = 70 - 43$

$$= 27$$

Hence the value of greater number

$$= 43.$$

28. Sum of ratios $= 7x + 5x + 3x + 4x$

$$= 19x$$

$$19x = 76$$

$\Rightarrow$ $x = \dfrac{76}{19}$

$$= 4$$

$\therefore$ Smallest part $= 3x$

$$= 3 \times 4$$

$$= 12.$$

29. $12x + 19x = 217$

$\Rightarrow$ $31x = 217$

$\Rightarrow$ $x = \dfrac{217}{31}$

$$= 7$$

$\therefore$ Value of smaller number

$$= 12x$$

$$= 12 \times 7$$

$$= 84.$$

30. $\because$ $\dfrac{x}{y} = \dfrac{5}{2}$

$\therefore$ $\dfrac{8x + 9y}{8x + 2y} = \dfrac{8\dfrac{x}{y} + 9\dfrac{y}{y}}{8\dfrac{x}{y} + 2\dfrac{y}{y}}$

[Divide numerator and denominator by y]

$$= \frac{8\left(\dfrac{5}{2}\right) + 9}{8\left(\dfrac{5}{2}\right) + 2}$$

$$= \frac{20 + 9}{20 + 2}$$

$$= \frac{29}{22}$$

$\therefore$ Value of $\dfrac{8x+9y}{8x+2y}$

$$= \dfrac{29}{22}.$$

31. We know that $x^\circ = 1$

Hence the value of $(100)^\circ = 1$.

32. $4^3 = 4 \times 4 \times 4 = 64$

Hence, Third power of 4 is equivalent to 64.

33. $\quad (3)^2 - (2)^3 = 9 - 8$

$$= 1.$$

34. $12\dfrac{1}{2}\%$ of ₹ 400

$$= \dfrac{25}{2 \times 100} \times 400$$

$$= ₹ 50.$$

35. 10% of 250 – 5% of 280

$$= \dfrac{10}{100} \times 250 - \dfrac{5}{100} \times 280$$

$$= 25 - 14$$

$$= 11.$$

36. Let the number be x

$$75\% \text{ of } x = 15$$

$$\Rightarrow \dfrac{75}{100} \times x = 15$$

$$\Rightarrow \quad x = \dfrac{100 \times 15}{75} = \dfrac{4}{3} \times 15$$

$$= 4 \times 5$$

$$= 20$$

$\therefore$ Number = 20.

37. Cost price of the Car

$$= 5200 + 1700$$

$$= ₹ 6900$$

Selling price of the Car

$$= ₹ 8200$$

Profit = SP – CP

$$= ₹ 8200 - ₹ 6900$$

$$= ₹ 1300.$$

38. $l = 8$ hectometer $= 8 \times 10$

$$= 80 \text{ decameter}$$

$b = 6$ decameter

Perimeter of rectangular garden

$$= 2(l + b)$$

$$= 2(80 + 6)$$

$$= 2 \times 86$$

$$= 172 \text{ decameter}$$

Time taken walking 4 decameter in 1 min

Time taken walking 172 decameter

$$= \dfrac{1}{4} \times 172 = 43 \text{ minutes.}$$

39. $\quad 36 \text{ km/hr} = \dfrac{36 \times 1000}{60 \times 60}$

$$= 36 \times \dfrac{5}{18}$$

$$= 10 \text{ m/s}$$

Speed = 10 m/s

Time = 36 seconds

$\therefore$ Distance = Speed $\times$ time

$$= 36 \times 10 = 360 \text{ m}$$

Hence the train will travel 360 m in 36 seconds.

40. Area of the tank $= 45 \times 34$

$$= 1530 \text{ m}^2$$

Cost of 1 m^2 = ₹ 625

Cost of 1530 m^2 = ₹ 1530 × 625

$$= ₹ 9,56,250$$

Hence contractor received money for the whole work = ₹ 9,56,250.

41. $52 + 8 = 60$

Number of persons who travel in all seven rounds

$$= 60 \times 7$$

$$= 420.$$

42. Cost of 5 tables

$$= \text{Cost of 7 chairs}$$

∵ Cost of 1 table

$$= ₹ 210$$

∴ Cost of 5 tables

$$= 210 \times 5$$

$$= ₹ 1050$$

Now, Cost of 7 chairs

$$= ₹ 1050$$

∴ Cost of 1 chair

$$= \frac{1050}{7}$$

$$= ₹ 150.$$

43. Total income of 8 members

$$= ₹ 900$$

Average income $= ₹ \dfrac{900}{8}$

$$= ₹ 112.50.$$

44. 40 boys can do a work in 6 days

1 boy can do this work in 6 × 40 days

10 boys can do the same work in

$$\frac{6 \times 40}{10} = 24 \text{ days.}$$

45. Speed = 72 km/hr

$$= \frac{72 \times 1000}{60 \times 60} \text{ m/s}$$

$$= 72 \times \frac{5}{18}$$

$$= 4 \times 5$$

$$= 20 \text{ m/s}$$

Time = 15 seconds

Distance = Speed × Time

$$= 20 \times 15$$

$$= 300 \text{ m}$$

∵ Train passes an electric pole

∴ Length of the train = 300 m.

46. Speed = 54 km/hr

$$= \frac{54 \times 1000}{60 \times 60} \text{ m/s}$$

$$= 54 \times \frac{5}{18}$$

$$= 3 \times 5$$

$$= 15 \text{ m/s}$$

Let the length of the bride

$$= x \text{ m}$$

Distance $= (300 + x)$ m

Time = 40 seconds

∵ Speed $= \dfrac{\text{Distance}}{\text{Time}}$

$$\Rightarrow \quad 15 = \frac{300 + x}{40}$$

$\Rightarrow \quad 300 + x = 15 \times 40$

$= 600$

$\Rightarrow \qquad x = 600 - 300$

$= 300$

$\therefore$ Length of the bridge

$= 300$ m.

47. $2(l + b) = 28$

$\Rightarrow \quad l + b = \dfrac{28}{2}$

$= 14$

$8 + b = 14$

$\Rightarrow \qquad b = 14 - 8$

$= 6$ m

Area of rectangle

$= l \times b$

$= 8 \times 6$

$= 48$ m^2.

48. Area of room which is in the form of square

$= 14 \times 14$

$= 196$ m^2

Cost of 196 m^2 of paving marbles

$= ₹ 5880$

Cost of 1 m^2 marble $= \dfrac{5880}{196}$

$= ₹ 30$

Hence cost of marble per square metre

$= ₹ 30.$

49. Total distance travelled in a day

$= 6 + 6 = 12$ km

Total distance travelled in one week (except Sunday)

$= 6 \times 12$

$= 72$ km

Now, we know that 5 miles

$= 8$ km

$\because \qquad 8$ km $= 5$ miles

72 km $= \dfrac{5}{8} \times 72$

$= 5 \times 9$

$= 45$ miles.

50. According to the question,

Perimeter of triangle

$= x + x + \dfrac{x}{2}$

$= \dfrac{2x + 2x + x}{2}$

$= \dfrac{5x}{2}$

$= 2\dfrac{1}{2} x.$

51. Except (D), others have four legs, while hen has two legs.

52. Except (B), others are bevergents, while curd is a milk product.

53. In the code the middle three letters are put in the reverse order.

54. In the code, the first, the middle and the last letters of the word are kept the same. The two letters between first and middle letters are replaced by the two letters between the middle and last letters and vice-versa. Also, the mutual arrangement of each of the two letters is reversed.

55. Every term is obtained by multiplying the previous term by 2

Hence,

$$4\text{th term} = 3\text{rd term} \times 2$$
$$= 16 \times 2 = 32$$
$$5\text{th term} = 4\text{th term} \times 2$$
$$= 32 \times 2 = 64$$
$$6\text{th term} = 5\text{th term} \times 2$$
$$= 64 \times 2 = 128$$

Hence, answers are 32, 64.

56. The difference between consecutive term is 2.

Hence,

$$4\text{th term} = 3\text{rd term} - 2$$
$$= 20 - 2 = 18$$
$$5\text{th term} = 4\text{th term} - 2$$
$$= 18 - 2 = 16$$

Hence, answers are 18, 16.

57. 'Bank' is the institute which deals with transaction of 'Money'. Likewise, 'Transport' deals with the movement of Goods.

58. 'Tree' originates from 'Root'. Likewise, 'Smoke' originates from 'Fire'.

59. $8 \div 2 - 3 \times 4 + 6$

$4 - 12 + 6 = -2$

60. $9 \div 3 \times 4 + 8 - 2$

$12 + 8 - 2 = 18$

61. In each subsequent figure one line is increasing., Hence, there should be 4 lines in figure 'D' but there are only two lines.

62. Except problem figure 'C', in all other figures, the design in the square is open.

63. Problem figure 2 is obtained from problem figure 1 by uniting the three sections to obtain a circle. Similarly, Answer figure 'B' is obtained from problem figure 3.

64. Problem figure PF/2 is obtained from PF/1 by turning the black cross (+) into the white cross. Similarly, Answer figure (AF) 'A' is obtained from PF/3 by turning white cross into black cross.

65. 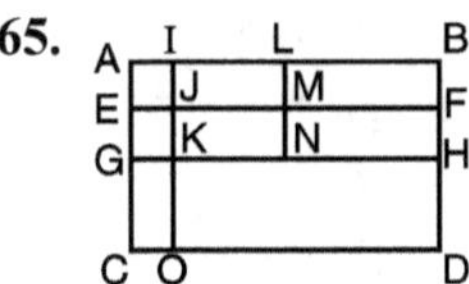

The main rectangle is ABDC, *i.e.,* 1 rectangle

The simplest rectangles are AIJE, ILMJ, LBFM, EJKG, JMNK, MFHN, GKOC and KHDO, *i.e.,* 8 rectangles.

The rectangles which have two parts are ALME, IBFJ, EMNG, JFHK, AIKG, IKNL, LBHN, EJOC and GHDC, *i.e.,* 9 rectangles.

The rectangles which have three parts are AIOC, ABFE and EFHG, *i.e.,* 3 rectangles

The rectangles which have four parts are ALNG and IBHK, *i.e.,* 2 rectangles

So, the total number of rectangles $1 + 8 + 9 + 3 + 2 = 23$.

66. The order in which the girls are positioned is:

Rajni, Mini, Ananta, Saya, Jaya

or

Saya, Jaya, Ananta

or

Saya, Ananta, Jaya

67.

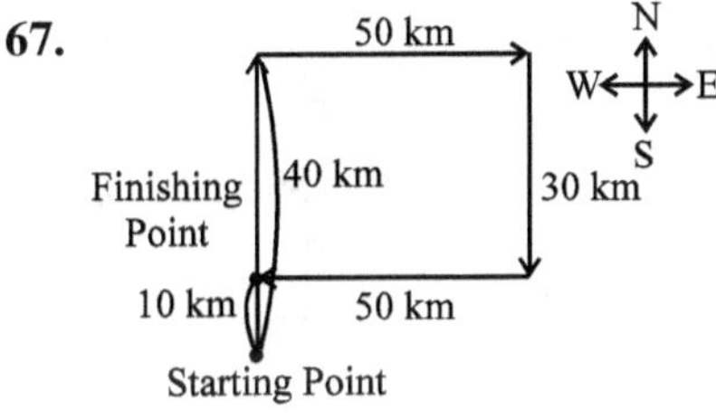

68. Grand father

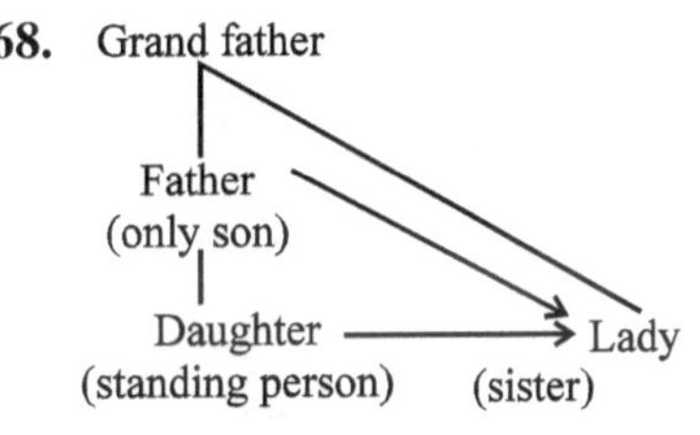

Lady's grandfather's son is lady's father and father's daughter will only be lady's sister.

69. First Sunday is on 1st December

First Tuesday is on 3rd December

3 weeks later, Fourth Tuesday will be on $3 + (7 \times 3)$

$= 24$th December.

70.

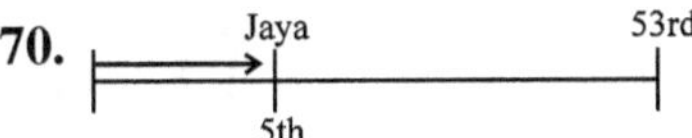

Jaya's rank from the bottom is :

$(53 - 5) + 1 = 49$th.

71. When all the players have to play with each other then the method of calculating the number of matches to be played is $\dfrac{n\,(n-1)}{2}$

where '*n*' is the number of players playing the match. So, the number of matches played will be:

$(6 \times 5) \div 2 = 30 \div 2 = 15$

72. Of the four letters in each set the two letters are vowels.

73.

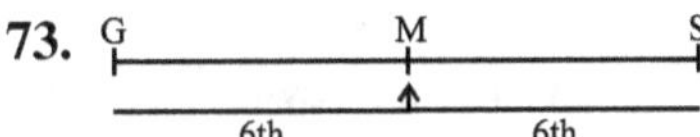

'M' is midway between G and S.

74. 15 horses eat 15 bags of grain in 15 days

15 horses eat 1 bag of grain in 1 day

1 horse eats 1 bag of grain in 15 days.

75. Mamuni goes to the movies on Thursday, so nine days ago was Thursday.

$\therefore$ Two days ago was also Thursday. So, today is Saturday.

R. Gupta's®
GENERAL KNOWLEDGE BOOKS

Book Name	Code	Price(₹)
General Knowledge 2019	R-1716	40
General Knowledge for All 2019	R-1641	25
R. Gupta's® GK & Current Affairs *including Latest Who's Who*	R-1	35
General Knowledge Hand Book (Junior)	R-3	50
General Knowledge & Current Affairs	R-5	60
General Knowledge At a Glance	R-7	75
Popular General Knowledge	R-9	160
General Knowledge Encyclopaedia	R-11	270
Delhi General Knowledge	R-464	70
Objective General Knowledge	R-177	170
Kerala General Knowledge	R-1588	95
Comprehensive J&K GK, Current Affairs & Who's Who	R-564	95
J&K General Knowledge (with latest Facts & Data)	R-1605	35
J&K General Knowledge – At a Glance	R-1066	55
Haryana General Knowledge	R-505	95
Himachal Pradesh General Knowledge	R-415	95
Uttarakhand General Knowledge	R-469	65
Odisha General Knowledge	R-518	140
West Bengal General Knowledge	R-1070	65
Arunachal Pradesh General Knowledge	R-1067	70
Manipur General Knowledge	R-1864	110
Manipur GK Handbook *(with Multiple Choice Questions)*	R-954	50
Maharashtra General Knowledge	R-1043	75

 **Ramesh Publishing House** | 1902 |

12-H, New Daryaganj Road, Opp. Officers' Mess, Delhi-110002

For Online Shopping: www.rameshpublishinghouse.com

GENERAL KNOWLEDGE

INDIAN HISTORY AND CULTURE

1. Which of following throws light on Harappan Culture?
   A. Rock edicts
   B. The writings in terracotta seals
   C. Archaeological excavations
   D. All of the above

2. The idol worship in India can be traced to:
   A. the Pre-Aryan period
   B. the later Vedic period
   C. the Mauryan period
   D. the Kushan period

3. Who was the court part of Samudra Gupta?
   A. Asvaghosha
   B. Nagarjuna
   C. Harishena
   D. Aryabhatta

4. The ruins of the glory of Vijayanagar and a place of historical importance for its architectural style is now found at:
   A. Belur
   B. Hampi
   C. Srirangapatnam
   D. Tanjore

5. The world famous rock cut Kailasa Temple at Ellora was built by the:
   A. Mauryas
   B. Pallavas
   C. Chalukyas
   D. Rashtrakutas

6. Which one of the following Silsilas of Sufism was against music:
   A. Chishtiya
   B. Suhrawardiya
   C. Qadiriya
   D. Naqshbandiya

7. From the excavations of which ancient site informations are gathered regarding brisk trade relations between India and Rome during early centuries of Christian era:
   A. Madurai   B. Tamralipti
   C. Tondi   D. Arikamedu

8. Greko-Roman Art has found a place in:
   A. Ellora
   B. Gandhara
   C. Kalinga
   D. Buddhist Art

9. How many 'Mandals' (Books) does the *Rig Veda* contain?
   A. 7   B. 10
   C. 11   D. 21

10. Which one of the following trees is shown in seals of the Indus Valley Civilisation in association with a deity?
    A. Neem tree
    B. Pipal tree
    C. Banyan tree
    D. Mango tree

11. Chinese pilgrim who visited India during Harshavardhan's period was:
    A. Fa-hien
    B. Itsing
    C. Nishka
    D. Hiuen Tsang

12. Chalukya King Pulakesin-II was defeated by:
    A. Mahendra Varman-I
    B. Narasimha Varman-I
    C. Parameswara Varman-I
    D. Jatila Parantaka

13. Lumbini, the birth place of Gautam Buddha, is in:
    A. Bihar
    B. Sikkim
    C. Nepal
    D. None of these

14. Which one of the following Sufis regarded Krishna among the awliyas:
    A. Shah Mohammad Ghaus
    B. Shah Waliullah
    C. Shah Abdul Azeez
    D. Khwaja Mir Dard

15. The Mughals borrowed the celebration of 'Nauroz' from:
    A. Parsis
    B. Jews
    C. Mangols
    D. Turks

16. The temple built in 1100 AD and dominating all other temples in Bhubaneshwar is:
    A. Raja Rani Temple
    B. Kandariya Mahadev
    C. Tribhuvaneswara Lingaraja
    D. Mukhteswara

17. The paintings in the Ajanta and Ellora caves are indicative of development of art under the:
    A. Rashtrakutas
    B. Pallavas
    C. Pandyas
    D. Chalukyas

18. Match List-I with List-II and select the correct answer with the help of the codes given below:

	List-I		*List-II*
(a)	Rigveda	1.	Musical hymns
(b)	Yajurveda	2.	Hymns and rituals
(c)	Samaveda	3.	Charms and spells
(d)	Atharvaveda	4.	Hymns and prayers

Codes:

	(a)	(b)	(c)	(d)
A.	4	2	1	3
B.	3	2	4	1
C.	4	1	2	3
D.	2	3	1	4

19. Mughal painting reached its zenith under:
    A. Shahjahan
    B. Akbar
    C. Jahangir
    D. Aurangzeb

20. Who among the following Sikh Gurus compiled the 'Adi Granth'?
    A. First Guru
    B. Fifth Guru
    C. Ninth Guru
    D. Tenth and the last Guru

21. 'Mongols' intruded into India for the first time during the reign of:
    A. Iltutmish
    B. Firoz Shah Tughlaq
    C. Balban
    D. Alauddin Khilji

22. Which dynasty was well-known for excellent village administration?
    A. Pallavas   B. Cholas
    C. Pandyas   D. Chalukyas

23. Who of the following was the biographer of Akbar?
    A. Abul Fazl
    B. Faizi
    C. Abdun Nabi Khan
    D. Birbal

24. Match the following:

List-I		*List-II*
(*a*)	Sanchi	1. Chandela Art
(*b*)	Khajuraho	2. Great Stupa
(*c*)	Thanjavur	3. Pallava temples
(*d*)	Kanchipuram	4. Chola temples

    Codes:

	(*a*)	(*b*)	(*c*)	(*d*)
A.	1	2	3	4
B.	2	1	4	3
C.	3	4	2	1
D.	4	1	2	3

25. Who was called the "Second Founder of the Maratha Kingdom"?
    A. Raja Ram
    B. Balaji Viswanath
    C. Baji Rao I
    D. Balaji Baji Rao

26. The Mughal emperor who discouraged *Sati* was:
    A. Babur   B. Humayun
    C. Akbar   D. Jahangir

27. Which one of the following Saints' name is associated with Shivaji?
    A. Rama Nand B. Ram Das
    C. Chaitanya   D. Tukaram

28. Tansen, the greatest musician of Akbar's court, belonged to:
    A. Gwalior   B. Kannauj
    C. Delhi   D. Agra

29. The tomb of Sufi saint Sheikh Salim Chishti is at:
    A. Jaunpur
    B. Sikandara
    C. Fatehpur Sikri
    D. Ajmer

30. Islam was abolished as the State religion during the rule of:
    A. Akbar
    B. Balban
    C. Ibrahim Lodi
    D. Ghias-ud-din Tughlaq

31. Who among the following founded the 'Sunga' dynasty?
    A. Bimbisara   B. Agnimitra
    C. Ajatashatru D. Pushyamitra

32. Who among the following founded the 'Brahmo Samaj'?
    A. Keshab Chandra Sen
    B. Ramakrishna
    C. Dayananda Saraswati
    D. Raja Ram Mohan Roy

33. Akbar built Ibadatkhana at Fatehpur Sikri to:
    A. Conduct mass prayer
    B. Hold darbar
    C. Hold religious discussions
    D. Hear public grievances

34. Which one of the given Mughal buildings bears the inscription "If on Earth be on Eden of Bliss it is this, it is this none but this"?
    A. Diwan-i-Aam

B. Diwan-i-Khas
C. Taj Mahal
D. Buland Darwaza

35. 'Mansabdars' during the Mughal period were:
A. Landlords and zamindars
B. Militia men
C. Officials of the state
D. Revenue Collectors

36. During Aurangzeb's reign which of the following were not employed by his government?
A. Rajputs
B. Pathans
C. Marathas
D. All of the above

37. The first Europeans who started trade with India were:
A. British   B. Danish
C. Portuguese   D. Dutch

38. The fulsome development of Mughal painting was the achievement of:
A. Humayun   B. Akbar
C. Babur   D. Jahangir

39. Moti Masjid in the Red Fort at Delhi was built by:
A. Akbar   B. Jahangir
C. Shahjahan   D. Aurangzeb

40. Who among the following Sultans of Delhi has been described by the historians as the 'mixture of opposites'?
A. Balban
B. Alauddin Khilji
C. Muhammad Bin Tughlaq
D. Ibrahim Lodi

41. Who was the last ruler of Lodi Dynasty?

A. Bahlol Lodi
B. Ibrahim Lodi
C. Daulat Khan Lodi
D. Sikander Lodhi

42. Which of the following Mughal emperors has vividly described Indian flora & fauna, seasons, fruits, etc. in his diary?
A. Akbar   B. Jahangir
C. Babur   D. Aurangzeb

43. The greatness of Shershah lies in his:
A. victories against Humayun
B. superior generalship
C. adminstrative reforms
D. religious tolerance

44. Who among the following Mughal emperors wrote his autobiography in Persian:
A. Babur   B. Akbar
C. Jahangir   D. Aurangzeb

45. Taxila was a famous site of:
A. Early Vedic Art
B. Mauryan Art
C. Gandhara Art
D. Gupta Art

46. The gold coins were introduced first time in India by:
A. The Kushanas
B. The Greeks
C. The Sakas
D. The Parthians

47. Which of the following dynasties conquered Sri Lanka and South-East Asian countries?
A. The Pandyas
B. The Chalukyas
C. The Cholas
D. The Rashtrakutas

48. Match the capitals of the ruling dynasties of early Medieval India:

List-I		*List-II*
(*a*) Pratiharas		1. Kannauj
(*b*) Chandelas		2. Khajuraho
(*c*) Paramaras		3. Dhar
(*d*) Chalukyas		4. Anhilwad

Codes:

	(*a*)	(*b*)	(*c*)	(*d*)
A.	1	2	3	4
B.	1	3	4	2
C.	2	4	1	3
D.	2	1	3	4

49. 'Al Hilal' was a newspaper started for propagating nationalism by:
A. Abul Kalam Azad
B. Mohammed Ali
C. Zafar Ali Khan
D. Dr. Syed Mahmud

50. The famous monastery of Vikramsila was founded by the:
A. Guptas
B. Senas
C. Palas
D. Rashtrakutas

51. Fahein, the first Chinese pilgrim, visited India during the reign of:
A. Chandragupta Maurya
B. Chandragupta Vikramaditya
C. Harshavardhana
D. Ashoka the Great

52. Who amongst the following rulers belonged to the Holkar dynasty?
A. Balaji B. Shivaji
C. Tukoji D. Prithviraj

53. Who levied the tax known by the name "Chauth"?
A. Marathas B. Mughals
C. Cholas D. Chandelas

54. The most important feature in the economic measures pursued by Allauddin Khilji was:
A. Foreign trade
B. Minting of new coins
C. Development of agriculture
D. Market control

55. The era which is counted from 78 AD is the:
A. Kollam Era
B. Vikrama Era
C. Saka Era
D. Salivahana Era

56. Provincial Autonomy was a significant feature of:
A. The Indian Independence Act, 1947
B. The Government of India Act, 1919
C. The Government of India Act, 1909
D. The Government of India Act, 1935

57. The Simon Commission was appointed in:
A. 1928 B. 1929
C. 1930 D. 1926

58. Swarajya was declared as the goal of the Congress at its session in 1906 at:
A. Bombay B. Calcutta
C. Lucknow D. Madras

59. Gandhiji started the Dandi march from:
A. Ahmedabad B. Allahabad
C. Dandi D. Calcutta

60. The Congress adopted the Quit India Resolution in the year:
A. 1940   B. 1938
C. 1946   D. 1942

61. The art style which combines Indian and Greek features is called:
A. Sikhara   B. Verna
C. Nagana   D. Gandhara

62. Match the following:

List-I		*List-II*
(a) Fascism	1.	Adolf Hitler
(b) Democracy	2.	Lenin
(c) Nazism	3.	Mussolini
(d) Socialism	4.	Woodrow Wilson

Codes:

	(a)	(b)	(c)	(d)
A.	1	4	2	3
B.	4	3	2	1
C.	3	4	1	2
D.	3	1	4	2

63. Which battle laid the foundation of Mughal rule in India?
A. Battle of Plassey
B. Battle of Talikota
C. First battle of Panipat
D. Battle of Haldighati

64. The site of Amritsar was bestowed by Mughal emperor Akbar upon:
A. Guru Tegh Bahadur
B. Guru Ram Das
C. Guru Amar Das
D. Guru Hari Kishan

65. Alexander advanced in India up to the river:
A. Ravi   B. Satluj
C. Beas   D. Yamuna

66. The water divide between Indus and Ganga river systems is formed by:
A. Vindhyan Range
B. Dhaula Dhar Range
C. Aravalli Range
D. Satpura Range

67. The Partition of Bengal was effected in 1905 by:
A. Lord Minto
B. Lord Lyton
C. Lord Curzon
D. Lord Lawrence

68. Revival of Vedas is associated with:
A. Swami Dayanand Saraswati
B. Swami Vivekananda
C. Acharya Rajneesh
D. Raja Ram Mohan Roy

69. At the time of independence of India in 1947, the Prime Minister of England was:
A. Lord Mountbatten
B. Clement Attlee
C. Winston Churchill
D. Neville Chamberlain

70. Who is known as the 'Iron man' of India?
A. Lala Lajpat Rai
B. Gopal Krishna Gokhale
C. Sardar Vallabhbhai Patel
D. Dr. B.R. Ambedkar

71. Iqtas were organised in India by:
A. Qutubuddin Aibak
B. Balban
C. Alauddin Khilji
D. Iltutmish

72. Literature in the Gupta period was written mostly in:
    A. Sanskrit   B. Telugu
    C. Tamil   D. Kannada

73. Who among the following was impeached on return to Britain for accepting bribes and committing atrocities on Indian rulers?
    A. Warren Hastings
    B. Sir John Share
    C. Lord Clive
    D. Lord Cornwallis

74. Gandhiji started **Satyagraha** in 1919 in protest against the:
    A. Salt Law
    B. Rowlatt Act
    C. Act of 1909
    D. Jallianwala Bagh Massacre

75. The immediate cause for the outbreak of the First World War was:
    A. the assassination of Archduke Francis Ferdinand
    B. the imprisonment of Lenin
    C. the ambition of America to dominate the world
    D. the sudden death of Lloyd George

76. The Opium Wars were fought between:
    A. Britain and China
    B. Britain and India
    C. India and China
    D. Britain and Japan

77. Of the following who was not a signatory to the historic Poona Pact of 1932?
    A. B.R. Ambedkar
    B. Madan Mohan Malviya
    C. C. Rajagopalachari
    D. M.K. Gandhi

78. On the first occasion, the Prime Minister of India was appointed by:
    A. The Governor General
    B. The British Emperor
    C. Mahatma Gandhi
    D. The Viceroy

79. The American publicist who was with Mahatma Gandhi during his 'Quit India' movement was:
    A. Louis Fischer
    B. William L. Shiver
    C. Web Miller
    D. Negley Farson

80. The most decisive battle that led to the establishment of supremacy of the British in India was:
    A. The battle of Plassey
    B. The battle of Buxar
    C. The battle of Wandiwash
    D. The third battle of Panipat

81. The person who returned his Token of Honour to Government of India on May 30, 1919 was:
    A. Jamnalal Bajaj
    B. Tej Bahadur Sapru
    C. Mahatma Gandhi
    D. Rabindranath Tagore

82. Match the following Lists I and II and select the correct answer from the codes given below:

List-I	*List-II*
(Authors)	*(Books)*
(a) Mahatma Gandhi	1. India Divided
(b) Ram Manohar Lohia	2. India Wins Freedom

(c) Dr Rajendra 3. Hind
    Prasad   Swaraj
(d) Abul Kalam 4. The Wheel
    Azad   of History
Codes:

	(a)	(b)	(c)	(d)
A.	1	3	4	2
B.	4	3	2	1
C.	3	4	1	2
D.	2	3	4	1

83. Karamchand Gandhi was a Dewan of:
A. Porbandar
B. Rajkot
C. Wakaner
D. All of the above states

84. The Asiatic Society of Bengal (founded in 1784) owes its origin to:
A. Warren Hastings
B. Sir William Jones
C. Sir James Mackintosh
D. James Princep

85. A prominent leader of the Ghadar Party was:
A. P. Mitra
B. Hardayal
C. B.G. Tilak
D. Bipin Chandra Pal

86. Who propounded the theory of 'Drain of Wealth' from India to Great Britain?
A. Gopal Krishna Gokhale
B. Dadabhai Naoroji
C. Surendranath Banerjee
D. Lala Lajpat Rai

87. Which one of the following was the first to impose censorship of the Press:
A. Wellesley   B. Hastings
C. John Adams D. Dalhousie

88. MacDonald's Communal Award did not provide separate electorates and reserved seats in provincial legislatures to:
A. Muslims
B. Sikhs
C. Scheduled Castes
D. Buddhists

89. On November 1, 1858 Queen Victoria Proclamation was read out at Allahabad by:
A. Lord William Bentinck
B. Lord Canning
C. Lord Burnham
D. Sir Harcourt Butler

90. The first census in India during the British period was held during the tenure of:
A. Lord Dufferin
B. Lord Lyton
C. Lord Mayo
D. Lord Ripon

91. Which one of the following names cannot be associated with the Revolt of 1857?
A. Begum Hazarat Mahal
B. Maulavi Ahmadullah
C. Peshwa Baji Rao II
D. Bahadur Shah II

92. The call 'Dilli Challo' was given by:
A. Lala Lajpat Rai
B. Dr Rajendra Prasad
C. Subhash Chandra Bose
D. Mahatma Gandhi

93. Who among the following attended all the three Round Table Conferences?

A. Jawaharlal Nehru
B. Dr B.R. Ambedkar
C. Vallabhbhai Patel
D. Dr Rajendra Prasad

94. The British Viceroy who took a number of measures for preserving ancient buildings and monuments of India was:
A. Lord Ripon
B. Lord Curzon
C. Lord Minto
D. Lord Irwin

95. Find the correct match:

	List-I		*List-II*
(a)	Abdul Gaffar Khan	1.	Mahatma
(b)	Dadabhai Naoroji	2.	Frontier Gandhi
(c)	Mohandas Karamchand Gandhi	3.	Grand Old Man of India
(d)	Rabindranath Tagore	4.	Gurudev

Codes:

	(a)	(b)	(c)	(d)
A.	3	1	4	2
B.	2	3	1	4
C.	4	1	2	3
D.	2	1	3	4

96. The first Governor-General of the East India Company in India was:
A. Robert Clive
B. Sir John Shore
C. Warren Hastings
D. Marquis of Hastings

97. The Stupa of Sanchi was built by:
A. Ashoka
B. Kanishka
C. Harshvardhan
D. Dharmpala

98. The prefix 'Mahatma' was added with the name of Gandhi:
A. During Champaran **Satyagraha**
B. During the **Satyagraha** against Rowlatt Act
C. In the Amritsar Session of the Indian National Congress 1919
D. At the beginning of **Khilafat** movement

99. The Harappans were the earliest people to produce:
A. Seals
B. Bronze implements
C. Cotton
D. Barley

100. The Megalithic culture (500 BC-AD 100) brings us to the historical period in South India. The Megaliths used:
A. weapons made of stone
B. tools and implements made of stone
C. graves encircled by big pieces of stones
D. articles of daily use made of stone

101. Which one of the following persons called Irwin and Gandhi as 'the two Mahatmas':
A. Mira Behn
B. Sarojini Naidu
C. Madan Mohan Malviya
D. Jawaharlal Nehru

102. Gandhi suspended his first non-cooperation movement because:
    A. it turned violent suddenly
    B. most of the leaders had been arrested and were in prison
    C. his experiment on all-India strike had succeeded
    D. he saw no chances of success for the movement

103. Indian National Army was headed by:
    A. Netaji Subhash Chandra Bose
    B. General Cariappa
    C. Field Marshal Manekshaw
    D. Chandra Shekhar Azad

104. 'Purna Swaraj' day was first celebrated in India on:
    A. 26 January, 1930
    B. 15 August, 1930
    C. 15 August, 1947
    D. 26 January, 1950

105. Who was the Viceroy of British India when Attlee's government decided to grant Independence to India?
    A. Lord Mountbatten
    B. Lord Linlithgow
    C. Lord Wavell
    D. Lord Wellington

106. When did the 'Quit India' movement begin?
    A. March 1930
    B. August 1942
    C. August 1945
    D. August 1947

107. The Mausoleum of Sher Shah Suri is at:
    A. Allahabad   B. Agra
    C. Jaunpur   D. Sasaram

108. The slogan 'Inquilab Zindabad' was given by:
    A. Chandra Shekhar Azad
    B. Mohammed Iqbal
    C. Bhagat Singh
    D. Mahatma Gandhi

109. 'Red Shirts' movement aimed at:
    A. creation of an independent Pakhtoonistan
    B. ensuring the creating of Pakistan
    C. making India a communist country at the dawn of independence
    D. throwing out the British from India

110. Bhagwad Gita was originally written in the language:
    A. Pali   B. Prakrit
    C. Sanskrit   D. Hindi

111. Megasthenes was sent by Seleukos Nikator to the court of
    A. Chandragupta Maurya
    B. Ashoka
    C. Chandragupta I
    D. Bimbisar

112. The aim of the Cripps Mission to India was to:
    A. appease the Indian public opinion
    B. decide the future of India immediately
    C. grant independence to India in stages
    D. decentralise power to provinces

113. Which party was in power in the UK when India became independent?

A. Labour
B. Conservative
C. Liberal
D. No party, since a National Government was there

114. Who evolved the national consciousness as a formal concept?
A. Bal Gangadhar Tilak
B. Mahatma Gandhi
C. Jawaharlal Nehru
D. Surendranath Banerjee

115. The Swaraj Party was founded by:
A. Motilal Nehru
B. Bal Gangadhar Tilak
C. C. Rajagopalachari
D. Vallabhbhai Patel

116. The aim of the Swaraj Party was to:
A. boycott the foreign goods
B. declare independence and establish a provisional Indian government
C. enter the Legislative Councils through elections in order to wreck the legislature from within
D. All of the above

117. The cause of the immediate precipitation of the Sepoy mutiny was:
A. the spread of Christianity
B. the Doctrine of Lapse
C. the disparity between the European soldiers and the native Sepoys in service conditions
D. The compulsion on the Sepoys to use cartridges greased with fat

118. When did Vikram era start?
A. 19 BC   B. 58 BC
C. 78 AD   D. 73 AD

119. Which of the following was a consequence of the invasion of Amir Timur?
A. Decline of the Mughal Empire
B. Fall of Lodi Dynasty
C. Decline of Tughlaq Dynasty
D. End of Khilji Dynasty

120. What is the correct chronological sequence of the following?
  I. Gandhi-Irwin Pact
  II. Nehru Report
  III. Non-cooperation Movement
  IV. Quit India Movement
A. III, IV, I, II   B. III, II, I, IV
C. II, III, IV, I   D. I, III, II, IV

121. What is the correct chronological order in which the following four appeared on the political scenario in India?
  I. Lord Minto
  II. Lord Reading
  III. Lord Curzon
  IV. Lord Irwin
A. II, III, I, IV   B. IV, I, III, II
C. I, III, II, IV   D. III, I, II, IV

122. Who was the first Governor-General of free India?
A. Lord Mountbatten
B. C. Rajagopalachari
C. Pandit Jawaharlal Nehru
D. Babu Rajendra Prasad

123. 'Jatakas' are the sacred books of the:
A. Vaishnavas B. Jains
C. Buddhists   D. Shaivas

124. The Ajanta paintings belong to the:
   A. Harappan period
   B. Mauryan period
   C. Buddhist period
   D. Gupta period

125. The famous King of legendary Bhoja, belonged to the dynasty of:
   A. the Pratiharas
   B. the Chauhans
   C. the Paramaras
   D. the Chandelas

126. The Gandhara School of Art was influenced most by the:
   A. Greeks   B. Kushans
   C. Persians   D. Sakas

127. Rock cut temples have been discovered in:
   A. Elephanta Caves
   B. Ajanta Caves
   C. Ellora Caves
   D. None of the above

128. 'Sufi Sect' developed in the religion:
   A. Hinduism   B. Islam
   C. Christianity D. Sikhism

129. The great Indian philosopher Sankara advocated:
   A. Dvaita
   B. Advaita
   C. Vishishtadvaita
   D. None of the above

130. The influence of Chaitanya was mainly confined to:
   A. The Eastern India
   B. The Southern India
   C. Gujarat
   D. North India

131. Which of the following classes participated the least in the Indian National Movement?
   A. Capitalists
   B. Princes of States
   C. Government officials
   D. The peasants

132. Who said first 'Swaraj is my birth right, and I shall have it'?
   A. Bal Gangadhar Tilak
   B. Gopal Krishna Gokhale
   C. M.K. Gandhi
   D. Lala Lajpat Rai

133. Who led the extremists before the arrival of Gandhi on the political scene for India's freedom struggle?
   A. Dadabhai Naoroji
   B. Surendranath Banerjee
   C. Gopal Krishna Gokhale
   D. Bal Gangadhar Tilak

134. The Home Rule movement was launched by:
   A. Annie Besant and Bal Gangadhar Tilak together
   B. Annie Besant and Bal Gangadhar Tilak separately
   C. Annie Besant and Mahatma Gandhi together
   D. The Congress when Mrs Besant was its President

135. Which of the following caves has the 'Trimurti' statue with the faces of Brahma, Vishnu and Mahesh?
   A. Kanheri   B. Ajanta
   C. Elephanta   D. Ellora

ANSWERS

1	2	3	4	5	6	7	8	9	10
C	A	C	B	D	D	D	B	B	B

11	12	13	14	15	16	17	18	19	20
D	B	C	A	A	C	A	A	C	B

21	22	23	24	25	26	27	28	29	30
A	B	A	B	B	C	B	A	C	A

31	32	33	34	35	36	37	38	39	40
D	D	C	B	C	C	C	D	D	C

41	42	43	44	45	46	47	48	49	50
B	B	C	C	C	A	C	A	A	C

51	52	53	54	55	56	57	58	59	60
B	C	A	D	C	D	A	B	A	D

61	62	63	64	65	66	67	68	69	70
D	C	C	B	C	C	C	A	B	C

71	72	73	74	75	76	77	78	79	80
D	A	A	B	A	A	B	A	A	B

81	82	83	84	85	86	87	88	89	90
D	C	B	B	B	B	A	D	B	C

91	92	93	94	95	96	97	98	99	100
C	C	B	B	B	C	A	B	C	B

101	102	103	104	105	106	107	108	109	110
C	A	A	A	C	B	D	C	D	C

111	112	113	114	115	116	117	118	119	120
A	A	A	D	A	C	D	B	C	B

121	122	123	124	125	126	127	128	129	130
D	A	C	D	A	A	A	B	B	A

131	132	133	134	135
B	A	D	B	C

INDIAN POLITY AND CONSTITUTION

1. The Constituent Assembly was presided over by:
   A. Dr Rajendra Prasad
   B. Dr B.R. Ambedkar
   C. Pandit Jawaharlal Nehru
   D. Dr K.M. Munshi

2. Under which article of the Constitution of India, a citizen can go to the Supreme Court for the enforcement of his Fundamental Rights?
   A. Article 31
   B. Article 29
   C. Article 32
   D. Article 10

3. Which of the following two words were added to the Preamble of the Indian Constitution by the 42nd Amendment?
   A. Sovereign and Democratic
   B. Secular and Socialist
   C. Secular and Democratic
   D. Democratic and Republic

4. By which Constitutional Amendment Bill was the voting age reduced from 21 years to 18 years?
   A. 48th
   B. 57th
   C. 61st
   D. 63rd

5. Which among the following is not a Fundamental Right now?
   A. Right to Equality
   B. Right to Property
   C. Right to Constitutional Remedies
   D. None of these

6. Secularism in the Constitution of India stands for:
   A. equal respect to all religions
   B. non-interference of the State in religious affairs
   C. according the status of state religion to all religions in India
   D. None of the above

7. Which of the following is not a condition for Indian citizenship?
   A. Property
   B. Birth
   C. Heredity
   D. Nationality

8. The President calls the joint sitting of both Houses of Parliament when:
   A. any constitutional amendment bill is to be passed
   B. a money bill is rejected by the Rajya Sabha
   C. an ordinary bill is not passed by both Houses of Parliament
   D. the President wished to do so

9. The Indian Constitution was adopted and enacted by the Constituent Assembly of India on:
   A. 9 December, 1949
   B. 26 January, 1946
   C. 26 November, 1949
   D. 26 January, 1950

10. The Preamble of our Constitution reads—India is a:
    A. Sovereign Socialist Secular Democratic Republic

    B. Sovereign Democratic Socialist Secular Republic
    C. Socialist Democratic Secular Republic
    D. Democratic Sovereign Secular Socialist Republic

11. The main feature of the Panchayati Raj in India is:
    A. Rolling plan
    B. Decentralisation of power
    C. Money plan
    D. Sharing of power between the Centre and the States

12. The President of India is elected by:
    A. the people of India
    B. all the members of Parliament
    C. all the elected Members of Parliament
    D. all the elected Members of the Parliament and of State Legislative Assemblies

13. The maximum strength of the Rajya Sabha is:
    A. 250   B. 270
    C. 300   D. 545

14. Who conducts elections to the Lok Sabha and Legislative Assemblies of the States?
    A. President and Governor respectively
    B. Prime Minister and Chief Minister respectively
    C. Speakers of the Lok Sabha and the Legislative Assemblies
    D. Chief Election Commissioner

15. The Comptroller and Auditor General of India may be removed:
    A. by the President in his discretion
    B. by the President on the advice of the Union Council of Ministers
    C. by the President on the advice of the UPSC
    D. by the President on an address by both Houses of Parliament

16. Salaries and allowances of the High Court judges are charged upon the:
    A. Consolidated Fund of India
    B. Consolidated Fund of the State
    C. Contingency Fund of India
    D. Contingency Fund of the State

17. Who was appointed as the Prime Minister without being a member of a House of the Parliament?
    A. Gulzarilal Nanda
    B. Rajiv Gandhi
    C. Chandrashekhar
    D. P.V. Narasimha Rao

18. What can be the maximum period of gap between any two sessions of the Indian Parliament?
    A. Six months
    B. Three months
    C. One year
    D. Ten weeks

19. The number of members nominated to Lok Sabha by the President is:
    - A. 2
    - B. 4
    - C. 5
    - D. 12

20. Which democratic country is said to be federal in form but unitary in character?
    - A. USA
    - B. India
    - C. Ireland
    - D. UK

21. Which of the following is not a charged expenditure on the Consolidated Fund of India?
    - A. Expenditure of Five-Year Plans
    - B. Expenditure on the Chairman and Members of the UPSC
    - C. Expenditure on the Judges of the Supreme Court
    - D. Debt charges of the Government of India

22. Which one of the following subjects is not contained in the Union list?
    - A. Currency
    - B. Agriculture
    - C. Foreign Affairs
    - D. Union Duties

23. The Speaker of the Lok Sabha is:
    - A. nominated by the President
    - B. nominated by the Prime Minister
    - C. nominated by the Vice-President
    - D. elected by the members of the Lok Sabha

24. Which writ is issued by a superior court to an individual or institution directing him to perform a public duty?
    - A. Habeas Corpus
    - B. Quo Warranto
    - C. Mandamus
    - D. Certiorari

25. The Council of Ministers of an Indian State is collectively responsible to the:
    - A. Legislative Council
    - B. Legislative Assembly
    - C. Governor of the State
    - D. Both houses of the State legislature

26. Who can legislate on those residual matters which are not mentioned in Central/State/Concurrent lists?
    - A. State legislatures exclusively
    - B. Parliament alone
    - C. Parliament after State legislatures concur
    - D. Parliament or State legislatures as adjudicated by the Supreme Court

27. The salary of the Members of Parliament is decided by:
    - A. the Parliament
    - B. the Central Cabinet
    - C. the President
    - D. the Speaker

28. Which one of the following Fundamental Rights was described by Dr B.R. Ambedkar as the heart and soul of the Constitution?
    - A. Right to Religion

B. Right to Constitutional Remedies
C. Right to Property
D. Right to Education

29. The President of India addresses both Houses of Parliament assembled together at the commencement of the first session:
A. of each year
B. after each general election to the House of the People
C. Both A and B
D. Neither A nor B

30. Of the following, who held the offices of judge of the Supreme Court and the Speaker of Lok Sabha?
A. M. Hidayatullah
B. K.S. Hegde
C. Subba Rao
D. P.N. Bhagwati

31. No person shall be a citizen of India if he has:
A. lived in a foreign country for more than five years
B. been convicted by a foreign court of law
C. voluntarily acquired citizenship of another country
D. accepted employment in another country

32. The Balwant Rai Mehta Committee made important recommendations concerning:
A. Industrial policy towards the small scale industries

B. Policy towards foreign capital
C. Panchayati raj
D. Foodgrain policy

33. The Constituent Assembly of India was set up under the:
A. Simon Commission Proposals
B. Cripps' Mission Proposals
C. Mountbatten Plan
D. Cabinet Mission Plan

34. A Judge of the Supreme Court retires at the age of:
A. 65 years   B. 55 years
C. 60 years   D. 58 years

35. Match List-I with List-II and select your answer from the code given below:

List-I *(Articles of the Constitution)*	*List-II* *(Subject Matter)*
(a) Art. 40	1. Organisation of village panchayat
(b) Art. 41	2. Right to work
(c) Art. 44	3. Uniform Civil Code
(d) Art. 48	4. Organisation of agriculture and animal husbandry

Codes:

	(a)	(b)	(c)	(d)
A.	1	2	3	4
B.	2	3	1	4
C.	1	3	4	2
D.	3	2	4	1

36. The Council of Ministers is collectively responsible to
A. the President of India
B. the Prime Minister
C. the Parliament
D. the People

37. When the office of the President of India falls vacant, it must be filled by an election within:
A. eight months
B. six months
C. two months
D. nine months

38. The provisions as to disqualification on grounds of defection by a member of Parliament are contained in:
A. Article 191
B. Article 102
C. The Seventh Schedule
D. The Tenth Schedule

39. According to our Constitution, the Rajya Sabha:
A. is dissolved once in 2 years
B. is dissolved every 5 years
C. is dissolved every 6 years
D. is not subject to dissolution

40. Fundamental Duties were introduced in the Constitution by:
A. 40th Amendment
B. 42nd Amendment
C. 43rd Amendment
D. 44th Amendment

41. The jurisdiction of a High Court may be extended by the:
A. President
B. Governor of the State
C. Parliament
D. State Legislature

42. Linguistic reorganisation of state took place in:
A. 1947
B. 1950
C. 1956
D. 1971

43. The Union Council of Ministers is collectively responsible to the:
A. President
B. Lok Sabha
C. Rajya Sabha and Lok Sabha
D. Prime Minister

44. Who administers the oath of the office to the President in India?
A. Prime Minister
B. Speaker of Lok Sabha
C. Chief Justice of India
D. Vice-President

45. Which of the following qualifications is not essential for a person to become the Vice-President of India?
A. He must be an Indian citizen
B. He should be a graduate
C. He must not be less than 35 years of age
D. He must be qualified to be a member of the Rajya Sabha

46. The term "Fourth Estate" is used for:
A. The Press and Newspaper
B. Parliament
C. Judiciary
D. The Executive

47. Implementing Laws is the function of:
A. Executive
B. Legislature
C. Judiciary
D. Cabinet

48. Which one of the following is a Fundamental Right guaranteed by the Constitution of India?
A. Right to Govern
B. Right to Property
C. Right to Information
D. Right to Equality

49. Education is included in which of the following lists?
A. Central list
B. State list
C. Concurrent list
D. Local list

50. The Chief Jusitce of a High Court is appointed by:
A. The President
B. Chief Justice of the Supreme Court
C. Governor of the State
D. Chief Minister of the State

51. Can a person who is not a member of Parliament by appointed as a minister?
A. No
B. Yes
C. Yes, provided the Parliament approves of such an appointment
D. Yes, but he has to become a member of Parliament within six months of his appointment

52. Through which Constitutional Amendment was the Nagarpalika Bill passed?
A. 70th   B. 72nd
C. 73rd   D. 74th

53. The fourth schedule of the Constitution of India contains:

A. Directive Principles of State Policy
B. the Anti Defection Act
C. Fundamental Duties
D. Allocation of seats in the Council of State

54. Which of the following Article/ Articles read with the word 'Socialist' used in the Preamble of the Indian Constitution enabled the Supreme Court to deduce a fundamental right to equal pay for equal work?
A. Article 14
B. Article 14 and 15
C. Article 14, 15 and 16
D. Article 14 and 16

55. Under the Cabinet Mission Plan, the total number of seats allotted to each province in the Constituent Assembly was roughly in the ratio of one representative to the population of:
A. 8 lakh persons
B. 10 lakh persons
C. 12 lakh persons
D. 15 lakh persons

56. Which Article of the Constitution of India deals with the appellate jurisdiction of the Supreme Court in connection with constitutional cases:
A. Article 131
B. Article 132
C. Article 132 read with Article 134 A
D. Article 133 read with Article 134 A

57. Article 356 of the Constitution of India deals with:
    A. autonomy of States
    B. the proclamation of President's Rule in a State
    C. the removal of a Chief Minister
    D. the appointment of a Governor

58. Which one of the following constitutional amendments gives a constitutional status of the Panchayati Raj institutions?
    A. 72nd
    B. 73rd
    C. 74th
    D. 75th

59. Panchayati Raj system involves a three-tier arrangement. Which one of the following correctly represents this system?
    A. Village level, corporation level, block level
    B. Village level, block level, district level
    C. Village level, town level, district level
    D. Village level, district level, State level

60. The Election Commission is:
    A. A legislative body
    B. A constitutional body
    C. An executive body
    D. A non-formal body

61. Who is normally the Chancellor of the State Universities?
    A. Chief Minister of the State
    B. Governor of the State
    C. Education Minister of the State
    D. Advocate-General of the State

62. The *ex officio* Chairman of the NITI Aagog of India is the:
    A. Planning Minister
    B. Finance Minister
    C. Prime Minister
    D. President

63. In which part of the Constitution the concept of Welfare State finds elaboration?
    A. Preamble
    B. Fundamental Rights
    C. Fundamental Duties
    D. Directive Principles of State Policy

64. Judges of the High Courts cannot practise, after retirement, in:
    A. The Supreme Court
    B. Any of the High Courts
    C. The High Courts served by them
    D. Any court in the country

65. The election of the President can be challenged:
    A. before the Chief Election Commissioner
    B. in the Supreme Court
    C. before Union Parliament
    D. before the Ministry of Law

ANSWERS

1	2	3	4	5	6	7	8	9	10
A	C	B	C	B	A	A	C	C	A

11	12	13	14	15	16	17	18	19	20
B	D	A	D	D	A	B	A	A	B

21	22	23	24	25	26	27	28	29	30
A	B	D	C	B	D	A	B	C	B

31	32	33	34	35	36	37	38	39	40
C	C	D	A	A	C	B	D	D	B

41	42	43	44	45	46	47	48	49	50
C	C	B	C	B	A	C	D	C	A

51	52	53	54	55	56	57	58	59	60
D	D	D	C	B	B	B	B	B	B

61	62	63	64	65
B	C	D	C	B

GEOGRAPHY OF INDIA AND WORLD

1. Which of the following soils in India is most fertile?
   A. Regur
   B. Alluvial soil
   C. Laterite soil
   D. Red soil

2. In which of the following States is the site of Nhava Sheva Port located?
   A. Kerala
   B. Karnataka
   C. Andhra Pradesh
   D. Maharashtra

3. Density of Earth's atmosphere is highest in the:
   A. Troposphere
   B. Stratosphere
   C. Mesosphere
   D. Ionosphere

4. Which one of the following is the driest region in India?
   A. Telengana
   B. Marwar
   C. Vidarbha
   D. Marathwada

5. The Equatorial Forests of the Amazon Basin in South America are known as:
   A. Selva
   B. Taiga
   C. Tundra
   D. Pampas

6. Which is a tropical food crop requiring a temperature of 27°C and a rainfall more than 100 cm?
   A. Wheat
   B. Maize
   C. Rice
   D. Barley

7. After which one of the following tribes of India; has a large continent of ancient geological history of the world been named?
   A. Santhals
   B. Bhils
   C. Marias
   D. Gonds

8. Which one of the following characteristics is associated with the 'Bread Basket' area of the USA?
   A. Moderate rainfall in winter
   B. Heavy rainfall throughout the year
   C. Low rainfall in summer
   D. Long winter with snow

9. Which of the following is largely used in textile industries in India?
   A. Cotton
   B. Wool
   C. Synthetic fibres
   D. Jute

10. Sun belt of USA is important for which one of the following industries?
    A. Cotton textile
    B. Petrochemical
    C. Hi-tech electronics
    D. Food processing

11. Coffee is a:
    A. Sub-tropical shrub
    B. Warm temperate shrub
    C. Tropical shrub
    D. Cool temperate shrub

12. The best variety of world's cotton is known as:
    A. Sea Island
    B. Upland American
    C. Egyptian
    D. Short staple Indian

13. How much land area in India is under forests?
  - A. About 17%
  - B. About 28%
  - C. About 18%
  - D. About 21.34%

14. Which one of the following statements is not true for laterite soils?
  - A. they are the soils of the humid tropical regions
  - B. they are highly leached soils
  - C. their fertility is low
  - D. they are rich in line

15. Which of the following States has the largest deposits of mica in India:
  - A. Andhra Pradesh
  - B. Karnataka
  - C. Rajasthan
  - D. Madhya Pradesh

16. The Industry for which Nepa Nagar is known is:
  - A. cement
  - B. fertilizer
  - C. handloom
  - D. newsprint paper

17. Which of the following is known as the morning star?
  - A. Saturn
  - B. Jupiter
  - C. Venus
  - D. Mars

18. The Nagarjuna Sagar project is constructed on the river:
  - A. Kaveri
  - B. Krishna
  - C. Godavari
  - D. Indus

19. The innermost layer of the earth is known as:
  - A. Lithosphere
  - B. Mesosphere
  - C. Asthenosphere
  - D. Barysphere

20. Which one of the following is not a cold ocean current?
  - A. California
  - B. Oyashio
  - C. Kuroshio
  - D. Canaries

21. The highest trophic level in an ecosystem is obtained by:
  - A. herbivores
  - B. carnivores
  - C. decomposers
  - D. omnivores

22. Which of the following absorbs part of the insolation and preserves earth's radiated hear?
  - A. Oxygen
  - B. Nitrogen
  - C. Water vapour
  - D. Carbon dioxide

23. Arakan Yoma is the extension of the Himalayas located in:
  - A. Baluchistan
  - B. Myanmar
  - C. Nepal
  - D. Kashmir (India)

24. The largest estuary in India is at the mouth of river:
  - A. Hooghly
  - B. Bhagirathi
  - C. Godavari
  - D. Krishna

25. Match Lists I and II and mark the correct answer using the codes given below:

List-I (Places)	List-II (Minerals)
(a) Ankaleshwar	1. Iron ore
(b) Dalli-Rajhara	2. Petroleum
(c) Kodarma	3. Copper
(d) Khetri	4. Mica

Codes:

	(a)	(b)	(c)	(d)
A.	1	2	3	4
B.	2	1	4	3
C.	4	3	2	1
D.	3	2	1	4

26. When it is noon at IST meredian, what would be the local time at 120° East longitude:
    A. 09.30   B. 14.30
    C. 17.30   D. 20.00

27. Which one of the following is correctly matched?
    A. Eskimo–Canada
    B. Oran–Japan
    C. Lapps–India
    D. Gonds–Africa

28. The coniferous forests are not found in:
    A. Amazonian
    B. Scandinavia
    C. Canada
    D. Finland

29. The largest Mica producing country in the world?
    A. India   B. USA
    C. China   D. Australia

30. Which food crop in India is sown in October-November and reaped in April?
    A. Coconut   B. Coffee
    C. Rice   D. Wheat

31. Which one of the following is the longest river in the world?
    A. Amazon
    B. Yangtze-Kiang
    C. Nile
    D. Mississipi-Missouri

32. The Alamatti Dam is constructed on the river:
    A. Kaveri
    B. Seeleru
    C. Krishna
    D. Tungabhadra

33. Which of the following States is most famous for its beautiful sea beaches?
    A. Gujarat   B. Goa
    C. Tamil Nadu D. Odisha

34. Grassland is called 'Pampas' in:
    A. Africa
    B. South America
    C. United Kingdom
    D. the USA

35. The coastal part of water bodies of the oceans which is structurally part of the mainland of the continents is called the:
    A. Isthmus
    B. Oceanic Ridge
    C. Continental Shelf
    D. Continental Slope

36. Which one of the following is not the result of underground water action?
    A. Stalactites   B. Stalagmites
    C. Sink holes   D. Fiords

37. Which one of the following practices is adopted for restoring the fertility of soil?
    A. Weeding   B. Levelling
    C. Fallowing   D. Harrowing

38. The Eastern Coast of India is known as:
    A. Eastern Plateau
    B. Bengal Coast
    C. Coromandel Coast
    D. Cyclonic Coast

39. Which of the following dams is the largest?
    A. Mython Dam
    B. Bhakra-Nangal Dam
    C. Hirakud Dam
    D. Nagarjuna Sagar Dam

40. Which of the following States is the largest producer of lignite?
A. Odisha
B. Bihar
C. West Bengal
D. Tamil Nadu

41. The International date line passes through:
A. Gibraltar strait
B. Bering strait
C. Florida strait
D. Malacca strait

42. The direction of ocean currents is reversed with seasons:
A. in the Pacific ocean
B. in the Indian ocean
C. in the Atlantic ocean
D. in the Mediterranean sea

43. The importance of ozone layer is that it shields:
A. plants from radiation
B. life on earth from cosmic bombardment
C. earth from meteorites
D. life on earth from the ultraviolet rays of the sun

44. The ideal monsoon system is developed in:
A. Mexico   B. India
C. Thailand   D. China

45. The State which occupies the first place in India in the production of Tobacco is:
A. Tamil Nadu
B. West Bengal
C. Andhra Pradesh
D. Maharashtra

46. Why is rent earned by land even in the long-run?
A. Land has original and indestructible powers
B. Land is a man-made factor
C. Its supply is inelastic in the short run
D. Its supply is inelastic in the long-run

47. The largest brackish water lake of India is in the State of:
A. Jammu & Kashmir
B. Maharashtra
C. Odisha
D. West Bengal

48. Which of the following represents the zone between Tropic of Cancer and Tropic of Capricorn?
A. Frigid Zone
B. Torrid Zone
C. Temperate Zone
D. Sub-tropical Zone

49. Maharashtrian Plateau is made up of:
A. alluvial soil B. coral reef
C. sandstone   D. lava

50. Which gets first monsoon in summer?
A. Western Ghats
B. Himalayas
C. Eastern Ghats
D. Gangetic Plains

51. Which country is called the Sugar Bowl of the world?
A. Cuba   B. India
C. Argentina   D. Brazil

52. What is the maximum known depth of an ocean?
A. 8 km   B. 10 km
C. 11 km   D. 22 km

53. A line drawn on a weather map connecting places that receive equal amounts of sunshine is called:
A. Isohyet   B. Isotherm
C. Isobar   D. Isohel

54. Palk Strait connects:
A. India and Sri Lanka
B. North Korea and South Korea
C. Saudi Arabia and Burma (Myanmar)
D. Britain and France

55. Black Pagoda is found at:
A. Konark   B. Khajuraho
C. Madurai   D. Egypt

56. Earthquakes occur owing to:
A. changes in earth crust
B. movements in the interior layers of the earth
C. volcanic eruptions
D. None of the above

57. What is the International Date Line?
A. A line connecting places of the same longitude as Greenwich
B. The line near 180° longitude, while crossing which date changes
C. The line of the Globe which will have daytime throughout the year
D. None of the above

58. In which region do we find the belt of doldrum?
A. Polar region
B. Sub-tropical region
C. Temperate region
D. Equatorial region

59. The grasslands of Argentina are called:
A. Steppes   B. Pampas
C. Campos   D. Prairies

60. On which one of the following longitudes is the Indian Standard Time determined?
A. 68½ E   B. 68½ W
C. 82½ E   D. 82½ W

61. The origin of earth dates back to approximately:
A. 3.6 billion years
B. 4.6 billion years
C. 5.6 billion years
D. 6.6 billion years

62. The period by which the entire country in India comes under southwest monsoon is:
A. Ist - 10th June
B. 10th - 20th June
C. 20th - 30th June
D. Ist - 15th July

63. The most extensive soil cover of India comprises:
A. laterite soils
B. black soils
C. alluvial soils
D. marshy soils

64. Evergreen rain forest is mainly found in regions having well distributed annual rainfall:
A. below 50 cm
B. 50 - 100 cm
C. 100 - 200 cm
D. more than 200 cm

65. Which one of the following organisations is responsible for publishing topographical sheets?

A. Geological Survey of India (GSI)
B. National Atlas & Thematic Mapping Organisation (NATMO)
C. Indian Meteorological Department (IMD)
D. Survey of India (SOI)

66. Humidity is measured by:
A. Lactometer
B. Polarimeter
C. Thermometer
D. Hygrometer

67. Which of the following is not a terrestrial planet?
A. Mercury
B. Earth
C. Jupiter
D. Mars

68. Access to raw material is the main basis for the location of:
A. sugarcane industry
B. aluminium industry
C. electronic industry
D. hi-tech industry

69. Which of the following Himalayan peaks is situated in Assam?
A. Nanda Devi
B. Namche Barwa
C. Dhaulagiri
D. Kedarnath

70. Among the world oceans, the widest continental shelves are observed around the:
A. Atlantic ocean
B. Arctic ocean
C. Indian ocean
D. Pacific ocean

71. Mozambique current forms part of currents of:
A. North Pacific
B. South Pacific
C. Indian Ocean
D. South Atlantic

72. The average time interval between successive high and low tides is:
A. 3 hours and 13 minutes
B. 6 hours and 26 minutes
C. 12 hours and 36 minutes
D. 24 hours and 52 minutes

73. Which of the following shipping canals joins the North sea and the Baltic sea?
A. Suez
B. Keil
C. Soo
D. Manchester

74. High temperature and low pressure over the Indian subcontinent during the summer season, draws air from the Indian ocean leading to the in blowing of the:
A. South-east monsoon
B. South-west monsoon
C. Trade winds
D. Westerlies

75. Through which of the following countries does the river Tigris flow?
A. Egypt
B. Iran
C. Italy
D. Iraq

76. Imaginary lines drawn on a global map from pole-to-pole and from the perpendicular to the equator are called:
A. Contours
B. Isobars
C. Meridians
D. Steppes

77. The 23½° South latitude is known as:
A. the Tropic of Cancer
B. the Tropic of Capricorn
C. the Equator
D. the Prime Meridian

78. 'Equinox' means:
A. days are longer than nights
B. days and nights are equal
C. days are shorter than nights
D. None of these

79. The hills that have the Dodda Bettah Peak are:
A. Annamalai   B. Nilgiri
C. Palani   D. Kutralam

80. Which one of the following processes is responsible for changing the colour of a rock into yellow or red?
A. Hydration   B. Exfoliation
C. Carbonation D. Oxidation

81. The food crop sown in the largest area in India is:
A. maize   B. paddy
C. wheat   D. jawar

82. Find the mismatched pair:
A. Mathura—Oil refinery
B. Visakhapatnam—Aircraft
C. Sindri—Fertiliser
D. Kapurthala—Railway coaches

83. Which one of the following is the largest lake in the world?
A. Lake Superior
B. Caspian Sea
C. Lake Baikal
D. Lake Victoria

84. Chilka Lake is located in:
A. Bihar
B. West Bengal
C. Assam
D. Odisha

85. Seasonal movement of people from mountains to plains and vice versa is called:
A. migration
B. transhumance
C. commutation
D. transportation

86. What do you call a narrow neck of land that connects two large landmarks?
A. Peninsula   B. Isthmus
C. Cape   D. Strait

87. What is the colour of laterite soil?
A. Yellow   B. Brown
C. Red   D. Pink

88. What are Doldrums?
A. The trade winds
B. Area of great humidity
C. A low pressure belt round the Equator where there are very light winds and calm seas
D. Area where seas are calm

89. The Thermal Equator coincides with the Tropic of Cancer on:
A. 21st March
B. 21st June
C. 23rd September
D. 22nd December

90. The total length of India's coastline is approximately:
A. 5500 km   B. 7516 km
C. 6500 km   D. 8500 km

ANSWERS

1	2	3	4	5	6	7	8	9	10
B	D	A	B	A	C	D	A	A	B

11	12	13	14	15	16	17	18	19	20
A	D	D	D	A	D	C	B	D	B

21	22	23	24	25	26	27	28	29	30
D	C	B	A	B	B	A	A	C	D

31	32	33	34	35	36	37	38	39	40
C	C	B	B	C	D	C	C	B	D

41	42	43	44	45	46	47	48	49	50
B	B	D	B	C	A	C	C	D	A

51	52	53	54	55	56	57	58	59	60
A	A	D	A	A	B	B	D	B	C

61	62	63	64	65	66	67	68	69	70
B	D	C	C	B	D	C	A	B	D

71	72	73	74	75	76	77	78	79	80
C	C	B	B	D	C	B	B	B	D

81	82	83	84	85	86	87	88	89	90
B	B	B	D	A	B	B	C	B	B

INDIAN ECONOMY

1. According to the 2011 Census the population of India is:
   A. 1 billion 21 crore
   B. 1 billion 2 crore
   C. 1 billion 2 crore 7 lakh
   D. 1 billion

2. What is the density of population in India?
   A. 273
   B. 382
   C. 416
   D. 216

3. The sex ratio (females per thousand males) in India is:
   A. 927
   B. 963
   C. 943
   D. 993

4. The decadal growth rate of population during the decade 2001-2011:
   A. 17.7 per cent
   B. 18.5 per cent
   C. 12.8 per cent
   D. 13.7 per cent

5. The principal means of transport of goods in India is:
   A. Railways
   B. Roadways
   C. Inland waterways
   D. Airways

6. Which one of the following is the most densely populated state of India?
   A. UP
   B. Bihar
   C. West Bengal
   D. Kerala

7. Which of the following states has the highest literacy rate?
   A. Kerala
   B. Arunachal Pradesh
   C. Nagaland
   D. Maharashtra

8. Which one of the following Union Territories has the highest literacy rate:
   A. Puducherry
   B. Daman and Diu
   C. Lakshadweep
   D. Chandigarh

9. Unemployment in India is due to:
   A. poor manpower planning
   B. population explosion
   C. inappropriate educational system
   D. All of the above

10. The policy of family planning was adopted by the government in:
    A. 1947
    B. 1952
    C. 1956
    D. 1962

11. The Second Five Year Plan focussed on:
    A. agriculture
    B. education
    C. heavy industries
    D. health

12. Which one of the following measures has been taken to modernise Indian agriculture?
    A. Area under irrigation increase
    B. High yielding variety seeds
    C. Credit and facilities to villages
    D. All of the above

13. Seasonal unemployment refers mainly to:
    A. Private sector industry
    B. Public sector industry
    C. Agriculture
    D. Banks

14. Open unemployment refers to people:
    A. who are not willing to work
    B. who are willing but do not get work
    C. who leave their jobs in search of better ones
    D. who have been dismissed because of incorrect practices

15. Which one of the following is not a source of revenue of the Union Government?
    A. Income tax
    B. Corporation tax
    C. Land revenue
    D. Customs duties

16. Bank rate means:
    A. the official rate of interest charged by the Central Bank of the country
    B. rate of profit of the banking institutions
    C. interest rate charged by the scheduled banks
    D. interest rate charged by the moneylenders

17. Marginal revenue will be zero if the elasticity of demand is:
    A. negative
    B. unity
    C. greater than one
    D. equal to zero

18. The term "market" in Economics means:
    A. a central place
    B. presence of competition
    C. place where goods are stored
    D. shops and superbazars

19. Commercial banking system in India is:
    A. mixed banking
    B. unit banking
    C. branch banking
    D. None of the above

20. The gilt edged market in the capital market of India refers to:
    A. long term private securities
    B. market dealing in existing securities
    C. market for corporate securities
    D. market for Government securities

21. Which of the following yields the largest revenue to the Government of India?
    A. Sales tax
    B. Corporate tax
    C. Income tax
    D. Entertainment tax

22. Sustainable agriculture means:
    A. Self-sufficiency
    B. To be able to export and import under WTO norms
    C. To utilise land so that its quality remains intact
    D. To utilise waste land for agricultural purposes

23. Which one of the following crops is the greatest beneficiary of the Green Revolution in both production and productivity?
    A. Jowar   B. Maize
    C. Rice   D. Wheat

24. Per capita income means:
A. average income of the wage-earners
B. income necessary for an individual to meet his daily expenses
C. total income of the group divided by the number of the people in the group
D. average income of family

25. The agency estimating the national income of India is:
A. NITI Aayog
B. Ministry of Finance
C. RBI
D. CSO

26. The most serious economic problems of India are:
A. underdevelopment, not poverty
B. poverty and unemployment
C. unemployment, not poverty
D. stagnation, not poverty

27. National product includes goods:
A. only those consumed by the producers
B. all whether exchanged or not
C. both exchanged in markets and retained by producers for addition to their stock
D. only exchanged in markets but not those consumed by producers

28. Marginal utility is:
A. total minus average utility
B. addition to total utility because of one unit increase in commodity
C. total utility divided by the number of units
D. total plus average utility

29. Demand of a commodity mainly depends on:
A. desire to purchase
B. power to purchase
C. tax policy
D. advertisement

30. Which one of the following is in the State list?
A. Railway Police
B. Corporation Tax
C. Census
D. Economic and Social Planning

31. In a highly developed country the relative contribution of agriculture to Gross Domestic Product (GDP) is:
A. relatively high
B. relatively low
C. the same as that of other sectors
D. zero

32. Match List-I with List-II and select the correct answer using the codes given below:

List-I *(Industry)*	*List-II* *(Production Centre)*
(a) Jute Textile	1. Bhadohi
(b) Silk Textile	2. Ludhiana
(c) Woollen Hosiery	3. Bangalore
(d) Woollen Carpet	4. Titagarh

Codes:

	(a)	(b)	(c)	(d)
A.	3	4	2	1
B.	4	3	2	1
C.	1	3	4	2
D.	4	1	3	2

33. The credit control operation in India is performed by:
   A. Rural banks
   B. Commercial banks
   C. Reserve Bank of India
   D. State Bank of India

34. Division of labour is limited by:
   A. the number of workers
   B. hours of work
   C. extent of the market
   D. working space

35. The four factors of production are:
   A. land, labour, capital, organisation
   B. land, electricity, water, labour
   C. labour, capital, land, rainfall
   D. labour, climate, land, tools

36. What is the main purpose of currency?
   A. Currency Chest
   B. Standard of Postponed Payments
   C. Standard of Money
   D. Medium of Exchange

37. National Income accounting is the study of the income and expenditure of the entire:
   A. family
   B. state
   C. economy
   D. organisation

38. The problem of Economics arises from:
   A. plenty of goods
   B. scarcity of goods
   C. more wants and less goods
   D. All of these

39. Agricultural income-tax is a source of revenue to:
   A. Central Government
   B. State Government
   C. Local Administration
   D. Central and State Governments

40. Beyond a certain point, deficit financing will certainly lead to:
   A. inflation
   B. deflation
   C. recession
   D. economic stagnation

41. In public budgets, zero-based budgeting was first introduced in:
   A. USA   B. UK
   C. France   D. Sweden

42. To achieve economic self-reliance was the main objective of which of the following Five-Year Plans?
   A. First Plan
   B. Second Plan
   C. Third Plan
   D. Fourth Plan

43. The preparation of National Income Estimates is the responsibility of the:
   A. NITI Aayog
   B. National Development Council
   C. National Sample Survey
   D. Central Statistical Organisation

44. Which one of the following is the most sensitive indicator of the health of a community?
   A. Birth rate

B. Infant mortality rate

C. Death rate

D. Maternal mortality rate

45. Banks in India were nationalised for the first time in the year:

A. 1950   B. 1960

C. 1969   D. 1979

46. The objectives of Indian Planning are:

A. increasing national income

B. reducing inequalities in income wealth

C. elimination of poverty

D. All of the above

47. The Gandhian economy was based on the principle of:

A. State control

B. Competition

C. Trusteeship

D. Rural cooperation

48. Fiscal policy is concerned with:

A. public revenue

B. public expenditure and debt

C. bank rate policy

D. Both A and B

49. Devaluation of a currency refers to:

A. decrease in the internal value of money

B. decrease in the external value of money

C. decrease both in the external and internal values of money

D. Government withdrawal of a currency not of a denomination

50. The maternal mortality rates in Asia are the highest in:

A. Bangladesh   B. India

C. Indonesia   D. Nepal

51. To get the Net National Product we deduct what from the Gross National Product?

A. Direct Taxes

B. Imports

C. Interim Payments

D. Loss

52. 'Protection' means:

A. restrictions imposed on import trade

B. protection to home industries

C. no free exchange of goods and services between two countries

D. All of these

53. The Reserve Bank of India:

A. provides direct finance to agriculture

B. provides finance to primary cooperative societies

C. provides finance to State cooperative banks

D. does not provide finance to agriculture

54. In which sector of the Indian economy is productivity the highest?

A. Manufacturing

B. Transport, Communication and Commerce

C. Agriculture

D. Other sectors

55. Which of the following is not a method of estimating national income?

A. Income method

B. Value-added method
C. Expenditure method
D. Export-import method

56. As per the 2011 Census, the literacy rate in India has gone up to:
A. 70.0%   B. 78.0%
C. 80.5%   D. 73.0%

57. Population explosion in a country means:
A. high birth rate and high death rate
B. high birth rate and low death rate
C. low birth rate and high death rate
D. low birth rate and low death rate

58. The measurement of poverty line is based on the criteria of:
A. their dwelling houses
B. the nature of employment
C. caloric consumption
D. level of education

59. Elasticity of demand is a tendency of demand to:
A. increase or decrease on the change of price
B. increase on the rising of price
C. decrease on the falling of price
D. consistency of demand on rising and falling prices

60. Capital is that wealth:
A. which is used for the production of wealth
B. which is kept in boxes and lockers
C. which is buried in the land
D. which is stored for consumption

61. Function of an entrepreneur is:
A. organisation of labour
B. collection of capital
C. showing efficiency in collection of loans from the banks and the market
D. risk-taking

62. How many banks were nationalised on 19th July, 1969?
A. 14   B. 20
C. 19   D. 23

63. The poverty line has been defined in the:
A. Seventh Five-Year Plan
B. Sixth Five-Year Plan
C. Eighth Five-Year Plan
D. Fifth Five-Year Plan

64. In Centre-State financial relations in India, the Gadgil Formula is used in:
A. division of tax revenue
B. formulating the policy for fresh borrowings
C. writing off states indebtedness to the Centre
D. allocating Central Plan assistance between States

65. Which of the following is a cash crop?
A. Wheat   B. Rice
C. Maize   D. Sugarcane

66. According to the Reserve Bank of India, the term 'Open Market Operation' means sale and purchase of:
A. gold

B. government securities
C. iron and steel
D. foreign exchange

67. Reserve Bank of India was established on:
A. January 1, 1934
B. April 1, 1934
C. January 1, 1935
D. April 1, 1935

68. What is India's trade policy?
A. Increase in both exports and imports
B. Decrease in both exports and imports
C. Neither increase nor decrease in both imports and exports
D. Export promotion and import substitution

69. The Centre gives grants-in-aid to States:
A. to augment the financial resources of the States
B. to maintain good relations with the States
C. to ensure balanced and quick economic growth throughout the country
D. to ensure social justice in India

70. Temporary tax levied to obtain additional revenue is called:
A. Cess
B. Rate
C. Fee
D. Surcharge

71. Finance Commission is constituted every:
A. three years
B. six years
C. four years
D. five years

72. 'Mixed economy' means co-existence of:
A. heavy industries and light industries
B. agrarian economy and industrialised economy
C. the poor and the rich
D. public sector and private sector

73. The largest share of India's National income originates in the:
A. Primary sector
B. Secondary sector
C. Tertiary sector
D. None of the above

74. Which one of the following taxes is levied by the State Government only?
A. Entertainment tax
B. Wealth tax
C. Income tax
D. Corporation tax

75. Which one of the following States has the lowest per capita income in India?
A. Odisha
B. Bihar
C. Jharkhand
D. Rajasthan

ANSWERS

1	2	3	4	5	6	7	8	9	10
A	B	C	A	A	B	A	C	D	B

11	12	13	14	15	16	17	18	19	20
C	D	C	D	C	A	B	B	C	C

21	22	23	24	25	26	27	28	29	30
B	C	D	A	D	B	B	B	B	A
31	32	33	34	35	36	37	38	39	40
B	B	C	B	A	D	C	B	B	A
41	42	43	44	45	46	47	48	49	50
A	D	D	B	C	D	C	D	B	A
51	52	53	54	55	56	57	58	59	60
D	D	D	C	D	D	B	C	A	A
61	62	63	64	65	66	67	68	69	70
D	A	D	A	D	B	D	D	A	D
71	72	73	74	75					
D	D	C	A	B					

SCIENCE

1. Which of the following is the hardest metal?
   A. Gold   B. Iron
   C. Platinum   D. Tungsten

2. Bakeries use yeast in bread-making because it:
   A. makes the bread hard
   B. makes the bread soft and spongy
   C. enhances the food values
   D. keeps the bread fresh

3. The chemical name of 'laughing gas' is:
   A. nitric oxide
   B. nitrogen dioxide
   C. nitrogen pentoxide
   D. nitrous oxide

4. Brass is an alloy of:
   A. lead and tin
   B. zinc and copper
   C. antimony, tin and lead
   D. zinc, tin and copper

5. The length of its day and tilt of its axis are almost identical to those of the earth. This is true of:
   A. Uranus   B. Neptune
   C. Saturn   D. Mars

6. The milky way is classified as:
   A. spiral Galaxy
   B. electrical Galaxy
   C. irregular Galaxy
   D. round Galaxy

7. The energy of the sun is produced by:
   A. ionisation
   B. nuclear fusion
   C. nuclear fission
   D. oxidation

8. Which one of the following is not correctly matched?
   A. Decibel—unit of loudness of sound
   B. Horse power—unit of power
   C. Nautical mile—unit of distance in navigation
   D. Celsius—unit of heat

9. The common name of Sodium Bicarbonate is:
   A. baking soda
   B. washing soda
   C. caustic soda
   D. soda lime

10. Which variety of glass is heat resistant?
    A. Flint glass   B. Hard glass
    C. Bottle glass   D. Pyrex glass

11. Which of the following is a source of ready energy that one athlete can use after strenuous exercises?
    A. Milk
    B. Glucose
    C. Sucrose
    D. Tomato soup

12. The renewable source of energy:
    A. petroleum   B. kerosene
    C. coal   D. tree

13. The filament of an electric bulb is made of:
    A. copper   B. soft iron
    C. cast iron   D. tungsten

14. The natural wax and lac are obtained as:
    A. petroleum products
    B. resins of forest plants
    C. by-products of sugar indsutry
    D. insect secretions

15. Which hormone is known as 'fight or flight' hormone:
    A. insulin   B. adrenaline
    C. estrogen   D. oxytocin

16. "Pacemaker" is associated with:
    A. kidney   B. brain
    C. heart   D. lungs

17. The velocity of sound is more in:
    A. water   B. air
    C. steel   D. wood

18. Which planet orbits closest to the earth?
    A. Mars   B. Jupiter
    C. Venus   D. Mercury

19. It causes clotting of blood:
    A. thrombin
    B. haemoglobin
    C. pectin
    D. All of the above

20. Hardness of water is caused by soluble salts of:
    A. sodium and potassium
    B. potassium and ammonium
    C. sodium and calcium
    D. calcium and magnesium

21. The purification of a substance which evaporates without melting can be carried out by:
    A. Crystallisation
    B. Distillation
    C. Steam distillation
    D. Sublimation

22. Which of the following is the largest part of the human brain?
    A. Cerebellum
    B. Midbrain
    C. Cerebrum
    D. Medulla Oblongata

23. The total number of ear bones are:
    A. 2   B. 4
    C. 6   D. 8

24. An element in the form of gaseous atoms is converted into negative ions is called:
    A. bond energy
    B. electron affinity
    C. electronegativity
    D. ionization energy

25. Match the following:

List-I (Name of Instruments)	List-II (The Quantitites they Measure)
(a) Anemometer	1. Speed Rotation
(b) Ammeter	2. High temperature
(c) Tachometer	3. Wind speed
(d) Pyrometer	4. Electric current
	5. Pressure difference

Codes:

	(a)	(b)	(c)	(d)
A.	4	3	1	5
B.	3	4	1	2
C.	3	5	2	1
D.	1	4	5	2

26. Diamond is a form of:
A. carbon   B. nitrogen
C. oxygen   D. hydrogen

27. The method used to obtain alcohol from molasses is called:
A. Distillation B. Hydrolysis
C. Fermentation D. Oxidation

28. Which of the following is the least inflammable fabric?
A. Cotton   B. Nylon
C. Rayon   D. Silk

29. Which of the following is required to build new tissues in the human body?
A. Carbohydrates
B. Fat
C. Protein
D. Water

30. The Vitamin which is required for proper clotting of blood in human body is:
A. vitamin E   B. vitamin A
C. vitamin B_{12} D. vitamin K

31. Electron was discovered by:
A. Ernest Rutherford
B. Max Planck
C. Joseph Thomson
D. Albert Einstein

32. The number of amino acids which are found in nature is:
A. 20   B. 10
C. 15   D. 105

33. Bacteria were first seen, described and sketched by:
A. Jenner
B. Linnaeus
C. Pasteur
D. Leeuwenhock

34. The outstanding discovery of J.C. Bose, the Indian Scientist, is:
A. crescograph B. boson
C. cosmic rays D. ionograph

35. Density of a metal—when it is heated:
A. remains the same
B. increases
C. decreases
D. melts

36. Which of the following elements has been known to man from prehistoric times?
A. Sulphur   B. Uranium
C. Platinum   D. Arsenic

37. Our Solar system is a small unit of:
A. milky way galaxy
B. crab nebula galaxy
C. an independent galaxy
D. None of the above

38. Nights are cooler in the deserts because:
A. the sky is generally clear
B. the sky is generally cloudy
C. sand radiates heat less quickly as compared to earth
D. sand radiates heat more quickly as compared to the earth

39. Storage batteries commonly contain:
A. copper   B. mercury
C. lead   D. iron

40. Which of the following is a polymer?
A. Vinyl chloride
B. Urea
C. Starch
D. Styrene

41. What is common between a whale and a monkey?
    A. Both have on external ear
    B. Both have a long balancing tail
    C. Both have body-hair throughout life
    D. Both give birth to young ones

42. The hormone which regulates the basal metabolism in our body is secreted from:
    A. pituitary
    B. thyroid
    C. adrenal cortex
    D. pancreas

43. The acid used in car battery is:
    A. hydrochloric acid
    B. boric acid
    C. sulphuric acid
    D. carbonic acid

44. The boiling point of water is unaffected by:
    A. the external pressure
    B. the temperature of heat source
    C. the kind of dissolved substances
    D. the amount of dissolved substances

45. What is the velocity of sound in the air?
    A. 330 cms per sec.
    B. 330 metres per sec.
    C. 760 metres per sec.
    D. 1120 cms per sec.

46. The gas used in discharge tubes for optical decoration and advertising is:
    A. carbon dioxide
    B. ammonia
    C. sulphur dioxide
    D. neon

47. The substances present at the centre of the sun are in:
    A. solid, liquid and gaseous states
    B. liquid state only
    C. gaseous state only
    D. Both B and C

48. Blank capsules used in dispensing are made of:
    A. egg-white   B. gum
    C. starch   D. gelatine

49. Which one of the following is not an explosive?
    A. trinitrotoluene
    B. trinitroglycerine
    C. cyclotrimethylene trinitramine
    D. nitrochloroform

50. An ordinary clock loses time in summer; this is because:
    A. the length of the pendulum increases and time period decreases
    B. the length of the pendulum increases and time period increases
    C. the length of the pendulum decreases and time period increases
    D. the length of the pendulum decreases and time period decreases

51. When ice cubes floating in a beaker of water melt, the level of water in the beaker:

A. goes up
B. goes down
C. remains same
D. fall or rise depending on the number of ice cubes present in the beaker

52. Which of the following is an element?
A. Silica
B. Magnesia
C. Glass
D. Graphite

53. A characteristic gas smells near the unclear public urinals. Which is this gas?
A. Ammonia
B. Chlorine
C. Sulphur dioxide
D. Carbon monoxide

54. Kilowatt is a unit to measure:
A. power
B. work
C. energy
D. current

55. The apparent weight of a man in a lift will be less than his real weight:
A. when the lift is stationary
B. at no time
C. when the lift is going up with uniform acceleration
D. when the lift is going down with uniform acceleration

56. A natural sweetening agent obtained from a plant (but not sugar) is:
A. saccharin
B. santonine
C. cyclomates
D. None of these

57. Alkaloids are by-products of the metabolism of:
A. animals
B. bacteria
C. plants
D. viruses

58. Atom bomb is based on:
A. artificial radioactivity
B. nuclear fission
C. nuclear fusion
D. chemical reaction

59. Which gas in the atmosphere absorbs ultraviolet rays?
A. Methane
B. Nitrogen
C. Ozone
D. Helium

60. Which of the following is essential for the plants to help them in the formation of chlorophyll?
A. Potassium
B. Magnesium
C. Calcium
D. Phosphorus

61. The material used for bleaching paper pulp is:
A. lime
B. alum
C. caustic soda
D. sodium hypochlorite

62. Which of the following is used as a preservative of food articles?
A. sodium bicarbonate
B. sodium benzoate
C. sodium carbonate
D. sodium chloride

63. Milk in natural form has a certain amount of sugar. This sugar is called:
A. fructose
B. glucose
C. sucrose
D. lactose

64. Blood is classified biochemically as a:
A. cell
B. liquid
C. tissue
D. cartilage

65. Foxglove plant yields a drug which is a stimulant to:
A. kidney   B. brain
C. lungs   D. heart

66. The function of a catalyst in a reaction is to:
A. decrease the rate of the reaction
B. increase the rate of the reaction
C. increase the pressure of the reactants
D. decrease the pressure of the reactants

67. Which of the following gases is used for refrigeration?
A. Sulphur dioxide
B. Chlorine
C. Freon
D. Phosphine

68. Which plant stores food in the stem?
A. Ginger   B. Carrot
C. Raddish   D. Groundnut

69. When a ship enters a sea from a river, its level:
A. remains same
B. falls
C. rises
D. rises or falls depending on the condition and material of the ship

70. The sky is blue in colour because of:
A. combination of various lights producing blue colour
B. the moisture present in the air

C. the accumulation of smoke in the sky
D. the scattering of light by dust particles or air molecules

71. If a body is taken from the earth to the moon:
A. its mass will not be affected
B. its mass will decrease
C. its weight will become more
D. Both its mass and weight will decrease

72. An iron nail floats on mercury but sinks in water because:
A. mercury is a metal and water is not
B. upper layer of mercury is strong
C. mercury is a liquid metal and iron is a solid metal
D. iron is less dense than mercury

73. An electric bulb produces a loud sound when broken, because:
A. the glass is brittle
B. the gas inside the bulb suddenly expands
C. the gas makes the explosion
D. the air rushes into the partial vacuum in the bulb

74. A person climbing a hill bends forward so as to:
A. reduce chances of slipping
B. increase his stability
C. increase his stamina
D. move faster

75. The freezer in a refrigerator is fitted near the top:
A. without any specific and particular purpose

B. because it is convenient
C. so that it can cool the whole interior by setting up convection current
D. to keep it away from the hot compressor

76. The cover of a solar cooker is made of glass:
A. because glass allows heat radiation from the sun into the container but not out of it
B. to enable us to see the food cooking
C. because heat is radiated without absorption by glass
D. as glass is a good conductor of heat and cheap

77. Chlorine is a/an:
A. halogen   B. alloy
C. metal   D. noble gas

78. Which of the following is not an alloy?
A. brass   B. bronze
C. steel   D. zinc

79. Which of the following is an insecticide?
A. TNT   B. DDT
C. Urea   D. Alcohol

80. 'IC chips' for computers are usually made of:
A. chromium   B. lead
C. silicon   D. gold

81. Which of the following is used as dry ice?
A. Carbon dioxide
B. Ammonia
C. Oxygen
D. Ice with raw dust

82. The normal unit of measurement of distance of a star is:
A. kilometre   B. light year
C. nautical mile D. knot

83. Solution of washing soda in water will be:
A. alkaline
B. acidic
C. neutral
D. None of these

84. Vitamin C is also called:
A. ascorbic acid
B. nucleic acid
C. lactic acid
D. hydrochloric acid

85. Pearls are found in:
A. turtles   B. snails
C. tortoises   D. oysters

86. Coal burns in air because air contains:
A. hydrogen
B. oxygen
C. nitrogen
D. carbon dioxide

87. A substance which glows and is used in watch dials is:
A. sodium   B. sulphur
C. phosphorus   D. chlorine

88. Which of the following chemical is used by photographers?
A. Sodium sulphide
B. Silver bromide
C. Potassium cyanide
D. Ivory powder

89. The process of coating iron with zinc is known as:
A. vulcanisation
B. electroplating
C. polishing
D. galvanising

90. The best source of iron is:
A. milk
B. egg
C. cauliflower
D. green vegetables

91. Vitamins are useful to the body for:
A. replacing the energy lost
B. the body growth
C. regulating the functions of the body
D. maintaining the body temperature

92. The metals used for the manufacture of stainless steel are:
A. chromium and carbon
B. aluminium and carbon
C. copper and nickel
D. chromium and zinc

93. In refrigerator, the refrigerant liquid is:
A. carbon dioxide
B. nitrogen
C. liquid helium
D. ammonia

94. Which of the following is the least inflammable fabric?
A. Cotton
B. Nylon
C. Rayon
D. Silk

95. Which of the following contains carbon?
A. Chromite
B. Bauxite
C. Lignite
D. Phosphorite

96. Which of the following blood groups is the universal donor?
A. A
B. B
C. AB
D. O

97. Which of the following fight infections in the body?
A. WBCs
B. RBCs
C. Blood plasma
D. Haemoglobin

98. The term 'refraction of light' means:
A. bending of light rays when they enter from one medium to another medium
B. splitting of white light into seven colours when it passes through the prism
C. bending of light round the corners of obstacles and apertures
D. coming back of light from a bright smooth surface

99. In the visible spectrum, the colour having the shortest wavelength is:
A. green
B. red
C. violet
D. blue

100. What is used to disintegrate bladder stones?
A. Infrared
B. Ultraviolet rays
C. X-rays
D. Ultrasonics

101. Mica is used in an electric iron, because it is a:
A. bad conductor of heat
B. good conductor of heat
C. good conductor of electricity
D. bad conductor of electricity

102. A line on a map joining places having equal atmospheric pressure is called:
A. Isotherm   B. Isobar
C. Isocryme   D. Isoheline

103. On addition of salt to water, its:
A. boiling point increases
B. boiling point decreases
C. boiling point is not affected
D. freezing point increases

104. If the velocity of a particle is reduced to half of its initial value, then the kinetic energy of the particle will:
A. get doubled
B. become four times
C. reduce to half its original value
D. reduce to one-fourth of its original value

105. A lunar eclipse occurs when:
A. Sun, Moon and Earth are not in the same line
B. Earth comes between the Sun and the Moon
C. Moon comes between the Sun and the Earth
D. Sun comes between the Earth and the Moon

106. Red light is used in traffic signals because:
A. it has the longest wavelength
B. it is beautiful
C. it is visible to people even with bad eyesight
D. None of these

107. The oil in the wick of a lamp rises up due to:
A. pressure difference
B. low viscosity of oil
C. capillary action
D. gravitational force

108. A thick glass tumbler cracks more easily than a thin one when hot water is poured into it. Why?
A. Thick glass is more brittle than thin glass
B. Thick glass is of inferior quality
C. The inner surface of the tumbler expands more than its outer surface
D. The outer surface of the tumbler expands more than its inner surface

109. How many cells are there in the hen's egg?
A. 1   B. 10
C. 100   D. 1000

110. The mirror placed near the driver of a bus is:
A. plane mirror
B. convex mirror
C. concave mirror
D. cooling mirror

111. Beri-Beri is a disease, caused by the deficiency of:
A. vitamin B   B. vitamin C
C. vitamin K   D. protein

112. Following are the great discoveries in physics:
1. X-rays
2. Theory of Relativity
3. Super Conductivity
4. Raman Effect

The chronological order in which they were discovered is:
A. 1, 3, 2, 4
B. 1, 2, 3, 4
C. 2, 1, 4, 3
D. 4, 1, 2, 3

113. Heliotropism is:
A. harmful effects of helium
B. helicopter flight control
C. medicine used to cure heart diseases
D. movement of plant organs towards sunlight

114. The isotope of uranium which is very much radioactive is:
A. U 235
B. U 238
C. U 233
D. All of the above

115. The human skull consists of:
A. 8 bones
B. 14 bones
C. 21 bones
D. 42 bones

ANSWERS

1	2	3	4	5	6	7	8	9	10
D	B	D	D	D	A	B	D	A	D

11	12	13	14	15	16	17	18	19	20
B	D	D	D	B	C	A	C	A	D

21	22	23	24	25	26	27	28	29	30
D	C	C	B	B	A	C	A	C	D

31	32	33	34	35	36	37	38	39	40
C	A	D	A	C	A	A	D	C	C

41	42	43	44	45	46	47	48	49	50
D	B	C	B	B	D	C	C	D	B

51	52	53	54	55	56	57	58	59	60
C	D	C	A	D	D	C	B	C	B

61	62	63	64	65	66	67	68	69	70
D	B	D	C	D	B	C	A	C	D

71	72	73	74	75	76	77	78	79	80
A	D	D	B	C	A	A	D	D	C

81	82	83	84	85	86	87	88	89	90
A	B	A	A	D	B	C	B	D	D

91	92	93	94	95	96	97	98	99	100
C	A	D	A	C	D	A	A	C	C

101	102	103	104	105	106	107	108	109	110
A	A	A	D	B	A	C	C	A	C

111	112	113	114	115
A	B	D	A	C

Science and Technology

1. Which one of the following techniques can be used to establish the paternity of child?
   A. Protein analysis
   B. Chromosome counting
   C. Quantitative analysis of DNA
   D. DNA finger printing

2. The first Indian artificial satellite was named:
   A. Aryabhatta B. Explorer-I
   C. Sputnik-1   D. Luna-3

3. The first computer of India is known as:
   A. Dharam   B. Siddharth
   C. Param   D. Gati

4. The symptom of anaemia is:
   A. loose or wrinkled skin
   B. difficulty in breathing
   C. yellowish eyes
   D. Oedema of liver

5. In surgery, what is arthroplasty:
   A. open heart surgery
   B. kidney transplant
   C. hip-joint replacement
   D. blood transfussion

6. The intermediate range nuclear-capable missile developed indigenously is named:
   A. Agni   B. Prithvi
   C. Nag   D. Trishul

7. The computer was invented by:
   A. Faraday   B. Maxwell
   C. Babbage   D. Bill Gates

8. Which of the following is the name of the first indigenously developed Indian Super Computer?
   A. Param   B. Shakti
   C. Dharam   D. Gati

9. The instrument which measures the movement of clouds by casting their images through a peephole on to a black mirrored surface is called:
   A. Periscope
   B. Nephoscope
   C. Stethoscope
   D. Gyroscope

10. Genetic engineering is possible only due to the role of certain specific enzymes that cut DNA at particular points of the sequence. These enzymes are called:
    A. nucleuses
    B. restriction enzymes
    C. DNA polymerases
    D. nitrogenases

11. The intensity of the waves generated by an earthquake and its time of occurrence is recorded by a:
    A. Barometer
    B. Thermometer
    C. Seismograph
    D. Galvanometer

12. A genetic disorder characterised by poor blood circulation and

abnormal haemoglobin molecules is better known as:
A. Sickel-cell anaemia
B. Haemophilia
C. Phenyl ketonuria
D. Huntington's chorea

13. The process of preparation of soap is known as:
A. Saponification
B. Calcification
C. Hydroxylation
D. Methylation

14. Who amongst the following initiated the age of genetic engineering in 1973 by inserting an amphibian ribosomal RNA gene into a bacterial plasmid?
A. Cohen and Boyer
B. J.C. Sanford
C. Watson and Crick
D. Roger Beachy

15. Superconductivity results when matter is:
A. heated to very high temperature
B. compressed to very high pressure
C. subjected to very low pressure
D. cooled to very low temperature

16. All of the following diseases are caused by viruses except:
A. jaundice
B. influenza
C. mumps
D. typhoid

17. Penicillin is given a patient in order to:
A. cure hereditary disease
B. cure all diseases
C. prevent any rise in body temperature
D. prevent the growth of several types of diseases caused by bacteria

18. BCG is:
A. curative medicine for tuberculosis
B. a preventive medicine for tuberculosis
C. a disinfectant
D. an antiseptic

19. What is "Lakshya"?
A. Pilotless target aircraft
B. Missile
C. Radar
D. Satellite Launch Vehicle

20. What is a 'Robot':
A. a type of rocket
B. a bomb
C. a machine that resembles a person and does mechanical routine tasks on command
D. an animal found in the jungles of Africa

21. MAB stands for:
A. Man and Biosphere Programme
B. Man and Biology Programme
C. Mammals and Biosphere Programme
D. None of the above

22. Element used for atomic power is:
A. calcium　　B. sodium
C. beryllium　D. uranium

23. A pure semiconductor:
    A. has low resistance
    B. is called an intrinsic semi-conductor
    C. Both of the above
    D. None of the above

24. AIDS disease is caused by:
    A. virus
    B. sexual contact
    C. bacteria
    D. protozoa

25. The first indigenously built missile boat is named as:
    A. INS Vibhuti
    B. INS Vikrant
    C. INS Shilpi
    D. INS Mana

26. Which of the following is an example of Bio-technology?
    A. Using electron microscope
    B. Using technology to stabilise the life processes
    C. Using modern techniques to understand the evolution of life
    D. Using micro-organisms to synthesise insulin

27. Autopsy means:
    A. curing a disease through self-medication
    B. postmortem examination of a human body
    C. curing a disease through auto-suggestion
    D. becoming diseased through abuse of drugs

28. Introduction of a steel plough in the place of a wooden plough is an instance of:
    A. advanced technology
    B. appropriate technology
    C. redundant technology
    D. absolute technology

29. For appropriate technology what factors are of immediate concern?
    I. skilled manpower
    II. capital
    III. infrastructure
    IV. latest innovation
    A. I and II   B. III and IV
    C. I and IV   D. II and IV

30. Eco mark is given to Indian products that are:
    A. pure and unadulterated
    B. rich in protein
    C. environment friendly
    D. economically viable

31. 'Dolly' is the first clone mammal in the world of:
    A. buffalo   B. goat
    C. sheep   D. monkey

32. India's biggest nuclear research reactor is known as:
    A. Apsara   B. Dhruva
    C. Cirus   D. Purnima

33. We use the term 'mach number' in connection with:
    A. sound
    B. submarines
    C. aircraft
    D. spacecraft

34. Which of the following units measures the memory of the computer?
    A. Volts   B. Amperes
    C. Ohms   D. Bits

35. Maximum 'gobar gas' is produced during:
A. summer
B. winter
C. rainy season
D. All seasons

36. The first Indian satellite, Aryabhatta, was launched into space from a cosmodrome of:
A. France
B. USA
C. USSR
D. West Germany

37. The Vikram Sarabhai Space Centre is at:
A. Ahmedabad
B. Bangalore
C. Sriharikota
D. Trivandrum

38. The science dealing with the study of inheritance and variation is called:
A. Genetics
B. Evolution
C. Morphology
D. Cytology

39. Games are made up of:
A. histones
B. non-histones
C. proteins
D. polynucleotides

40. Which is the first artificial satellite to be put into orbit on October 4, 1957?
A. Sputnik-1
B. Apollo-7
C. Explorer-1
D. Solar Max

41. CNG (Compressed Natural Gas) is used for:
A. protecting pollution
B. saving diesel
C. avoiding the use of petrol
D. All of the above

42. Bronchitis is a disease of:
A. blood
B. liver
C. intestine
D. respiratory tract

43. The molecules responsible for storing the genetic code are:
A. DNA
B. RNA
C. protein
D. chromosome

44. Test tube baby means:
A. ovum fertilised and developed in test tube
B. ovum fertilised in test tube and developed in test tubes
C. ovum fertilised in test tubes and developed in uterus
D. ovum developed without fertilisation in test tubes

45. What is the basic characteristic of antigens:
A. They are capable of stimulating the formation of haemoglobin in the blood
B. They destroy haemoglobin
C. They are capable of defending themselves against attack by antibodies
D. They are capable of stimulating the formation of antibodies

46. What was the disease that led to the discovery of first anti viral vaccine?
  A. Cancer   B. Tetanus
  C. Polio   D. Small pox

47. Which is the most fast spreading disease?
  A. Malaria
  B. Plague
  C. Poliomyelitis
  D. Leprosy

48. The Central Food Technological Research Institute is located at:
  A. Kolkata   B. Kanpur
  C. Mysore   D. Ranchi

49. The International Rice Research Institute is located in:
  A. Philippines   B. Thailand
  C. Indonesia   D. Malaysia

50. "AIDS" affects:
  A. blood cells of human body
  B. immune system of human body
  C. growth of human body
  D. All of the above

51. Which of the following fertilisers is used after sowing the seeds:
  A. nitrate
  B. potash
  C. green manure
  D. phosphorus

52. Swelling of a strained foot is reduced by soaking in hot water containing a large amount of common salt. This is because of phenomenon called:
  A. Osmosis
  B. Plasmolysis
  C. Electrolysis
  D. None of these

53. Match List-I with List-II and select the correct answer using the codes given below the lists:

List-I	List-II
(a) Trishul	1. Anti-tank missile
(b) Prithvi	2. Intermediate range ballistic system
(c) Agni	3. Short range surface to air missile
(d) Nag	4. Surface to surface missile

Codes:

	(a)	(b)	(c)	(d)
A.	1	2	3	4
B.	4	3	2	1
C.	3	4	2	1
D.	2	1	4	3

54. In paints, the pigment is responsible for:
  A. durability   B. colour
  C. smoothness   D. glossy face

55. The working principle of a washing machine is:
  A. centrifugation
  B. dialysis
  C. reverse osmosis
  D. diffusion

56. Who invented 'radar':
  A. J.H. Van Tassell
  B. Wilhelm K. Roentgen
  C. P.T. Farnsworth
  D. A.H. Taylor and Zeo C. Young

57. Which one of the following is a useful functional association between fungi and the roots of higher plants?
 A. Biofertiliser
 B. Coralloid root
 C. Lichen
 D. Mycorrhiza

58. Low temperatures (cryogenics) find application in:
 A. space travel, surgery and magnetic levitation
 B. surgery, magnetic levitation and telemetry
 C. space travel, surgery and telemetry
 D. space travel, magnetic levitation and telemetry

59. Pure silicon is used as a:
 A. conductor
 B. insulator
 C. non-conductor
 D. semiconductor

60. The most common type of fingerprint encountered are:
 A. whorls
 B. loops
 C. arches
 D. composites

61. Indian farmers are unhappy over the introduction of 'Terminator Seed Technology' because the seeds produced by this technology are expected to:
 A. show poor germination
 B. form low-yielding plants despite the high quality

C. give rise to sexually sterile plants
 D. give rise to plants incapable of forming viable seeds

62. Which one of the following genetic diseases is sex linked?
 A. Royal haemophilia
 B. Tay Sachs disease
 C. Cystic fibrosis
 D. Hypertension

63. Guided missiles are:
 A. missiles that guide the soldiers in the army
 B. unmanned self-propelled space or air vehicles carrying explosive war head
 C. missiles that are launched by the gliders
 D. ordinary war planes with a very sharp striking power and deep thrust

64. Prithvi is:
 A. indigenously developed intermediate range ballistic missile
 B. indigenously developed nuclear bomb
 C. indigenously developed nuclear reactor
 D. indigenously developed surface to surface missile

65. National Institute of Immunology and National Institute of Science, Technology and Development Studies are located in:
 A. Hyderabad
 B. Bangalore
 C. Mumbai
 D. New Delhi

ANSWERS

1	2	3	4	5	6	7	8	9	10
C	A	B	D	C	A	C	A	B	B

11	12	13	14	15	16	17	18	19	20
C	A	C	A	D	D	D	B	A	C

21	22	23	24	25	26	27	28	29	30
A	D	B	A	A	B	B	A	A	C

31	32	33	34	35	36	37	38	39	40
C	B	C	D	C	C	D	A	D	A

41	42	43	44	45	46	47	48	49	50
D	D	A	C	D	D	B	C	A	B

51	52	53	54	55	56	57	58	59	60
A	A	C	B	A	D	A	A	B	B

61	62	63	64	65
D	A	B	D	D

AWARDS AND HONOURS

1. Who among the following is the first person to receive the Bharat Ratna award?
   A. C. Rajagopalachari
   B. S. Radhakrishnan
   C. C.V. Raman
   D. M. Visweswaraiya

2. Who among the following is the first person who was given the Bharat Ratna award posthumaously?
   A. K. Kamraj
   B. Lal Bahadur Shastri
   C. B.R. Ambedkar
   D. Vallabhbhai Patel

3. Which of the following is the highest order of gallantry award in India?
   A. Mahavir Chakra
   B. Vir Chakra
   C. Paramveer Chakra
   D. Ashok Chakra

4. The Arjuna awards are given to outstanding persons in the field of:
   A. science
   B. sports
   C. social services
   D. literature

5. The Bhartiya Jnanpith award is given to:
   A. sportspersons
   B. scientists
   C. coaches
   D. creative writers

6. Dada Saheb Phalke award is given in the field of:
   A. social services
   B. cinema
   C. creative writing
   D. politics

7. Who among the following is the first to receive 'Dada Saheb Phalke award'?
   A. Sivaji Ganesan
   B. Dr. Raj Kumar
   C. Devika Rani
   D. Majrooh Sultanpuri

8. Which of the following awards is given to the eminent coaches who successfully trained international sportspersons and teams:
   A. Dronacharya award
   B. K.K. Birla Foundation sports award
   C. Jamnalal Bajaj award
   D. Arjuna award

9. Lata Mangeshkar award is given by Madhya Pradesh Government in the field of:
   A. music   B. cinema
   C. drama   D. dance

10. The Kalinga Prize is given for the popularisation of Science and Research, by which of the following:
    A. UNICEF   B. UNESCO
    C. Odisha Govt.   D. Indian Govt.

11. Indira Gandhi International award is given in the field of:
    A. peace
    B. disarmament

C. development
D. All of the above

12. Which of the following prizes is considered to be the most prestigious in the world?
A. Magsaysay award
B. Nobel prize
C. Japan prize
D. Pulitzer award

13. Dhanvantari prize is given in which of the following fields:
A. medicine
B. agriculture
C. journalism
D. international understanding

14. The Nobel prize is not given in which of the following fields:
A. peace   B. physics
C. economics   D. agriculture

15. Match the following:

List-I *(Nobel Prize Recipients)*	*List-II* *(Fields in which given)*
(a) C.V. Raman	1. Economics
(b) Hargobind Khorana	2. Peace
(c) Mother Teresa	3. Medicine
(d) Amartya Sen	4. Literature
(e) Rabindra Nath Tagore	5. Physics

Codes:

	(a)	(b)	(c)	(d)	(e)
A.	5	3	2	1	4
B.	5	2	3	1	4
C.	3	4	2	1	5
D.	3	4	2	5	1

16. Who was first Nobel prize winner in the field of Physics?
A. Meriy Curie
B. Wilhelm Rontgen
C. C.V. Raman
D. Thomas Alva Edison

17. Which of the following is not a Civilian award?
A. Padma Vibhushan
B. Bharat Ratna
C. Padma Bhushan
D. Param Vishist Seva Medal

18. Which of the following is not a Gallantry award?
A. Paramveer Chakra
B. Mahavir Chakra
C. Padma Shri
D. Ashoka Chakra

19. Vikram Sarabhai Puraskar is given for:
A. outstanding contribution in science and technology
B. the popularisation of science and research
C. outstanding contribution in space and research
D. significant contribution in medicine

20. Which of the following is the highest order of Scientific award in India?
A. Shanti Swaroop Bhatnagar Puraskar
B. Homi Jahangir Bhabha Puraskar
C. Vikram Sarabhai Puraskar
D. G.D. Birla Science Puraskar

21. Which of the following awards is not conferred by Indian Government?
A. Ambedkar International award

B. Mahatma Gandhi Peace award
C. Padma Bhushan
D. Mahatma Gandhi award

22. C.K. Naidu award is given to a person for:
A. excellence in athletics
B. outstanding performance in games
C. outstanding contribution in cricket
D. best performance in hockey

23. Who among the following cinestars is awarded Pakistan's highest civil award in recognition of his services in improving Indo-Pak relations:
A. Manoj Kumar
B. Dilip Kumar
C. Raj Kumar
D. Ashok Kumar

24. The Saraswati Samman the highest and most prestigious literacy award of the country is given by:
A. Bharati Jnanpith
B. Sahitya Akademi
C. K.K. Birla Foundation
D. Human Resources Ministry, Indian Government

25. The Nobel prize for economics was awarded for the first time in 1969 by:
A. Swedish Central Bank
B. World Bank
C. International Monetary Fund
D. Nobel Foundation Committee

26. The UNESCO peace award is regarded as little Nobel prize conferred by:

A. UNESCO
B. Nobel Foundation Committee, Sweden
C. US Government
D. None of these

27. Govind Ballabh Pant award is given to:
A. the honestman of the year
B. the best parliamentarian
C. the best sportsman of the year
D. None of these

28. Which of the following samman is not conferred by Madhya Pradesh Government?
A. Tansen Samman
B. Kalidas Samman
C. Tulsi Samman
D. Vyas Samman

29. What name is given to the highest award for self-sacrifice or brave, daring and proeminent act of valour?
A. Param Vishist Seva Medal
B. Mahavir Chakra
C. Paramveer Chakra
D. Vir Chakra

30. 'Global 500' awards are given for achievements in:
A. population control
B. campaign against terrorism
C. protection of environment
D. campaign against drugs

31. The first Indian to win Nobel prize was:
A. C.V. Raman
B. Rabindra Nath Tagore
C. Hargobind Khorana
D. Amartya Sen

32. In which one of the following scientific fields Borlaug award is given:
- A. medicine
- B. space research
- C. agriculture
- D. atomic physics

33. 'Stri Shakti Puraskar' is given to women for:
1. excellence in athletics
2. outstanding performance in games
3. courage and enterprise for betterment of women
4. contribution to the nation and the people

Select your answer from the codes given below:

Codes:
- A. 1 and 2
- B. 2 and 3
- C. 3 and 4
- D. 1 and 4

34. The highest civilian award of India, Bharat Ratna has been awarded to only two foreigners so far. One of them is Khan Abdul Ghaffar Khan, the other is:
- A. Mikhail Gorbachev
- B. George Bush
- C. Nelson Mandela
- D. Helmut Kohl

35. Match the following:

I. Arjuna award	(a) Persons of cine world
II. Oscar award	(b) Journalists
III. Dronacharya award	(c) Sports persons
IV. Pulitzer prize	(d) Coaches

Codes:
- A. I-(a), II-(b), III-(d), IV-(c)
- B. I-(c), II-(a), III-(d), IV-(b)
- C. I-(b), II-(a), III-(c), IV-(d)
- D. I-(c), II-(d), III-(a), IV-(b)

36. Match List-I with List-II and select the correct answer by using the codes given below the lists:

List-I (Field in which given)	List-II (Name of Award)
(a) Science	1. Ghalib award
(b) Films	2. Arjuna award
(c) Poetry and prose	3. Phalke award
(d) Sports	4. Shanti Swarup Bhatnagar Memorial award

Codes:

	(a)	(b)	(c)	(d)
A.	4	3	2	1
B.	3	4	1	2
C.	3	4	2	1
D.	4	3	1	2

37. Which India-born scientist was awarded the Nobel prize in Astrophysics?
- A. Prof. Chandrasekhar
- B. Sir C.V. Raman
- C. Satyendra Nath Bose
- D. Vikram Sarabhai

38. Which of the following awards is not conferred by K.K. Birla Foundation?
- A. Bihari award
- B. Shankar award
- C. Bharat Bharti Samman
- D. Vyas Samman

39. The Vachaspati award is given for the outstanding contribution in the field of:
A. Hindi literature
B. Sanskrit literature
C. Bengali literature
D. Malayalam literature

40. The Ramon Magsaysay award, considered to be the Asia's Nobel prize is not given in which of the following fields:
A. government services
B. public services
C. community leadership
D. peace and disarmament

ANSWERS

1	2	3	4	5	6	7	8	9	10
A	B	C	B	D	B	C	A	A	B
11	12	13	14	15	16	17	18	19	20
D	B	A	D	A	B	D	C	C	A
21	22	23	24	25	26	27	28	29	30
D	C	B	C	A	A	B	D	C	C
31	32	33	34	35	36	37	38	39	40
B	C	C	C	B	D	A	C	B	D

GAMES AND SPORTS

1. Which is the national game of India?
   A. Football   B. Cricket
   C. Hockey   D. Kabaddi

2. Who among the following sportsmen is called the 'magician of Hockey'?
   A. Dhyanchand
   B. Dhanraj Pillai
   C. Pargat Singh
   D. Baljit Singh Dhillon

3. Which one of the following teams won the First One-Day Cricket World Cup held in 1975?
   A. England   B. Australia
   C. Pakistan   D. West Indies

4. In India the game of polo was introduced by the:
   A. Greeks
   B. Englishmen
   C. Turks
   D. Mughals

5. The term 'Tricks' is associated with which of the following games?
   A. Polo   B. Billiards
   C. Bridge   D. Croquet

6. P.V. Sindhu is associated with which of the following sport?
   A. Weightlifting
   B. Swimming
   C. Tennis
   D. Badminton

7. The name of Abhinav Bindra is associated with this sport?
   A. Shooting   B. Cricket
   C. Football   D. Basketball

8. 'Deodhar Trophy' is associated with which of the following games?
   A. Hockey   B. Cricket
   C. Football   D. Basketball

9. 'Free-throw' is given in which of the following sports?
   A. Volleyball
   B. Basketball
   C. Badminton
   D. Cricket

10. Match the following:

List-I	*List-II*
(Countries)	*(Sports)*
1. Australia	(a) Bull fighting
2. USA	(b) Ice hockey
3. Spain	(c) Cricket
4. Japan	(d) Basketball
	(e) Ju Jitsu

Codes:
   A. 1-(c), 2-(d), 3-(b), 4-(a)
   B. 1-(d), 2-(b), 3-(c), 4-(e)
   C. 1-(c), 2-(d), 3-(a), 4-(e)
   D. 1-(c), 2-(b), 3-(a), 4-(e)

11. How many players participate in a polo team?
   A. 4   B. 8
   C. 11   D. 7

12. In a cricket game when the umpire raises his right hand's index finger high:

A. batsman is not out
B. batsman is out
C. batsman is retired
D. batsman scores a six

13. What is the maximum duration of playing a football match?
A. 60 minutes   B. 90 minutes
C. 80 minutes   D. 70 minutes

14. The longest swimming course in the world is:
A. Dardenelles strait
B. Palk strait
C. English channel
D. Magellan strait

15. 'Subroto Cup' is associated with which of the following games?
A. Hockey   B. Football
C. Basketball   D. Cricket

16. Which of the following is the distance of running in a Marathon race?
A. 26 miles
B. 26 miles, 385 yards
C. 26 miles, 225 yards
D. 26 miles, 365 yards

17. Which is the correct weight of the cricket ball?
A. 4¼ oz   B. 5¾ ioz
C. 4 oz   D. 6 oz

18. The term 'butterfly stroke' is associated with which of the following games?
A. Swimming B. Cricket
C. Gliding   D. Football

19. The term 'put' is associated with the sport:
A. Billiards   B. Golf
C. Cricket   D. Baseball

20. The Olympic Symbol (Summer Games) comprises of five rings or circles linked together to represent:
A. the sporting friendship of all
B. the five continents
C. Both A and B
D. None of these

21. Select a pair which is not properly matched:
A. Diego Maradona—Hockey
B. Gary Kasparov—Chess
C. Pete Sampras—Tennis
D. Ronaldo—Football

22. Santosh Trophy is associated with this sport:
A. Hockey   B. Cricket
C. Badminton D. Football

23. Who was the first Indian woman to swim across the English channel?
A. Rita Faria
B. Shanta Rangaswami
C. Arati Saha
D. P.T. Usha

24. The 'Hall of Fame' tournament is associated with which of the following games:
A. Cricket   B. Football
C. Hockey   D. Tennis

25. The term 'Silly Point' is associated with the sport:
A. Billiards   B. Bridge
C. Chess   D. Cricket

26. The term 'Bunker' is associated with:
A. Polo
B. Golf

C. Basketball
D. Table Tennis

27. 'Arthur Walker Trophy' is associated with the sport:
A. Basketball
B. Billiards
C. Boat rowing
D. Bridge

28. Geet Sethi is associated with the sports:
A. Athletics
B. Billiards
C. Shooting
D. Weightlifting

29. Saina Nehwal is associated with the sport:
A. Shooting
B. Badminton
C. Boxing
D. Weightlifting

30. How many players participate in a volleyball team?
A. 6　　　　B. 7
C. 8　　　　D. 9

31. The Sports Day is observed on:
A. August 27　B. August 29
C. October 25　D. October 27

32. The first Asian Games were held in 1951 at:
A. Tokyo, Japan
B. Jakarta, Indonesia
C. Bangkok, Thailand
D. New Delhi, India

33. Ryder Cup is related with which sports?
A. Football　　B. Tennis
C. Golf　　　　D. Hockey

34. 'Checkmate' is associated with which of the following sports:
A. Boxing
B. Bridge
C. Chess
D. Golf

35. Eden Gardens is a famous place associated with which of the following games?
A. Football
B. Hockey
C. Lawn Tennis
D. Cricket

36. The first Modern Olympic Games were held in 1896 in which of the following places?
A. Athens
B. Paris
C. Los Angeles
D. Sarajevo

37. The Winter Olympic Games came into being in 1924 was held at:
A. Chamonix (France)
B. St. Moritz (Switzerland)
C. Lake Placid (New York)
D. Oslo (Norway)

38. In the game of Baseball, distance between each base in a Diamond shaped ground is:
A. 56 ft　　　B. 72 ft
C. 80 ft　　　D. 90 ft

39. The Davis Cup is associated with which of the following games?
A. Lawn Tennis
B. Tennis
C. Cricket
D. Soccer

40. The Olympic Games are held every:
A. two years
B. four years
C. five years
D. six years

41. In which of the following years, the Olympic Games were not held:
A. 1916   B. 1940
C. 1944   D. All of these

42. Baron Pierre de Coubertin, father of the modern Olympic Games, belongs to:
A. Greece   B. USA
C. France   D. Italy

43. What is the national sport of Japan?
A. Karate   B. Sumo
C. Ju-Jitsu   D. Mikado

44. Which of the following cups is not associated with Hockey?
A. Agha Khan Cup
B. Azlan Shah Cup
C. Singer Cup
D. Indira Gandhi Gold Cup

45. Match the following:

List-I	*List-II*
(Game)	*(Term)*
1. Badminton	(*a*) Dribbling
2. Basketball	(*b*) Smash
3. Baseball	(*c*) Cue
4. Billiards	(*d*) Strike

Codes:
A. 1-(*b*), 2-(*a*), 3-(*d*), 4-(*c*)
B. 1-(*a*), 2-(*b*), 3-(*c*), 4-(*d*)
C. 1-(*d*), 2-(*b*), 3-(*a*), 4-(*c*)
D. 1-(*b*), 2-(*a*), 3-(*c*), 4-(*d*)

46. Who among the following has become the first women in the world to swim across seven seas?
A. Shikha Tandon
B. Bula Chowdhury
C. Amanda Beard
D. Arati Saha

47. In which of the following years were women athetes admitted to Olympic Games?
A. 1900   B. 1904
C. 1908   D. 1912

48. The term 'Gambit' is associated with the game of:
A. Golf   B. Boating
C. Bridge   D. Chess

49. 'Thomas Cup Trophy' is associated with which of the following sports?
A. World Chess
B. World Badminton
C. World Cricket
D. World Hockey

50. Match the following:

List-I	*List-II*
(Sportsmen)	*(Sports)*
I. Pele	(*a*) Ocean swimming
II. Sachin Tendulkar	(*b*) Athletics
III. Anju B. George	(*c*) Cricket
IV. Bula Chowdhury	(*d*) Football

Codes:
A. I-(*a*), II-(*b*), III-(*c*), IV-(*d*)
B. I-(*d*), II-(*c*), III-(*b*), IV-(*a*)
C. I-(*d*), II-(*c*), III-(*a*), IV-(*b*)
D. I-(*c*), II-(*d*), III-(*b*), IV-(*a*)

ANSWERS

1	2	3	4	5	6	7	8	9	10
C	A	D	C	C	D	A	B	B	C

11	12	13	14	15	16	17	18	19	20
D	B	B	C	B	B	B	A	B	C

21	22	23	24	25	26	27	28	29	30
A	D	C	D	D	A	B	B	B	A

31	32	33	34	35	36	37	38	39	40
B	D	C	C	D	A	A	D	A	B

41	42	43	44	45	46	47	48	49	50
D	C	C	C	A	B	A	D	B	B

———————

MISCELLANEOUS

1. Who is popularly known as the 'Nightingale of India'?
   A. Saronjini Naidu
   B. M.S. Subbulakshmi
   C. Mahadevi Verma
   D. Lata Mangeshkar

2. The first Speaker of the Lok Sabha was:
   A. Rabi Ray
   B. M. Ananthasayanam Ayangar
   C. Hukam Singh
   D. G.V. Mavalankar

3. The book *Prison Diary* was written by:
   A. Mahatma Gandhi
   B. V.D. Savarkar
   C. Jaya Prakash Narain
   D. Morarji Desai

4. The new name given to Calcutta city is:
   A. Kalighat   B. Kalicutta
   C. Kolkatta   D. Kolkata

5. ISI mark is not given to which of the following products?
   A. Electrical goods
   B. Hosiery goods
   C. Biscuits
   D. Cloth

6. Which day every year is observed as the World Health Day?
   A. May 13
   B. June 30
   C. April 7
   D. September 30

7. The origin of the phrase "United Nations" is associated with which one of the following personalities?
   A. Jawaharlal Nehru
   B. Franklin Roosevelt
   C. Charles de Gaulle
   D. Woodraw Wilson

8. The Economic and Social Commission for Asia and Pacific (ESCAP) is located at:
   A. Kuala Lumpur
   B. Bangkok
   C. Manila
   D. Singapore

9. Which of the following is the headquarters of the World Bank?
   A. The Hague
   B. Washington
   C. Paris
   D. London

10. Which one of the following countries is not a member of the Shanghai Cooperation Organisation (SCO)?
    A. China
    B. Kazakhistan
    C. Russia
    D. Vietnam

11. What is the currency of South Africa?
    A. Guilder   B. Pound
    C. Shekel   D. Rand

12. Who was the first woman the following to become the Prime Minister of a country in the world?
A. Benazir Bhutto
B. Indira Gandhi
C. Margaret Thatcher
D. Sirimavo Bandarnaika

13. Which animal is the symbol of the World Wildlife Fund?
A. Tiger
B. Giant Panda
C. Hornbill
D. White Bear

14. Who was the first President of All India Trade Union Congress?
A. Dewan Chaman Lal
B. Lala Lajpat Rai
C. N.G. Ranga
D. Swami Sahajanand

15. Which one of the following is an important tribe of the Dhauladha Range?
A. Abor   B. Gaddi
C. Lepcha   D. Tharu

16. Which one of the following cities is not connected by National Highway No. 3?
A. Agra   B. Bhopal
C. Dhule   D. Gwalior

17. Shakti-Sthal is situated in
A. Delhi   B. Lucknow
C. Allahabad   D. Surat

18. India's first lunar spacecraft Chandrayaan-1 was launched in
....

A. 2010   B. 2012
C. 2015   D. 2008

19. Who took the charge of Prime Ministership immediately after the death of Jawaharlal Nehru?
A. Indira Gandhi
B. Morarji Desai
C. Gulzarilal Nanda
D. Lal Bahadur Shastri

20. Which one among the following is least like the others?
A. Kathakali
B. Bhangra
C. Kuchipudi
D. Bharat Natyam

21. Which one of the following is not correctly matched?
A. Fiji—Suva
B. Finland—Oslo
C. Guyana—George Town
D. Lebanon—Beirut

22. The author of the book "Animal Farm" is:
A. Leo Tolstoy
B. George Orwell
C. John Dryden
D. S.M. Ali

23. Which one of the following is referred to as the 'Golden Hand Shake'?
A. Honouring VIP's
B. Voluntary Retirement Scheme
C. Wishing bon voyage
D. Receiving distinguished guests

24. "India House" is located in:
A. New Delhi   B. Kolkata
C. London   D. NewYork

25. The largest flightless bird which can run at a great speed:
A. Penguin B. Kiwi
C. Ostrich D. Emu

26. International Finance Corporation is the ancillary institution of the:
A. UNO B. IDO
C. IMF D. IBRD

27. The Pradhan Mantri Gram Sadak Yojna is:
A. to augment road connectivity and provide foodgrains to the poorest of the poor at cheaper rates.
B. to facilitate patrolling of the area to prevent misuse of electricity by unauthorised persons
C. to help the police to reach the place of crime more swiftly to control crime-spurt
D. to develop community life in villages which are not well connected

28. Losoong is a festival which is celebrated in:
A. Tibet
B. Arunachal Pradesh
C. Sikkim
D. Kerala

29. Which of the following countries is now known as Myammar?
A. Kampuchea
B. Northern Rhodesia
C. Burma
D. Laos

30. Who said 'Man is a political animal'?
A. Socrates B. Plato
C. Aristotle D. Dante

31. "Persons may change but rules should not change" is the principle of:
A. Absolute Monarchy
B. Constitutional Government
C. Unwritten Constitution
D. Republic

32. 'Kuchipudi' is a dance style which originated from:
A. Kerala
B. Andhra Pradesh
C. Manipur
D. Tamil Nadu

33. Currency of Japan is called:
A. Yen B. Dollar
C. Pound D. Lira

34. The first Secretary-General of the United Nations was:
A. Dag Hammarskjoeld
B. U. Thant
C. Kurt Waldheim
D. Trygve Lie

35. Padma Subramaniam is an exponent of classical dance:
A. Kuchipudi
B. Odissi
C. Bharatnatyam
D. Manipuri

36. Shiv-Hari, the popular musical duo, plays which of the following instruments?
A. Tabla and Guitar
B. Santoor and Flute
C. Piano and Drums
D. None of these

37. Which of the following is called the 'Mother of Parliaments'?
    A. The German Parliament
    B. The American Parliament
    C. The French Parliament
    D. The British Parliament

38. Which of the following places is not in Pak-occupied Kashmir?
    A. Gilgit
    B. Skardu
    C. Muzaffarabad
    D. Kargil

39. Who amongst the following was not a Vice-President before becoming President of India?
    A. V.V. Giri
    B. R. Venkataraman
    C. S. Radhakrishnan
    D. Giani Zail Singh

40. Which one of the following projections is used chiefly in navigation?
    A. Mercator's   B. Mollweid's
    C. Bonne's   D. Lambert'

41. Which of the following years is known as the "Year of great divide" with regard to population growth in India?
    A. 1911   B. 1921
    C. 1947   D. 1951

42. Which one of the following is the World Environment Day?
    A. 22nd April   B. 1st May
    C. 31st May   D. 5th June

43. The cost of next-best alternative is known as:
    A. Real Cost
    B. Social Cost
    C. Opportunity Cost
    D. Over-head Cost

44. "Kamasutra" is written by:
    A. Kalamandalam Nair
    B. Ananda Coomaraswamy
    C. Birju Maharaj
    D. S.H. Vatsyayan

45. December 10, is regarded as a red-letter-day for the whole world because it is the:
    A. International Labour Day
    B. Human Rights Day
    C. United Nations Day
    D. Science Day

46. Given below is a list of traditional dresses of women along with States. Which one of them is not correctly matched?
    A. Boku–Sikkim
    B. Mekhala–Assam
    C. Mundu–Chhattisgarh
    D. Pheran–Kashmir

47. The book "The Proudest Day" deals with the story of:
    A. Integration of Indian States
    B. India's independence
    C. Pokhran nuclear explosion
    D. Formation of the NDA Government at the Centre

48. March 8th, is observed as:
    A. World Environment Day
    B. Heritage Day
    C. International Women's Day
    D. Youth Day

49. The 'Kumbha Mela' comes round once in:
    A. 7 years   B. 5 years
    C. 10 years   D. 12 years

50. Who among the following has written the book entitled 'Autobiography of an Unknown Indian'?
A. Kuldip Nayyar
B. V.S. Naipaul
C. Nirad C. Choudhuri
D. N.A. Palkhivala

51. The abbrivation IGNOU stands for:
A. Indian Government's Nuclear Option Ultimatum
B. Indira Gandhi National Open University
C. Inter-Governmental and Non-Official Understandings
D. Informal Group on National Occupational Utilities

52. The author of the book 'The Gin Drinkers' is:
A. Arundhati Roy
B. Anita Desai
C. Sagarika Ghose
D. Shobha De

53. 1st December, of every year is observed to mark:
A. World Habitat Day
B. Universal Children's Day
C. World AIDS Day
D. Anniversary of United Nations

54. The famous Salar Jung Museum is situated in:
A. Assam
B. Telangana
C. Jammu and Kashmir
D. Uttar Pradesh

55. The International Nautical Mile is equal to:
A. 1852 metres
B. 1825 metres
C. 2000 metres
D. 1582 metres

56. Consumer Day is celebrated every year on:
A. April 1
B. October 23
C. March 15
D. December 5

57. Subhas Mukhopadhyay is associated with which one of the following fields?
A. Politics
B. Sports
C. Literature
D. Social service

58. The Asian Development Bank has its headquarters in:
A. Kathmandu B. Manila
C. Colombo   D. Tokyo

59. Who among the following Indians has presided over the UNESCO?
A. Dr. Zakir Hussain
B. Dr. Ramaswami Mudaliar
C. Dr. S. Radhakrishnan
D. Maulana Abul Kalam Azad

60. World Health Day is observed on:
A. April 7   B. April 9
C. April 18   D. April 20

61. Which of the following countries is now known as Cambodia?
A. Northern Rhodesia
B. Laos
C. Kampuchea
D. Comoros

62. Who was the first Indian to become the member of British Parliament?
A. W.C. Bannerjee
B. M. Malabari
C. D.N. Wacha
D. Dadabhai Naoroji

63. Who is the writer of the book 'Interpreter of Maladies'?
A. Jhumpa Lahiri
B. Arundhati Roy
C. Vikram Seth
D. Geeta Mehta

64. Which of the following is a morning 'Raag'?
A. Sohini   B. Bhairavi
C. Kalabati   D. Sarang

65. Who is the writer of the poetry 'Deep Shikha'?
A. Ramdhari Singh Dinkar
B. Shankar Dayal Sharma
C. Subhadara Kumari Chauhan
D. None of these

66. The compilation of 'Meri Ekawan Kavitayen' (My 51 Poems) is written by:
A. Atal Behari Vajpayee
B. Harivanshrai Bachchan
C. Dharam Vir Bharati
D. Shivmangal Singh 'Suman'

67. Who among the following is the writer of 'Anand Math'?
A. Harindra Nath Chattopadhyay
B. Rabindranath Tagore
C. Mulk Raj Anand
D. Bankim Chandra Chatterjee

68. In which Shakespearian drama is *Desdemona* a character?
A. Hamlet
B. Othello
C. Merchant of Venice
D. As You Like It

69. The famous work of Leo Tolstoy is:
A. Merchant of Venice
B. Illiad
C. War and Peace
D. Great Expectations

70. Who said, "Fools rush in where angels fear to tread"?
A. The Bible
B. John Milton
C. Alexander Pope
D. Dr. Samuel Johnson

71. Who is the writer of the novel "God of Small Things"?
A. Arundhati Roy
B. Jhumpa Lahiri
C. Kamal Subramaniyam
D. Mahashweta Devi

72. The capital of Mizoram is:
A. Imphal   B. Shillong
C. Kohima   D. Aizawl

73. Who is the author of the book 'The Namesake'?
A. Shashi Desh
B. Jhumpa Lahiri
C. Kapil Dev
D. Benazir Bhutto

74. Which of the following is the 29th State of India?
A. Telangana
B. Uttarakhand
C. Chhattisgarh
D. Goa

75. Guernica was painted by:
    A. Leonardo da Vinci
    B. Michelangelo
    C. Picasso
    D. Raphael

76. The 'Last Supper' is a world famous painting by:
    A. Paul Gaugin
    B. Leonardo da Vinci
    C. Raphael
    D. Rembrandt

77. 'Bhogali Bihu' is a festival of:
    A. Assam   B. Odisha
    C. Gujarat   D. Rajasthan

78. Classical dance having its roots in Tamil Nadu is:
    A. Kathakali
    B. Kathak
    C. Kuchipudi
    D. Bharat Natyam

79. Jamini Roy distinguished himself in:
    A. dancing
    B. colour photography
    C. instrumental music
    D. painting

80. Which of the following countries is not a member of the UNO?
    A. Sweden   B. Taiwan
    C. Australia   D. Norway

81. Which Indian jurist held the office of the President of International Court of Justice?
    A. H.R. Khanna
    B. K.S. Hegde
    C. Nagendra Singh
    D. R.S. Pathak

82. Who was the first Indian to be the President of UN General Assembly?
    A. Natwar Singh
    B. V.K. Krishna Menon
    C. Mrs. Vijayalakshmi Pandit
    D. Romesh Bhandari

83. What is the correct sequence of the formation of the following States of India?
    1. Andhra Pradesh
    2. Haryana
    3. Kerala
    4. Meghalaya
    A. 1, 3, 2, 4
    B. 1, 3, 4, 2
    C. 3, 1, 2, 4
    D. 3, 1, 4, 2

84. The 'first lady' of the Indian silver screen is:
    A. Madhubala
    B. Devika Rani
    C. Durga Khote
    D. Nargis Dutt

85. Arunachal Pradesh has borders with:
    A. Bhutan, China and Myanmar
    B. Bhutan, Bangladesh and Myanmar
    C. Bangladesh, China and Myanmar
    D. Bhutan, China and Bangladesh

86. The talkie film Alam Ara was produced in:
    A. 1912   B. 1913
    C. 1931   D. 1934

87. The headquarters of UNESCO is:
    A. Paris
    B. Washington DC
    C. Geneva
    D. Switzerland

88. The headquarters of WHO is:
    A. Paris
    B. Geneva
    C. Washington DC
    D. Rome

89. The author of the book 'India Wins Freedom' is:
    A. Abul Kalam Azad
    B. Rajendra Prasad
    C. Annie Besant
    D. Lala Lajpat Rai

90. Television was introduced in India in:
    A. 15 September, 1959
    B. 5 September, 1959
    C. 25 September, 1959
    D. 30 September, 1959

ANSWERS

1	2	3	4	5	6	7	8	9	10
A	D	C	D	D	C	B	B	B	D

11	12	13	14	15	16	17	18	19	20
D	D	B	B	B	B	A	D	C	B

21	22	23	24	25	26	27	28	29	30
B	B	B	C	C	D	D	C	C	C

31	32	33	34	35	36	37	38	39	40
B	B	A	D	C	B	D	D	D	A

41	42	43	44	45	46	47	48	49	50
B	D	C	D	B	C	C	C	D	C

51	52	53	54	55	56	57	58	59	60
B	C	C	B	B	C	C	B	C	A

61	62	63	64	65	66	67	68	69	70
C	D	A	B	D	A	D	B	C	C

71	72	73	74	75	76	77	78	79	80
A	D	B	A	C	B	A	D	D	B

81	82	83	84	85	86	87	88	89	90
C	C	A	B	A	C	A	B	A	A

MATHEMATICS

ARITHMETIC

1 — Number System

The development of the number system started with natural numbers. These are generally known as counting numbers.

Natural Numbers

Numbers which start from 1 are known as natural numbers. It is denoted by N. The smallest natural number is 1. It is written as, $N = \{1, 2, 3, ..., \infty\}$

Whole Numbers

A number which starts from zero (0) is known as whole number. It is denoted by W. It is written as, $W = \{0, 1, 2, 3, ..., \infty\}$

Integers

Natural numbers along with 0 and their negatives are known as integers. It is denoted by I. It is written as, $I = \{..., -4, -3, -2, -1, 0, 1, 2, 3, 4, ...\}$

Even Numbers

A number which is divisible by 2 is known as even numbers. Such as, 2, 4, 6, 10, 12, 128, 432 etc.

Odd Numbers

A number which is not divisible by 2 is known as odd numbers: Such as, 1, 3, 5, 7, 9, 11, 13, 21, 29, 123 etc.

Prime Numbers

A number which is divided by itself is known as prime numbers. The smallest prime number is 2. Such as, 2, 3, 5, 7, 11, 13, 17, 19, 23, ... etc.

The formulae given below are quite useful for quick multiplication:

$$(i)\ (a + b)^2 = a^2 + 2ab + b^2$$
$$(ii)\ (a - b)^2 = a^2 - 2ab + b^2$$
$$(iii)\ a^2 - b^2 = (a + b)(a - b)$$
$$(iv)\ a^2 + b^2 = (a + b)^2 - 2ab$$
$$(v)\ (a + b)^3 = a^3 + b^3 + 3ab(a + b)$$

$(vi)\ (a - b)^3 = a^3 - b^3 - 3ab\ (a - b)$

$(vii)\ a^3 + b^3 = (a + b)\ (a^2 - ab + b^2)$

$(viii)\ a^3 - b^3 = (a - b)\ (a^2 + ab + b^2)$

Example : Simplify the following : $\dfrac{261 \times 261 \times 261 - 77 \times 77 \times 77}{261 \times 261 + 261 \times 77 + 77 \times 77}$

Solution : $\dfrac{261 \times 261 \times 261 - 77 \times 77 \times 77}{261 \times 261 + 261 \times 77 + 77 \times 77}$

Let $261 = a$

and $77 = b$

$$\therefore\ \frac{a^3 - b^3}{a^2 + ab + b^2} = \frac{(a-b)(a^2 + ab + b^2)}{(a^2 + ab + b^2)} = a - b$$

$$\therefore\ 261 - 77 = 184.$$

MULTIPLE CHOICE QUESTIONS

1. The face value of 8 in the numeral 458926 is:

 A. 8000   B. 8   C. 1000   D. 458000

2. $106 \times 106 + 94 \times 94 = x$, the value of x is:

 A. 21032   B. 20032   C. 23032   D. 20072

3. If $m \times 48 = 173 \times 240$ then the value of m is:

 A. 545   B. 685   C. 865   D. 495

4. $\left(1 - \dfrac{1}{3}\right)\left(1 - \dfrac{1}{4}\right)\left(1 - \dfrac{1}{5}\right)...\left(1 - \dfrac{1}{n}\right) = x$, then the value of x is:

 A. $\dfrac{1}{n}$ B. $\dfrac{2}{n}$ C. $\dfrac{2(n-1)}{n}$ D. $\dfrac{2}{n(n+1)}$

5. When simplified the product $\left(2 - \dfrac{1}{3}\right)\left(2 - \dfrac{3}{5}\right)\left(2 - \dfrac{5}{7}\right)...\left(2 - \dfrac{997}{999}\right)$ is equal to:

 A. $\dfrac{5}{999}$ B. $\dfrac{1001}{999}$ C. $\dfrac{1001}{3}$ D. None of these

6. Which number should replace both the asterisks in $\left(\dfrac{*}{21}\right) \times \left(\dfrac{*}{189}\right) = 1$?

 A. 21   B. 63   C. 3969   D. 147

7. In a division sum, the divisor is 12 times the quotient and 5 times the remainder. If the remainder be 48, then the dividend is:
   A. 240   B. 576   C. 4800   D. 4848

8. What least number must be subtracted from 1294 so that the remainder when divided by 9, 11, 13 will leave in each case the same remainder 6?
   A. 0   B. 1   C. 2   D. 3

9. If $\sqrt{\left(1+\dfrac{27}{169}\right)} = \left(1+\dfrac{x}{13}\right)$, then the value of x is:
   A. 1   B. 3   C. 5   D. 7

10. If $\dfrac{x}{y} = \dfrac{3}{4}$, then the value of $\left(\dfrac{6}{7} + \dfrac{y-x}{y+x}\right)$ equals:
    A. $\dfrac{5}{7}$ B. $1\dfrac{1}{7}$ C. 1   D. 2

11. The largest natural number by which the product of three consecutive even natural numbers is always divisible, is:
    A. 16   B. 24   C. 48   D. 96

12. The least number of five digits which is exactly divisible by 12, 15 and 18 is:
    A. 10080   B. 10800   C. 18000   D. 81000

13. The least number which when divided by 8, 9, 12, 16 and 20 leaves the same remainder 1 in each case is:
    A. 712   B. 271   C. 721   D. 720

14. The value of 0.8693 + 0.092 + 0.87 + 0.4 equals:
    A. 2.3213   B. 2.2331   C. 3.2313   D. 2.2313

15. The prime numbers between 1 to 50 are:
    A. 8   B. 12   C. 15   D. 10

16. If $\dfrac{a}{b} = \dfrac{4}{3}$, then $\dfrac{3a+2b}{3a-2b}$ equals:
    A. 6   B. 3   C. 5   D. −1

17. If $\sqrt{3^n} = 81$, then n equals:
    A. 2   B. 4   C. 6   D. 8

18. If $\sqrt{\dfrac{x}{196}} = \dfrac{72}{56}$, then x equals:
    A. 18   B. 14   C. 324   D. 212

19. If $a \times 48 = 173 \times 240$, then the value of a is:
    A. 545   B. 685   C. 865   D. 495

20. If $\dfrac{80}{x} = \dfrac{x}{20}$, then the value of x is:
    A. 40   B. 400   C. 800   D. 1600

21. If 'x' and 'y' are both odd numbers, which of the following numbers must be an even number?
    A. $x + y$ B. $x \times y$ C. $xy + 2$ D. $2x + y$

22. 'a' is less than 'b' then, which of the following numbers is greater than 'a' and less than 'b'?
    A. $\dfrac{a+b}{2}$ B. $\dfrac{ab}{2}$ C. $b^2 - a^2$ D. ab

23. $a + b + c + d$ is a positive number, a minimum of 'x' of the number a, b, c and d must be positive, where 'x' is equal to—
    A. -1 B. 2   C. 3   D. 4

24. There are four numbers A, B, C and D. Average of the first three i.e., A, B and C is 15 and that of B, C and D is 16. If the last number, i.e., D is 19, then the first number is—
    A. 15   B. 16   C. 17   D. 18

25. Think of a number, divide it by 9 and add 9 to it, if the result is 27, the number is—
    A. 18   B. 21   C. 100   D. 162

26. Of the three numbers, the first is twice the second and thrice the third. If the average of three is 22, the three numbers are—
    A. 12, 18, 36   B. 18, 12, 36   C. 36, 12, 18   D. 36, 18, 12

27. The number which when added to itself 10 times gives 264. The number is—
    A. 20   B. 22   C. 24   D. 26

28. If a person is standing on the sixth number in the queue from both the ends, the total persons in the queue are—
    A. 9   B. 11   C. 12   D. 13

29. A number 'x' when multiplied by 5 and added to three times its own gives 64, the number is—
    A. 8   B. 12   C. 14   D. 18

30. If the sum of two numbers 'x' and 'y' is equal to twice the first number, the second number 'y' is—
    A. $> x$ B. $< x$
    C. $= x$ D. negative number

ANSWERS

1	2	3	4	5	6	7	8	9	10
B	D	C	B	C	B	D	B	A	C

11	12	13	14	15	16	17	18	19	20
C	A	C	D	C	B	D	C	C	A

21	22	23	24	25	26	27	28	29	30
A	A	A	B	D	D	C	B	A	C

EXPLANATORY ANSWERS

1. The face value of 8 in the numeral 458926 is 8.

3. $\because m = \dfrac{173 \times 240}{48} = 865.$

7. Let quotient = Q and remainder = R
   Then, divisor = 12Q = 5R   Now, R = 48
   $\Rightarrow$ 12Q = 5 × 48 $\Rightarrow$ Q = 20 $\therefore$ Dividend = (20 × 240 + 48) = 4848

11. It is 2 × 4 × 6 = 48

15. The prime numbers between 1 to 50 are 2, 3, 5, 7, 11, 13, 17, 19, 23, 29, 31, 37, 41, 43, 47.
    Hence, there are 15 prime numbers between 1 to 50.

17. $\because \sqrt{3^n} = 81 \Rightarrow 3^{\frac{n}{2}} = 3^4 \Rightarrow \dfrac{n}{2} = 4 \Rightarrow n = 8.$

20. $\because \dfrac{80}{x} = \dfrac{x}{20} \Rightarrow x^2 = 80 \times 20 \Rightarrow x^2 = 1600 \Rightarrow x = 40$

21. Since the sum of two odd numbers is always even number, therefore, $x + y$ is even number.

22. Average of two different numbers is always between the two numbers.

23. If all numbers were not positive, then the sum could not be positive. If a, b, c were all -1 and d were 5, then $a + b + c + d$ would be positive, so *(b), (c), (d)* are incorrect.

25. Let the number is x.

    $\therefore \dfrac{x}{9} + 9 = 27$ or, $\dfrac{x}{9} = 27 - 9 = 18$ $\therefore x = 18 \times 9 = 162.$

29. $5 \times x + 3x = 64 \Rightarrow 8x = 64$ $\therefore x = \dfrac{64}{8} = 8$

30. $x + y = 2x$ $\therefore y = 2x - x = x$

❖ ❖ ❖

2

HCF and LCM

Highest Common Factor

The HCF of two or more than two numbers is the greatest number that divides each of them exactly. The highest common factor is also known as Greatest Common Divisor or Greatest Common Measure.

There are two methods of determining the HCF of two or more numbers.

(*i*) HCF by Factorization method

(*ii*) HCF by Division method.

HCF by Factorization Method

Express each one of the given number as the product of prime factors. Now choose common factors and take the product of these factors to obtain the required HCF.

EXAMPLE : Find the HCF of 126, 396 and 5400.

SOLUTION :
$$126 = 2 \times 3 \times 3 \times 7$$
$$396 = 2 \times 2 \times 3 \times 3 \times 11$$
$$5400 = 2 \times 2 \times 2 \times 3 \times 3 \times 3 \times 5 \times 5$$

Common factors are 2, 3 and 3.

Hence, the HCF = $2 \times 3 \times 3 = 18$.

HCF by Division Method

Divide the larger number by the smaller one. Now, divide the divisor by the remainder. Repeat the process of dividing the preceding divisor by the remainder last obtained till zero is obtained as remainder. The last divisor is the required HCF.

EXAMPLE: Find the HCF of 48, 168 and 324.

SOLUTION: Firstly, we find the HCF of 48 and 168.

```
     48) 1 6 8 (3
         -1 4 4
        ----------
        24) 4 8 (2
           - 4 8
           --------
             0
```

Thus, HCF of 48 and 168 = 24.

Now, HCF of 24 and 324

```
        24) 3 2 4 (13
           - 2 4
           ----------
             8 4
             7 2
            ----------
            1 2) 2 4 (2
                 2 4
                --------
                  0
```

Hence, HCF of 48, 168 and 324 = 12

Lowest Common Multiple

The LCM of two or more numbers is the lowest or least number which is exactly divisible by each of them.

LCM by Factorization

Resolve each one of the given numbers into a product of prime factors. Then LCM is the product of highest powers of all the factors.

    EXAMPLE: Find the LCM of 72, 189 and 1026.

    SOLUTION: $\quad 72 = 2^3 \times 3^2$

$$189 = 3^3 \times 7$$

and $\quad\quad 1026 = 2 \times 3^3 \times 19$

$\therefore \quad\quad\quad$ LCM $= 2^3 \times 3^3 \times 7 \times 19$

$$= 8 \times 27 \times 7 \times 19 = 28728$$

FORMULA

    Product of two numbers = HCF × LCM.

$$\text{LCM} = \frac{\text{Product of numbers}}{\text{HCF}} \qquad\qquad \text{HCF} = \frac{\text{Product of numbers}}{\text{LCM}}$$

$$\text{First number} = \frac{\text{LCM} \times \text{HCF}}{\text{2nd number}} \qquad \text{2nd number} = \frac{\text{LCM} \times \text{HCF}}{\text{First number}}$$

HCF and LCM of Fractions

$$(i) \ \text{HCF} = \frac{\text{HCF of numerators}}{\text{LCM of denominators}} \qquad (ii) \ \text{LCM} = \frac{\text{LCM of numerators}}{\text{HCF of denominators}}$$

MULTIPLE CHOICE QUESTIONS

1. HCF of 1485 and 4356 is:

    A. 189   B. 89   C. 99   D. 83

2. LCM of 18, 24, 42, 63 is:

    A. 302   B. 604   C. 504   D. 404

3. Which of the following fractions is the greatest of all? $\dfrac{7}{8}, \dfrac{6}{7}, \dfrac{4}{5}, \dfrac{5}{6}$

    A. $\dfrac{6}{7}$ B. $\dfrac{4}{5}$ C. $\dfrac{5}{6}$ D. $\dfrac{7}{8}$

4. Which of the following is in ascending order?

    A. $\dfrac{5}{7}, \dfrac{7}{8}, \dfrac{9}{11}$ B. $\dfrac{5}{7}, \dfrac{9}{11}, \dfrac{7}{8}$ C. $\dfrac{7}{8}, \dfrac{5}{7}, \dfrac{9}{11}$ D. $\dfrac{9}{11}, \dfrac{7}{8}, \dfrac{5}{7}$

5. HCF of three numbers is 12. If they be in the ratio 1 : 2 : 3, the numbers are:
   A. 12, 24, 36   B. 10, 20, 30   C. 5, 10, 15   D. 4, 8, 12

6. The largest natural number which exactly divides the product of any four consecutive natural numbers is:
   A. 6   B. 12   C. 24   D. 120

7. The traffic lights at three different road crossings change after every 48 seconds, 72 seconds and 108 seconds respectively. If they all change simultaneously at 8 : 20 : 00 hrs; then they will again change simultaneously at:
   A. 8 : 27 : 12 hrs   B. 8 : 27 : 24 hrs
   C. 8 : 27 : 36 hrs   D. 8 : 27 : 48 hrs

8. The HCF of two numbers is 16 and their LCM is 160. If one of the number is 32, then the other number is:
   A. 48   B. 80   C. 96   D. 112

9. The HCF of two numbers is 12 and their difference is also 12. The numbers are:
   A. 66, 78   B. 70, 82   C. 94, 106   D. 84, 96

10. The largest number which exactly divides 210, 315, 147 and 161 is:
   A. 3   B. 7   C. 21   D. 4410

11. The least perfect square number which is divisible by 3, 4, 5, 6 and 8 is:
   A. 900   B. 1200   C. 2500   D. 3600

12. The smallest number which is divisible by 12, 15 and 20 is a perfect square, is:
   A. 400   B. 900   C. 1600   D. 3600

13. The sum of two numbers is 216 and their HCF is 27. The numbers are:
   A. 54, 162   B. 108, 108   C. 27, 189   D. None of these

14. The HCF and LCM of two numbers are 44 and 264 respectively. If the first number is divided by 2, the quotient is 44. The other number is:
   A. 33   B. 66   C. 132   D. 264

15. The number of prime factors in $2^{222} \times 3^{333} \times 5^{555}$ is:
   A. 3   B. 1107   C. 1110   D. 1272

16. The number of prime factors in the expression $(6)^{10} \times (7)^{17} \times (11)^{27}$ is:
   A. 54   B. 64   C. 71   D. 81

17. Three measuring rods are 64 cm, 80 cm and 96 cm in length. The least length of cloth that can be measured exact number of times using any one of the above rod is:
   A. 0.96 m   B. 19.20 m   C. 9.60 m   D. 96.00 m

18. The product of two numbers is 1600 and their HCF is 5. The LCM of the numbers is:

    A. 320   B. 1605   C. 1595   D. 8000

19. About the number of pairs which have 16 as their HCF and 136 as their LCM, we can definitely say that:

    A. Only one such pair exists   B. Only two such pairs exist

    C. Many such pairs exist   D. No such pair exist

20. The total number of prime factors of the product $(8)^{20} \times (15)^{24} \times (7)^{15}$ is:

    A. 59   B. 98   C. 123   D. 138

21. A number n is said to be perfect, if the sum of all its divisors (excluding n itself) is equal to n. A perfect number is

    A. 21   B. 15   C. 9   D. 6

22. HCF of $4 \times 27 \times 3125$, $8 \times 9 \times 25 \times 7$ and $16 \times 81 \times 5 \times 11 \times 49$ is

    A. 1260   B. 540   C. 360   D. 180

23. Which is of the following is a co-primes?

    A. (23, 92)   B. (21, 35)   C. (18, 25)   D. (16, 62)

24. The LCM of $2^3 \times 3^2 \times 5 \times 11$, $2^4 \times 3^4 \times 5^2 \times 7$

    and $2^5 \times 3^3 \times 5^3 \times 7^2 \times 11$ is :

    A. $2^5 \times 3^4 \times 5^3$ B. $2^3 \times 3^2 \times 5$

    C. $2^5 \times 3^4 \times 5^3 \times 7^2 \times 11$ D. $2^3 \times 3^2 \times 5 \times 7 \times 11$

25. The G.C.D. of 1.08, 0.36 and 0.9 is

    A. 0.108   B. 0.18   C. 0.9   D. 0.03

26. H.C.F. of 3240, 3600 and a third number is 36 and their L.C.M. is $2^4 \times 3^5 \times 5^2 \times 7^2$. The third number is

    A. $2^3 \times 3^5 \times 7^2$ B. $2^5 \times 5^2 \times 7^2$ C. $2^2 \times 5^3 \times 7^2$ D. $2^2 \times 3^5 \times 7^2$

27. The ratio of two numbers is 3 : 4 and their H.C.F. is 4. Find their L.C.M.

    A. 48   B. 24   C. 16   D. 12

28. Three numbers are in the ratio 1 : 2 : 3 and their HCF is 12. Find the numbers.

    A. 12, 24, 36   B. 10, 20, 30   C. 5, 10, 15   D. 4, 8, 12

29. If the sum of two numbers is 55 and the H.C.F. and L.C.M. of these numbers are 5 and 120 respectively. Find the sum of their reciprocals.

    A. $\dfrac{120}{11}$ B. $\dfrac{11}{120}$ C. $\dfrac{601}{55}$ D. $\dfrac{55}{601}$

30. The L.C.M. of two numbers is 495 and their HCF is 5. If the sum of the numbers is 100, then find their difference.

    A. 90   B. 70   C. 46   D. 10

ANSWERS

1	2	3	4	5	6	7	8	9	10
C	C	D	B	A	C	A	B	D	B

11	12	13	14	15	16	17	18	19	20
D	D	C	C	C	B	C	A	D	C

21	22	23	24	25	26	27	28	29	30
D	D	C	C	B	D	A	A	B	D

EXPLANATORY ANSWERS

2.

```
2 | 18,  24,  42,  63
3 |  9,  12,  21,  63
3 |  3,   4,   7,  21
7 |  1,   4,   7,   7
  |  1,   4,   1,   1
```

LCM of 18, 24, 42, 63 = $2 \times 3^2 \times 7 \times 4 = 504$.

5. Let the numbers be x, $2x$ and $3x$.
Then, their HCF = x
According to the question, $x = 12$
$\therefore$ The numbers are 12, 24, 36.

6. $1 \times 2 \times 3 \times 4 = 24$
$\therefore$ Required number = 24.

10. HCF of 210, 315, 147 and 161 = 7 Hence, the required number = 7.

12. LCM of 12, 15 and 20 = 60
Hence, required number = $60 \times 60 = 3600$.

15. The number of prime factors in the given product
= (222 + 333 + 555) = 1110

19. HCF is always a factor of LCM. So no two numbers exist with HCF = 16 and LCM = 136.

24. $2^3 \times 3^2 \times 5 \times 11$; $2^4 \times 3^4 \times 5^2 \times 7$

and $2^5 \times 3^3 \times 5^3 \times 7^2 \times 11$
$\therefore$ LCM = $2^5 \times 3^4 \times 5^3 \times 7^2 \times 11$

25. GCD of 108, 36 and 90 = 18
Hence, GCD of 1.08, 0.36 and 0.9 = 0.18.

27. Let the numbers be $3x$ and $4x$; HCF = 4; Hence, $x = 4$
Then, numbers will be 12 and 16;
$\therefore$ Their LCM = 48.

28. Let the numbers are x, $2x$ and $3x$;
Their HCF = 12
Then, $x = 12$,
so the numbers will be 12, 24, 36.

29. Let the number be x and y.
Then, $x + y = 55$;
$xy = \text{HCF} \times \text{LCM} = 5 \times 120$

$\therefore$ Sum of their reciprocals $= \dfrac{1}{x} + \dfrac{1}{y} = \dfrac{x+y}{xy} = \dfrac{55}{5 \times 120} = \dfrac{11}{120}$

30. Let the number be x and $(100 - x)$
Now, $x(100 - x) = 5 \times 495$
$\Rightarrow x^2 - 100x + 2475 = 0$
$\Rightarrow x^2 - 55x - 45x + 2475 = 0$
$\Rightarrow x(x - 55) - 45(x - 55) = 0$
$\Rightarrow (x - 45)(x - 55) = 0$
Either, $x = 45$ or, $x = 55$
Hence, the numbers are 45 and 55
So, their difference $= 55 - 45 = 10$

❖ ❖ ❖

3

Simplification

Simplification means expressing in a simpler form. In order to simplify an expression we use the operations in the following order which is easily remembered as "BODMAS".

(*i*) Bracket (*ii*) Of (*iii*) Division (*iv*) Multiplication (*v*) Addition (*vi*) Subtraction.

'Of' means multiplication but it is operated even before division.

While removing brackets, first of all bar bracket '—' and after that small bracket '( )' is removed. Thereafter curley bracket '{ }' and at last square bracket '[ ]' is removed.

EXAMPLE: Simplify: $10 - \left[6 - \left\{7 - \left(6 - \overline{8 - 5}\right)\right\}\right]$

SOLUTION: $10 - \left[6 - \left\{7 - \left(6 - 3\right)\right\}\right]$

$$= 10 - [6 - \{7 - 3\}] \qquad = 10 - [6 - 4] = 10 - 2 = 8.$$

MULTIPLE CHOICE QUESTIONS

1. $\dfrac{48 - 12 \times 3 + 9}{12 - 9 \div 3}$ equals:

   A. 3   B. 21   C. $\dfrac{7}{3}$ D. $\dfrac{1}{3}$

2. $\dfrac{69 - 14 \times 3 + 2}{9 \times 5 - (5)^2}$ equals:

   A. 1.45   B. 2.75   C. 26.5   D. 265

3. If $\dfrac{17.28 \div x}{3.6 \times 0.2} = 2$ then, the value of x is:

   A. 120   B. 1.20   C. 12   D. 0.12

4. $171 \div 19 \times 9$ equals:

   A. 0   B. 1   C. 18   D. 81

5. $3120 \div 26 + 13 \times 30$ equals:

   A. 2400   B. 3900   C. 536   D. None of these

6. $\dfrac{31}{10} \times \dfrac{3}{10} + \dfrac{7}{5} \div 20$ equals:

   A. 0   B. 1   C. 100   D. $\dfrac{107}{200}$

7. The simplification of $1 + \dfrac{1}{2 + \dfrac{1}{1 - \dfrac{1}{3}}}$ yields the result:

   A. $\dfrac{2}{7}$ B. $\dfrac{7}{9}$ C. $\dfrac{9}{7}$ D. $\dfrac{13}{7}$

8. The value of $1 + \dfrac{1}{4 \times 3} + \dfrac{1}{4 \times 3^2} + \dfrac{1}{4 \times 3^3}$ up to four places of decimals is:

   A. 1.1202   B. 1.1203   C. 1.1204   D. None of these

9. $\dfrac{\dfrac{1}{2} \div 4 + 20}{\dfrac{1}{2} \times 4 + 20}$ equals:

   A. $\dfrac{81}{88}$ B. $2\dfrac{3}{11}$ C. $\dfrac{161}{176}$ D. 1

10. $3 \div \left[(8 - 5) \div \left\{ (4 - 2) \div \left(2 + \dfrac{8}{13} \right) \right\} \right]$ equals:

   A. $\dfrac{13}{17}$ B. $\dfrac{68}{13}$ C. $\dfrac{17}{13}$ D. $\dfrac{13}{68}$

11. $10 - [9 - \{8 - (7 - 6)\}] - 5$ is equal to:

   A. -5 B. 1   C. 3   D. 9

12. $\dfrac{\dfrac{1}{5} \div \dfrac{1}{5} \text{ of } \dfrac{1}{5}}{\dfrac{1}{5} \text{ of } \dfrac{1}{5} \div \dfrac{1}{5}}$ is equal to:

   A. 1   B. 5   C. $\dfrac{1}{5}$ D. 25

13. The value of $1 + \dfrac{1}{1 + \dfrac{1}{1 + \dfrac{1}{9}}}$ is:

   A. $\dfrac{29}{19}$ B. $\dfrac{10}{19}$ C. $\dfrac{29}{10}$ D. $\dfrac{10}{9}$

14. $\dfrac{3}{48}$ is what part of $\dfrac{1}{12}$?

   A. $\dfrac{3}{7}$ B. $\dfrac{1}{12}$ C. $\dfrac{4}{3}$ D. None of these

15. How many $\dfrac{1}{8}$s are there in $37\dfrac{1}{2}$?

   A. 300   B. 400

   C. 500   D. Cannot be determined

16. $\dfrac{885 \times 885 \times 885 + 115 \times 115 \times 115}{885 \times 885 + 115 \times 115 - 885 \times 115}$ is equal to:

   A. 115   B. 770   C. 885   D. 1000

17. The value of $\dfrac{9^2 \times 18^4}{3^{16}}$ is:

   A. $\dfrac{2}{3}$ B. $\dfrac{4}{9}$ C. $\dfrac{16}{81}$ D. $\dfrac{32}{243}$

18. $\left(1\dfrac{3}{5} - \dfrac{2}{3} \div \dfrac{12}{13} + \dfrac{7}{5} \times \dfrac{1}{3}\right)$ is equal to:

   A. $1\dfrac{31}{90}$ B. $\dfrac{19}{30}$ C. $\dfrac{11}{30}$ D. 30

19. The value of $48 \div 12 \times \left(\dfrac{9}{8}\,\text{of}\,\dfrac{4}{3} \div \dfrac{3}{4}\,\text{of}\,\dfrac{2}{3}\right)$ is:

   A. $1\dfrac{1}{3}$ B. $5\dfrac{1}{3}$ C. 3   D. 12

20. $(20 \div 5) \div 2 + (16 \div 8) \times 2 + (10 \div 5) \times (3 \div 2)$ is equal to

   A. 9   B. 12   C. 15   D. 18

21. The sum of 1/9, 1/3, 1/6 and 7/18 of a number is 150. The number is

   A. 120   B. 130   C. 140   D. 150

22. Which is the greatest? .999, .1011, .1995, .9985

   A. .999   B. .1011   C. .1995   D. .9985

23. In decimal system, $9\dfrac{1}{8}$ may be represented as

   A. 9.18   B. 9.125   C. 9.025   D. 9.225

24. $2.205 \div 0.15 = ?$

   A. 1.47   B. 14.7   C. 147   D. 0.147

25. G.C.M. of .24, 3.2 and 16.0 is

    A. 80   B. 8   C. .8   D. .08

26. L.C.M. of .24, 3.2 and 16.0 is

    A. .48   B. 4.8   C. 48   D. 480

27. A pole has 0.5 of its length in mud, 0.25 of its length in water and 2 metres above water. The total length of the pole is

    A. 8 metres   B. 5 metres   C. 4 metres   D. 2 metres

28. $\sqrt{1/3}$ is equal to

    A. 0.57   B. 0.35   C. 0.30   D. 3.00

29. How many times does 2/3 of 1/2 go into half of third?

    A. 2   B. 1/2   C. 1/3   D. 2/3

30. The eleventh part of $990\dfrac{990}{990}$ is

    A. 99.0   B. 99.99   C. 90   D. 90.9

ANSWERS

1	2	3	4	5	6	7	8	9	10
C	A	C	D	D	B	C	B	C	A
11	12	13	14	15	16	17	18	19	20
C	D	A	D	A	D	C	A	D	A
21	22	23	24	25	26	27	28	29	30
D	A	B	B	D	C	A	A	B	C

EXPLANATORY ANSWERS

4. $171 \div 19 \times 9 = 9 \times 9 = 81$.

5. $3120 \div 26 + 13 \times 30 = 120 + 390 = 510$.

6. $\dfrac{31}{10} \times \dfrac{3}{10} + \dfrac{7}{5} \div 20 = \dfrac{31}{10} \times \dfrac{3}{10} + \dfrac{7}{5} \times \dfrac{1}{20}$

$= \dfrac{93}{100} + \dfrac{7}{100} = \dfrac{93 + 7}{100} = \dfrac{100}{100} = 1$

11. $10 - [9 - \{8 - (7 - 6)\}] - 5$

$= 10 - [9 - \{8 - 1\}] - 5$

$= 10 - [9 - 7] - 5$

$= 10 - 2 - 5 = 10 - 7 = 3$

22. .999 is the greatest.

23. $9\dfrac{1}{8} = 9 + \dfrac{1}{8} = 9 + .125 = 9.125$

26. L.C.M. of .24, 3.2 and 16.0 = L.C.M. of $\dfrac{24,\,320\text{ and }1600}{100}$

$\qquad = \dfrac{4800}{100} = 48.$

27. Let total length of the pole $= x$
Pole above water $= x - [0.5x + 0.25x]$
$= 0.25x$; But, $0.25x = 2$ metres

$\qquad \therefore x = \dfrac{2 \times 100}{25} = 8$ metres

28. $\qquad \sqrt{\dfrac{1}{3}} = \dfrac{1}{\sqrt{3}} \times \dfrac{\sqrt{3}}{\sqrt{3}} = \dfrac{\sqrt{3}}{3} = \dfrac{1.732}{3} = .57$

29. $\qquad \dfrac{2}{3} \text{ of } \dfrac{1}{2} = \dfrac{2}{3} \times \dfrac{1}{2} = \dfrac{1}{3}$

$\qquad \dfrac{1}{2} \text{ of } \dfrac{1}{3} = \dfrac{1}{6}$

$\therefore \qquad \dfrac{1}{6} \div \dfrac{1}{3} = \dfrac{1}{6} \times \dfrac{3}{1} = \dfrac{1}{2}$

30. $\qquad$ Eleventh part of $990\dfrac{990}{990} = 990\dfrac{990}{990} \div 11 = \dfrac{990}{11} = 90$

4

Surds and Indices

Surds

If 'a' is a rational number and n is a positive integer such that nth root of 'a', i.e., $a^{1/n}$ or $\sqrt[n]{a}$ is an irrational number, then $a^{1/n}$ is called a surd or radical.

For example, $\sqrt{2} = 2^{1/2} =$ Square root of 2

$\sqrt[3]{5} = 5^{1/3} =$ Cube root of 5

Important Formulae Based on Surds

$\sqrt[n]{a} = a^{1/n}$ and it is called a surd of order n.

(i) $\sqrt[n]{a^n} = a$

(ii) $\sqrt[n]{ab} = \sqrt[n]{a}\,\sqrt[n]{b}$

(iii) $\sqrt{a} \times \sqrt{b} = \sqrt{ab}$

(iv) $\left(\sqrt{a} + \sqrt{b}\right)^2 = a + b + 2\sqrt{ab}$

(v) $\left(\sqrt{a} - \sqrt{b}\right)^2 = a + b - 2\sqrt{ab}$

(vi) $\left(\sqrt{a} + \sqrt{b}\right)\left(\sqrt{a} - \sqrt{b}\right) = a - b$ where a and b are positive rational numbers.

Indices

The expression a^n is termed as power function or simply power, a is called the base and n is called index or exponent of the power a^n.

For example, $2^2 =$ square of 2, $2^3 =$ cube of 2, etc.

Laws of Indices

(i) $a^m \times a^n = a^{m+n}$

(ii) $a^m \times a^n \times a^p \times \ldots = a^{m+n+p+\ldots}$

(iii) $\dfrac{a^m}{a^n} = a^{m-n}$, if $m > n$

(iv) $(a^m)^n = a^{mn}$

(v) $(ab)^n = a^n b^n$

(vi) $a^0 = 1$

(vii) If $a^m = a^n$ then $m = n$

(viii) If $a^m = b^m$ then $a = b$

MULTIPLE CHOICE QUESTIONS

1. If the infinite series is $x = \sqrt{6 + \sqrt{6 + \sqrt{6 + \ldots}}}$ then the value of x is:

   A. 2.5   B. 3   C. 6   D. 8

2. If $\dfrac{9^n \cdot 3^2 \cdot 3^n - (27)^n}{3^{3m} \cdot 2^3} = \dfrac{1}{27}$, then the value of $(m - n)$ is:

   A. 1   B. 2   C. $\sqrt{3}$ D. $\sqrt{\dfrac{2}{3}}$

3. If $x = \dfrac{\sqrt{5} + \sqrt{3}}{\sqrt{5} - \sqrt{3}}$ and $y = \dfrac{\sqrt{5} - \sqrt{3}}{\sqrt{5} + \sqrt{3}}$, then $(x + y)$ is equal to:

   A. 8   B. 6   C. $2\sqrt{15}$ D. $2\left(\sqrt{5} + \sqrt{3}\right)$

4. $2^{x+1} + 2^{x+3} = 2560$, then x is equal to:

   A. 12   B. 11   C. 8   D. 6

5. If $\dfrac{5 + 2\sqrt{3}}{7 + 4\sqrt{3}} = a + b\sqrt{3}$, then b is equal to:

   A. –6   B. 6   C. –11   D. 11

6. If $\dfrac{(21)^{5.36}}{(21)^{3.47}} = (21)^x$, then the value of x is:

   A. 8.88   B. 1.54   C. 9.32   D. 1.89

7. $\sqrt{24} + \sqrt{12}$ equal to:

   A. $\sqrt{36}$ B. $2\sqrt{6} + 2\sqrt{3}$ C. $6\sqrt{2}$ D. $\sqrt{288}$

8. If $a^b = 64$, where a and b are positive integers then $(a - b)^{a+b-4}$ is:

   A. 0   B. 1   C. 2   D. $\dfrac{1}{2}$

9. The value of $\dfrac{5^{10+n} \cdot 25^{3n-4}}{5^{7n}}$ is:

   A. 5   B. 8   C. 25   D. 16

10. $3^x - 3^{x-1} = 18$, then the value of x^x is:

   A. 3   B. 8   C. 27   D. 216

11. If $x = \sqrt{10 + \sqrt{25 + \sqrt{121}}}$, then x is equal to:

   A. –2 only   B. 2 only   C. $\pm\,4$ D. 4 only

12. If $a^x = b^y = c^z$ and $b^2 = ac$, then y is equal to:

   A. $\dfrac{xz}{x + z}$ B. $\dfrac{xz}{2(x - z)}$ C. $\dfrac{xz}{2(z - x)}$ D. $\dfrac{2xz}{x + z}$

13. $\dfrac{5^{n+3} - 6 \times 5^{n+1}}{9 \times 5^n - 5^n \times 2^2}$ is equal to:

A. 5 B. 19 C. 25 D. 95

14. The value of $\left(\dfrac{x^a}{x^b}\right)^{(a+b)} \times \left(\dfrac{x^b}{x^c}\right)^{(b+c)} \times \left(\dfrac{x^c}{x^a}\right)^{(c+a)}$ is equal to:

A. 0 B. 2 C. 1 D. 3

15. If $\sqrt{3^n} = 729$, then the value of n is:

A. 12 B. 8 C. 10 D. 6

16. The value of $4\sqrt{3} - 3\sqrt{12} + 2\sqrt{75}$ is:

A. $2\sqrt{3}$ B. $4\sqrt{3}$ C. $6\sqrt{3}$ D. $8\sqrt{3}$

17. The value of $\sqrt{50} - \sqrt{98} + \sqrt{162}$ is:

A. $5\sqrt{2}$ B. $7\sqrt{2}$ C. $3\sqrt{2}$ D. $4\sqrt{2}$

18. If $x = 1 - \sqrt{2}$, the value of $\left(x - \dfrac{1}{x}\right)^3$ is:

A. 1 B. 4 C. 8 D. 2

19. If $a = 7 - 4\sqrt{3}$, then the value of $\sqrt{a} + \dfrac{1}{\sqrt{a}}$ is equal to:

A. 1 B. 4 C. 2 D. 3

20. The value of $\dfrac{4\sqrt{18}}{\sqrt{12}} - \dfrac{8\sqrt{75}}{\sqrt{32}} + \dfrac{9\sqrt{2}}{\sqrt{3}}$ is:

A. 0 B. 2 C. 1 D. 3

21. If $(625)^2 = 390625$, then the value of $\sqrt{.00390625}$ will be:

A. .0625 B. 0.625 C. .00625 D. .000625

22. $x \otimes y = \sqrt{(x+1)(y+1)^2}$, then the value of $3 \otimes 7$ will be:

A. 21 B. 16 C. 18 D. 28

23. The cube root of 8^4 is:

A. 16 B. 8 C. 4 D. 64

24. By what smallest number 270 be multiplied so that the resulting number becomes a perfect cube?

   A. 121   B. 109   C. 100   D. 99

25. By what smallest number 675 be multiplied so that the product becomes a perfect square number?

   A. 2   B. $\dfrac{3}{5}$ C. 4   D. 3

26. If the approximate square root of 80 is 8.94. What will be the value of $\sqrt{20}$?

   A. 3.37   B. 4.47   C. 4.87   D. 4.40

27. What will be the value of $\sqrt[3]{32+\sqrt{1012+\sqrt{144}}}$?

   A. 4   B. 6   C. 5   D. 8

28. What will be the square root of $\left(\sqrt[3]{0.00000064}\right) \times \sqrt{2.56}$?

   A. .06   B. .08   C. .05   D. .04

29. If $\dfrac{\sqrt{?}}{4} = \dfrac{1}{3}$, what will be in place of (?)?

   A. $\dfrac{16}{3}$ B. $\dfrac{16}{9}$ C. $\dfrac{21}{16}$ D. $\dfrac{4}{3}$

30. If 30% of $\sqrt{?}$ + 15% of 40 = 11, what should replace the sign of interrogation (?)?

   A. $\dfrac{2500}{9}$ B. $\dfrac{2400}{7}$ C. $\dfrac{2300}{11}$ D. $\dfrac{2200}{7}$

ANSWERS

1	2	3	4	5	6	7	8	9	10
B	A	A	C	A	D	B	B	C	C

11	12	13	14	15	16	17	18	19	20
D	D	B	C	A	D	B	C	B	A

21	22	23	24	25	26	27	28	29	30
A	B	A	C	D	B	A	B	B	A

EXPLANATORY ANSWERS

6.
$$\frac{(21)^{5.36}}{(21)^{3.47}} = (21)^x$$

$$\Rightarrow \quad (21)^{5.36 - 3.47} = (21)^x$$
$$\Rightarrow \qquad\qquad x = 1.89$$

7. $\sqrt{24} + \sqrt{12} = 2\sqrt{6} + 2\sqrt{3}$

8. $a^b = 64 = (4)^3 \Rightarrow a = 4, b = 3$
$$\therefore \ (a - b)^{a+b-4} = (4 - 3)^{4+3-4} = (1)^3 = 1$$

13.
$$\frac{5^{n+3} - 6 \times 5^{n+1}}{9 \times 5^n - 5^n \times 2^2} = \frac{5^n \times 5^3 - 6 \times 5^n \times 5}{9 \times 5^n - 4 \times 5^n}$$

$$= \frac{5^n(125 - 30)}{5^n(9 - 4)} = 5^0 \times \frac{95}{5}$$

$$= 1 \times 19 = 19.$$

15. $\sqrt{3^n} = 729 \Rightarrow 3^{n/2} = 3^6$

$$\Rightarrow \qquad\qquad \frac{n}{2} = 6$$
$$\Rightarrow \qquad\qquad n = 12.$$

25. $675 = 3 \times 3 \times 3 \times 5 \times 5 = 3 \times 3^2 \times 5^2$
From the above, we find that only a factor 3 is left unpaired
$\therefore$ If we multiply 675 by 3 the product would be $\underline{3 \times 3} \times 3^2 \times 5^2$ which
is a perfect square.
$\therefore$ The required smallest number is 3.

27. $\because \sqrt[3]{32 + \sqrt{1012 + \sqrt{144}}} = \sqrt[3]{32 + \sqrt{1012 + 12}}$

$$= \sqrt[3]{32 + \sqrt{1024}} = \sqrt[3]{32 + 32} = \sqrt[3]{64} = \sqrt[3]{4 \times 4 \times 4} = 4$$

29. $\dfrac{\sqrt{?}}{4} = \dfrac{1}{3} \Rightarrow \sqrt{?} = \dfrac{4}{3} \qquad \Rightarrow ? = \dfrac{4}{3} \times \dfrac{4}{3} = \dfrac{16}{9}$

$\therefore$ Sign of interrogation (?) should be replaced by $\dfrac{16}{9}$.

❖ ❖ ❖

5

Ratio, Proportion & Partnership

Ratio

When comparison is made by dividing one quantity by another of the same kind, the result is called ratio. If a and b are two numbers, ratio of a to b is denoted by $a : b$ or $\dfrac{a}{b}$. The first term a is called antecedent and the second term b is called consequent.

Proportion

Equality of two ratios is called proportion. If $a : b = c : d$, then a, b, c, d are called in proportion. In a proportion $a : b : : c : d$, then a and d are called extremes and b and c are called means.

Product of extremes = Product of means

Comparison of Ratio: Suppose $\dfrac{a}{b} > \dfrac{c}{d}$ then we say that $a : b > c : d$.

Compounded Ratio: The compound ratio of the ratios $a : b$, $c : d$ and $e : f$ is $ace : bdf$.

Duplicate Ratio: The duplicate ratio of $a : b$ is $a^2 : b^2$.

Triplicate Ratio: The triplicate ratio of $a : b$ is $a^3 : b^3$.

EXAMPLE: If A : B = 3 : 4 and B : C = 8 : 9 then find A : C.

SOLUTION: $A : B = 3 : 4 \Rightarrow \dfrac{A}{B} = \dfrac{3}{4}$

$B : C = 8 : 9 \Rightarrow \dfrac{B}{C} = \dfrac{8}{9}$ $\qquad$ $\dfrac{A}{C} = \dfrac{A}{B} \times \dfrac{B}{C} = \dfrac{3}{4} \times \dfrac{8}{9} = \dfrac{2}{3}$

$\Rightarrow A : C = 2 : 3$

Partnership

Partnership is a form of association of two or more persons who contribute resources like money together in order to carry on a business. It may be of simple or compound type.

Simple partnership is one in which the capitals of the partners are invested for the same time. The profits or losses are divided among the partners in the ratio of their investments.

Compound partnership is one in which the capitals of the partners are invested for different periods. In such cases, equivalent capitals are calculated for each partner by multiplying their capital contributions with time. The profits or losses are then divided in the ratio of these equivalent capitals.

The partner who invests the money in the business as well as takes part in its management, is known as **Working partner.**

The partner who only invests the money in the business and does not work, is known as **Sleeping partner.**

MULTIPLE CHOICE QUESTIONS

1. If A : B = 2 : 3 and B : C = 4 : 5, then C : A is equal to:
   A. 15 : 8
   B. 12 : 10
   C. 8 : 5
   D. 8 : 15

2. If 10% of x is the same as 20% of y, then $x : y$ is equal to:
   A. 1 : 2
   B. 2 : 1
   C. 5 : 1
   D. 10 : 1

3. The mean proportional to $6 + \sqrt{27}$ and $6 - \sqrt{27}$ is:
   A. 3
   B. 9
   C. 10
   D. $\sqrt{10}$

4. If $x : y = 9 : 11$, the value of $\dfrac{5x + 3y}{3x + 5y}$ is:
   A. 45 : 55
   B. 18 : 22
   C. 37 : 41
   D. 39 : 41

5. If $a + b : b + c : c + a = 6 : 7 : 8$ and $a + b + c = 14$, then the value of c is:
   A. 14
   B. 7
   C. 8
   D. 6

6. Two numbers are in the ratio 2 : 3. If 5 is added to each number, the ratio becomes 5 : 7. The bigger number is:
   A. 30
   B. 40
   C. 60
   D. 20

7. What should be added to each of the numbers 12, 30, 40 and 86, so that they are in proportion?
   A. 6
   B. 4
   C. –6
   D. –4

8. The ratio of males and females of a village is 5 : 3. If there are 800 males in the village, females are:
   A. 240
   B. 480
   C. 840
   D. 488

9. In a mixture of 60 litres, the ratio of ethanol to ether is 4 : 1. How much ether must be added to the mixture to make this ratio 2 : 1?
   A. 10 litres
   B. 12 litres
   C. 18 litres
   D. 24 litres

10. The proportion of zinc and copper in a brass piece is 4 : 5. How much zinc will be there in 180 kg of such a piece?

    A. 40 kg   B. 80 kg   C. 100 kg   D. 120 kg

11. The prices of a scooter and a television set are in the ratio 3 : 2. If a scooter costs ₹ 6000 more than the television set, the price of the television set is:

    A. ₹ 18000   B. ₹ 12000   C. ₹ 10000   D. ₹ 6000

12. The weight of a 13 metres long iron rod be 23.4 kg. The weight of 6 metres long of such rod will be:

    A. 7.2 kg   B. 12.4 kg   C. 10.8 kg   D. 18 kg

13. The ratio between the ages of Gayatri and Savitri is 6 : 5 and the sum of their ages is 44 years. The ratio of their ages after 8 years will be:

    A. 5 : 6   B. 7 : 8   C. 8 : 7   D. 14 : 13

14. Two numbers are such that the ratio between them is 3 : 5 but if each is increased by 10, the ratio between them becomes 5 : 7. The numbers are:

    A. 3, 5   B. 7, 9   C. 13, 22   D. 15, 25

15. A, B and C share the profit in the ratio of 3 : 5 : 7. If the gain is ₹ 2040, then C's share is:

    A. ₹ 360   B. ₹ 600   C. ₹ 952   D. ₹ 120

16. A, B and C started a business with ₹ 47000. A puts in ₹ 5000 more than B and B ₹ 3000 more than C. The share of A out of the profit of ₹ 14100 will be:

    A. ₹ 3600   B. ₹ 4500   C. ₹ 6000   D. ₹ 6300

17. A starts a business with ₹ 5000. After 4 months B joins him with a sum of ₹ 4000. In the end of the year there is a profit of ₹ 8970. The share of A in the profit will be:

    A. ₹ 3120   B. ₹ 4020   C. ₹ 5850   D. ₹ 6360

18. A, B, C are three partners in a business. The profit share of A is $\dfrac{3}{16}$ of the profit and B's share is $\dfrac{1}{4}$ of the profit. If C receives ₹ 243, then the amount received by B will be:

    A. ₹ 90   B. ₹ 96   C. ₹ 108   D. ₹ 120

19. A, B and C share the profit in the ratio 2 : 3 : 7. If the average gain is ₹ 8000, then B's share is:

    A. ₹ 2000   B. ₹ 1000   C. ₹ 1500   D. ₹ 3000

20. Ashok started a business investing ₹ 90,000. After 3 months Shabir joined him with a capital of ₹ 1,20,000. If at the end of one year the total profit made by them was ₹ 96,000, what will be the difference between their shares?

A. ₹ 24000 　　 B. ₹ 8000 　　 C. ₹ 20000 　　 D. None of these

21. If a : b = 2 : 3, b : c = 4 : 5 and c : d = 6 : 7, then a : d is equal to:

A. 2 : 7 　　 B. 7 : 8 　　 C. 4 : 13 　　 D. 16 : 35

22. The mean proportional between 0.32 and 0.02 is:

A. 0.34 　　 B. 0.3 　　 C. 0.16 　　 D. 0.08

23. The sum of three numbers is 98. If the ratio between the first and second be 2 : 3 and that between the second and third be 5 : 8, then what is the second number?

A. 20 　　 B. 30 　　 C. 10 　　 D. 40

24. One man adds 3 litres of water to 12 litres of milk and another 4 litres of water to 10 litres of milk. What is the ratio of the strenghts of the milk in the two mixtures?

A. 15 : 25 　　 B. 25 : 28 　　 C. 28 : 25 　　 D. None of these

25. ₹ 425 is divided among 4 men, 5 women and 6 boys such that the share of a man, a woman and a boy may be in the ratio of 9 : 8 : 4. What is the share of a woman?

A. ₹ 34 　　 B. ₹ 24 　　 C. ₹ 44 　　 D. None

26. A vessel contains liquids P and Q in the ratio 5 : 3. If 6 litres of the mixture are removed and the same quantity of liquid q is added, the ratio becomes 3 : 5. What quantity does the vessel hold?

A. 40 litres 　　 B. 50 litres 　　 C. 30 litres 　　 D. None of these

27. A bucket contains a mixture of two liquids P and Q in the proportion 7 : 5. If 9 litres of the mixture is replaced by 9 litres of liquid Q, then the ratio of the two liquid becomes 7 : 9. How much of the liquid P was there in the bucket?

A. 11 litres 　　 B. 21 litres 　　 C. 31 litres 　　 D. None of these

28. Three glasses P, Q and R with their capacities in the ratio 2 : 3 : 4 are filled with a mixture of spirit and water. The ratio of spirit to water in P, Q and R is 1 : 5, 3 : 5 and 5 : 7 respectively. If the contents of these glasses are mixed together, what is the ratio of spirit to water in the mixture?

A. 14 : 27 　　 B. 23 : 47 　　 C. 25 : 47 　　 D. None of these

29. A and B are two alloys of gold and copper prepared by mixing metals in proportions 7 : 2 and 7 : 11 respectively. If equal quantities of the alloys are melted to form a third alloy C, the proportion of gold and copper in C will be

A. 5 : 9   B. 5 : 7   C. 7 : 5   D. 9 : 5

30. Gold is 19 times as heavy as water and copper 9 times as heavy as water. The ratio in which these two metals be mixed so that the mixtures is 15 times as heavy as water is:

A. 1 : 2   B. 2 : 3   C. 3 : 2   D. 19 : 135

ANSWERS

1	2	3	4	5	6	7	8	9	10
A	B	A	D	D	A	A	B	B	B

11	12	13	14	15	16	17	18	19	20
B	C	C	D	C	C	C	C	A	D

21	22	23	24	25	26	27	28	29	30
D	D	B	C	A	A	B	C	C	C

EXPLANATORY ANSWERS

3. Mean proportional $= \sqrt{\left(6+\sqrt{27}\right)\left(6-\sqrt{27}\right)}$

$$= \sqrt{36-27} = \sqrt{9} = 3$$

8. Ratio of Males : Females = 5 : 3

$$\Rightarrow \frac{800}{x} = \frac{5}{3} \Rightarrow 5x = 3 \times 800$$

$$\Rightarrow x = \frac{3 \times 800}{5} = 3 \times 160 = 480$$

Hence, number of females = 480.

10. In 9 kg of brass, zinc = 4 kg

$$\therefore \text{ In 180 kg of brass, zinc} = \frac{4}{9} \times 180 = 80 \text{ kg.}$$

12. Weight of 13 m long iron rod = 23.4 kg

Weight of 6 m long iron rod

$$= \frac{23.4}{13} \times 6 \text{ kg} = 1.8 \times 6 = 10.8 \text{ kg.}$$

15. C's share $= \dfrac{7}{15} \times 2040 = ₹\ 952.$

19. B's share $= \dfrac{3}{2+3+7} \times 8000 = \dfrac{3 \times 8000}{12} = ₹\ 2000$

22. Mean proportional $= \sqrt{0.32 \times 0.02} = \sqrt{0.0064} = 0.08$

23. The ratio among the three numbers is

$$2 \quad : \quad 3$$
$$5 \quad : \quad 8$$
$$\text{and} \quad 10 \quad : \quad 15 \quad : \quad 24$$

$\therefore$ The second number $= \dfrac{98}{10+15+24} \times 15 = 30$

25. The ratio of shares of group of men, women and boys
$$= 9 \times 4 : 8 \times 5 : 4 \times 6 = 9 : 10 : 6$$

$\therefore$ Share of 5 women $= \dfrac{425}{9+10+6} \times 10 = ₹\ 170$

$\therefore$ Share of 1 woman $= \dfrac{170}{5} = ₹\ 34$

29. Gold in C $= \left(\dfrac{7}{9} + \dfrac{7}{18}\right) = \dfrac{21}{18} = \dfrac{7}{6}$

Copper in C $= \left(\dfrac{2}{9} + \dfrac{11}{18}\right) = \dfrac{15}{18} = \dfrac{5}{6}$

$\therefore$ Gold : Copper $= \dfrac{7}{6} : \dfrac{5}{6} = 7 : 5$

6

Average

The sum of all the quantities of same kind divided by their number is called average (or mean) of those quantities.

FORMULAE

1. Average $= \left(\dfrac{\text{Sum of observations}}{\text{Number of observations}} \right)$

2. Sum of the first n natural numbers $= 1 + 2 + 3 + \dots + n = \dfrac{n(n+1)}{2}$

3. Sum of the squares of the first n natural numbers

$$= 1^2 + 2^2 + \dots + n^2 = \frac{n(n+1)(2n+1)}{6}$$

4. Sum of the cubes of the first n natural numbers

$$= 1^3 + 2^3 + \dots + n^3 = \left\{ \frac{n(n+1)}{2} \right\}^2$$

5. Sum of the first n odd numbers $= 1 + 3 + 5 + \dots + (2n - 1) = n^2$

Different kinds of mean or average:

(*a*) Arithmetic mean, (*b*) Geometric mean, (*c*) Harmonic mean

$$\text{A.M.} = \frac{x_1 + x_2 + x_3 + \dots + x_n}{n}$$

$$\text{G.M.} = (x_1 \cdot x_2 \cdot x_3 \dots x_n)^{1/n}$$

$$\text{H.M.} = \frac{n}{\dfrac{1}{x_1} + \dfrac{1}{x_2} + \dots + \dfrac{1}{x_n}}.$$

EXAMPLE 1. : Find the average of first ten prime numbers.

SOLUTION: First ten prime numbers are 2, 3, 5, 7, 11, 13, 17, 19, 23 and 29.

$$\therefore \text{ Average} = \frac{2+3+5+7+11+13+17+19+23+29}{10}$$

$$= \frac{129}{10} = 12.9$$

EXAMPLE 2. : The average of 11 results is 50. If the average of first six results is 49 and that of last six is 52, find the sixth result.

SOLUTION: Sum of 11 results $= 11 \times 50 = 550$

Sum of first 6 results $6 \times 49 = 294$

Sum of last 6 results $= 6 \times 52 = 312$

∴ 6th result $= 294 + 312 - 550 = 56$

EXAMPLE 3. : The average age of three boys is 15 years. If their ages are in the ratio 3 : 5 : 7. What is the age of the youngest boy?

SOLUTION: Let the ages of the three boys be $3x$, $5x$ and $7x$.

$$\text{Average age} = \frac{3x + 5x + 7x}{3} = 5x \text{ and } 5x = 15 \Rightarrow x = 3$$

The age of the youngest boy $= 3x = 3 \times 3 = 9$ years.

MULTIPLE CHOICE QUESTIONS

1. The average of first five multiples of 3 is:
   A. 3 B. 9 C. 12 D. 15

2. The average of 25 results is 18, that of first 12 is 14 and of the last 12 is 17. Thirteenth result is:
   A. 78 B. 85 C. 28 D. 72

3. Out of three numbers, the first is twice the second and is half of the third. If the average of the three numbers is 56, the three numbers in order are:
   A. 48, 96, 24 B. 48, 24, 96 C. 96, 24, 48 D. 96, 48, 24

4. The sum of three numbers is 98. If the ratio between first and second be 2 : 3 and that between second and third be 5 : 8, then the second number is:
   A. 30 B. 20 C. 58 D. 48

5. The average age of a committee of seven trustees is the same as it was 5 years ago; a young man having been substituted for one of them. The new man compared to the replaced old man, is younger in age by:
   A. 5 years B. 7 years C. 12 years D. 35 years

6. The average expenditure of a man for the first five months is ₹ 120 and for the next seven months is ₹ 130. His monthly average income if he saves ₹ 290 in that year, is:
   A. ₹ 160 B. ₹ 170 C. ₹ 150 D. ₹ 140

7. The average salary of 20 workers in an office is ₹ 1900 per month. If the manager's salary is added, the average becomes ₹ 2000 per month. The manager's salary is:
   A. ₹ 24000 B. ₹ 25200 C. ₹ 45600 D. None of these

8. The average temperature of first 3 days is 27°C and of the next 3 days is 29°C. If the average of the whole week is 28.5°C, the temperature of the last day is:

   A. 31.5°C   B. 10.5°C   C. 21°C   D. 42°C

9. A cricketer scored 180 runs in the first test and 258 runs in the second. How many runs should he score in the third test so that his average score in the three tests would be 230 runs?

   A. 219   B. 242   C. 334   D. None of these

10. The average of first five prime numbers is:

   A. 5.0   B. 5.2   C. 5.6   D. 6.0

11. The average weight of 3 men A, B and C is 84 kg. Another man D joins the group and the average now becomes 80 kg. If another man E, whose weight is 3 kg more than that of D, replaces A, then average weight of B, C, D and E becomes 79 kg. The weight of A is:

   A. 70 kg   B. 72 kg   C. 75 kg   D. 80 kg

12. The average age of A, B, C, D and E is 45 years. By including x, the present average of all the six is 49 years. The present age of x is:

   A. 64 years   B. 69 years   C. 45 years   D. 40 years

13. The average height of 30 boys, out of a class of 50, is 160 cm. If the average height of the remaining boys is 165 cm, the average height of the whole class (in cm) is:

   A. 161   B. 162   C. 163   D. 164

14. The average age of an adult class is 40 years. 12 new students with an average age of 30 years join the class, thereby decreasing the average of the class by 4 years. The original strength of the class was:

   A. 10   B. 18   C. 12   D. 15

15. If a, b, c, d, e are five consecutive even numbers, their average is:

   A. $5(a + 4)$ B. $\dfrac{abcde}{5}$

   C. $5(a + b + c + d + e)$ D. None of these

16. Of the three numbers, second is twice the first and is also thrice the third. If the average of the three numbers is 44, the largest number is:

   A. 24   B. 36   C. 72   D. 108

17. The average of 50 numbers is 38. If two numbers namely, 45 and 55 are discarded, the average of remaining number is:

   A. 36.50   B. 37.00   C. 37.50   D. 37.52

18. The average height of 30 girls out of a class of 40 is 160 cm and that of the remaining girls is 156 cm. The average height of the whole class is:
A. 158 cm   B. 158.5 cm   C. 159 cm   D. 159.5 cm

19. The average of n numbers is x. If 36 is subtracted from any two numbers each, then new average is $(x - 8)$. The value of n is:
A. 6   B. 8   C. 9   D. 72

20. The average salary of male employees in a firm is ₹ 520 and that of female employees is ₹ 420. The mean salary of all the employees is ₹ 500. The percentage of female employees is:
A. 40%   B. 30%   C. 25%   D. 20%

21. Out of three numbers, the first is twice the second and is half of the third. If the average of the three numbers is 56, the three numbers in order are
A. 48, 96, 24   B. 48, 24, 96   C. 96, 24, 48   D. 96, 48, 24

22. The average age of 30 students in a class is 12 years. The average age of a group of 5 of the students is 10 years and that of another group of 5 of them is 14 years. The average age of the remaining students is
A. 8 years   B. 10 years   C. 12 years   D. 14 years

23. Out of four numbers, the average of first three is 15 and that of the last three is 16. If the last number is 19, the first is
A. 15   B. 16   C. 18   D. 19

24. The average age of an adult class is 40 years. 12 new students with an average age of 32 years join the class, thereby decreasing the average by 4 years. The original strength of the class was
A. 10   B. 11   C. 12   D. 15

25. The average age of 24 students in a class is 10. If the teacher's age is included, the average increases by one. The age of the teacher is
A. 25   B. 30   C. 35   D. 40

26. The average age of A, B, C and D five years ago was 45 years. By including X, the present age of all the five is 49 years. The present age of X is
A. 64 years   B. 48 years   C. 45 years   D. 40 years

27. The average expenditure of a man for the first five months is ₹ 120 and for the next seven months it is ₹ 130. If he saves ₹ 290 in that year, his monthly average income is
A. ₹ 1000   B. ₹ 1800   C. ₹ 2000   D. ₹ 2500

28. The average weight of a class of 40 students is 40 kg. If the weight of the teacher be included, the average weight increases by 500 gms. The weight of the teacher is

A. 40.5 kg   B. 60 kg   C. 60.5 kg   D. 62 kg

29. The average weight of 8 persons is increased by 2.5 kg when one of them whose weight is 56 kg is replaced by a new man. The weight of the new man is

A. 66 kg   B. 75 kg   C. 76 kg   D. 86 kg

30. If a, b, c, d, e are five consecutive odd numbers, their average is

A. $5 (a + 4)$ B. $\dfrac{abcde}{5}$

C. $5(a + b + c + d + e)$ D. None of these

ANSWERS

1	2	3	4	5	6	7	8	9	10
B	A	B	A	D	C	D	A	D	C

11	12	13	14	15	16	17	18	19	20
C	B	B	B	D	C	C	C	C	D

21	22	23	24	25	26	27	28	29	30
B	C	B	C	C	C	B	C	C	D

EXPLANATORY ANSWERS

1. Average = $\dfrac{3(1+2+3+4+5)}{5} = \dfrac{(3 \times 15)}{5} = 9$

6. Total income for 12 months = ₹ (120 × 5 + 130 × 7 + 290) = ₹ 1800

Average monthly income = ₹$\dfrac{1800}{12}$ = ₹150

10. Average = $\dfrac{2+3+5+7+11}{5} = \dfrac{28}{5} = 5.6.$

13. Total height of 30 boys = 30 × 160 = 4800
Total height of 20 boys = 20 × 165 = 3300
Total height of 50 boys = 8100

Average height of 50 boys = $\dfrac{8100}{50} = 162.$

19. $\dfrac{nx - 36 - 36}{n} = x - 8$

$\Rightarrow nx - 72 = nx - 8n$

$\Rightarrow 8n = 72 \Rightarrow \quad n = 9$

23. Sum of four numbers $= (15 \times 3 + 19) = 64$

Sum of last three numbers $= (16 \times 3) = 48$

$\therefore$ First number $= (64 - 48) = 16$

24. Let the original strength $= x$

Then, $40x + 12 \times 32 = (x + 12) \times 36$

$\Rightarrow \qquad 40x + 384 = 36x + 432$

$\Rightarrow \qquad 4x = 48$

$\Rightarrow \qquad x = 12$

25. Age of the teacher $= (25 \times 11 - 24 \times 10)$ years $= 35$ years

26. Present age of $x = [(49 \times 5) - (4 \times 45 + 4 \times 5)]$ years

$= 45$ years

27. Total income $= (120 \times 5 + 130 \times 7 + 290) = ₹\ 1800$

28. Weight of the teacher $= (41 \times 40.5 - 40 \times 40)$ kg $= 60.5$ kg

29. Total increase $= (8 \times 2.5)$ kg $= 20$ kg

Weight of new man $= (56 + 20)$kg $= 76$ kg

30. Average $= \dfrac{a + (a + 2) + (a + 4) + (a + 6) + (a + 8)}{5}$

$= (a + 4)$

❖ ❖ ❖

7

Percentage

The word 'per cent' or 'percentage' means 'for every one hundred'. In other words, it gives an indication of rate per hundred. It is denoted by the symbol %.

For example, 5% means 5 out of one hundred or $\dfrac{5}{100}$.

Important Facts:

For quickly solving the problems related to percentage, remember following rules:

(a) Of the given two numbers if the first is $x\%$ more than the second, then the second will be $\left(\dfrac{100 \times x}{100 + x}\right)\%$ less than the first.

(b) Of the given two numbers if the first is $x\%$ less than the second, then the second will be $\left(\dfrac{100 \times x}{100 - x}\right)\%$ more than the first.

(c) If two numbers are respectively $x\%$ and $y\%$ more than a third number, then the first number will be $\left(\dfrac{100 + x}{100 + y} \times 100\right)\%$ of the second.

(d) If two numbers are respectively $x\%$ and $y\%$ less than a third number, then the first number will be $\left(\dfrac{100 - x}{100 - y} \times 100\right)\%$ of the second.

Example 1. : A's income is 150% more than B's income. By how much per cent is B's income less than A's income?

Solution : Here, A's income is 150% more than B's income, *i.e.*, $x = 150$

$\therefore$ B's income will be $\left(\dfrac{100 \times 150}{100 + 150}\right)\%$ less than A's income,

$\left(\dfrac{100 \times 150}{100 + 150}\right)\% = \dfrac{100 \times 150}{250}\% = 60\%$

Example 2. : If a number is increased by 10% and thereafter decreased by 10%, then by how much per cent the number has been increased or decreased?

Solution : $\because$ The number is first increased by 10% and later the new number is decreased by 10%

$\therefore$ Percentage decrease in the number $= \left(\dfrac{(10)^2}{100}\right)\% = 1\%$

Example 3. : The population of a town is 40,000. If the population increases 20% every year, find the population after 3 years.

Solution: Population after 3 years $= 40000\left(1+\dfrac{20}{100}\right)^3$

$= 40000 \times \dfrac{6}{5} \times \dfrac{6}{5} \times \dfrac{6}{5} = 69120$

MULTIPLE CHOICE QUESTIONS

1. If x is 90% of y, then what per cent of x is y?
   A. 90   B. 190   C. 101.1   D. 111.1

2. A number exceeds 20% of itself by 40. The number is :
   A. 50   B. 60   C. 80   D. 320

3. The price of an article is cut by 10%. To restore it to the former value, the new price must be increased by :
   A. 10%   B. $9\dfrac{1}{11}\%$ C. $11\dfrac{1}{9}\%$ D. 11%

4. The income of a broker remains unchanged though the rate of commission is increased from 4% to 5%. The percentage of slump business is :
   A. 8%   B. 1%   C. 20%   D. 80%

5. 5% income of A is equal to 15% income of B and 10% income of B is equal to 20% income of C. If income of C is ₹ 2000, then total income of A, B and C is :
   A. ₹ 6000   B. ₹ 18000   C. ₹ 20000   D. ₹ 14000

6. A student who secures 20% marks in an examination fails by 30 marks. Another student who secures 32% gets 42 marks more than those required to pass. The percentage of marks required to pass is:
   A. 20   B. 25   C. 28   D. 30

7. In a college election, a candidate secured 62% of the votes and is elected by a majority of 144 votes. The total number of votes polled is :
   A. 600   B. 800   C. 925   D. 1200

8. What will be 80% of a number whose 200% is 90?
   A. 144   B. 72   C. 36   D. None of these

9. p is six times as large as q. The per cent that q is less than p, is :
   A. $83\dfrac{1}{3}$ B. $16\dfrac{2}{3}$ C. 90   D. 60

10. The price of an article has been reduced by 25%. In order to restore the original price, the new price must be increased by :
   A. $33\dfrac{1}{3}\%$ B. $11\dfrac{1}{9}\%$ C. $9\dfrac{1}{11}\%$ D. $66\dfrac{2}{3}\%$

11. The price of cooking oil has increased by 25%. The percentage of reduction that a family should effect in the use of cooking oil so as not to increase the expenditure on this account is :
   A. 25%   B. 30%   C. 20%   D. 15%

12. In an organisation, 40% of the employees are matriculates, 50% of the remaining are graduates and the remaining 180 are postgraduates. How many employees are graduates?
   A. 360   B. 240   C. 300   D. 180

13. In 40% of the people read newspaper X, 50% read newspaper Y, and 10% read both the papers. What percentage of the people read neither newspaper?
   A. 10%   B. 15%   C. 20%   D. 25%

14. The population of a town increases by 5% annually. If its population in 2008 was 138915, what it was in 2005?
   A. 110000   B. 100000   C. 120000   D. 90000

15. The population of a village is 4500. $\dfrac{5}{9}$ th of them are males and rest females. If 40% of the males are married, then the percentage of married female is :
   A. 35   B. 40   C. 50   D. 60

16. A's income is 10% more than B's. How much per cent is B's income is less than A's?
   A. 10%   B. 7%   C. $9\dfrac{1}{11}\%$ D. $6\dfrac{1}{2}\%$

17. A mixture of 40 litres of milk and water contains 10% water. How much water must be added to make water 20% in the new mixture?
   A. 10 litres   B. 7 litres   C. 5 litres   D. 3 litres

18. If $z = \dfrac{x^2}{y}$ and x, y both are increased in value by 10%, then the value

of z is :
A. unchanged   B. increased by 10%
C. increased by 11%   D. increased by 20%

19. In an examination, 35% of the examinees failed in G.K. and 25% in English. If 10% of the examinees failed in both, then the percentage of examinees passed will be:
A. 40%   B. 45%   C. 48%   D. 50%

20. If the price of a television set is increased by 25%, then by what percentage should the new price be reduced to bring the price back to original level?
A. 15%   B. 20%   C. 25%   D. 30%

21. A candidate needs 35% marks to pass. If he gets 96 marks and fails by 16 marks, then the maximum marks are :
A. 250   B. 320   C. 300   D. 425

22. In an election one of the two candidates gets 40% votes and loses by 100 votes. Total number of votes is :
A. 500   B. 400   C. 600   D. 1000

23. If the income tax is decreased by 26%, a man's net income increases by $\dfrac{2}{3}\%$. The rate of income tax is:

A. $3\dfrac{1}{2}\%$ B. $2\dfrac{1}{2}\%$ C. $1\dfrac{1}{2}\%$ D. 3%

24. The gross income of a person is ₹ 20000. 10% of his income is exempted from income tax and his net income is ₹ 19100. The rate of income tax is :
A. 3%   B. 2%   C. 4%   D. 5%

25. If the rate of income tax is 5%, the net income of a person is ₹ 17100. If the rate of income tax is 6%, how much will be the net income?
A. 15820   B. 16920   C. 17820   D. 18920

26. The gross income of a person is ₹ 15000, 20% of his income is exempted from income tax and the rate of income tax is ₹ 4%. The net income is :
A. 14520   B. 14620   C. 15520   D. 15620

27. The gross income of a person is ₹ 16000. A part of his income is exempted from income tax and his net income is ₹ 14480. If the rate of income tax is 8%, the income exempted from income tax is :
A. 1600   B. 1700   C. 1800   D. 1500

28. One-eight of a number is 17.25. What will 73% of number be?

    A. 82.66   B. 96.42   C. 100.74   D. 138.00

29. If 58% of 960 – x% of 635 = 277.4, find the value of x.

    A. 24   B. 36   C. 44   D. 58

30. There are 1225 employees in an organisation, out of which 40% got transferred to different places. How many such employees got transferred?

    A. 490   B. 540   C. 630   D. 710

ANSWERS

1	2	3	4	5	6	7	8	9	10
D	A	C	C	B	B	A	C	A	A

11	12	13	14	15	16	17	18	19	20
C	D	C	C	C	C	C	B	D	B

21	22	23	24	25	26	27	28	29	30
B	A	B	D	B	A	D	C	C	A

EXPLANATORY ANSWERS

2. $x - 20\%$ of $x = 40$

$$\Rightarrow x - \frac{x}{5} = 40 \Rightarrow \frac{4x}{5} = 40$$

$$\Rightarrow x = \frac{40 \times 5}{4} = 50$$

3. Required percentage $= \dfrac{10}{100 - 10} \times 100$

$$= \frac{10}{90} \times 100 = 11\frac{1}{9}\%$$

7. $(62\%$ of $x - 38\%$ of $x) = 144$

$$\Rightarrow 24\% \text{ of } x = 144$$

$$\Rightarrow x = \frac{144 \times 100}{24}$$

$$= 600$$

10. Required percentage $= \dfrac{25}{100 - 25} \times 100 = \dfrac{25}{75} \times 100 = 33\frac{1}{3}\%$

13. Number of people read either one or both = 40 + 50 − 10 = 80%

Hence, number of people read neither newspaper = 100 − 80 = 20%

16. Required percentage $= \left[\dfrac{10}{(100+10)} \times 100\right]\% = 9\dfrac{1}{11}\%$

21. 35% of $x = 96 + 16 = 112$

$$\Rightarrow \frac{35}{100} \times x = 112 \Rightarrow x = \frac{112 \times 100}{35} = 320$$

22. Out of 100, difference in votes = (60 − 40) = 20

20% of $x = 100$

$$\therefore \quad x = \frac{100 \times 100}{20} = 500$$

25. Gross income $= \dfrac{100}{95} \times 17100 = ₹\,18000$

New net income $= \dfrac{94}{100} \times 18000 = ₹\,16920$

28. The number = 8 × 17.25 = 138.00

73% of the number $= \dfrac{73}{100} \times 138 = \dfrac{10074}{100} = 100.75$

30. The number of employess got transferred $= \dfrac{40}{100} \times 1225 = 490$

8

Profit & Loss

Cost Price (CP)

The price at which an article is purchased is called the cost price of the article.

Selling Price (SP)

The price at which an article is sold is called the selling price of the article.

Profit or Gain

If SP is greater than the CP, the seller is said to have a profit or gain.

Clearly,   Gain = SP – CP

Loss

If SP is less than CP, the seller is said to have a loss.

Clearly,   Loss = CP – SP

Profit or loss per cent is calculated on cost price.

$$\text{Profit \%} = \frac{\text{Profit}}{\text{CP}} \times 100$$

$$\text{Loss \%} = \frac{\text{Loss}}{\text{CP}} \times 100$$

If an article is sold at a gain of 20%,
then,   SP = (120% of CP)
If an article is sold at a loss of 20%,
then,   SP = (80% of CP)

EXAMPLE 1. : Ravi buys an article for ₹ 5000 and sells it at 20% gain. Find it selling price.

$$\text{SOLUTION:} \quad \text{Profit} = 20\% \text{ of CP} = \frac{20}{100} \times 5000$$

$\Rightarrow$ Profit = ₹ 1000
              SP = CP + Profit
                 = 5000 + 1000
                 = ₹ 6000

EXAMPLE 2. : A man sells an article at 20% gain for ₹ 3600. Find its cost price.

SOLUTION: Let CP = ₹ 100
then   SP = 100 + 20 = ₹ 120

When SP ₹ 120 then CP = ₹ 100

When SP ₹ 3600 then CP = $\dfrac{100}{120} \times 3600$

Hence　　　　　CP = ₹ 3000

MULTIPLE CHOICE QUESTIONS

1. A loss of 5% was suffered by selling a plot for ₹ 4085. The cost price of the plot was:
    A. ₹ 4350　　　B. ₹ 4259.25　　C. ₹ 4200　　D. ₹ 4300

2. On selling an article for ₹ 240, a trader loses 4%. In order to gain 10%, he must sell that article for:
    A. ₹ 264.00　　B. ₹ 273.20　　C. ₹ 275.00　　D. ₹ 280.00

3. A man purchased a watch for ₹ 400 and sold it at a gain of 20% of the selling price. The selling price of the watch is:
    A. ₹ 300　　　B. ₹ 320　　　C. ₹ 440　　　D. ₹ 500

4. If 5% more is gained by selling an article for ₹ 350 than by selling it for ₹ 340, the cost of the article is:
    A. ₹ 50　　　　B. ₹ 160　　　C. ₹ 200　　　D. ₹ 225

5. Profit after selling a commodity for ₹ 425 is same as loss after selling it for ₹ 355. The cost of the commodity is:
    A. ₹ 385　　　B. ₹ 390　　　C. ₹ 395　　　D. ₹ 400

6. The cost price of an article, which on being sold at a gain of 12% yields ₹ 6 more than when it is sold at a loss of 12%, is:
    A. ₹ 30　　　　B. ₹ 25　　　C. ₹ 20　　　　D. ₹ 24

7. The CP of an article which is sold at a loss of 25% for ₹150, is:
    A. ₹ 125　　　B. ₹ 175　　　C. ₹ 200　　　D. ₹ 225

8. When the price of pressure cooker was increased by 15%, its sale fell down by 15%. The effect on the money receipt was:
    A. no effect　　　　　　　　　B. 15% decrease
    C. 7.5% increase　　　　　　　D. 2.25% decrease

9. A man sells 320 mangoes at the cost price of 400 mangoes. His gain per cent is:
    A. 10%　　　　B. 25%　　　C. 15%　　　　D. 20%

10. By selling 12 oranges for one rupee a man loses 20%. How many for a rupee should he sell to get a gain of 20%?
    A. 5　　　　　B. 8　　　　C. 10　　　　D. 15

11. A man sells a car to his friend at 10% loss. If the friend sells it for ₹ 54000 and gains 20%, the original CP of the car was:
A. ₹ 25000   B. ₹ 37500   C. ₹ 50000   D. ₹ 60000

12. The loss incurred on selling an article for ₹ 270 is as much as the profit made after selling it at 10% profit. The CP of the article is:
A. ₹ 90   B. ₹ 110   C. ₹ 363   D. ₹ 300

13. An item costing ₹ 200 is being sold at 10% loss. If the price is further reduced by 5%, the selling price will be:
A. ₹ 179   B. ₹ 175   C. ₹ 171   D. ₹ 170

14. A trader lists his articles 20% above CP and allows a discount of 10% on cash payment. His gain per cent is:
A. 10%   B. 6%   C. 8%   D. 5%

15. A discount series of 10%, 20% and 40% is equal to a single discount of:
A. 50%   B. 56.80%   C. 70%   D. 70.28%

16. An umbrella marked at ₹ 80 is sold for ₹ 68, the rate of discount is:

A. 12%   B. 15%   C. $17\dfrac{11}{17}\%$ D. 20%

17. A reduction of 20% in the price of mangoes enables a person to purchase 12 more for ₹ 15. The price of 16 mangoes before reduction was:
A. ₹ 5   B. ₹ 6   C. ₹ 7   D. ₹ 9

18. Tarun bought a TV with 20% discount on the labelled price. Had he bought it with 25% discount, he would have saved ₹ 500. At what price did he buy the TV?
A. ₹ 5,000   B. ₹ 10,000   C. ₹ 12,000   D. None of these

19. If a commission of 10% is given on the marked price of a book, the publisher gains 20%. If the commission is increased to 15%, the gain is:

A. $16\dfrac{2}{3}\%$ B. $13\dfrac{1}{3}\%$ C. $15\dfrac{1}{6}\%$ D. None of these

20. There would be 10% loss if rice is sold at ₹ 5.40 per kg. At what price per kg should it be sold to earn a profit of 20%?
A. ₹ 7.20   B. ₹ 7.02   C. ₹ 6.48   D. ₹ 6

21. At what price must Kantilal sell a mixture of 80 kg sugar at ₹ 6.75 per kg with 120 kg at ₹ 8 per kg to gain 20%?
A. ₹ 7.50 per kg   B. ₹ 8.20 per kg
C. ₹ 8.35 per kg   D. ₹ 9 per kg

22. Subhash purchased a taperecorder at $\dfrac{9}{10}$ of its selling price and sold it at 8% more than its S.P. His gain is :
A. 8%   B. 10%   C. 18%   D. 20%

23. A dealer marks his goods 20% above cost price. He then allows some discount on it and makes a profit of 8%. The rate of discount is :
A. 12%   B. 10%   C. 6%   D. 4%

24. A trader lists his articles 20% above C.P. and allows a discount of 10% on cash payment. His gain per cent is :
A. 10%   B. 8%   C. 6%   D. 4%

25. Tarun bought a T.V. with 20% discount on the labelled price. Had he bought it with 25% discount, he would have saved Rs. 500. At what price did he buy the T.V.?
A. ₹ 5000   B. ₹ 8000   C. ₹ 10000   D. ₹ 12000

26. While selling a watch, a shopkeeper gives a discount of 5%. If he gives a discount of 7%, he earns ₹ 15 less as profit. The marked price of the watch is :
A. ₹ 697.50   B. ₹ 712.50   C. ₹ 787.50   D. None of these

27. Kabir buys an article with 25% discount on its marked price. He makes a profit of 10% by selling it at ₹ 660. The marked price is :
A. ₹ 600   B. ₹ 700   C. ₹ 800   D. ₹ 885

28. A person bought an article and sold it at a loss of 10%. If he had bought it for 20% less and sold it for ₹ 55 more, he would have had a profit of 40%. The C.P. of the article is :
A. ₹ 200   B. ₹ 225   C. ₹ 250   D. None of these

29. The purchase tax on an article is levied at the rate of $66\dfrac{2}{3}\%$ of its wholesale price, while the retailer's profit amounts to 20% of the retail price of the article. What is the wholesale price of an article which is retailed at ₹ 12.50?
A. ₹ 4   B. ₹ 6   C. ₹ 8   D. ₹ 2

30. The catalogue price of a radio is ₹ 720. If it is sold at a discount of $16\dfrac{2}{3}\%$ of the catalogue price, the gain is 25%. Find the gain or loss per cent, if it is sold for ₹ 160 below the catalogue price.

A. $16\dfrac{2}{3}\%$ B. 16%   C. 18%   D. 20%

ANSWERS

1	2	3	4	5	6	7	8	9	10
D	C	D	C	B	B	C	D	B	B
11	12	13	14	15	16	17	18	19	20
C	D	C	C	B	B	A	D	B	A
21	22	23	24	25	26	27	28	29	30
D	D	B	B	B	D	C	C	B	A

EXPLANATORY ANSWERS

1. Loss = 5%, SP = ₹ 4085

$$\text{Let CP} = ₹\ 100$$
$$\therefore \quad \text{SP} = ₹\ 100 - 5 = ₹\ 95$$

When SP ₹ 95 then CP = ₹ 100

When SP ₹ 4085 then CP = $\dfrac{100}{95} \times 4085 = 4300$

Hence, the cost price of the plot was ₹ 4300.

5. Let CP = ₹ x, then, $425 - x = x - 355 \Rightarrow 2x = 780 \Rightarrow x = 390$
Hence, the cost of commodity is ₹ 390.

7. $100 - 25 = 75$

When SP 75 then CP = ₹ 100

When SP 150 then CP = ₹ $\dfrac{100}{75} \times 150 = ₹\ 200$

9. Let CP of each mango be ₹ 1.

$$\text{Then,} \quad \text{CP of 400 mangoes} = ₹\ 400$$
$$\therefore \quad \text{CP of 320 mangoes} = ₹\ 320$$
$$\text{SP of 320 mangoes} = ₹\ 400$$
$$\text{Profit} = 400 - 320 = ₹\ 80$$

$$\text{Profit\%} = \dfrac{80}{320} \times 100 = 25\%$$

11. SP = ₹ 54000 and gain earned = 20%

$$\text{CP} = ₹\left(\dfrac{100}{120} \times 54000\right) = ₹\ 45000$$

Now, SP = ₹ 45000 and Loss = 10%

$$\therefore \text{CP} = ₹\left(\dfrac{100}{90} \times 45000\right) = ₹\ 50000$$

13. SP = 90% of ₹ 200 = ₹ 180
Further, SP = (95% of ₹180) = ₹ 171

16. Marked price = ₹ 80, SP = ₹ 68
Discount = MP − SP = 80 − 68 = ₹ 12

$$\text{Discount \%} = \frac{\text{discount}}{\text{MP}} \times 100 = \frac{12}{80} \times 100 = 15\%$$

22. Let S.P. = ₹ 100; C.P. for Subhash = $\frac{9}{10} \times 100$ = ₹ 90 and S.P. = ₹ 108

Hence, gain % for Subhash = $\frac{108 - 90}{90} \times 100 = 20\%$

23. Let C.P. be ₹ 100; then Marked price = ₹ 120 and S.P. = ₹ 108

$$\therefore \text{ Discount} = \left(\frac{12}{120} \times 100\right)\% = 10\%$$

24. Let C.P. be ₹ 100
Then, marked price = ₹ 120

$$\text{S.P.} = ₹\left(\frac{90}{100} \times 120\right) = ₹ 108 \therefore \text{ Gain \%} = \left(\frac{8}{100} \times 100\right)\% = 8\%$$

26. Let the marked price = ₹ x

Then, $\dfrac{7x}{100} - \dfrac{5x}{100} = 15$

$$\Rightarrow \frac{x}{50} = 15 \qquad \therefore x = ₹\, 750$$

27. C.P. = $\dfrac{100}{110} \times 660$ = ₹ 600

Hence, M.P. = $\dfrac{100}{75} \times 600$ = ₹ 800

❖ ❖ ❖

9

Simple & Compound Interest

In any money transaction there is a **lender** who gives money, and a **borrower** who receives money. The amount of loan borrowed, is called the principal (P). The borrower pays a certain amount for the use of this money. This is called **Interest (I)**. Interest is always calculated on the principal borrowed. The borrowing is for a specified **Time (t)** and on specified terms. The specified term is expressed as per cent of the principal and is called rate of interest. The sum of the principal and the interest is called the **Amount (A)**.

Interest is of two kinds—**Simple Interest and compound Interest**. If the interest is calculated only, on a certain sum borrowed it is called Simple Interest. The simple interest (SI) on a principal P at R% per annum for T years is given by: $SI = \dfrac{P \times R \times T}{100}$

Compound Interest differs from Simple Interest that in CI the interest for the future period is calculated not only on the principal but also on the interest earned until the previous period. The difference between the final amount (A) obtained at the last unit of time and the original principal is called the **Compound Interest**.

Important Relations

Principal	=	₹ P (in rupees)
Rate	=	R % (in per cent per annum)
Time period	=	T years (in years)
Amount	=	₹ A (in rupees)

When interest is compounded annually, $A = P\left[1+\dfrac{R}{100}\right]^{T}$

When interest is compounded half-yearly,

$$A = P\left[1+\dfrac{R/2}{100}\right]^{2T} = P\left[1+\dfrac{R}{200}\right]^{2T}$$

[R is divided by 2 and T is multiplied by 2.]

$CI = A - P$

EXAMPLE 1. : Find the simple interest on ₹ 1000 for 3 years at 10% p.a.

SOLUTION: $SI = \dfrac{P \times R \times T}{100} = \dfrac{1000 \times 10 \times 3}{100} = ₹\ 300$

EXAMPLE 2. : Find the amount of ₹ 600 in 4 years at 3% p.a.

SOLUTION: $\text{SI} = \dfrac{P \times R \times T}{100} = \dfrac{600 \times 3 \times 4}{100} = ₹\ 72$

∴   Amount = P + SI = 600 + 72 = ₹ 672

EXAMPLE 3. : In what time will ₹ 7000 give ₹ 3675 as interest at the rate of 7% p.a. simple interest?

SOLUTION: $T = \dfrac{\text{SI} \times 100}{P \times R} = \dfrac{3675 \times 100}{7000 \times 7} = \dfrac{15}{2} = 7\dfrac{1}{2}$ years.

MULTIPLE CHOICE QUESTIONS

1. The simple interest on ₹ 500 for 6 years at 5% p.a. is:
   A. ₹ 250   B. ₹ 150   C. ₹ 140   D. ₹ 120

2. A certain sum of money at SI amounts to ₹ 1012 in $2\dfrac{1}{2}$ years and to ₹ 1067.20 in 4 years. The rate of interest per annum is:
   A. 2.5%   B. 3%   C. 4%   D. 5%

3. ₹ 1200 amounts to ₹ 1632 in 4 years at a certain rate of simple interest. If the rate of interest is increased by 1%, it would amount to how much?
   A. ₹ 1635   B. ₹ 1644   C. ₹ 1670   D. ₹ 1680

4. A man will get ₹ 87 as simple interest on ₹ 725 at 4% per annum in:
   A. 3 years   B. 3½ years   C. 4 years   D. 5 years

5. At simple interest, a sum doubles after 20 years. The rate of interest per annum is:
   A. 5%   B. 10%
   C. 20%   D. Data inadequate

6. A lent ₹ 600 to B for 2 years and ₹ 150 to C for 4 years and received altogether from both ₹ 90 as simple interest. The rate of interest is:
   A. 12%   B. 10%   C. 5%   D. 4%

7. Interest on a certain sum of money for $2\dfrac{1}{3}$ years at $3\dfrac{3}{4}\%$ per annum is ₹ 210. The sum is:
   A. ₹ 2800   B. ₹ 1580   C. ₹ 2400   D. None of these

8. A certain sum of money at simple interest amounts to ₹ 1260 in 2 years and to ₹ 1350 in 5 years. The rate per cent per annum is:
   A. 2.5%   B. 3.75%   C. 5%   D. 7.5%

9. A sum of money doubles itself in 5 years. It will become 4 times itself in:
   A. 10 years B. 12 years C. 15 years D. 20 years

10. The simple interest on a sum of money will be ₹ 600 after 10 years. If the principal is trebled after 5 years, the total interest at the end of 10 years will be:
    A. ₹ 600 B. ₹ 900
    C. ₹ 1200 D. Data inadequate

11. ₹ 800 amounts to ₹ 920 in 3 years at simple interest. If the interest rate is increased by 3%, it would amount to how much?
    A. ₹ 1056 B. ₹ 1112 C. ₹ 1182 D. ₹ 992

12. A sum of money at simple interest amounts to ₹ 2240 in 2 years and ₹ 2600 in 5 years. The sum is:
    A. ₹ 1880 B. ₹ 2000
    C. ₹ 2120 D. Data inadequate

13. If ₹ 7500 are borrowed at CI at the rate of 4% per annum, then after 2 years the amount to be paid is:
    A. ₹ 8082 B. ₹ 7800 C. ₹ 8100 D. ₹ 8112

14. Simple interest on a sum at 4% per annum is ₹ 80 in 2 years. The compound interest on the same sum for the same period is:
    A. ₹ 81.60 B. ₹ 160 C. ₹ 1081.60 D. None of these

15. ₹ 800 at 5% per annum compound interest will amount to ₹ 882 in:
    A. 1 year B. 2 years C. 3 years D. 4 years

16. What is the principal amount which earns ₹ 132 as compound interest for the second year at 10% per annum?
    A. ₹ 1000 B. ₹ 1200 C. ₹ 1320 D. None of these

17. The difference between the compound interest and the simple interest on a certain sum at 5% per annum for 2 years is ₹ 1.50. The sum is:
    A. ₹ 600 B. ₹ 500 C. ₹ 400 D. ₹ 300

18. The compound interest on a certain sum of money for 2 years at 10% per annum is ₹ 420. The simple interest on the same sum at the same rate and for the same time will be:
    A. ₹ 350 B. ₹ 375 C. ₹ 380 D. ₹ 400

19. A sum amounts to ₹ 2916 in 2 years and to ₹ 3149.28 in 3 years at compound interest. The sum is :
    A. ₹ 1500 B. ₹ 2000 C. ₹ 2500 D. ₹ 3000

20. A sum of money amounts to ₹ 10648 in 3 years and ₹ 9680 in 2 years. The rate of interest is:
    A. 5% B. 10% C. 15% D. 20%

21. If the simple interest on a certain sum of money at 6% per annum for 3 years is ₹ 90, the sum will be:
A. ₹ 500   B. ₹ 450   C. ₹ 525   D. ₹ 560

22. If the simple interest on Re. 1 for 1 month is 1 paise, the rate per cent p.a. will be :
A. 10%   B. 8%   C. 12%   D. 6%

23. A sum of money doubles itself in 20 years. In how many years will it triple itself at the same rate of simple interest?
A. 30 years   B. 50 years   C. 40 years   D. 45 years

24. If the simple interest on Rs. 500 for 4 years is Rs. 40, find the rate per cent p.a.
A. 3½%   B. 2%   C. 2½%   D. 3%

25. After what time will the sum of ₹ 2000 become ₹ 2240 at 4% per annum simple interest?
A. 3 years   B. 2 years   C. 5 years   D. 4 years

26. What will be the compound interest on ₹ 8000 for 3 years at 5% p.a.?
A. ₹ 1361   B. ₹ 1261   C. ₹ 1260   D. ₹ 1250

27. What will be the amount if a sum of ₹ 2500 is invested for 1 year at 4% per annum compound interest, interest being compounded half-yearly?
A. ₹ 2625   B. ₹ 2601   C. ₹ 2830   D. ₹ 2901

28. Find the compound interest on ₹ 2560 for ½ year at 12½% per annum, interest payable quarterly.
A. ₹ 3720.50   B. ₹ 2722.50   C. ₹ 2752.50   D. ₹ 2250.50

29. After how many years will ₹ 3375 become ₹ 4096 at $6\frac{2}{3}\%$ per annum compound interest?
A. 4 years   B. 2 years   C. 2½ years   D. 3 years

30. A certain sum of money placed at compound interest amounts to Rs. 110 in 1 year and to Rs. 121 in 2 years. The rate of interest per annum is :
A. 5%   B. 10%   C. 8%   D. 4%

ANSWERS

1	2	3	4	5	6	7	8	9	10
B	C	D	A	A	C	C	A	C	C

11	12	13	14	15	16	17	18	19	20
D	B	D	A	B	B	A	D	C	B

21	22	23	24	25	26	27	28	29	30
A	C	C	B	A	B	B	B	D	B

EXPLANATORY ANSWERS

1. $\text{SI} = \dfrac{P \times R \times T}{100} = \dfrac{500 \times 5 \times 6}{100} = ₹\ 150$

3. $R = \dfrac{\text{SI} \times 100}{P \times T} = \dfrac{432 \times 100}{1200 \times 4} = 9\%$

   New rate = $(9 + 1)\% = 10\%$

   $$\text{SI} = \dfrac{P \times R \times T}{100} = \dfrac{1200 \times 10 \times 4}{100} = ₹\ 480$$

   Amount = P + SI = $1200 + 480 = ₹\ 1680$

4. $T = \dfrac{\text{SI} \times 100}{P \times R} = \dfrac{87 \times 100}{725 \times 4} = 3$ years

5. Let P be $₹\ x$ then A = $₹\ 2x$

   SI = A – P = $2x - x = ₹\ x$

   $$R = \dfrac{\text{SI} \times 100}{P \times T} = \dfrac{x \times 100}{x \times 20} = 5\%$$

12. SI for 3 years = $2600 - 2240 = ₹\ 360$

   $$\text{SI for 2 years} = \dfrac{360}{3} \times 2 = ₹\ 240$$

   $\therefore$ Sum = $2240 - 240 = ₹\ 2000$

13. $A = P\left(1 + \dfrac{R}{100}\right)^{T} = 7500\left(1 + \dfrac{4}{100}\right)^{2}$

   $$= 7500 \times \dfrac{26}{25} \times \dfrac{26}{25} = ₹\ 8112$$

21. $P = \dfrac{90 \times 100}{6 \times 3} = ₹\ 500$

22. $\text{Rate} = \dfrac{1 \times 100}{100 \times \dfrac{1}{12}} = 12\%.$

23. Let principal = $₹\ x$; Amount = $₹\ 2x$; then I = $2x - x = ₹\ x$

   $$\therefore R = \dfrac{x \times 100}{x \times 20} = 5\%$$

Again, if principal = ₹ x; Amount = ₹ $3x$; then I = $3x - x$ = ₹ $2x$

Hence, T = $\dfrac{2x \times 100}{x \times 5}$ = 40 years

24. Rate = $\dfrac{40 \times 100}{500 \times 4}$ = 2%

25. Here, I = 2240 − 2000 = ₹ 240

$\therefore$ T = $\dfrac{240 \times 100}{2000 \times 4}$ = 3 years

26. $\therefore$ C.I. = $8000\left[\left(1+\dfrac{5}{100}\right)^3 - 1\right]$ = $8000\left[\left(\dfrac{21}{20}\right)^3 - 1\right]$

   = $\dfrac{8000 \times 1261}{8000}$ = ₹ 1261

27. A = $2500\left(1+\dfrac{2}{100}\right)^2$ = $2500\left(\dfrac{51}{50}\right)^2$ = $\dfrac{2500 \times 51 \times 51}{50 \times 50}$ = ₹ 2601

28. Amount = $2560\left(1+\dfrac{25}{8 \times 100}\right)^2$ = $\dfrac{2560 \times 33 \times 33}{32 \times 32}$ = ₹ 2722.50

29. Here, $4096 = 3375\left(1+\dfrac{20}{3 \times 100}\right)^n$ $\Rightarrow \dfrac{4096}{3375} = \left(1+\dfrac{1}{15}\right)^n$

   $\Rightarrow \left(\dfrac{16}{15}\right)^3 = \left(\dfrac{16}{15}\right)^n$ $\therefore n$ = 3 years

10

Time & Work

The problems on Time and Work can be solved by following two methods:

   (*i*) **Ratio and Proportion Method:** Since problems concerning to Time and Work have proportional relation, these can be solved by this method.

   (*ii*) **Unitary Method:** In this method, we first proceed to reduce the problem to either work done by one person or work done in 1 day and so on as per the requirement of the problem.

If M_1 persons can do W_1 works in D_1 days and M_2 persons can do W_2 works in D_2 days then we have a very general formula in the relationship of

$$M_1 D_1 W_2 = M_2 D_2 W_1$$

The above relationship can be taken as a very basic and all-in-one formula we also derive:

   (*i*) More men less days and conversely more days less men.

   (*ii*) More men more work and conversely more work more men.

  (*iii*) More days more work and conversely more work more days.

$$M_1 D_1 T_1 W_2 = M_2 D_2 T_2 W_1$$

EXAMPLE: 5 men can prepare 10 toys in 6 days working 6 hrs a day. How many days can 12 men prepare 16 toys working 8 hrs a day?

SOLUTION: $M_1 D_1 T_1 W_2 = M_2 D_2 T_2 W_1$

$$5 \times 6 \times 6 \times 16 = 12 \times D_2 \times 8 \times 10$$

$$D_2 = \frac{5 \times 6 \times 6 \times 16}{12 \times 8 \times 10} = 3 \text{ days.}$$

EXAMPLE: A and B together can do a piece of work in 12 days, B alone can finish it in 30 days. In how many days can A alone finish the work?

SOLUTION: (A + B)'s 1 day's work $= \dfrac{1}{12}$

B's 1 day's work $= \dfrac{1}{30}$

$\therefore$ A's 1 day's work $= \dfrac{1}{12} - \dfrac{1}{30} = \dfrac{5-2}{60} = \dfrac{3}{60} = \dfrac{1}{20}$

Hence, A alone can finish the work in 20 days.

MULTIPLE CHOICE QUESTIONS

1. A and B can together do a piece of work in 15 days. B alone can do it in 20 days. In how many days can A alone do it?
   A. 30 days   B. 40 days   C. 45 days   D. 60 days

2. A can do a piece of work in 30 days while B can do it in 40 days. A and B working together can do it in:
   A. 70 days   B. $42\dfrac{3}{4}$ days   C. $27\dfrac{1}{7}$ days   D. $17\dfrac{1}{7}$ days

3. A can do $\dfrac{1}{3}$ of the work in 5 days and B can do $\dfrac{2}{5}$ of the work in 10 days. In how many days both A and B together can do the work?
   A. $7\dfrac{3}{4}$ days   B. $8\dfrac{4}{5}$ days   C. $9\dfrac{3}{8}$ days   D. 10 days

4. A, B and C can do a piece of work in 6, 12 and 24 days respectively. They altogether will complete the work in:
   A. $3\dfrac{3}{7}$ days   B. $\dfrac{7}{24}$ days   C. $4\dfrac{4}{5}$ days   D. $\dfrac{5}{24}$ days

5. A, B and C contract a work for ₹ 550. Together A and B are to do $\dfrac{7}{11}$ of the work. The share of C should be:
   A. ₹ $183\dfrac{1}{3}$ B. ₹ 200   C. ₹ 300   D. ₹ 400

6. A and B finish a job in 12 days while A, B and C can finish it in 8 days. C alone will finish the job in:
   A. 20 days   B. 14 days   C. 24 days   D. 16 days

7. 12 men can complete a work in 8 days. Three days after they started the work, 3 more men joined them. In how many days will all of them together complete the remaining work?
   A. 2   B. 4   C. 5   D. 6

8. Mahesh and Umesh can complete a work in 10 and 15 days respectively. Umesh starts the work and after 5 days Mahesh joins him. In all, the work would be completed in:
   A. 9 days   B. 7 days   C. 11 days   D. None of these

9. Sunil completes a work in 4 days whereas Dinesh completes the work in 6 days. Ramesh works $1\frac{1}{2}$ times as fast as Sunil. How many days it will take for the three together to complete the work?

  A. $\dfrac{7}{12}$ B. $1\dfrac{5}{12}$ C. $1\dfrac{5}{7}$ D. None of these

10. A can complete a work in 6 days and B in 5 days. They work together, finish the job and receive ₹ 220 as wages. B's share should be:
A. ₹ 120   B. ₹ 110   C. ₹ 100   D. ₹ 90

11. 12 men and 8 children can finish a piece of work in 9 days. If each child takes twice the time taken by a man to finish the work, in how many days will 12 men finish the same work?
A. 8 days   B. 15 days   C. 9 days   D. 12 days

12. A, B and C together earn ₹ 150 per day while A and C together earn ₹ 94 and B and C together earn ₹ 76. The daily earning of C is:
A. ₹ 75   B. ₹ 56   C. ₹ 34   D. ₹ 20

13. If 5 men or 9 women can finish a piece of work in 19 days, 3 men and 6 women will do the same work in:
A. 10 days   B. 12 days   C. 13 days   D. 15 days

14. A can do a piece of work in 12 days. B is 60% more efficient than A. The number of days, it takes B to do the same piece of work, is:

  A. $7\dfrac{1}{2}$ days   B. $6\dfrac{1}{4}$ days   C. 8 days   D. 6 days

15. A and B can do a piece of work in 45 and 40 days respectively. They began the work together, but A leaves after some days and B finished the remaining work in 23 days. After how many days did A leave?
A. 6 days   B. 8 days   C. 9 days   D. 12 days

16. 12 men can complete a work within 9 days. After 3 days they started the work, 6 men joined them to replace 2 men. How many days will they take to complete the remaining work?

  A. 2 days   B. 3 days   C. 4 days   D. $4\dfrac{1}{2}$ days

17. 10 men can finish a piece of work in 10 days whereas it takes 12 women to finish it in 10 days. If 15 men and 6 women undertake to complete the work, how many days will they take to complete it?
A. 2 days   B. 4 days   C. 5 days   D. 11 days

18. A can do a piece of work in 80 days. He works at it for 10 days and then B alone finishes the work in 42 days. The two together could complete the work in:
A. 24 days   B. 25 days   C. 30 days   D. 35 days

19. A and B can together finish a work in 30 days. They worked for it for 20 days and then B left. The remaining work was done by A alone in 20 more days. A alone can finish the work in:
A. 48 days   B. 50 days   C. 54 days   D. 60 days

20. A can complete a job in 9 days, B in 10 days and C in 15 days. B and C start the work and are forced to leave after 2 days. The time taken by A alone to complete the remaining work is:
A. 13 days   B. 10 days   C. 9 days   D. 6 days

21. 12 boys can do a piece of work in 16 days. In how many days can 6 boys do the same work?
A. 16 days   B. 32 days   C. 23 days   D. 24 days

22. A can do a piece of work in 8 days while B can do the same work in 16 days. If they start working together, how long would they take to complete half portion of this work?
A. $2\dfrac{2}{3}$ days   B. $3\dfrac{5}{7}$ days   C. $4\dfrac{1}{2}$ days   D. $3\dfrac{1}{2}$ days

23. A can do a piece of work in 4 days. B is 50% more efficient than A. How long would B alone take to finish this work?
A. $3\dfrac{1}{3}$ days   B. $5\dfrac{1}{4}$ days   C. $2\dfrac{2}{3}$ days   D. $1\dfrac{2}{3}$ days

24. A and B working together complete a work in 35 days. If A takes 60 days to complete it, how long would B alone take to complete it?
A. 64 days   B. 72 days   C. 81 days   D. 84 days

25. A few children working together can do a piece of work in 18 days. If the number of children employed on the work is made double, how long would they take to complete half of the work?
A. $4\dfrac{1}{2}$ days   B. $2\dfrac{1}{3}$ days   C. $8\dfrac{3}{4}$ days   D. $6\dfrac{1}{2}$ days

26. 10 men or 18 boys can do a piece of work in 15 days. In how many days would 25 men and 15 boys complete the same work working together?
A. $5\dfrac{1}{2}$ days   B. $4\dfrac{1}{2}$ days   C. $6\dfrac{2}{3}$ days   D. $2\dfrac{1}{3}$ days

27. A can do a piece of work in 40 days. He starts working, but having some other engagements he drops out after 5 days. Thereafter B completes this work in 21 days. How many days would A and B take to complete this work working together?

A. 15 days   B. 16 days   C. 17 days   D. 11 days

28. Two persons A and B can complete a piece of work in 8 hours and 16 hours respectively. If they work at it alternately for an hour, A starting first, in how many hours will the work be finished?

A. $9\dfrac{1}{3}$ hours   B. $10\dfrac{1}{2}$ hours   C. $11\dfrac{1}{2}$ hours   D. $8\dfrac{1}{2}$ hours

29. 15 men can complete a work in 210 days. They started the work but at the end of 10 days 15 additional men, with double efficiency, were inducted. How many days, in whole, did they take to finish the work?

A. $76\dfrac{2}{3}$ days   B. $84\dfrac{3}{4}$ days   C. $72\dfrac{1}{2}$ days   D. 70 days

30. A and B working together can complete a piece of work in 12 days and B and C working together can complete the same work in 16 days. A worked at it for 5 days and B worked at it for 7 days. C finished the remaining work in 13 days. How many days would C alone take to complete it?

A. 10 days   B. 24 days   C. 32 days   D. 40 days

ANSWERS

1	2	3	4	5	6	7	8	9	10
D	D	C	A	B	C	B	A	D	A

11	12	13	14	15	16	17	18	19	20
D	D	D	A	C	D	C	C	D	D

21	22	23	24	25	26	27	28	29	30
B	A	C	D	A	B	A	B	A	B

EXPLANATORY ANSWERS

1. (A + B)'s 1 day's work $= \dfrac{1}{15}$

B's 1 day's work $= \dfrac{1}{20}$

A's 1 day's work $= \dfrac{1}{15} - \dfrac{1}{20} = \dfrac{4-3}{60} = \dfrac{1}{60}$

∴ A can do this work alone in 60 days.

5. Work to be done by C $= \left(1 - \dfrac{7}{11}\right) = \dfrac{4}{11}$

$\therefore$ (A + B) : C $= \dfrac{7}{11} : \dfrac{4}{11} = 7 : 4$

$\therefore$ C's share $= ₹\dfrac{4}{11} \times 550 = ₹\ 200$

10. Ratio of time taken by A and B = 6 : 5
Ratio of work done in same time = 5 : 6
So, the money is to be divided among A and B in the ratio 5 : 6.

$\therefore$ B's share $= ₹\dfrac{6}{11} \times 220 = ₹\ 120$

11. 2 children = 1 man
$\therefore$ 8 children + 12 men = 4 + 12 = 16 men
Now, less men, more days

$12 : 16 :: 9 : x \Rightarrow \dfrac{12}{16} = \dfrac{9}{x} \Rightarrow x = 12$ days

12. B's daily earning $= ₹\ (150 - 94) = ₹\ 56$
A's daily earning $= ₹\ (150 - 76) = ₹\ 74$
C's daily earning $= ₹\ [150 - (56 + 74)] = ₹\ 20$

17. 10 men = 12 women $\Rightarrow$ 1 man $= \dfrac{6}{5}$ women

$\therefore$ 15 men + 6 women $= 15 \times \dfrac{6}{5} + 6$
$\qquad = 18 + 6 = 24$ women

12 women can do the work in 10 days

24 women can do the same work in $\dfrac{10 \times 12}{24} = 5$ days

20. (B + C)'s 2 day's work $= 2\left(\dfrac{1}{10} + \dfrac{1}{15}\right) = \dfrac{1}{3}$

Remaining work $= 1 - \dfrac{1}{3} = \dfrac{2}{3}$

Now, $\dfrac{1}{9}$ work is done by A in 1 day

$\therefore \dfrac{2}{3}$ work will be done by A in $9 \times \dfrac{2}{3} = 6$ days

21. $\because$ 12 boys can do a piece of work in 16 days.

$\therefore$ 1 boy will do the same piece of work in 16 × 12 days.

$\therefore$ 6 boys will do the same piece of work in $\dfrac{16 \times 12}{6}$ days = 32 days.

23. A's 1 day's work $= \dfrac{1}{4}$;   Hence, B's 1 day's work $= \dfrac{150}{100} \times \dfrac{1}{4} = \dfrac{3}{8}$

So, B will do the whole work in $\dfrac{8}{3} = 2\dfrac{2}{3}$ days.

25. Let number of children be x;

Now x children can do the work in 18 days.

Hence, $2x$ children will do $\dfrac{1}{2}$ of the work in $\dfrac{18 \times x}{2x \times 2} = \dfrac{9}{2}$ days $= 4\dfrac{1}{2}$ days.

27. A's 5 days' work $= 5 \times \dfrac{1}{40} = \dfrac{1}{8}$

Remaining work $= 1 - \dfrac{1}{8} = \dfrac{7}{8}$, which is done by B in 21 days.

Hence, B's 1 day's work $= \dfrac{7}{8 \times 21} = \dfrac{1}{24}$

Now, (A + B)'s 1 day's work $= \dfrac{1}{40} + \dfrac{1}{24} = \dfrac{8}{120} = \dfrac{1}{15}$

Hence, (A + B) will complete the work in 15 days.

28. In 2 hours the part of work $= \dfrac{1}{8} + \dfrac{1}{16} = \dfrac{3}{16}$ will be completed.

Hence, in 5 pairs of hours the part of work

$= 5 \times \dfrac{3}{16} = \dfrac{15}{16}$ will be completed

Remaining work $= 1 - \dfrac{15}{16} = \dfrac{1}{16}$ which will be done by A.

Time taken by A to complete the $\dfrac{1}{16}$ work $= \dfrac{{}^{1}/_{16}}{{}^{1}/_{8}} = \dfrac{1}{2}$ hour.

Hence, required number of hours $= 10 + \dfrac{1}{2} = 10\dfrac{1}{2}$ hours.

❖ ❖ ❖

11

Time & Distance

Important Formulae:

1. Speed = Distance ÷ Time

2. Distance = Time × Speed

3. Time = Distance ÷ Speed

4. x km/hr = $\left(x \times \dfrac{5}{18}\right)$ m/sec

5. x metres/sec = $\left(x \times \dfrac{18}{5}\right)$ km/hr.

6. If the speed of a body is changed in the ratio $m : n$, then the ratio of the time taken changes in the ratio $n : m$.

7. When a man covers a certain distance with a speed of x km/h and another equal distance at the rate of y km/h, then for the whole journey, the average speed is given by Average speed = $\dfrac{2xy}{x+y}$ km/h.

Example : A boy goes to school at a speed of 4 km/h and returns to the house at a speed of 3 km/h. If he takes 5 hrs. in all, what is the distance between the house and the school?

Solution: Let the distance between house and the school be x km.

$$\frac{x}{4}+\frac{x}{3}=5 \qquad \Rightarrow \qquad \frac{7x}{12}=5 \qquad \therefore \quad x=\frac{60}{7}\ \text{km}$$

MULTIPLE CHOICE QUESTIONS

1. A car moving at 48 km/hr completes a journey in 10 hours. By how much the speed of this car should be increased so as to do this journey in 8 hours?
   A. 8 km/hr.   B. 12 km/hr   C. 10 km/hr   D. 15 km/hr

2. Starting from a point at a speed of 4 km/hr a man reaches at a cerain place and returns back to the point from where he had started journey on bicycle at the speed of 16 km/hr. His average speed during the entire journey will be :
   A. 6.4 km/h   B. 8.4 km/h   C. 5.4 km/h   D. 10 km/h

3. A motorist covers a certain distance at a average speed of 48 km/h in 45 minutes. What speed in km/h he must maintain to cover the same distance in 30 minutes?
   A. 66 km/h   B. 79 km/h   C. 80 km/h   D. 72 km/h

4. Two points A and B are 150 km apart. A man completes his onward journey from A to B in 3 hours 20 minutes and return journey from B to A in 4 hours 10 minutes. His average speed during the entire journey will be less than his average speed during the journey from A to B by :
   A. 5 km/h   B. 7.5 km/h   C. 9 km/h   D. 3 km/h

5. A policeman saw a thief at a distance of 200 m. The policeman and the thief started running at the same time. If the policeman runs at a speed of $4\frac{1}{6}$ m per second and the thief at a speed of $3\frac{1}{3}$ m per second, after what time the policeman will catch the thief?
   A. 12 min   B. 10 min   C. 9 min   D. 4 min

6. Kanchan walks from her home at 4 kms per hour and reaches her school 5 minutes late. If she walks at 5 kms per hour, she reaches the school 2½ minutes earlier. How far is the school from her home?
   A. 3.5 kms   B. 2.5 kms   C. 2.75 kms   D. 3.2 kms

7. A monkey wants to climb up a glazed pole. He climbs 12 metres in 1 minute and then he slips back 3 metres in the next minute. If the pole is 63 metre high, how long does he take to climb at the top of the pole?
   A. $11\frac{1}{4}$ min   B. $12\frac{1}{2}$ min   C. $12\frac{3}{4}$ min   D. $14\frac{3}{4}$ min

8. A and B start walking at the same time on a circular path with circumference 35 metre. If they walk in the same direction at 4 km/hr and 5 km/hr respectively, after what time will they meet together?
   A. 35 hours   B. 27 hours   C. 24 hours   D. 40 hours

9. While walking at $\frac{3}{5}$ of his usual speed Kamalkant reaches at his destination late by 30 minutes. His usual time consumed in reaching to his destination is:
   A. 32 min   B. 40 min   C. 45 min   D. 42 min

10. The distance between two stations A and B is 300 km. A train leaves the station A with a speed of 40 km/hr. At the same time another train departs from the station B with a speed of 50 km/hr. How much time will these two trains take to cross each other?
    A. 3 hrs 40 min   B. 3 hrs 20 min   C. 2 hrs 20 min   D. 3 hrs 45 min

11. Gulshan starts from a place P at 2 p.m. and walks to Q at 5 km per hour. Tarun starts from P at 3 p.m. and follows Gulshan on bicycle at 10 km per hour. By when Tarun will catch Gulshan?
    A. At 5.30 p.m.   B. At 4.00 p.m.   C. At 4.30 p.m.   D. At 6.00 p.m.

12. Nilesh goes to school from his village at the speed of 4 km/hr and returns from school to village at the speed of 2 km/hr. If he takes 6 hours in all, then what is the distance between the village and the school?
A. 8 km   B. 6 km   C. 5 km   D. 4 km

13. A school bus covers a distance from a village to school at the speed of 12 km/hr and reaches the school 8 minute late. The next day the bus covers the same distance at the speed of 20 km/hr and reaches the school 10 minutes early. What is the distance between village and the school?
A. 6 km   B. 9 km   C. 12 km   D. 15 km

14. By increasing the speed of the bus by 10 km/hr the time of journey for 72 km is reduced by 36 minutes. What was the original speed of the bus?
A. 30 km/hr   B. 35 km/hr   C. 40 km/hr   D. 45 km/hr

15. A car completes a fixed journey in 8 hours. It covers half distance at the speed of 40 km/hr and rest at the 60 km/hr, the distance of the journeyTis:
A. 400 km   B. 420 km   C. 384 km   D. 350 km

16. A car covers four consecutive extensions of 3 km each at the speeds of 10 km/hr, 20 km/hr, 30 km/hr and 60 km/hr. Its average speed of journey is:
A. 30 km/hr   B. 25 km/hr   C. 20 km/hr   D. 10 km/hr

17. A girl rides her bicycle 10 km at an average speed of 12 km/hr and another 12 km at an average speed of 10 km/hr. Her average speed for the entire journey is approximately:
A. 12.2 km/hr   B. 11.2 km/hr   C. 10.8 km/hr D. 10.4 km/hr

18. Raman drove from home to a neighbouring town at the speed of 50 km/hr and on his returning journey, he drove at the speed of 45 km/hr and also took an hour longer to reach home. What distance did he cover each way?
A. 900 km   B. 500 km   C. 450 km   D. 225 km

19. A man takes 6 hours 35 minutes in walking to a certain place and riding back. He would have taken 2 hours less by riding both ways. What would be the time he would take to walk both ways?
A. 10 hours   B. 8 hours 35 minutes
C. 8 hours 25 minutes   D. 8 hrs

20. A man covers a distance of 6 km at the rate of 4 km/hr and other 4 km at 3 km/hr this average speed is

A. $3\dfrac{5}{9}$ km/hr   B. $3\dfrac{9}{17}$ km/hr   C. $5\dfrac{9}{17}$ km/hr D. $9\dfrac{3}{17}$ km/hr

21. A cyclist rides 24 km at 16 km/h and further 36 km at 15 km/hr. Find his average speed for the journey.
A. 15.38 km/hr   B. 15.5 km/hr   C. 16 km/hr   D. 16.5 km/hr

22. A car is running at a speed of 108 km/hr. Find the distance covered by it in 15 seconds.
A. 450 m   B. 475 m   C. 500 m   D. 550 m

23. How long will a boy take to run round a square field of side 35 meters, If he runs at the rate of 9 km/hr?
A. 56 sec.   B. 54 sec.   C. 52 sec.   D. 50 sec.

24. A person crosses a 600 m long street in 5 minutes. Find his speed in km/hr.
A. 10   B. 8.4   C. 7.2   D. 3.6

25. A man walking at the rate of 5 km/hr crosses a bridge in 15 minutes. What is the length of the bridge in meters?
A. 1250   B. 1000   C. 750   D. 600

26. A truck covers a distance of 550 m in 1 minute whereas a bus covers a distance of 33 km in 45 minutes. The ratio of their speeds is:
A. 50 : 3   B. 3 : 5   C. 4 : 3   D. 3 : 4

27. A train travels at an average of 50 miles/hr for $2\frac{1}{2}$ hrs and then travels at a speed of 70 miles/hr for $1\frac{1}{2}$ hrs. Find the distance travelled by the train in entire 4 hrs.
A. 230 miles   B. 200 miles   C. 150 miles   D. 120 miles

28. Sound is said to travel in air at about 1100 feet/sec. A man hears the axe striking the tree $\frac{11}{5}$ seconds after he sees it strike the tree. Find the distance between the man and the wood chopper.
A. 2629 ft.   B. 2500 ft.   C. 2420 ft.   D. 2197 ft.

29. A motor car starts with the speed of 70 km/hr with its speed increasing every two hours by 10 km/hr. What is the time taken (in hours) in covering 345 km by it?
A. 5 hrs.   B. $4\frac{1}{2}$ hrs.   C. 4 hrs 5 min.   D. 4 hrs

30. A person has to cover a distance of 6 km in 45 minutes. If he covers one-half of the distance in two-thirds of the total time. Find his speed (in km/hr) to cover the remaining distance in remaining time.
A. 15   B. 12   C. 8   D. 6

ANSWERS

1	2	3	4	5	6	7	8	9	10
B	A	D	A	D	B	C	A	C	B

11	12	13	14	15	16	17	18	19	20
B	A	B	A	C	C	C	C	B	B

21	22	23	24	25	26	27	28	29	30
A	A	A	C	A	D	A	C	B	B

EXPLANATORY ANSWERS

2. Average speed during the entire journey

$$= \frac{2xy}{x+y} = \frac{2 \times 4 \times 16}{4+16} = \frac{8 \times 16}{20} = 6.4 \text{ km/hr.}$$

3. Let required speed be x km/hr; then

$$x \times \frac{1}{2} = 48 \times \frac{3}{4} \qquad \therefore \ x = 48 \times \frac{3}{4} \times 2 = 72 \text{ km/hr}$$

5. Suppose the policeman will catch the thief after t seconds

then, $\left(\dfrac{25}{6} - \dfrac{10}{3} \right) t = 200 \Rightarrow \dfrac{5}{6} t = 200 \quad \therefore \ t = \dfrac{200 \times 6}{5} = 240$ sec = 4 min.

11. Let Tarun will catch Gulshan after t hours the starting of Tarun; then,
$10t = 5(t + 1) \Rightarrow 5t = 5 \ \therefore \ t = 1$ hr
Hence, required time = 3 p.m. + 1 hr. = 4 p.m.

21. Required average speed $= \dfrac{24+36}{\dfrac{24}{16}+\dfrac{36}{15}} = \dfrac{60}{\dfrac{3}{2}+\dfrac{12}{5}} = \dfrac{60 \times 10}{39} = 15.38$ km/hr

22. Required distance $= 108 \times \dfrac{15}{60 \times 60}$ km $= \dfrac{9}{20}$ km $= \dfrac{9}{20} \times 1000 = 450$ m

23. 9 km/hr $= 9 \times \dfrac{5}{18} = \dfrac{5}{2}$ m/s

Time taken $= \dfrac{4 \times 35}{5/2} = 4 \times 7 \times 2 = 56$ sec.

24. Speed $= \dfrac{600 \text{m}}{5 \times 60 \text{ s}} = 2 \text{m}/s = 2 \times \dfrac{18}{5}$ km/hr $= \dfrac{36}{5} = 7.2$ km/hr.

❖ ❖ ❖

12

Mensuration

Perimeter

Perimeter of a geometrical figure is the total length of the sides enclosing the figure.

Triangle

A triangle is a plane figure bounded by three sides. It includes three angles. It is denoted by the symbol Δ. The sum of angles of a triangle is 180°.

(*i*) **Equilateral Triangle:** A triangle in which all sides are equal is called an equilateral triangle.

(*ii*) **Isosceles Triangle:** A triangle in which two sides are equal is called an isosceles triangle.

(*iii*) **Scalene Triangle:** A triangle in which all sides are different or unequal is called scalene triangle.

(*iv*) **Right Angled Triangle:** A triangle having one of the angles equal to 90° is called a right angled triangle. The side opposite to the right angle of a triangle is called its hypotenuse.

Quadrilateral

A plane figure bounded by four straight lines is called a quadrilateral.

Various Types of Quadrilaterals:

(*i*) **Rectangle:** A quadrilateral whose opposite sides are equal and all angles are at right angles. The diagonals of a rectangle are equal.

(*ii*) **Square:** A rectangle having all sides are equal is called a square.

(*iii*) **Parallelogram:** A quadrilateral whose opposite sides are equal and parallel is called parallelogram.

(*iv*) **Rhombus:** A parallelogram having all the sides equal is called a rhombus. Diagonals of a rhombus are not equal and they bisect each other at right angles.

(*v*) **Trapezium:** A quadrilateral having one pair of opposite sides parallel, is called a trapezium.

Circle

The path traced by a point which moves in such a way that its distance from a fixed point is always same, is called a circle. The fixed point is called its centre and fixed distance is called its radius.

R-165 (Math)-5-II

(*i*) **Arc:** Any part of the circumference of a circle is called an arc.

(*ii*) **Chord:** The straight line joining the ends of an arc of a circle is called a chord.

(*iii*) **Diameter:** The chord passing through the centre of a circle is called its diameter.

(*iv*) **Segment:** The area enclosed by an arc and a chord is called a segment.

(*v*) **Sector:** The area bounded by an arc and two radii is called a sector.

Formulae for Area of Various Figures:

(*i*) **Rectangle:**

Area of rectangle $= l \times b$ Perimeter of rectangle $= 2\,(l + b)$.

(*ii*) **Square:**

Area of square $= (\text{side})^2$ Perimeter of square $= 4 \times \text{side}$

Area of room $= l \times b$

Area of 4 walls of a room $= 2(l + b) \times h$

(*iii*) **Parallelogram:**

Area of Parallelogram $= b \times h$ Area of rhombus $= \dfrac{1}{2} \times d_1 \times d_2$.

(*iv*) **Trapezium:**

Area of trapezium $= \dfrac{1}{2}$ (sum of parallel sides) $\times$ (distance between them)

(*v*) **Triangle:**

(*a*) Area of right triangle $= \dfrac{1}{2} \times b \times h$

(*b*) Area of equilateral triangle $= \dfrac{\sqrt{3}}{4} \times (\text{side})^2$

(*c*) Area of scalene triangle $= \sqrt{s(s-a)(s-b)(s-c)}$ where, $s = \dfrac{a+b+c}{2}$

(*vi*) **Circle:**

(*a*) Area of circle $= \pi r^2$ (*b*) Circumference of a circle $= 2\pi r$

(*c*) Length of arc $= \dfrac{\theta}{360} \times 2\pi r$ (*d*) Area of sector $= \dfrac{\theta}{360} \times \pi r^2$

Polygon

A polygon is plane figure bounded by multiple number of sides. Normally, it is used for figures enclosed by more than four sides: *e.g.,* pentagon, hexagon, octagon etc.

Regular Polygon

It is a polygon whose all sides are equal. For a regular polygon of n equal sides,

its vertex angle θ is given by $\theta = \left(\dfrac{n-2}{n}\right) \times 180°$

EXAMPLE: Find the area and perimeter of a rectangle whose length is 25 m and breadth is 15 m.

SOLUTION: Area of rectangle $= l \times b = 25 \times 15 = 375$ m^2

Perimeter of rectangle $= 2(l + b) = 2(25 + 15) = 80$ m

EXAMPLE: Find the area of a parallelogram whose base is 35 m and altitude 18 m.

SOLUTION: Area of parallelogram $= b \times h = 35 \times 18 = 630$ m^2

EXAMPLE: Find the circumference and the area of a circle of radius 3.5 cm.

SOLUTION: Circumference $= 2\pi r = 2 \times \dfrac{22}{7} \times 3.5 = 22$ cm

Area of circle $= \pi r^2 = \dfrac{22}{7} \times 3.5 \times 3.5 = 38.5$ cm^2

Volume and Surface Area

Cuboid:

Volume of cuboid	$= l \times b \times h$ cubic units
Whole surface area	$= 2(lb + bh + hl)$ square units
Diagonal of cuboid	$= \sqrt{l^2 + b^2 + h^2}$ units
Area of 4 walls of a room	$= 2(l + b) \times h$ square units

Cube:

Volume of cube	$= a^3$ cubic units
Side of cube	$= \sqrt[3]{\text{Volume}}$
Lateral surface area	$= 4a^2$ square units
Total surface area	$= 6a^2$ square units
Diagonal of the cube	$= \left(\sqrt{3}\,a\right)$ units

Cylinder:

Volume of cylinder	$= \pi r^2 h$ cubic units
Lateral surface area	$= 2\pi rh$ square units
Total surface area	$= 2\pi r(h + r)$ square units

Cone:

Volume of cone	$= \dfrac{1}{3}\pi r^2 h$ cubic units
Lateral surface area	$= \pi rl$ square units

Total surface area	$= \pi r(l + r)$ square units
Slant height (l)	$= \sqrt{r^2 + h^2}$

Sphere:

Volume of sphere	$= \dfrac{4}{3}\pi r^3$ cubic units
Surface area	$= 4\pi r^2$ square units

Hemisphere:

Volume	$= \dfrac{2}{3}\pi r^3$ cubic units
Lateral surface area	$= 2\pi r^2$ square units
Total surface area	$= 3\pi r^2$ square units

Frustum:

Volume	$= \dfrac{1}{3}\pi h(r_1^2 + r_1 r_2 + r_2^2)$ cubic units
Curved surface area	$= \pi(r_1 + r_2) \times l$ square units
Total surface area	$= \pi\left[r_1^2 + r_2^2 + (r_1 + r_2)l\right]$ square units

Pyramid: Volume $= \dfrac{1}{2} \times$ (area of base) $\times$ height cubic units

Example: Three cubes whose edges measure 3 cm, 4 cm and 5 cm respectively form a single cube. Find the total surface area of the new cube.

Solution: Let the edge of new cube $= x$ cm

$$
\begin{aligned}
x^3 &= 3^3 + 4^3 + 5^3 \\
&= 27 + 64 + 125 = 216 \text{ cm}^3 \\
\Rightarrow x^3 &= 6 \times 6 \times 6 \Rightarrow x = 6 \text{ cm}
\end{aligned}
$$

Total surface area of cube $= 6(x)^2 = 6 \times 6 \times 6 = 216$ cm^2

Hence, total surface area of new cube $= 216$ cm^2.

MULTIPLE CHOICE QUESTIONS

1. The length of a plot is four times its breadth. A playground measuring 1200 square metres occupies a third of the total area of the plot. What is the length of the plot, in metres?

   A. 20 B. 30 C. 60 D. None of these

2. The width of a rectangular hall is $\dfrac{3}{4}$ of its length. If the area of the hall is 300 m^2, then the difference between its length and width is:

   A. 3 m B. 4 m C. 5 m D. 15 m

3. The length and breadth of a rectangular piece of land are in ratio of 5 : 3. The owner spent ₹ 3000 for surrounding it from all the sides at ₹ 7.50 per metre. The difference between its length and breadth is:
   A. 50 m   B. 100 m   C. 150 m   D. 200 m

4. A room 8 m × 6 m is to be carpeted by a carpet 2 m wide. The length of carpet required is:
   A. 12 m   B. 36 m   C. 24 m   D. 48 m

5. The length of a rectangle is increased by 60%. By what per cent would the width have to be decreased to maintain the same area?

   A. $37\frac{1}{2}\%$ B. 60%   C. 75%   D. 120%

6. A man walked 20 m to cross a rectangular field diagonally. If the length of the field is 16 m, the breadth of the rectangle is:
   A. 4 m   B. 16 m
   C. 12 m   D. Cannot be determined

7. If the ratio of the areas of two squares is 9 : 1, the ratio of their perimeters is:
   A. 9 : 1   B. 3 : 1   C. 3 : 4   D. 1 : 3

8. The perimeter of both, a square and a rectangle are each equal to 48 m and the difference between their areas is 4 m². The breadth of the rectangle is:
   A. 10 m   B. 12 m   C. 14 m   D. None of these

9. Area of a square with side x is equal to the area of a triangle with base x. The altitude of the triangle is:

   A. $\dfrac{x}{2}$ B. x C. $2x$ D. $4x$

10. If only the length of the rectangular plot is reduced to $\frac{2}{3}$rd of its original length, the ratio of original area to reduced area is:
    A. 2 : 3   B. 3 : 2   C. 1 : 2   D. None of these

11. If the radius of a circle be reduced by 50%, its area is reduced by:
    A. 25%   B. 50%   C. 75%   D. 100%

12. The perimeter of a rhombus is 52 m while its longer diagonal is 24 m. Its other diagonal is:
    A. 5 m   B. 10 m   C. 20 m   D. 28 m

13. The circumference of a circle is 352 m, then its area in m² is:
    A. 9856   B. 8956   C. 6589   D. 5986

14. A wheel makes 100 revolutions in covering a distance of 88 km. The diameter of the wheel is:
A. 240 m   B. 400 m   C. 280 m   D. 140 m

15. If the diameter of a circle is increased by 100%, its area is increased by:
A. 100%   B. 200%   C. 300%   D. 400%

16. The area of a sector of a circle of radius 5 cm formed by an arc of length 3.5 cm, is:
A. 35 cm^2 B. 17.5 cm^2 C. 8.75 cm^2 D. 55 cm^2

17. A circular wire of radius 42 cm is cut and bent in the form of a rectangle whose sides are in the ratio 6 : 5. The smaller side of the rectangle is:
A. 30 cm   B. 60 cm   C. 72 cm   D. 132 cm

18. The length of a minute hand on a wall clock is 7 cm. The area swept by the minute hand in 30 minutes is:
A. 147 cm^2 B. 210 cm^2 C. 154 cm^2 D. 77 cm^2

19. A circle and a square have same area. The ratio of the side of the square and the radius of the circle is:
A. $\sqrt{\pi}:1$ B. $1:\sqrt{\pi}$ C. $1:\pi$ D. $\pi:1$

20. The dimensions of the floor of a rectangular hall are 4 m × 3 m. The floor of the hall is to be tiled fully with 8 cm × 6 cm rectangular tiles without breaking tiles to smaller sizes. The number of tiles required is:
A. 4800   B. 2600   C. 2500   D. 2400

21. The surface area of a cube is 726 m^2. The volume of cube is:
A. 1300 m^3 B. 1331 m^3 C. 1452 m^3 D. 1542 m^3

22. Sum of the length, width and depth of a cuboid is s and its diagonal is d. Its surface area is:
A. s^2 B. d^2 C. $s^2 - d^2$ D. $s^2 + d^2$

23. A wooden box of dimensions 8 m × 7 m × 6 m is to carry rectangular boxes of dimensions 8 cm × 7 cm × 6 cm. The maximum number of boxes that can be carried in 1 wooden box is:
A. 1200000   B. 1000000   C. 9800000   D. 7500000

24. The length of the longest rod that can be placed in a room 30 m long, 24 m broad and 18 m high is:
A. 30 m   B. $15\sqrt{2}$ m   C. 60 m   D. $30\sqrt{2}$ m

25. If the volume of two cubes are in the ratio 8 : 1, the ratio of their edges is:
A. 8 : 1   B. $2\sqrt{2}:1$ C. 2 : 1   D. None of these

26. A metal sheet 27 cm long 8 cm broad and 1 cm thick is melted into a cube. The difference between the surface areas of two solids will be:
A. 284 cm^2 B. 296 cm^2 C. 286 cm^2 D. 300 cm^2

27. If each edge of a cube is increased by 50%, the percentage increase in surface area is:
A. 50% B. 75% C. 100% D. 125%

28. If a right circular cone of vertical height 24 cm has a volume of 1232 cm^3, then the area of its curved surface in cm^2 is:
A. 1254 B. 704 C. 550 D. 154

29. Two cubes have volumes in the ratio 1 : 27. The ratio of their surface areas is:
A. 1 : 3 B. 1 : 8 C. 1 : 9 D. 1 : 18

30. If the volumes of two cones are in the ratio 1 : 4 and their diameters are in the ratio 4 : 5, then the ratio of their heights is:
A. 1 : 5 B. 5 : 4 C. 5 : 16 D. 25 : 64

31. The radius of a wire is decreased to one-third. If volumes remains the same, length will increase:
A. 1 time B. 3 times C. 6 times D. 9 times

32. A cylindrical piece of metal of radius 2 cm and height 6 cm is shaped into a cone of same radius. The height of cone is:
A. 18 cm B. 14 cm C. 12 cm D. 8 cm

33. If 1 cubic cm of cast iron weight 21 g then the weight of a cast iron pipe of length 1 m with a bore of 3 cm and in which the thickness of the metal is 1 cm, is:
A. 21 kg B. 24.2 kg C. 26.4 kg D. 18.6 kg

34. The number of solid spheres, each of diameter 6 cm, that could be moulded to form a solid metal cylinder of height 45 cm and diameter 4 cms, is:
A. 3 B. 4 C. 5 D. 6

35. A right cylinder and a right circular cone have the same radius and the same volume. The ratio of the height of the cylinder to that of the cone is:
A. 3 : 5 B. 2 : 5 C. 3 : 1 D. 1 : 3

36. If a solid sphere of radius 10 cm is moulded into 8 spherical solid balls of equal radius, then surface area of each ball (in cm^2) is:
A. 100π B. 75π C. 60π D. 50π

37. The radii of two spheres are in the ratio 1 : 2. The ratio of their surface areas, is:
A. 1 : 2 B. 1 : 4 C. 1 : $\sqrt{2}$ D. 3 : 8

38. The radii of two cylinders are in the ratio 2 : 3 and their heights are in the ratio 5 : 3, then their volumes will be in ratio:
A. 4 : 9   B. 27 : 20   C. 20 : 27   D. 9 : 4

39. The volume of a hemisphere is 19404 cm^3. The total surface area is:
A. 2772 cm^2 B. 4158 cm^2 C. 5544 cm^2 D. 1386 cm^2

40. If the volume and surface area of a sphere are numerically the same, then its radius is:
A. 1 unit   B. 2 units   C. 3 units   D. 4 units

41. A rectangle measures 50 cm × 25 cm. Its area is
A. 1150 sq. cm.   B. 1250 sq. cm.   C. 1275 sq. cm.   D. 1280 sq. cm.

42. A field is in the form of a square whose perimeter is 580 m. Area of this field is
A. 21025 sq. m.   B. 20225 sq. m.
C. 30025 sq. m.   D. 19975 sq. m.

43. Find the area of the square whose each side measures 20 cm.
A. 300 sq. cm.   B. 380 sq. cm.
C. 360 sq. cm.   D. 400 sq. m.

44. Area of a circle is 154 sq. cm. Its circumference will be
A. 44 cm   B. 48 cm   C. 54 cm   D. 68 cm

45. The base and the height of a triangle is 8 cm and 10 cm respectively. Its area will be
A. 40 sq. cm.   B. 20 sq. cm.   C. 49 sq. cm.   D. 64 sq. cm.

46. A solid in the form of a cuboid is 4 cm × 3 cm × 2 cm. Its volume will be
A. 20 cu cm   B. 22 cu cm   C. 28 cu cm   D. 24 cu cm

47. A reservoir is 3 m long, 2 m wide and 1 m deep. Its capacity in litres is
A. 8000 litres   B. 10000 litres
C. 6500 litres   D. 6000 litres

48. Surface area of a cube is 1014 sq. cm. Its volume will be
A. 2197 cu cm   B. 2297 cu cm
C. 2179 cu cm   D. 2117 cu cm

49. If the volumes of two cubical blocks are in the ratio of 8 : 1, what will be the ratio of their edges?
A. 1 : 2   B. 2 : 1   C. 4 : 1   D. 2 : 3

50. Two spheres have their surface areas in the ratio 9 : 16. Their volumes are in the ratio of
A. 64 : 27   B. 27 : 64   C. 16 : 27   D. 11 : 27

ANSWERS

1	2	3	4	5	6	7	8	9	10
D	C	A	C	A	C	B	A	C	B

11	12	13	14	15	16	17	18	19	20
C	B	A	C	C	C	B	D	A	C

21	22	23	24	25	26	27	28	29	30
B	C	B	D	C	C	D	C	C	D

31	32	33	34	35	36	37	38	39	40
D	A	C	C	D	A	B	C	B	C

41	42	43	44	45	46	47	48	49	50
B	A	D	A	A	D	D	A	B	B

EXPLANATORY ANSWERS

1. Area of the plot = 3 × 1200 = 3600 m²
    Let breadth be x m. Then length = $4x$ m
    According to the question,
    $4x \times x = 3600 \Rightarrow x^2 = 900 \Rightarrow x = 30$
    Hence, length of the plot = 4 × 30 = 120 m.

4. Length of the carpet = $\dfrac{8 \times 6}{2}$ = 24 m.

6. Breadth $= \sqrt{(20)^2 - (16)^2}$

    $= \sqrt{400 - 256} = \sqrt{144}$ = 12 m.

12. Side of rhombus = $\dfrac{52}{4}$ = 13 m

    In $\triangle ABM$,
    $$x^2 = (13)^2 - (12)^2$$
    $$x^2 = 169 - 144$$
    $$x^2 = 25$$
    $$\Rightarrow \qquad x = 5 \text{ m}$$
    ∴ Another diagonal = 2 × 5 = 10 m

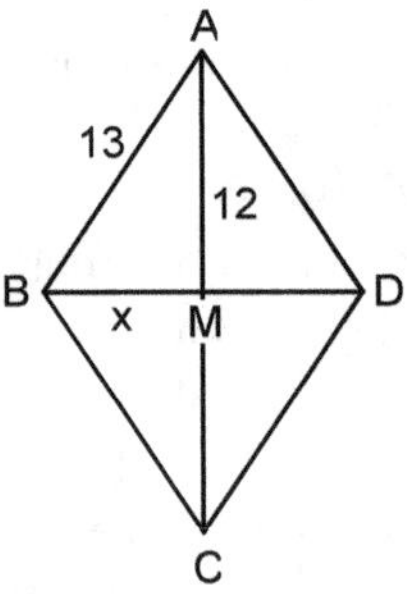

16. Area of sector = $\left(\dfrac{1}{2} \times r^2 \times \dfrac{\text{arc}}{r} \right)$

    $= \dfrac{1}{2} \times 5 \times 3.5$ = 8.75 cm²

21. Surface area of cube $= 6a^2$

$$6a^2 = 726 \Rightarrow a^2 = \frac{726}{6} = 121 \Rightarrow a = 11 \text{ m}$$

Volume of cube $= a^3 = 11 \times 11 \times 11 = 1331 \text{ m}^3$

23. Number of boxes $= \dfrac{800 \times 700 \times 600}{8 \times 7 \times 6} = 1000000$

25. Let their volumes be $8x^3$ and x^3.
Then, their sides are $2x$ and x
$\therefore$ Ratio of their edges $= 2 : 1$

38. Let the radii of cylinders are $2r$ and $3r$ and heights are $5x$ and $3x$

$$\text{Ratio of their volumes} = \frac{\pi(2r)^2 \times 5x}{\pi(3r)^2 \times 3x} = \frac{4r^2 \times 5}{9r^2 \times 3} = \frac{20}{27}$$

39. Volume of hemisphere $= 19404$

$$\Rightarrow \qquad \frac{2}{3}\pi r^3 = 19404 \Rightarrow \frac{2}{3} \times \frac{22}{7} r^3 = 19404$$

$$\Rightarrow \qquad r^3 = \frac{3 \times 19404 \times 7}{2 \times 22} = 9261$$

$$\Rightarrow \qquad r = 21 \text{ cm}$$

$$\text{Surface area} = 3\pi r^2 = 3 \times \frac{22}{7} \times 21 \times 21 = 4158 \text{ cm}^2$$

40. $\dfrac{4}{3}\pi r^3 = 4\pi r^2$

$$\Rightarrow \frac{r}{3} = 1 \Rightarrow r = 3 \text{ units}$$

41. Area of the rectangle $= l \times b = 50 \times 25 = 1250$ sq. cm

42. Here, $4 \times \text{side} = 580 \Rightarrow \text{side} = \dfrac{580}{4} = 145 \text{ m}$

$$\therefore \text{Area} = (\text{side})^2 = (145)^2 = 21025 \text{ sq. m.}$$

43. Area of the square $= (\text{side})^2 = (20)^2 = 400$ sq. cm.

44. Area of the circle $= \pi r^2 \Rightarrow \pi r^2 = 154 \Rightarrow r^2 = \dfrac{154 \times 7}{22} \Rightarrow r = 7 \text{ cm}$

$$\therefore \text{Circumference of the circle} = 2\pi r = 2 \times \frac{22}{7} \times 7 = 44 \text{ cm.}$$

45. Area of the triangle $= \dfrac{1}{2} \times 8 \times 10 = 40$ sq. cm.

46. Volume of the cuboid $= l \times b \times h = 4 \times 3 \times 2 = 24$ cu. cm.

47. Volume of the reservoir $= l \times b \times h = 3 \times 2 \times 1 = 6$ cu. m

($\because$ 1 cu m $= 1000$ litre)

$\therefore$ Capacity of the reservoir $= 6 \times 1000 = 6000$ litre.

48. Here, $6 \times (\text{side})^2 = 1014 \Rightarrow (\text{side})^2 = \dfrac{1014}{6} = 169$

$\therefore$ side $= \sqrt{169} = 13$ cm

Hence, Volume of the cube $= (\text{side})^3 = (13)^3 = 2197$ cu cm.

49. Here, $a_1{}^3 : a_2{}^3 = 8 : 1$

$\therefore \left(\dfrac{a_1}{a_2}\right)^3 = \left(\dfrac{2}{1}\right)^3 \Rightarrow a_1 : a_2 = 2 : 1$

Therefore, ratio of their edges $= 2 : 1$.

50. Here, $4\pi r_1^2 : 4\pi r_2^2 = 9 : 16 \Rightarrow r_1^2 : r_2^2 = 9 : 16$

$\Rightarrow \left(\dfrac{r_1}{r_2}\right)^2 = \left(\dfrac{3}{4}\right)^2 \Rightarrow r_1 : r_2 = 3 : 4$

$\Rightarrow \dfrac{r_1^3}{r_2^3} = \dfrac{27}{64}$

$\Rightarrow r_1^3 : r_2^3 = 27 : 64.$

Therefore, ratio of their volumes $= \dfrac{4}{3}\pi r_1^3 : \dfrac{4}{3}\pi r_2^3 = r_1^3 : r_2^3$

$= 27 : 64$

$\mathbf{A}$LGEBRA

13 | *Set Theory*

Set : It is a well defined collection of objects. The objects which belong to a set are called its member or elements.

Method of Representing a Set

(a) Tabular Form or the Roster Form

(b) Set Builder Form or Rule Method

Tabular Form : In this form all the elements of the set are separated by commas and enclosed between brackets { }, *e.g.,* : N = {1, 2, 3, 4, ...}.

Rule Method : In this form, the elements of the set are represented in terms of one or several characteristic properties, *e.g.,* N = {$x \mid x \in$ N}

Empty or Null Set : The set which contains no element is called the empty set. The symbols for the empty set is ϕ, *e.g.,* ϕ = { }.

The set of odd numbers is divisible by 2.

Singleton : A set containing only one element is called a singleton, *e.g.,* {1}, {a} etc.

Equal Sets : Two sets A ana B are said to be equal if both have the same elements. e.g., A = {a, b, c, d} and B = {b, c, a, d}, Then A = B.

Equivalent Sets : Two sets A and B are said to be equivalent if we can find a one-to-one correspondence between the element of the two sets.

e.g., A = {1, 2, 3, 4} and {b, c, a, d}, Then A ~ B but A ≠ B.

Note : Equal sets are always equivalent but vice-versa is not true.

Finite and Infinite Set : The set which contains a definite number of element is called a finite set. *e.g.,* The set of days in a week. The set which contains an infinite number of element is called an infinite set. *e.g.,* The set of natural numbers.

Disjoint Sets : Two sets A and B are said to be disjoint if they do not have any elements in common. *e.g.,* A = {1, 2, 3}, B = {4, 5, 6} are disjoint set.

Subsets : If every member of set A is also in set B then A is said to be a subset of B and B is called a super set A. e.g., : A = {1, 2, 3}, B = {1, 2, 3, 4, 5, 6} ∴ A ⊂ B.

Power Set : The set of all the subset of a set is called the power set. If n

is the number of element of a set A then the number of subset of A, *i.e.,* the no. of elements of $P(A) = 2^n$. $A = \{1, 2, 3\}$ $\therefore$ $P(A) = 2^3 = 8$.

Universal Set : The largest set containing every set is called universal set. It is denoted by U.

Union of Sets : The union of two sets A and B is the set of all elements of A with all the elements of B. It is denoted by $A \cup B$.

e.g., $A = \{1, 2, 3\}$, $B = \{1, 3, 4\}$, $\therefore$ $A \cup B = \{1, 2, 3, 4\}$

Intersection of Sets : The intersection of two sets is the set of all elements which are in A and also in B. It is written as $A \cap B$.

e.g., $A = \{1, 2, 3\}$, $B = \{2, 3, 4\}$, $\therefore$ $A \cap B = \{2, 3\}$.

Complement of a Set : The set of three elements of universal set (U) which are not the element of A is called the complement of A and is denoted by A^1 of A^c. e.g., If $U = \{1, 2, 3, 4, 5, 6\}$ and $A = \{1, 3, 5\}$, $A^1 = \{2, 4, 6\}$.

Complement of a Union and Intersection of Two Sets :

(*a*) $(A \cup B)^1 = A^1 \cap B^1$ (*b*) $(A \cap B)^1 = A^1 \cup B^1$.

Important Result

(*a*) $n(A \cup B) = n(A) + n(B)$, If A and B are disjoint set.

(*b*) $n(A \cup B) = n(A) + n(B) - n(A \cap B)$.

MULTIPLE CHOICE QUESTIONS

1. Let $a = \{x : x$ is a multiple of $3\}$ and $B = \{x : x$ is a multiple of $5\}$. Then $A \cap B$ is given by
   A. $\{3, 6, 9, ...\}$ B. $\{5, 10, 15, 20, ...\}$
   C. $\{15, 30, 45, ...\}$ D. None of these

2. If X and Y are two sets, then $X \cup (Y \cap X)'$ equals
   A. X   B. Y   C. ϕ D. None of these

3. Let $A = \{1, 2, 3, 4, 5\}$, $B = 2, 3, 6, 7\}$. Then the number of elements in $(A \times B) \cap (B \times A)$ is
   A. 18   B. 6   C. 4   D. 0

4. In a group of 52 persons, 16 drink tea but not coffee and 33 drink tea. It is assumed that every person takes tea or coffee. Then the number of persons who take coffee but not tea is given by
   A. 19   B. 36
   C. Cannot be found by the given data D. None of these

5. A survey of 100 Indians shows that 60 like cheese whereas 70 like apples. let n be the number of persons who like both cheese and apple. Then
   A. $n = 30$ B. $n = 60$ C. $n = 10$ D. None of these

6. Let $n(U) = 700$, $n(A) = 200$, $n(B) = 300$, $n(A \cap B) = 100$. Then $n(A' \cap B') = $
   A. 400   B. 600   C. 300   D. None of these

7. Two finite sets have m and n elements. The total number of subsets of the first set is 56 more than the total number of subsets of the second set. The values of m and n are
A. 7, 6   B. 6, 3   C. 5, 1   D. 8, 7

8. Let A = {1, 2, 3}, B = {1, 3, 5}. A relation R : A $\rightarrow$ B is defined by R = {(1, 3), (1, 5), (2, 1)}. Then R^{-1} is defined by
A. {(1, 2), (3, 1), (1, 3), (1, 5)}   B. {(1, 2), (3, 1), (2, 1)}
C. {(1, 2), (5, 1), (3, 1)}   D. None of these

9. The relation R is defined on the set of natural numbers as {(a, b): $a = 2b$}. Then R^{-1} is given by
A. {(2, 1), (4, 2), (6, 3)...}   B. {(1, 2), (2, 4), (3, 6)...}
C. R^{-1} is not defined   D. None of these

10. The relation R defined on the set of natural numbers as {(a, b) : a differs from b by 3}, is given by
A. {(1, 4), (2, 5), (3, 6), ...}   B. {(4, 1), (5, 2), (6, 3), ...}
C. {(1, 3), (2, 6), (3, 9), ...}   D. None of these

11. A relation R defined on the set of integers by R = {(a, b): a divides b}. Then R is
A. reflexive   B. symmetric   C. transitive   D. equivalence

12. Given two finite sets A and B such that $n(A) = 2$, $n(B) = 3$. Then total number of relations from A to B is
A. 4   B. 8   C. 64   D. None of these

13. The solution set of $8x \equiv 6 \pmod{14}$, $x \in Z$, are
A. [8] $\cup$ [6]   B. [8] $\cup$ [14]
C. [6] $\cup$ [13]   D. [8] $\cup$ [6] $\cup$ [13]

14. Let $n(A) = n$. Then the number of all relations on A is
A. 2^n B. $2^{(n)!}$ C. 2^{n^2} D. None of these

15. If A and B be two subsets of a set U, then which of the following is false?
A. $A \cap B = A$ B. $A \cap U = A$ C. $A \cap B \in A$ D. $B \cup A \cap B$

16. It is given that $n(P(S)) = 64$, where P (S) is power set of S, then $n(S)$ is:
A. 2   B. 4   C. 8   D. 6

17. If A and B are two sets, then A $\cup$ (A $\cap$ B) is:
A. $A \cap B$ B. A   C. B   D. none of these

18. If A and B are two subsets of universal set U, then A – B is equal to:
A. $A \cap B$ B. $A \cap B'$ C. $A' \cap B$ D. $A' \cap B'$

19. If P, Q $\subset$ U, then P $\cap$ (P $\cup$ Q); is equal to:
A. P   B. Q   C. f   D. none of these

20. In a town of 840 persons, 450 persons read Hindi, 300 read English and 200 read both. The number of persons who read neither, is:
A. 210   B. 290   C. 180   D. 260

21. Let A and B have 2 and 5 elements respectively. What can be the maximum and minimum number of elements in $A \cap B$?
A. 5 and 2   B. 5 and 0   C. 25 and 4   D. 2 and 0

22. If $A = \{a, c, d, g\}$ and $B = \{b, d, j, k\}$, then which of the following is true?
A. $A \cap B$ is a null set   B. A and B are disjoint sets
C. $A \cap B$ is a singleton set   D. All of the above are true

23. If A and B are subsets of a set X, then $[A \cap (X - B)] \cup B$ is equal to:
A. $A \cup B$ B. $A \cap B$ C. A   D. B

24. If $A = \{1, 2\}$, $B = \{2, 5\}$, $C = \{5, 7\}$ then
$(A \times B) \cap (A \times C)$ is equal to:
A. $\{(2, 5), (1, 5)\}$ B. $\{(2, 2), (5, 5)\}$
C. $\{(2, 7), (1, 5)\}$ D. none of these

25. Let $A = \{a, b, c, d, \}$, which one of the following subsets of $A \times A$ is not a function on A?
A. $\{(a, d), (d, a), (a, b), (d, c)\}$ B. $\{(d, a), (a, b), (b, c), (c, d)\}$
C. $\{(a, d), (b, a), (c, b), (d, c)\}$ D. $\{(d, a), (a, d), (b, a), (c, c)\}$

ANSWERS

1	2	3	4	5	6	7	8	9	10
C	C	C	A	A	C	B	C	B	D

11	12	13	14	15	16	17	18	19	20
C	C	C	C	A	D	B	B	C	B

21	22	23	24	25
D	C	A	A	A

EXPLANATORY ANSWERS

2.
$$X \cap (Y \cup X)' = X \cap (Y' \cap X')$$
$$= (X \cap X') \cap Y'$$
$$= \phi \cap X' = \phi$$

5. Let A = Apples, C ≡ Cheese
Then $n(A \cap C) \le n(A)$
$n(A \cap C) \le n(C)$
$\Rightarrow n(A \cap C) \le 60$
Also $n(A \cap C) = n(A) + n(C) - n(A \cup C)$

$\geq 70 + 60 - 100 = 30$

$\therefore 30 \leq n(A \cap C) \leq 60$

6. $n(A' \cap B') = n(A \cup B)'$
$$= 700 - n(A \cup B)$$
$$= 700 - [200 + 300 - 100]$$
$$= 300$$

7. $2^m = 2^n + 56$

which is satisfied when $m = 6$, $n = 3$.

8. $(x, y) \in R \Leftrightarrow (y, x) \in R^{-1}$,

$\therefore R^{-1} = \{(3, 1), (5, 1), (1, 2)\}$

9. $R = \{(2, 1), (4, 2), (6, 3), ...\}$

so $R^{-1} = \{(1, 2), (2, 4), (3, 6), ...\}$

10. $R = \{(a, b): a, b \in N, A \sim b = 3\}$
$$= \{(n, n + 3), (n + 3, n) : n \in N\}$$
$$= \{(1, 4), (4, 1), (2, 5), (5, 2), ...\}$$

23. See the figures

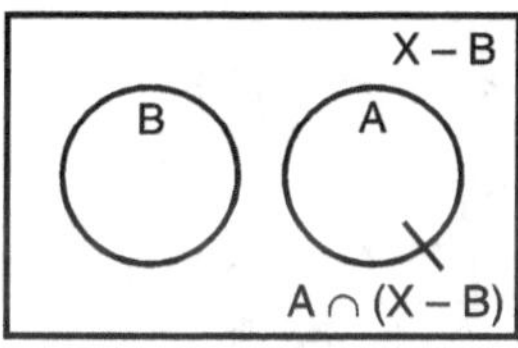

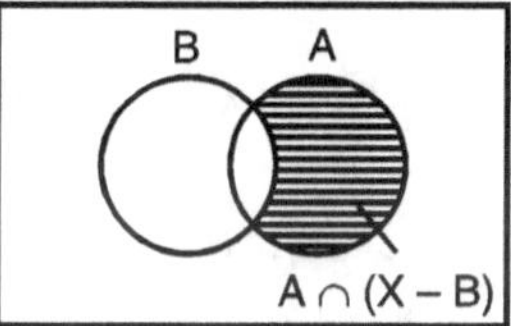

In both cases

24. $A \times B = \{(1, 2)(1, 5), (2, 2), (2, 5)\}$

$A \times C = \{(1, 5), (1, 7), (2, 5), (2, 7)\}$

$\therefore (A \times B) \cap (A \times C) = \{(1, 5), (2, 5)\}$

14

Simplification & Factorization

A function $p(x)$ defined by $p(x) = a_0 + a_1x + a_2 x^2 + ... + a_nx^n$ is called a polynomial function in x.

Where, $a_0, a_1 ... a_n$ are real numbers and called co-efficient of the polynomial.

Factor Theorem: If $f(x)$ is completely divisible by $(x - a)$, then $f(a) = 0$ Thus, $(x - a)$ is a factor of $f(x)$.

Some Important Formulae

1. $(a + b)^2 = a^2 + 2ab + b^2$

2. $(a - b)^2 = a^2 - 2ab + b^2$

3. $a^2 - b^2 = (a + b)(a - b)$

4. $a^2 + b^2 = (a + b)^2 - 2ab$

5. $(a + b + c)^2 = a^2 + b^2 + c^2 + 2ab + 2bc + 2ca$

6. $(a + b)^3 = a^3 + 3a^2b + 3ab^2 + b^3$

$\qquad = a^3 + b^3 + 3ab(a + b)$

7. $(a - b)^3 = a^3 - 3a^2b + 3ab^2 - b^3$

$\qquad = a^3 - b^3 - 3ab(a - b)$

8. $a^3 + b^3 = (a + b)(a^2 - ab + b^2)$ [for factorisation]

$a^3 + b^3 = (a + b)^3 - 3ab(a + b)$ [for evaluation when $a+b$ and ab are given]

9. $a^3 - b^3 = (a - b)(a^2 + ab + b^2)$ [for factorisation]

$a^3 - b^3 = (a - b)^3 + 3ab(a - b)$ [for evaluation]

10. If $a + b + c = 0$, then $a^3 + b^3 + c^3 = 3abc$

MULTIPLE CHOICE QUESTIONS

1. If $\left(x + \dfrac{1}{x}\right) = 5$, then $\left(x^2 + \dfrac{1}{x^2}\right)$ is equal to:

   A. 20   B. 24   C. 27   D. 23

2. If $\left(x + \dfrac{1}{x}\right) = 4$, then $\left(x^4 + \dfrac{1}{x^4}\right)$ is equal to:

   A. 190   B. 180   C. 193   D. 194

3. If $\left(x^2 + \dfrac{1}{x^2}\right) = 66$, then $\left(x - \dfrac{1}{x}\right)$ is equal to:

   A. 6   B. 12   C. 8   D. 9

4. If $a + b = 8$, $a - b = 4$, then $a^2 + b^2$ is equal to:

   A. 20   B. 40   C. 10   D. 30

5. If $x^2 + 5x - 2k$, is exactly divisible by $(x - 1)$, then the value of k is:

   A. 1   B. 2   C. 3   D. 4

6. If $(x - 2)$, is a factor of $x^2 + 4x - 2k$, then the value of k is:

   A. 1   B. 3   C. 4   D. 6

7. If $x^{100} + 2x^{99} + k$, is divisible by $(x + 1)$, then the value of k is:

   A. 1   B. 4   C. 3   D. 0

8. Value of k for which $(x - 2)$ is a factor of $(x^2 - kx + 2)$ is:

   A. 2   B. 3   C. 4   D. 5

9. If $x - \dfrac{1}{x} = 3$. The value of $x^2 + \dfrac{1}{x^2}$ is :

   A. 2   B. 12   C. 10   D. 11

10. If $x - \dfrac{1}{x} = 2$, then $x^3 - \dfrac{1}{x^3}$ is :

   A. 14   B. 16   C. 15   D. 12

11. If $x - 2$ is a factor of $x^2 + 3ax - 2a$, then a is equal to

   A. 2   B. -2 C. 1   D. -1

12. The value of k for which $x - 1$ is a factor of $4x^3 + 3x^2 - 4x + k$, is :

   A. 3   B. 1   C. -2 D. -3

13. If $x - a$ is a factor of $x^3 - 3x^2a + 2a^2x + b$, then the value of b is :

   A. 0   B. 2   C. 1   D. 3

14. If $x^{140} + 2x^{151} + k$ is divisible by $x + 1$, then the value of k is :

   A. 1   B. -3 C. 2   D. -2

15. If $x + 2$ and $x - 1$ are the factors of $x^3 + 10x^2 + mx + n$, then the values of m and n are respectively :

   A. 5 and -3 B. 17 and -8 C. 7 and -18 D. 23 and -19

16. Let $f(x)$ be a polynomial such that $f\left(-\dfrac{1}{2}\right) = 0$, then a factor of $f(x)$ is :

   A. $2x - 1$ B. $2x + 1$ C. $x - 1$ D. $x + 1$

17. When $x^3 - 2x^2 + ax - b$ is divided by $x^2 - 2x - 3$, the remainder is $x - 6$. The values of a and b are respectively :
   A. –2, –6   B. 2 and –6   C. –2 and 6   D. 2 and 6

18. One factor of $x^4 + x^2 - 20$ is $x^2 + 5$. The other factor is :
   A. $x^2 - 4$ B. $x - 4$ C. $x^2 - 5$ D. $x + 2$

19. If $(x - 1)$ is a factor of polynomial $f(x)$ but not of $g(x)$, then it must be a factor of :
   A. $f(x)\, g(x)$ B. $-f(x) + g(x)$
   C. $f(x) - g(x)$ D. $\{f(x) + g(x)\}\, g(x)$

20. $(x + 1)$ is a factor of $x^n + 1$ only if :
   A. n is an odd integer   B. n is an even integer
   C. n is a negative integer   D. n is a positive integer

21. If $x^2 + \dfrac{1}{x^2} = 7$, then the values of $x + \dfrac{1}{x}$ is :
   A. 2   B. 3   C. 5   D. 6

22. If $x + \dfrac{1}{x} = 4$, then the value of $x^3 + \dfrac{1}{x^3}$ is :
   A. 52   B. 64   C. 68   D. 76

23. The factors of $x^8 + x^4 + 1$ are :
   A. $\left(x^4 + 1 - x^2\right), \left(x^2 + 1 + x\right), \left(x^2 + 1 - x\right)$
   B. $\left(x^4 + 1 - x^2\right), \left(x^2 - 1 + x\right), \left(x^2 + 1 + x\right)$
   C. $\left(x^4 - 1 + x^2\right), \left(x^2 - 1 + x\right), \left(x^2 + 1 + x\right)$
   D. $\left(x^4 - 1 + x^2\right), \left(x^2 + 1 - x\right), \left(x^2 + 1 + x\right)$

24. The expression $10xy^4 - 10x^4 y$ can be expressed in factors as :
   A. $10xy\left(x - y\right)\left(x^2 + xy + y^2\right)$ B. $10xy\left(y - x\right)\left(x^2 - xy + y^2\right)$
   C. $10xy\left(y - x\right)\left(x^2 + xy + y^2\right)$ D. None of these

25. The algebraic expression $4x^2 + 9y^2 + 25z^2 + 12xy - 30yz - 20zx$ can be factorised as :
   A. $\left(2x + 3y + 5z\right)^2$ B. $\left(2x + 3y - 5z\right)^2$
   C. $\left(2x - 3y + 5z\right)^2$ D. None of these

26. One of the factors of the expressions $x^2 + 5x + 25$ is :

A. $x + 5$ B. $x - 5$

C. $x + \sqrt{5}$ D. Cannot be factorised

27. If $x + y = 8$ and $xy = 7$ then the value of $x^3 + y^3$ is :

A. 344   B. 342   C. 345   D. 340

28. The expression $49x^2 + 64$ when expressed as factors is :

A. $(7x + 8)^2$ B. $(7x + 8)(7x - 8)$

C. $(7x - 8)^2$ D. Cannot be factorised

29. $(4x + 3y)^2 + (4x - 3y)^2$ is equal to :

A. $16x^2 - 9y^2$ B. $32x^2 + 18y^2$ C. $16x^2 + 9y^2$ D. $32x^2 + 9y^2$

30. The expression $32x^3 + 108y^3$ can be expressed in factors as :

A. $(4x + 3y)(4x^2 - 6xy + 9y^2)$ B. $(4x - 3y)(4x^2 + 6xy + 9y^2)$

C. $(4x + 3y)(4x^2 + 6xy + 9y^2)$ D. None of these

ANSWERS

1	2	3	4	5	6	7	8	9	10
D	D	C	B	C	D	A	B	D	A
11	12	13	14	15	16	17	18	19	20
D	D	A	A	C	B	C	A	A	A
21	22	23	24	25	26	27	28	29	30
B	A	A	C	B	D	A	D	B	D

EXPLANATORY ANSWERS

1. $\because \left(x + \dfrac{1}{x} \right) = 5$

$$\therefore \ x^2 + \frac{1}{x^2} = \left(x + \frac{1}{x} \right)^2 - 2 = 25 - 2 = 23$$

4. $\because$ $(a + b)^2 + (a - b)^2 = 2a^2 + 2b^2 = 2(a^2 + b^2)$

$\Rightarrow$ $(8)^2 + (4)^2 = 2(a^2 + b^2)$

$64 + 16 = 2(a^2 + b^2)$

$\Rightarrow$ $80 = 2(a^2 + b^2)$

$\therefore$ $a^2 + b^2 = 40$

8. $\because$ $x - 2 = 0 \Rightarrow x = 2$

$x^2 - kx + 2 = 0 \Rightarrow 4 - k(2) + 2 = 0$

$6 - 2k = 0 \Rightarrow 2k = 6$

$k = 3.$

10. $\because$ $x - \dfrac{1}{x} = 2$

$\therefore$ $x^3 - \dfrac{1}{x^3} = \left(x - \dfrac{1}{x}\right)^3 + 3x \cdot \dfrac{1}{x}\left(x - \dfrac{1}{x}\right)$

$= (2)^3 + 3(2) = 8 + 6 = 14.$

18. $\because$ One factor of $x^4 + x^2 - 20$ is $x^2 + 5$

$(x^2 + 5)(x^2 - 4) = x^4 + x^2 - 20$

$\therefore$ Other factor $= x^2 - 4.$

22. $\because$ $x + \dfrac{1}{x} = 4$

$\therefore$ $x^3 + \dfrac{1}{x^3} = \left(x + \dfrac{1}{x}\right)^3 - 3 \cdot x \cdot \dfrac{1}{x}\left(x + \dfrac{1}{x}\right)$

$= (4)^3 - 3(4)$

$= 64 - 12 = 52$

27. $\because$ $x + y = 8$ and $xy = 7$

$\therefore$ $x^3 + y^3 = (x + y)^3 - 3xy(x + y)$

$= (8)^3 - 3(7)(8)$

$= 512 - 168 = 344.$

29. $(4x + 3y)^2 + (4x - 3y)^2 = 2(4x)^2 + 2(3y)^2$

$= 32x^2 + 18y^2$

$[\because \ (a + b)^2 + (a - b)^2 = 2a^2 + 2b^2].$

15

Linear equation &
Quadratic Equation

The System of Equations

$a_1x + b_1y + c_1 = 0$ and $a_2x + b_2y + c_2 = 0$ may be either unique solution or no solution or infinitely many solutions.

Unique solution is known as consistent or not parallel. No solution is known as inconsistent or parallel, while many solutions are known as coincident or dependent.

(a) **For unique solution:** $\dfrac{a_1}{a_2} \neq \dfrac{b_1}{b_2}$

(b) **For no solution:** $\dfrac{a_1}{a_2} = \dfrac{b_1}{b_2} \neq \dfrac{c_1}{c_2}$

(c) **For many solutions:** $\dfrac{a_1}{a_2} = \dfrac{b_1}{b_2} = \dfrac{c_1}{c_2}$

Algebraic Methods of Solving Simultaneous Linear Equations in Two Variables

(a) Substitution Method
(b) Elimination Method
(c) Cross Multiplication Method

Quadratic Equation

Definition : A polynomial equation in which the highest power of the unknown variable is two. The general form of a quadratic equation in the variable x is

$$ax^2 + bx + c = 0$$

where, a, b and c are constant.

Solution of a Quadratic Equation

$$x = \frac{-b \pm \sqrt{b^2 - 4ac}}{2a}$$

$b^2 - 4ac = D$ is called discriminant.

(*a*) If D > 0 then there are real and distinct roots given by

$$\alpha = \frac{-b+\sqrt{b^2-4ac}}{2a}, \quad \beta = \frac{-b-\sqrt{b^2-4ac}}{2a}$$

(*b*) If D = 0, there are real and equal roots

$$\alpha = \beta = \frac{-b}{2a}$$

(*c*) If D < 0, there are no real roots.

Sum of the roots

$$\alpha + \beta = \frac{-b}{a}$$

Product of the roots

$$\alpha\beta = \frac{c}{a}$$

Ex. 1 : The roots of the equation $6x^2 - 5x - 21 = 0$ are

Sol.
$$6x^2 - 14x + 9x - 21 = 0$$
$$\Rightarrow \quad 2x(3x - 7) + 3(3x - 7) = 0$$
$$\Rightarrow \quad (3x - 7)(2x + 3) = 0$$
$$\Rightarrow \quad x = \frac{7}{3}, \ x = -\frac{3}{2}$$

Ex. 2 : If α and β are the roots of the quadratic equation $3x^2 + 3x + 2 = 0$ then $\alpha^3 + \beta^3 = $ ......

Sol.
$$a = 3, \ b = 3, \ c = 2$$
$$\Rightarrow \quad \alpha + \beta = -1, \ \alpha\beta = \frac{2}{3}$$
$$\alpha^3 + \beta^3 = (-1)^3 - 3 \times \frac{2}{3} \times (-1)$$
$$= -1 + 2 = 1$$

MULTIPLE CHOICE QUESTIONS

1. The system of linear equations $2x + 3y = 7$ and $4x + 6y = 10$ has :
   A. no solution   B. unique solution
   C. infinite solution   D. no conclusion can be drawn

2. The value of k for which the system of equations $x + 2y + 7 = 0$ and $2x + ky + 14 = 0$ will have infinitely many solutions is :
   A. 2   B. 4   C. 6   D. 8

3. For what value of α, the system of equations $\alpha x + 3y = \alpha - 3$ and $12x + \alpha y = \alpha$ will have a unique solution?
A. $\alpha \neq \pm 6$ B. $\alpha \neq \pm 3$ C. $\alpha \neq \mp 6$ D. None of these

4. For what value of k, the system of equations will represent the coincident lines $x + 5y - 7 = 0$ and $4x + 20y + k = 0$?
A. 28   B. –28   C. –26   D. None of these

5. A lady has 50 paise and ₹ 1 coins in her purse. If in all, she has 40 coins totally ₹ 25.50 how many of each type of coins does she have?
A. 26, 11   B. 11, 29   C. 29, 11   D. None of these

6. A father is three times as old as his son. After twelve years his age will be twice as the age of his son. Find their present ages in years.
A. 12, 26   B. 24, 36   C. 36, 12   D. None of these

7. Ten years ago, father was twelve times as old as his son. Ten years after, he will be twice as old as his son will be. Find their present ages in years.
A. 12, 36   B. 12, 24   C. 12, 34   D. None of these

8. The present age of a father is 3 years more than three times the age of son. Three years hence father's age will be 10 years more than twice the age of son. Determine their present ages in years.
A. 10, 33   B. 33, 10   C. 10, 30   D. None of these

9. In a triangle ABC, $\angle C = 3\angle B = 2(\angle A + \angle B)$.
Find three angles in degrees.
A. 20°, 50°, 120°   B. 30°, 40°, 120°
C. 20°, 40°, 120°   D. None of these

10. The fraction becomes 2 when 1 is added to both the numerator and the denominator, and it becomes 3 when 1 is subtracted from both the numerator and denominator. The given fraction is :
A. $\dfrac{7}{3}$ B. $\dfrac{4}{7}$ C. $\dfrac{3}{7}$ D. $\dfrac{7}{4}$

11. In the system of equations $x + y = 13$ and $2x + 3y = 32$, the values of x and y are:
A. 5 and 6   B. 7 and 8   C. 7 and 6   D. 6 and 7

12. If $y = 4$, find the value of x in the equation $3x + 4y = 25$.
A. 3   B. 8   C. 5   D. 4

13. The equation whose roots are 5, 9 is :
A. $x^2 - 5x + 14 = 0$ B. $x^2 - 14x + 14 = 0$
C. $x^2 - 45x + 14 = 0$ D. $x^2 - 14x + 45 = 0$

14. If α, β be the values of x satisfying the equation $x^2 - px + q = 0$, the value of $\dfrac{1}{\alpha} + \dfrac{1}{\beta}$ is :

A. $\dfrac{q}{p}$　　　　B. $-\dfrac{p}{q}$　　　　C. $\dfrac{p}{q}$　　　　D. $\dfrac{1}{q}$

15. If one of the roots of the equation is $2 + \sqrt{3}$, the other has to be :

A. $\sqrt{3} - 2$　　　B. 2　　　C. $2 - \sqrt{3}$　　　D. $\sqrt{3}$

16. If α, β are the roots of $2x^2 - x + 1 = 0$, the value of $\alpha^2 + \beta^2$ is :
A. 1　　　　B. 0　　　　C. $5/4$　　　　D. $-3/4$

17. Find the values of 'p' for which the quadratic equation $px^2 + 4x + 1 = 0$ has real roots.
A. $p \le 4$　　　B. $p \ge 6$　　　C. $p \ge 4$　　　D. None of these

18. Determine 'k' such that the quadratic equation $x^2 + 7(3 + 2k) - 2x(1 + 3k) = 0$ has equal roots.
A. $2, -10/9$　　　B. $3, -10/9$　　　C. $2, 10/9$　　　D. None of these

19. For what value of 'k' the equation $(k + 3)x^2 - (5 - k)x + 1 = 0$ has coincident roots?
A. $1, 13$　　　B. $1, 12$　　　C. $3, 13$　　　D. None of these

20. Find the value of 'k' so that the sum of the roots of equation $3x^2 + (2x + 1)x - k + 5 = 0$ is equal to the product of roots.
A. 4　　　　B. 2　　　　C. 3　　　　D. -6

21. Find the value of 'p' so that equation $4x^2 - 8px + 9 = 0$ has roots whose difference is 4.
A. ± 3　　　B. $\pm 2/5$　　　C. $\pm 5/2$　　　D. None of these

22. Find the value of 'm' so that the equation $9x^2 - 8mx - 9 = 0$ has one root as the negative of the other.
A. 0　　　　B. 1　　　　C. 2　　　　D. None of these

23. If α and β are the roots of $x^2 - 2x - 1 = 0$, find the value of $\alpha^2\beta + \beta^2\alpha$.
A. -3　　　　B. -2　　　　C. 2　　　　D. None of these

24. If a and b are the roots of the equation $x^2 - 5x + 6 = 0$, find the value of $(a^2 - b^2)$.
A. ± 3　　　　B. ± 5　　　　C. ± 4　　　　D. None of these

25. For what values of 'p' for which the quadratic equation $px^2 - 4x + p$ has real linear factors?
A. $-2 \le p < 3$　　B. $-2 \le p \le 2$　　C. $-2 \ge p \le 2$　　D. None of these

26. The numerical difference of the roots of $x^2 - 6x + 6 = 0$ is
　　A. 0　　　　　　B. $\sqrt{6}$　　　　　C. $\sqrt{(12)}$　　　　D. $\sqrt{(18)}$

27. If one root of $5x^2 + 13x + k = 0$ is reciprocal of the other, then k is equal to
　　A. 0　　　　　　B. 5　　　　　C. 1/6　　　　D. 6

28. If one root of the equation
　　$x^2 + px + 12 = 0$ is 4, while the equation
　　$x^2 + px + q = 0$ has equal roots, the value of q is
　　A. 49/4　　　　B. 4/49　　　　C. 4　　　　D. None of these

29. If α and β are the roots of the equation
　　$ax^2 + bx + c = 0$, then $(1 + \alpha + \alpha^2)(1 + \beta + \beta^2) =$
　　A. 0　　　　　　B. positive　　　C. negative　　D. None of these

30. If the roots of $ax^2 + bx + c = 0$ are α, β and the roots of $Ax^2 + bx + C = 0$ are
　　$\alpha - k, \beta - k$ then $(B^2 - 4AC)/(b^2 - 4ac)$ is equal to
　　A. 0　　　　　　B. 1　　　　　C. $(A/a)^2$　　　D. $(a/A)^2$

ANSWERS

1	2	3	4	5	6	7	8	9	10
A	B	A	B	C	A	C	A	C	A

11	12	13	14	15	16	17	18	19	20
C	A	D	C	C	D	A	A	A	D

21	22	23	24	25	26	27	28	29	30
C	A	B	B	B	C	B	A	B	C

EXPLANATORY ANSWERS

3. Since, the given equations have unique solution.

$$\therefore \quad \frac{a_1}{a_2} \neq \frac{b_1}{b_2}$$

$$\frac{\alpha}{12} \neq \frac{3}{\alpha} \Rightarrow \alpha^2 \neq 36 \Rightarrow \alpha \neq \pm 6$$

4. Since, the given set of equations represent coincident lines.

$$\text{then,} \quad \frac{1}{4} = \frac{5}{20} = \frac{-7}{K} \Rightarrow K = -28$$

12. $3x + 4y = 25$
　　$\Rightarrow \quad 3x + 4 \times 4 = 25 \quad (\because y = 4)$

or $\qquad 3x + 16 = 25 \Rightarrow 3x = 25 - 16$

$\Rightarrow \qquad 3x = 9 \Rightarrow x = 9/3 = 3$

13. Roots are 5 and 9

Sum of the roots $= 5 + 9 = 14$

Product of roots $= 5 \times 9 = 45$

$\therefore x^2 -$ Sum of roots $(x) +$ Product of roots $= 0$

$\Rightarrow x^2 - 14x + 45 = 0$

14. $\alpha + \beta = p, \quad \alpha\beta = q$

$$\therefore \frac{1}{\alpha} + \frac{1}{\beta} = \frac{\alpha+\beta}{\alpha\beta} = \frac{p}{q}$$

17. For real roots $D \geq 0$

$$\Rightarrow (4)^2 - 4.p.1 \geq 0 \qquad\qquad \Rightarrow 16 \geq 4p$$

$$\Rightarrow 4p \leq 16 \qquad\qquad \Rightarrow p \leq 4$$

20. $\alpha + \beta = \alpha\beta$

$$\frac{-(2k+1)}{3} = \frac{-k+5}{3}$$

$$-2k-1 = -k+5 \qquad k = -6$$

23. Here, $\qquad \alpha + \beta = 2, \ \alpha\beta = -1$

Now, $\quad \alpha^2\beta + \alpha\beta^2 = \alpha\beta(\alpha + \beta)$

$$= -1(2) = -2$$

26. $\alpha + \beta = 6, \alpha\beta = 6$

$\therefore \alpha - \beta = \sqrt{[(\alpha + \beta)^2 - 4\alpha\beta]} = \sqrt{(12)}$

27. Let α and $1/\alpha$ be the roots.

$\therefore$ Product of roots $= \alpha(1/\alpha) = 1$

$\qquad = k/5 \Rightarrow k = 5$

28. $\because$ One root of equation

$x^2 + px + 12 = 0$ is 4

$\therefore 16 + 4p + 12 = 0 \Rightarrow p = -7$

If equation $x^2 + px + q = 0$ has equal roots,

then $p^2 - 4q = 0 \Rightarrow q = p^2/4 = 49/4$

❖ ❖ ❖

16

Logarithm

Definition

The logarithm of any number to a given base is the index of the power to which the base must be raised in order to equal the given number.

If b be any number and p and N two other numbers such that $b^p = N$, then p is called the logarithm of N to the base b and is written as $\log_b N$. Thus the exponential identity $b^p = N$ is equivalent to logarithmic identity $\log_b N = p$.

Exponential	*Logarithmic*
$b^p = n$	$\log_b N = p$
$3^2 = 9$	$\log_3 9 = 2$
$4^{-2} = \dfrac{1}{16}$	$\log_4\left(\dfrac{1}{16}\right) = -2$
$4^{-2} = 0.0625$	$\log_4 (0.0625) = -2$
$64^{1/3} = 4$	$\log_{64}(4) = \dfrac{1}{3}$

Properties of Logarithms:

(i) $a^{\log_a^x} = x;\ a \neq 0, \pm 1, x > 0.$

(ii) $a^{\log_b^x} = x^{\log_b^a}$; $a > 0, b > 0, \neq 1, x > 0.$

(iii) $\log_a a = 1,\ \log_a 1 = 0;\ a > 0, \neq 1.$

(iv) $\log_a x = \dfrac{1}{\log_x a};\ x, a > 0, \neq 1.$

(v) $\log_a x = \log_b x . \log_a b = \dfrac{\log_b x}{\log_b a}$; $a, b > 0, \neq 1, x > 0.$

(vi) For $x, y > 0, a > 0, \neq 1$

    (a) $\log_a (x.y) = \log_a x + \log_a y$

    (b) $\log_a (x/y) = \log_a x - \log_a y$

    (c) $\log_a (x^n) = n \log_a x.$

Example : Compute $\log_{30} 8$ if $\log_{30} 3 = a$ and $\log_{30} 5 = b.$

Solution : $\log_{30} 8 = 3 \log_{30} 2 = 3\log_{30} \dfrac{30}{15} = 3[1 - \log_{30} 3 - \log_{30} 5]$

$= 3 (1 - a - b)$

MULTIPLE CHOICE QUESTIONS

1. $\log_5 5 \, \log_4 9 \, \log_3 2$ simplifies to:

   A. 2   B. 1   C. 5   D. None of these

2. $\log_3 11 . \log_{11} 13 . \log_{13} 15 . \log_{15} 27 = ?$

   A. 1   B. 2   C. 3   D. None of these

3. $\log_{2\sqrt{2}} 512 = ?$

   A. 4   B. 5   C. 6   D. 7

4. If $A = \log_2 \log_2 \log_4 256 + 2\log_{\sqrt{2}} 2$, then A equals:

   A. 2   B. 3   C. 5   D. 7

5. $25^{\left(1/2 + \log_{1/5} 27 + \log_{125} 81\right)} = ?$

   A. 0   B. 1   C. 10/81   D. $5\sqrt[3]{9/81}$

6. The domain of the function $\sqrt{(\log_{0.5} x)}$ is:

   A. $(1, \infty)$ B. $(0, \infty)$ C. $(0, 1)$ D. $(0.5, 1)$

7. If $\log_{10} 3 = 0.477$, the no. of digits in 3^{40} is:

   A. 18   B. 19   C. 20   D. 21

8. If $a^x = b$, $b^y = c$, $c^z = a$, then value of xyz is:

   A. 0   B. 1   C. 2   D. 3

9. $7 \log (16/15) + 5 \log (25/24) + 3 \log (81/80) = ?$

   A. 0   B. 1   C. log 2   D. log 3

10. If $\log_{16} x + \log_4 x + \log_2 x = 14$, then $x = ?$

   A. 16   B. 32   C. 64   D. None of these

11. If $N = m!$ (m is a fixed positive integer > 2), then

$$\frac{1}{\log_2 N} + \frac{1}{\log_3 N} + \cdots\cdots + \frac{1}{\log_m N} \text{ is equal to:}$$

   A. -1 B. 0   C. 1   D. 2

12. $\log (\log_{ab} a + 1/\log_b ab) = ?$

   A. 0   B. 1   C. log ab D. None of these

13. The value of $\sqrt{(\log^2_{0.5} 4)}$ is:

   A. -2 B. $\sqrt{(-4)}$ C. 2   D. None of these

14. If $\dfrac{\log_8 17}{\log_9 23} - \dfrac{\log_{2\sqrt{2}} 17}{\log_3 23} = ?$

   A. 0   B. 1   C. 17/8   D. 23/17

15. $\dfrac{1}{\log_{xy} xyz} + \dfrac{1}{\log_{yz} xyz} + \dfrac{1}{\log_{zx} xyz} = ?$

   A. 0   B. 1   C. 2   D. $\log_x xyz$

16. The equation $\log_e x + \log_e (1 + x) = 0$ can be written as:

   A. $x^2 + x - 1 = 0$ B. $x^2 + x + 1 = 0$

   C. $x^2 + x - e = 0$ D. $x^2 + x + e = 0$

17. If $2 \log_{16} (x^2 + x) - \log_4 (x + 1) = 2$, then $x = ?$

   A. $- 1$ B. 16   C. 2   D. None of these

18. If $\dfrac{1}{\log_a x} + \dfrac{1}{\log_c x} = \dfrac{2}{\log_b x}$, then $a,\ b,\ c$ are in:

   A. A.P.   B. G.P.   C. H.P.   D. None of these

19. $\log_{10} \tan 1° + \log_{10} \tan 2° + ... + \log_{10} \tan 89° = ?$

   A. 0   B. 1   C. 2   D. 3

20. The number $\log_2 7$ is:

   A. an integer   B. a rational number

   C. an irrational number   D. a prime number

21. If $\log_{10} 3 = 0.477$, the number of digits in 3^{50} is:

   A. 23   B. 24   C. 50   D. 150

22. If $\log_8 m + \log_8 1/6 = \dfrac{2}{3}$; then m is equal to:

   A. 4   B. 12   C. 18   D. 24

23. If the logarithm of a number of the base $\sqrt{8}$ is 6, then the number is:

   A. $\sqrt{48}$ B. $\dfrac{\sqrt{8}}{6}$ C. $6\sqrt{8}$ D. 512

24. If $\log 2 = 0.3010$ and $\log 3 = 0.4771$, then the value of $\log 48$ is

   A. 1.6731   B. 1.6811   C. 1.6911   D. 1.8611

25. If $\log_4 7 = x$, then $\log_7 16$ is equal to:

   A. $2/x$ B. x C. $2x$ D. x^2

26. The value of the real number x satisfying $\log_9 x - \log_9 \left(\dfrac{x}{10} + \dfrac{1}{9}\right) = 1$ is:

   A. 2   B. 4   C. 9   D. 10

27. The value of $\log_2 \log_2 \log_3 \log_3 27^3$ is

   A. 0   B. 1   C. 2   D. 3

28. $\log_{10} 10 + \log_{10} 100 + ... + \log_{10} 1\underbrace{0000...0}_{n}$ is equal to:

    A. n B. $(n+1)$ C. (n^2+n+1) D. $\dfrac{n(n+1)}{2}$

29. If $\log_{10}(x+5) + \log_{10} 10 = 4$, then the value of x is:

    A. 795   B. 890   C. 995   D. 1000

30. If $\log_4 x^{2}(x-1)^{2} - \log_2(x-1) = 1,$ then the value of x will be:

    A. 1   B. 2   C. 3   D. 4

ANSWERS

1	2	3	4	5	6	7	8	9	10
B	C	C	C	D	C	C	B	C	D

11	12	13	14	15	16	17	18	19	20
C	A	C	A	C	A	B	B	A	C

21	22	23	24	25	26	27	28	29	30
B	D	D	B	A	D	A	D	C	B

EXPLANATORY ANSWERS

1. Given expression $= 1.\log_{2^2} 3^2.\log_3 2$

$$= \frac{2}{2}\log_2 3.1/(\log_2 3) = 1.$$

2. Given expression $= \log_3 27 = \log_3 3^3 = 3\log_3 3 = 3.$

3. $\log_{2\sqrt{2}} 512 = \log_{2^{3/2}} 2^9 = \{9/(3/2)\}\log_2 2 = 6.$

8. $a = c^z = (b^y)^z = b^{yz} = (a^x)^{yz}$
$$= a^{xyz} \Rightarrow xyz = 1.$$

21. Let $x = 3^{50}$
$\Rightarrow \log x = 50\log 3 = 50 \times 0.477 = 23.850$
Hence, requried number of digits $= 23 + 1 = 24$

22. $\log_8 m + \log_8 1^{1/6} = \dfrac{2}{3} \Rightarrow \log_8^{\left(m\times\frac{1}{6}\right)} = \dfrac{2}{3}$

$\Rightarrow m\times\dfrac{1}{6} = 8^{2/3} \quad \Rightarrow \dfrac{m}{6} = \left(2^3\right)^{2/3}$

$\Rightarrow \dfrac{m}{6} = 4 \quad \therefore m = 24$

23. $\log_{\sqrt{8}} x = 6 \qquad \Rightarrow x = \left(\sqrt{8}\right)^6 = \left(2^{3/2}\right)^6$

$\therefore x = 2^9 = 512$

24. $\log 48 = \log(2^4 \times 3) = 4\log 2 + \log 3$

$= 4 \times 0.3010 + 0.4771 = 1.6811$

25. $\log_4 7 = x \qquad \Rightarrow \log_7 4 = \dfrac{1}{x} \qquad \Rightarrow 2\log_7 4 = \dfrac{2}{x}$

$\Rightarrow \log_7 4^2 \qquad \Rightarrow \log_7 16 = \dfrac{2}{x}$

26. $\log_9 x - \log_9\left(\dfrac{x}{10}+\dfrac{1}{9}\right) = 1 \qquad \Rightarrow \log_9 x - \log_9\left(\dfrac{x}{10}+\dfrac{1}{9}\right) = \log_9 9$

$\Rightarrow \log_9 x/\left(\dfrac{x}{10}+\dfrac{1}{9}\right) = \log_9 9 \qquad \Rightarrow \log_9\left(\dfrac{90x}{9x+10}\right) = \log_9 9$

$\Rightarrow \dfrac{90x}{9x+10} = 9 \qquad \Rightarrow 90x = 81x + 90 \qquad \Rightarrow 9x = 90 \qquad \Rightarrow x = 10$

27. $\log_2 \log_2 \log_3 \log_3 27^3 = \log_2 \log_2 \log_3 \log_3 \left(3^3\right)^3 = \log_2 \log_2 \log_3 9\log_3 3$

$= \log_2 \log_2 \log_3 3^{3^2} \times 1 = \log_2 \log_2 2 \log_3 3^3 = \log_2 \log_2 2 \times 1$

$= \log_2 2 \times 1 = \log_2 2^1 = 0$

28. $\log_{10} 10 + \log_{10} 100 + \ldots + \log_{10} 1\underbrace{00000\ldots0}_{n}$

$= \log_{10} 10 + \log_{10} 10^2 + \ldots + \log_{10} 10^n$

$= \log_{10} 10 + 2\log_{10} 10 + \ldots + n\log_{10} 10$

$= 1 + 2 + \ldots + n = \dfrac{n(n+1)}{2}$

29. $\log_{10}(x+5) + \log_{10} 10 = 4 \qquad \Rightarrow \log_{10}(x+5) + 1 = 4$

$\Rightarrow \log_{10}(x+5) = 3 \quad \Rightarrow x + 5 = 10^3 \qquad \therefore x = 1000 - 5 = 995$

30. $\log_4 x^2(x-1)^2 - \log_2(x-1) = 1 \qquad \Rightarrow \log_{2^2}[x(x-1)]^2 - \log_2(x-1) = 1$

$\Rightarrow \dfrac{2}{2}\log_2 x(x-1) - \log_2(x-1) = 1 \Rightarrow \log_2 \dfrac{x(x-1)}{x-1} = 1$

$\Rightarrow \log_2 x = 1 \qquad \therefore x = 2^1 = 2$

17

Geometry

Important Definations and facts

Line : To connect two points on a plane is called a line. It may be straight line, a curved line (a line has only length, it has no breadth).

Point : On a given point there passes infinitely many lines.

Parrallel straight lines : Two lines on a plane which never intersect each other are called parrallel lines.

Angle : An angle is the union of two non-collinear rays with a common initial point.

1. **Right angle :** An angle whose measure is 90° is called a right angle.
2. **Actute angle :** An angle whose measure is less than 90° is called an actue angle.
3. **Obtuse angle :** An angle whose measure is more than 90° less than 180° is called an obtuse angle.
4. **Reflex angle :** An angle having measure more than 180° and less than 360° is called a reflex angle.
5. **Supplementary angle :** Two angles, the sum of whose measures is 180° are called supplementary angle.
6. **Complementary angle :** Two angles, the sum of whose measure is 90° are called complementary angles.
   For example : 70 and 110 are a pair of summple- mentary angles while 50 and 40 are a pair of complementary angles.
7. **Adjacent angle :** Two angles are called adjacent angle if they have the same vertex, they have a common arm and uncommon arms are on either side of the common arm.

Triangle

Triangle : Figure on a plane formed by three lines.

Types of Triangles

(*a*) Types of triangle on the basis of sides.
(*i*) Equilateral Triangle : All three sides are equal.
(*ii*) Isosceles Triangle : Two sides are equql.
(*iii*) Scalence Triangle : Non of side is equal (unequal)
(*b*) Types of triangle on the bases of angle :
(*i*) Right angle triangle : One angle is of a right angle (90°)
(*ii*) Obtuse angle triangle : Triangle with one angle an obtuse angle.
   Note : The sum of the three angles of a triangle is 180°.

R-165 (Math)-7-II

Quadrilateral

Quadrilateral : Figure on a plane formed by four lines. The sum is interior angles is 360°

The Types of Triangles Quadrilateral

(*i*) **Square :** All the four sides are equal and each angle is of 90°. The diagnonals are equal and intersect at 90°.

(*ii*) **Rhombus :** All the four sides are equal and angles are not necessary to be right angle. In a rhombus. (a) Diagonals intersect at 90° to each other. (b) Diagonals bisect each other.

(*iii*) **Rectangle :** It is a parallelogram having all the angles of 90° but the length and breadth are unequal.

(*iv*) **Parallelogram :** A quadrilateral which has both pairs of opposite sides parallel.

In a parallelogram : (a) Each pair of opposite side are equal. (b) Each pair of opposite angles are equal.

(*v*) **Trapezium :** A qudrilateral which has one pair of opposite sides parallel.

Interior Angles of a Polygon:

1. Sum of the exterior angles of any polygon is 360°.

2. Sum of the interior angles of any polygon is $(2n - 4)$ 90, here n stands for number of sides.

   For example :

(*i*) Find the sum of the interior angles of a hexagon (figure with six angles).

   Sol. $(2 \times 6 - 4)$ 90 = 8 × 90 = 720°.

(*ii*) Find the sum of the interior angles of a pentagon (figure with five angle).

   Sol. $(2 \times 5 - 4)$ 90 = 6 × 90 = 540°.

(*iii*) Each angle of a regular polygon $= \dfrac{2(n-4)\,90}{n}$

   For example :

(*iv*) Find the value of each angle of a regular hexagon.

   Sol. $\dfrac{(2 \times 6 - 4)90}{6}$ or $\dfrac{8 \times 90}{6} = 120°$

MULTIPLE CHOICE QUESTIONS

1. A tangent to a circle is a line that intersect the circle in only:
   A. two points   B. three points   C. four points   D. one point

2. A line intersecting a circle in two points is called:
   A. tangent   B. secant
   C. point of contact   D. None of these

3. The longest chord of a circle is called its:
   A. radius   B. secant   C. diameter   D. tangent

4. A tangent PQ at a point P of a circle of radius 5 cm meets a line through the centre O at a point Q, so that OQ = 12 cm. Length PQ is:
   A. $\sqrt{119}$ cm   B. 13 cm   C. 10 cm   D. 12 cm

5. In a right angled triangle hypotenuse is:
   A. Any side of the triangle   B. Side opposite to right angle
   C. Side opposite to acute angle   D. None of these

6. If the perimeter and area of a circle are numerically equal, then the radius of the circle is :
   A. 6 units   B. π units   C. 4 units   D. 2 units

7. The area of a circle is 301.84 cm². Then its radius is :
   A. 9.2 cm   B. 9.3 cm   C. 9.8 cm   D. 9.6 cm

8. If three altitudes of a triangle are equal then the triangle is :
   A. Right angled   B. Equilateral   C. Isosceles   D. Scalene

9. The height of an equilateral triangle is :

   A. $\dfrac{\sqrt{3}}{4} \times \text{Side}$ B. $\dfrac{\sqrt{3}}{2} \times \text{Side}$ C. $\dfrac{\sqrt{3}}{4} \times \text{Side}^2$ D. None of these

10. ABC is an isosceles right triangle. If $AB^2 = 2AC^2$ then right angle is at:
    A. C   B. A   C. B   D. None of these

11. The length of an altitude of an equilateral triangle of side $2a$ is :
    A. $\sqrt{2}\,a$ cm   B. $\sqrt{3}\,a$ cm   C. 2 cm   D. 1 cm

12. If $\angle A = 100°$, AB = AC, CD bisects $\angle ACB$ and BD bisects $\angle ABC$. The values of x and y are:
    A. 15° and 70°   B. 20° and 140°
    C. 10° and 160°   D. 20° and 125°

13. A perpendicular at the end of the radius of a circle is :
    A. diameter   B. tangent   C. chord   D. anyline

14. ABC and BDF are two equilateral triangles such that D is the mid-point of BC. The ratio of the areas of triangles ABC and BDF is :
    A. 2 : 1　　　　B. 1 : 2　　　　C. 4 : 1　　　　D. 1 : 4

15. The exterior angle of a quadrilateral are $x°$, $(x + 5)°$, $(x + 10)°$ and $(x + 25)°$, then value of x is :
    A. 50°　　　　B. 80°　　　　C. 60°　　　　D. 70°

16. The point equidistant from the three sides of a triangle is :
    A. circumference　　B. centroid　　　C. incentre　　　D. orthocentre

17. In $\triangle ABC$, AB = $6\sqrt{3}$ cm AC = 12 cm and BC = 6 cm. The $\angle CAB$ and $\angle ABC$ are:
    A. 90° and 60°　　　　　　　　　B. 30° and 90°
    C. 60° and 90°　　　　　　　　　D. 90° and 30°

18. Chords AC and BD of a circle intersect each other, than the figure ABCD formed will be :
    A. square　　　　　　　　　　　B. rectangle
    C. parallelogram　　　　　　　　D. quadrilateral

19. Sides of two similar triangles are in the ratio of 4 : 9 then area of these triangles are in the ratio :
    A. 2 : 3　　　　B. 4 : 9　　　　C. 81 : 16　　　　D. 16 : 81

20. In the given figure $\angle AOB = 80°$. The value of x is :

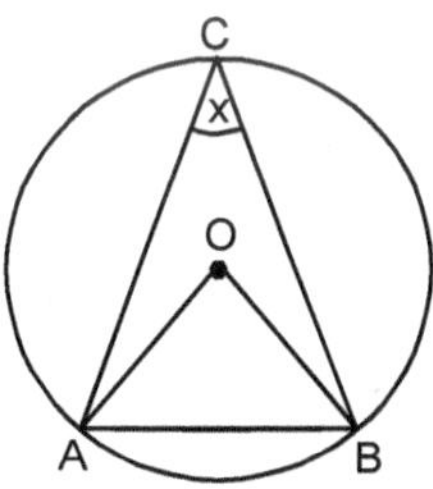

    A. 10°　　　　B. 25°　　　　C. 40°　　　　D. 160°

ANSWERS

1	2	3	4	5	6	7	8	9	10
D	B	C	A	B	D	C	B	B	A

11	12	13	14	15	16	17	18	19	20
B	B	D	C	B	C	B	B	D	C

EXPLANATORY ANSWERS

1. A line meeting a circle in one point is called a tangent to the circle.
2. A line, which intersects a cirlce in two distinct points is called secant of the circle.

5. 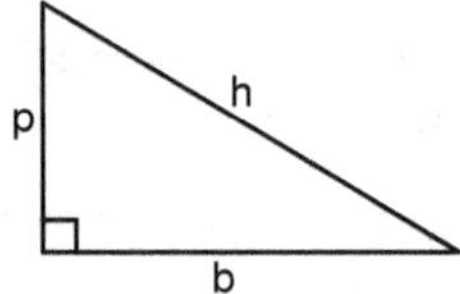

   In any right-angled triangle hypotenuse is opposite to right angle.

6. From question,
   circumference of circle = Area of circle
   $$2\pi r = \pi r^2$$
   $$\Rightarrow \quad r = 2$$
   $$\therefore \quad \text{Radius} = 2 \text{ units.}$$

7. Area of the circle $= \pi r^2$
   According to the question,
   $$\pi r^2 = 301.84$$
   $$\Rightarrow \quad \frac{22}{7}r^2 = 301.84$$
   $$r^2 = \frac{7 \times 301.84}{22} = 96.04$$
   $$\therefore \quad r = \sqrt{96.04} = 9.8 \text{ cm.}$$

8. If the altitudes of a triangle are equal then it is equilateral.

10. Let $\angle C = 90°$
    In $\triangle ACB$,
    $$(AB)^2 = (AC)^2 + (BC)^2$$
    $$(AB)^2 = (AC)^2 + (AC)^2$$
    $$AB^2 = 2AC^2$$
    $$\therefore \quad \angle C = 90°.$$

13. A tangent to a circle is at right angle to the radius.

15. We have,
    $$x° + (x + 5)° + (x + 10)° + (x + 25)° = 360°$$
    $$4x + 40° = 360°$$

$$4x = 320°$$
$$x = 80°.$$

16. Point of concurrence of the bisector of the angles of a triangle is called incentre.

17. In $\triangle ABC$

$$(12)^2 = (6)^2 + \left(6\sqrt{3}\right)^2$$
$$144 = 36 + 108 = 144$$

$\therefore$ $\triangle ABC$ is right-angled triangle

$\therefore$ $\qquad \angle B = 90°$

$$\sin A = \frac{BC}{AC} = \frac{6}{12} = \frac{1}{2}$$

$\Rightarrow \qquad \sin A = \sin 30°$

$$A = 30°$$

$\therefore$ The angles $\angle CAB$ and $\angle ABC$ are 30° and 90° respectively.

18. Chords AC and BD must pass through the centre of the circle and will intersect at the centre,

$\therefore$ $\square ABCD$ is a rectangle.

19. $\because$ $\triangle ABC \sim \triangle DEF$

$\therefore$ $\dfrac{ar\triangle ABC}{ar\triangle DEF} = \dfrac{(4)^2}{(9)^2} = \dfrac{16}{81} = 16 : 81.$

20. We have,

$$\angle AOB = 2\angle ACB$$

[Angle of the centre is twice at the angle of circumference]

$$80° = 2x$$

$\therefore$ $\qquad x = \dfrac{80}{2} = 40°.$

Trigonometry

The word 'trigonometry' literally means the science which deals with the measurement of triangles.

Angle

An angle is a figure formed by two rays (called the arms) with the common initial point (called the vertex).

It is determined by rotating a ray about its end point.

Positive and Negative Angles

Angles determined by a **counter clockwise** rotation are said to be **positive** and angles determined by **clockwise** rotation are said to be **negative**.

The six trigonometric ratios of the acute angle θ are defined as follows :

$$\sin\theta = \frac{p}{h} = \frac{AB}{AC} \qquad\qquad \cos\theta = \frac{b}{h} = \frac{BC}{AC}$$

$$\tan\theta = \frac{p}{b} = \frac{AB}{BC} \qquad\qquad \cot\theta = \frac{b}{p} = \frac{BC}{AB}$$

$$\sec\theta = \frac{h}{b} = \frac{AC}{BC} \qquad\qquad \mathrm{cosec}\,\theta = \frac{h}{p} = \frac{AC}{AB}$$

$$\left[\begin{array}{l} p = \text{perpendicular} \\ \quad\ \text{or opposite} \\ b = \text{base or adjacent} \\ h = \text{hypotenuse} \end{array}\right]$$

IMPORTANT FORMULAE

A.   (*i*) $\tan\theta = \dfrac{\sin\theta}{\cos\theta} = \dfrac{1}{\cot\theta}$ (*ii*) $\cot\theta = \dfrac{\cos\theta}{\sin\theta} = \dfrac{1}{\tan\theta}$

     (*iii*) $\sec\theta = \dfrac{1}{\cos\theta}$ (*iv*) $\mathrm{cosec}\,\theta = \dfrac{1}{\sin\theta}$

B.   (*i*) $\sin^2\theta + \cos^2\theta = 1$

         $\sin^2\theta = 1 - \cos^2\theta \Rightarrow \sin\theta = \sqrt{1 - \cos^2\theta}$

         $\cos^2\theta = 1 - \sin^2\theta \Rightarrow \cos\theta = \sqrt{1 - \sin^2\theta}$

   (*ii*) $1 + \tan^2\theta = \sec^2\theta$

       $\sec^2\theta - \tan^2\theta = 1$

       $\sec^2\theta - 1 = \tan^2\theta$

   (*iii*) $1 + \cot^2\theta = \operatorname{cosec}^2\theta$

       $\operatorname{cosec}^2\theta - \cot^2\theta = 1$

       $\operatorname{cosec}^2\theta - 1 = \cot^2\theta$

   (*iv*) $\tan^2\theta = \dfrac{\sin^2\theta}{\cos^2\theta}$

   (*v*) $\cot^2\theta = \dfrac{\cos^2\theta}{\sin^2\theta}$

   (*vi*) $\sec^2\theta = \dfrac{1}{\cos^2\theta}$

   (*vii*) $\operatorname{cosec}^2\theta = \dfrac{1}{\sin^2\theta}$

C. (*i*) $\sin(90 - \theta) = \cos\theta$ (*ii*) $\cos(90 - \theta) = \sin\theta$

   (*iii*) $\tan(90 - \theta) = \cot\theta$ (*iv*) $\cot(90 - \theta) = \tan\theta$

   (*v*) $\sec(90 - \theta) = \operatorname{cosec}\theta$ (*vi*) $\operatorname{cosec}(90 - \theta) = \sec\theta$

D. (*i*) $\sin(A \pm B) = \sin A \times \cos B \pm \cos A \times \sin B$

   (*ii*) $\cos(A \pm B) = \cos A \times \cos B \mp \sin A \times \sin B$

E. (*i*) $\sin 2\theta = 2\sin\theta \cdot \cos\theta$

   (*ii*) $\cos 2\theta = \cos^2\theta - \sin^2\theta = 1 - 2\sin^2\theta = 2\cos^2\theta - 1$

   (*iii*) $\tan 2\theta = \dfrac{2\tan\theta}{1 - \tan^2\theta}$

F. (*i*) $\sin 3\theta = 3\sin\theta - 4\sin^3\theta$ (*ii*) $\cos 3\theta = 4\cos^3\theta - 3\cos\theta$

T-Ratios of Standard Angles

θ	$0°$	$30°$	$45°$	$60°$	$90°$
$\sin\theta$	0	$\dfrac{1}{2}$	$\dfrac{1}{\sqrt{2}}$	$\dfrac{\sqrt{3}}{2}$	1
$\cos\theta$	1	$\dfrac{\sqrt{3}}{2}$	$\dfrac{1}{\sqrt{2}}$	$\dfrac{1}{2}$	0
$\tan\theta$	0	$\dfrac{1}{\sqrt{3}}$	1	$\sqrt{3}$	∞
$\cot\theta$	∞	$\sqrt{3}$	1	$\dfrac{1}{\sqrt{3}}$	0
$\sec\theta$	1	$\dfrac{2}{\sqrt{3}}$	$\sqrt{2}$	2	∞
$\operatorname{cosec}\theta$	∞	2	$\sqrt{2}$	$\dfrac{2}{\sqrt{3}}$	1

MULTIPLE CHOICE QUESTIONS

1. If $\cos \theta = \dfrac{1}{2}$, find the value of $\dfrac{2\sec\theta}{1+\tan^2\theta}$

    A. 1   B. 2   C. 3   D. 4

2. If $\sin \theta = \dfrac{5}{13}$ and $0 < \theta < 90°$, find out the value of $\cos \theta$.

    A. $\dfrac{5}{12}$ B. $\dfrac{12}{13}$ C. $\dfrac{13}{12}$ D. $\dfrac{12}{5}$

3. If $5 \tan \theta = 4$, find the value of $\dfrac{5\sin\theta - 3\cos\theta}{5\sin\theta + 2\cos\theta}$

    A. 2   B. $\dfrac{3}{2}$ C. $\dfrac{1}{6}$ D. $\dfrac{2}{3}$

4. If $3 \cot \theta = 2$, find the value of $\dfrac{4\sin\theta - 3\cos\theta}{2\sin\theta + 6\cos\theta}$

    A. $\dfrac{2}{3}$ B. $\dfrac{3}{2}$ C. $\dfrac{1}{3}$ D. 3

5. If $3 \tan \theta = 2$, find the value of $\dfrac{4\sin\theta - \cos\theta}{2\sin\theta + \cos\theta}$

    A. $\dfrac{3}{2}$ B. $\dfrac{5}{7}$ C. $\dfrac{3}{7}$ D. 1

6. If $3 \cot \theta = 4$, find the value of $\dfrac{5\sin\theta - 3\cos\theta}{5\sin\theta + 3\cos\theta}$

    A. $\dfrac{1}{9}$ B. $\dfrac{2}{7}$ C. 3   D. 4

7. If $\tan \theta = \dfrac{3}{4}$, find the value of $\dfrac{4\sin\theta - 2\cos\theta}{4\sin\theta + 3\cos\theta}$

    A. $\dfrac{2}{3}$ B. $\dfrac{4}{3}$ C. $\dfrac{1}{6}$ D. $\dfrac{5}{6}$

8. If $\tan A = \dfrac{5}{12}$, find the value of $\sin A + \cos A$, where A is an acute angle.

    A. $\dfrac{13}{17}$ B. $\dfrac{17}{13}$ C. $\dfrac{12}{5}$ D. $\dfrac{5}{17}$

9. If $\tan \theta = \dfrac{2}{3}(0° < \theta < 90°)$, then find the value of $\sin \theta$

A. $\dfrac{2}{\sqrt{13}}$ B. $\dfrac{3}{\sqrt{12}}$ C. 1   D. 0

10. If $2 \tan \theta = 1$, find the value of $\dfrac{3\cos\theta + 2\sin\theta}{2\cos\theta - \sin\theta}$

A. $\dfrac{8}{3}$ B. $\dfrac{5}{3}$ C. $\dfrac{2}{3}$ D. 2

11. Evaluate : $(\operatorname{cosec} \theta - \sin \theta)(\sec \theta - \cos \theta)(\tan \theta + \cot \theta)$
A. 1   B. 2   C. 3   D. 0

12. Evaluate : $(\sin A + \cos A)(\tan A + \cot A)$
A. $\sin A + \cos A$ B. $\sec A + \operatorname{cosec} A$
C. $\sin A$ D. $\cos A$

13. Evaluate $\dfrac{\sin \theta}{1 + \cos\theta} + \dfrac{1 + \cos\theta}{\sin \theta}$

A. 2 sin A   B. 2 cosec A   C. 2 tan A   D. 2 cos A

14. Evaluate $\dfrac{\tan A + \sec A - 1}{\tan A - \sec A + 1}$

A. sec A + tan A   B. sin A   C. 1   D. 0

15. If $\sin x + \sin^2 x = 1$, then $\cos^2 x + \cos^4 x$ is :
A. 1   B. 2   C. 3   D. 4

16. If $\cos \theta - \sin \theta = \sqrt{2} \sin \theta$, then $\cos \theta + \sin \theta$ is:

A. $\sqrt{2} \sin \theta$ B. $\sqrt{2} \cos \theta$ C. $\sin \theta$ D. $\cos \theta$

17. Find the value of
$4(\sin^4 30° + \cos^4 60°) - 3(\sin^2 45° - 2 \cos^2 45°)$.
A. 1   B. 2   C. 0   D. 3

18. Express $\cos 79° + \sec 79°$ in terms of angles between 0° and 45°
A. 1   B. 2
C. sin 11° + cosec 11°   D. cos 11° + sec 11°

19. Using the formula
$\cos (A - B) = \cos A \cos B + \sin A \sin B$, find the value of cos 15°.

A. $\dfrac{\sqrt{3} - 1}{2\sqrt{2}}$ B. $\sqrt{3} - 1$ C. $\dfrac{\sqrt{3} + 1}{2\sqrt{2}}$ D. $\sqrt{3} + 1$

20. Using the formula
$\sin (A - B) = \sin A \cos B - \cos A \sin B$, find the value of $\sin 15°$

A. $\sqrt{3}$ 　　　B. $\sqrt{3} + 1$ 　　　C. $\dfrac{\sqrt{3} - 1}{2\sqrt{2}}$ 　　　D. $\dfrac{\sqrt{3} + 1}{2\sqrt{2}}$

21. $\sin \theta \cos (90° - \theta) + \cos \theta \sin (90° - \theta)$ equal to :
A. 0 　　　B. 1 　　　C. –1 　　　D. 2

22. $\cos^2 72° + \cos^2 18° = ?$
A. 0 　　　B. 1 　　　C. –1 　　　D. 2

23. $3 \tan^2 30° + \sec^4 45° - \tan^2 60°$ is equal to :
A. 0 　　　B. 1 　　　C. 2 　　　D. 3

24. The value of $\sin 79° \cos 11° + \cos 79° \sin 11°$.
A. 1 　　　B. 0 　　　C. 2 　　　D. –2

25. $(\sin \theta + \cos \theta) (1 - \sin\theta \cos \theta)$ can be written as :
A. $\sin \theta + \cos \theta$ 　　　B. $\sin^3 \theta - \cos^3 \theta$
C. $\sin^3 \theta + \cos^3 \theta$ 　　　D. $\sin \theta - \cos \theta$

26. If $\cot^2 \theta = \dfrac{7}{8}$ and $0 < \theta < 90°$, then the value of $\dfrac{(1 + \sin \theta)(1 - \sin \theta)}{(1 + \cos \theta)(1 - \cos \theta)}$ is equal to :

A. $\dfrac{7}{8}$ 　　　B. $\dfrac{7}{6}$ 　　　C. $\dfrac{7}{5}$ 　　　D. $\dfrac{7}{4}$

27. $\sin 40°.\sec 50° - \dfrac{\tan 40°}{\cot 50°} + 1 =$
A. 0 　　　B. 1 　　　C. –1 　　　D. 2

28. The value of $\sin 20° - \cos 70°$ is :
A. 1 　　　B. 2 　　　C. 3 　　　D. 0

29. The value of $\csc^2 (90° - \theta) - \tan^2 \theta$ is
A. 2 　　　B. 3 　　　C. 0 　　　D. 1

30. If $\theta = 45$ then $\dfrac{2\tan\theta}{1 + \tan^2 \theta}$ is :
A. 1 　　　B. 0 　　　C. 2 　　　D. 3

31. The value of $\cos 1° \cos 2° ... \cos 100°$ is
A. 1 　　　B. – 1 　　　C. 0 　　　D. None of these

32. $\cos 24° + \cos 5° + \cos 175° + \cos 204° + \cos 300° =$
A. 1/2 　　　B. – 1/2 　　　C. $\sqrt{(3/2)}$ 　　　D. None of these

33. $\tan 5° \tan 25° \tan 45° \tan 65° \tan 85° =$
    A. 1   B. 1/2   C. 3/4   D. None of these

34. $\tan \dfrac{\pi}{20} \tan \dfrac{3\pi}{20} \tan \dfrac{5\pi}{20} \tan \dfrac{7\pi}{20} \tan \dfrac{9\pi}{20} =$
    A. 1   B. -1 C. 1/2   D. None of these

35. $\sin^2 (\pi/18) + \sin^2 (\pi/9) + \sin^2 (7\pi/18) + \sin^2 (4\pi/9)$
    A. 1   B. 2   C. 4   D. None of these

36. $\tan \theta \sin (\pi/2 + \theta) \cos (\pi/2 - \theta) =$
    A. 1   B. -1 C. 1/2 $\sin 2\theta$ D. None of these

37. $\log \sin 1° \, \log \sin 2° \, ... \, \log \sin 179° =$
    A. 1   B. 0   C. $1/\sqrt{2}$ D. None of these

38. $\log \tan 1° + \log \tan 2° + ... + \log \tan 89° =$
    A. 1   B. 0   C. $\pi/4$ D. None of these

39. The value of $\sin 12° \sin 48° \sin 54°$ is
    A. 1/2   B. 1/3   C. 1/6   D. 1/8

40. If $f(x) = \cos^2 x + \sec^2 x$, its value always is
    A. $f(x) < 1$ B. $f(x) = 1$ C. $2 > f(x) > 1$ D. $f(x) \geq 2$

41. If $A = \cos^2 \theta + \sin^4 \theta$, then for all values of θ
    A. $1 \leq A \leq 2$ B. $13/16 \leq A \leq 1$
    C. $3/4 \leq A \leq 13/16$ D. $3/4 \leq A \leq 1$

42. If $x = r \cos \theta \cos \phi$, $y = r \cos \theta \sin \phi$, $z = r \sin \theta$, then $x^2 + y^2 + z^2 =$
    A. 0   B. 1   C. r D. r^2

43. If $x = a \cos^3 \theta$, $y = b \sin^3 \theta$, then
    A. $(x/a)^{2/3} + (y/b)^{2/3} = 1$ B. $(x/b)^{2/3} + (y/a)^{2/3} = 1$
    C. $(a/x)^{2/3} + (b/y)^{2/3} = 1$ D. $(b/x)^{2/3} + (a/y)^{2/3} = 1$

44. The equation $x = \dfrac{2a\theta}{1+\theta^2}, y = \dfrac{a\left(1-\theta^2\right)}{1+\theta^2}$, where a is a constant, is the parametric equation of the curve:
    A. $x - y^2 = a^2$ B. $x^2 + y^2 = a^2$ C. $x^2 + 4y^2 = 4a^2$ D. $x = 2y$

45. The expression

$$3 \left[\sin^4 \left\{ \frac{3}{2}\pi - \alpha \right\} + \sin^4 (3\pi + \alpha) \right] - 2 \left[\sin^6 \left(\frac{1}{2}\pi + \alpha \right) + \sin^6 (5\pi - \alpha) \right] \text{ is}$$

equal to

    A. 0   B. 1   C. 3   D. $\sin 4\alpha + \cos 6\alpha$

46. $\dfrac{1}{\sin 10°} - \dfrac{\sqrt{3}}{\cos\ 10°}$ is equal to

    A. 2   B. 4   C. 3   D. None of these

47. $\sqrt{3}$ cosec 20° − sec 20° is equal to

    A. 2   B. 2 sin 20°/sin 40°

    C. 4   D. 4 sin 20°/sin 40°

48. If $\tan A = \dfrac{a}{a+1}$ and $\tan B = \dfrac{1}{2a+1}$, then the value of A + B is

    A. 0   B. π/2   C. π/3   D. π/4

49. In a triangle PQR, ∠ R = π/2. If tan (P/2) and tan (Q/2) are the roots of the equation $ax^2 + bx + c = 0$, then

    A. $a + b = c$ B. $b + c = a$ C. $a + c = b$ D. $b = c$

50. $\sqrt{(\log_3 \tan x)}$ is real for

    A. $n\pi + \pi/4 \le x < n\pi + \pi/2$ B. $n\pi < x < n\pi + \pi/2$

    C. $n\pi \pm \pi/4 \le x < n\pi \pm \pi/2$ D. None of these

ANSWERS

1	2	3	4	5	6	7	8	9	10
A	B	C	C	B	A	C	B	A	A
11	**12**	**13**	**14**	**15**	**16**	**17**	**18**	**19**	**20**
A	B	B	A	A	B	B	C	C	C
21	**22**	**23**	**24**	**25**	**26**	**27**	**28**	**29**	**30**
B	B	C	A	C	A	B	D	D	A
31	**32**	**33**	**34**	**35**	**36**	**37**	**38**	**39**	**40**
C	A	A	A	B	D	B	B	D	D
41	**42**	**43**	**44**	**45**	**46**	**47**	**48**	**49**	**50**
D	D	A	B	B	B	C	D	A	A

EXPLANATORY ANSWERS

18. cos 79° + sec 79°

    = cos (90° − 11°) + sec (90° − 11°)

    = sin 11° + cosec 11°.

28. sin 20° − cos(90° − 20°) = sin 20° − sin 20° = 0.

29. $\sec^2\theta - \tan^2\theta = \dfrac{1}{\cos^2\theta} - \dfrac{\sin^2\theta}{\cos^2\theta} = \dfrac{1-\sin^2\theta}{\cos^2\theta} = \dfrac{\cos^2\theta}{\cos^2\theta} = 1.$

30. $\dfrac{2\tan 45°}{1+\tan^2 45°} = \dfrac{2\times 1}{1+1} = \dfrac{2}{2} = 1.$

31. $\because \cos 90° = 0$
$\therefore$ Given expression
$= \cos 1° \cos 2° \dots \cos 89°.0 \cos 91°$ $\dots \cos 100° = 0.$

32. Given expression
$= \cos 24° + \cos 5° + \cos (180° - 5°) + \cos (180° + 24°) + \cos (360° - 60°)$
$= \cos 24° + \cos 5° - \cos 5° - \cos 24° + \cos 60° = 1/2.$

33. Given expression
$= \tan 5° \tan 25°.1 \tan (90° - 25°) \times \tan(90° - 5°)$
$= \tan 5° \tan 25° \cot 25° \cot 5° = 1.$

37. $\because \log \sin 90° = \log 1 = 0$
$\therefore$ Given expression $= 0.$

38. Given expression
$= \log (\tan 1°.\tan 2° \dots \tan 44°. \tan 45°.\cot 44°.\cot 43° \dots \cot 1°)$
$= \log 1 = 0.$

39. $\sin 12° \sin 48°. \sin 54°$

$= \dfrac{1}{2} (\cos 36° - \cos 60°) \cos 36°$

$= \dfrac{1}{4} (2 \cos^2 36° - \cos 36°)$

$= \dfrac{1}{4} (1 + \cos 72° - \cos 36°)$

$= \dfrac{1}{4} (1 + \sin 18° - \cos 36°) = \dfrac{1}{4}\cdot\left(\dfrac{1}{2}\right) = \dfrac{1}{8}.$

40. $f(x) = (\cos x - \sec x)^2 + 2 \Rightarrow f(x) \geq 2$

47. Given expression

$= \dfrac{\sqrt{3}\cos 20° - \sin 20°}{\cos 20° \sin 20°}$

$$= \frac{2\left[\left(\frac{1}{2}\sqrt{3}\right)\cos 20° - \frac{1}{2}\sin 20°\right]}{\frac{1}{2}\sin 40°}$$

$$= \frac{4\sin(60°-20°)}{\sin 40°} = 4.$$

48. $\tan(\theta + \phi) = (\tan \theta + \tan \phi)/(1 - \tan \theta \tan \phi)$
$= 1 \Rightarrow \theta + \phi = \pi/4.$

49. $\tan(P/2) + \tan(Q/2) = -b/a,$
$\tan(P/2).\tan(Q/2) = c/a$
$\angle P + \angle Q = \pi/2$

$$\tan\left(\frac{1}{2}P + \frac{1}{2}Q\right) = 1$$

$$= \frac{\tan(P/2) + \tan(Q/2)}{1 - \tan(P/2)\tan(Q/2)}$$

$$= \frac{-b/a}{1 - c/a} = \frac{-b}{a-c}$$

$\Rightarrow a + b = c.$

50. $\sqrt{(\log_3 \tan x)}$ is real if $\log_3 \tan x \geq 0$
i.e., $\tan x \geq 1$ (as base $= 3 > 1$)
$\therefore \pi/4 \leq x < \pi/2$. General values are given by
$n\pi + \pi/4 \leq x < n\pi + \pi/2.$

GENERAL INTELLIGENCE

VERBAL TEST

SERIES

In questions on series, a series of four numbers is given. The numbers of the series bear some relationship among themselves. You will have to find out the relationship that obtains among the numbers. Then, on the basis of the knowledge of that relationship you can find out the next number(s) in the series.

Series questions may contain a series of letters as well as alphabets.

To begin with, we give some questions on series, each with four options, of which only one is correct. You have to mark the correct answer. Then follow the *Questions for Practice* without options. Detailed answers to questions are given at the end.

Directions: *In each of the following questions on series, a series of numbers or letters is given with one space blank. Choose the correct option out of the four options given under each question.*

These questions are based on the samples of questions set for the examination.

1. 1, 3, 7, 15, ...

A. 25   B. 31
C. 33   D. 35

2. 4, 9, 16, 25, ...

A. 36   B. 38
C. 40   D. 42

3. 1, 13, 25, 37, ...

A. 41   B. 45
C. 49   D. 53

4. 64, 32, 16, 8, ...

A. 1   B. 2

C. 4   D. 6

5. AZ, DW, GT, ...

A. CX   B. TG
C. JQ   D. EV

6. A, D, G, ...

A. I   B. K
C. H   D. J

7. Z, A, Y, B, ...

A. X   B. C
C. D   D. W

8. If 3 + 2 = 25 and 3 + 4 = 49, then 2 + 3 = ?

A. 6   B. 15
C. 25   D. 18

9. 2, 4, 8, 16, ...

A. 20   B. 24
C. 32   D. 28

10. 20, 15, 11, 8, ...

A. 3   B. 4
C. 5   D. 6

QUESTIONS FOR PRACTICE

11. 76, 63, 50, 37, ...

12. 5, 10, 17, 26, ...

13. 2, 6, 12, 20, ...

14. 3, 6, 9, 12, ...

15. 3, 7, 11, 13, ...

16. 1, 4, 9, 16, ...

17. 0, 3, 8, 15, ...

18. 3, 6, 12, 24, ...

19. 1, 4, 8, 13, ...

20. 1, 3, 6, 10, ...

21. 1, 5, 17, 53, ...

22. 3, 8, 15, 24, ...

23. 25, 19, 14, 10, ...
24. 3, 7, 15, 31, ...
25. 80, 40, 20, 10, ...
26. 1, 6, 11, 16, ...
27. 59, 52, 45, 38, ...
28. 2, 5, 11, 23, ...
29. 13, 17, 19, 23, ...
30. 13, 23, 33, 43, ...
31. 1, 4, 10, 22, ...
32. 1, 4, 9, 16, ...
33. 96, 48, 24, 12, ...
34. 14, 10, 13, 9, 12, 8, ...
35. 4, 7, 14, 17, 34, 37, ...
36. 32, 16, 20, 10, 14, ...
37. 2, 3, 3, 5, 4, 7, ...
38. 5, 6, 8, 11, 15, 20, ...
39. 2, 9, 28, 65, ...
40. 0, 2, 6, 12, 20, ...
41. 2, 5, 10, 17, 26, ...
42. 1, 5, 11, 19, 29, ...
43. $\dfrac{11}{12}$, $\dfrac{10}{11}$, $\dfrac{9}{10}$, $\dfrac{8}{9}$ .....
44. 4, 5, 9, 14, 23, ...
45. 5, 10, 15, 25, 40, ...
46. 360, 180, 60, 15, ...
47. 4, 9, 16, 25, 36, ...
48. 4, 8, 3, 6, 2, 4, ...
49. 1, 8, 27, 64, ...
50. 4, 8, 16, 28, ...
51. 1, 2, 5, 10, 17, ...
52. 720, 120, 24, 6, ...
53. 1, 2, 4, 8, 16, ...
54. 1, 3, 6, 10, 15, ...
55. 0, 1, 4, 9, 16, ...
56. 810, 270, 90, 30, ...
57. 9, 16, 25, 36, ...
58. 6, 9, 12, 15, ...
59. 4, 8, 13, 19, ...
60. 3, 7, 15, 31, ...
61. 89, 79, 70, 72, ...
62. 2, 3, 4, 6, 8, ...
63. 3, 4, 9, 16, 27, ...
64. 45, 35, 26, 18, ...
65. 2, 9, 16, 23, ...
66. 40, 32, 26, 22, ...
67. 1, 3, 6, 10, ...
68. 66, 47, 28, ...
69. 5, 7, 11, 19, ...
70. 12, 6, 3, 1½, ...
71. 2, 3, 4, 6, 6, 9, ...
72. 5, 36, 10, 18, 20, ...
73. 5, 7, 11, 13, ...
74. 2, 4, 8, 16, ...
75. 45, 36, 27, ...
76. 1, 7, 13, 19, ...
77. 1, 4, 9, 16, ...
78. 54, 63, 72, ...
79. 42, 53, 63, 72, ...
80. 20, 8, 10, 4, 5, ...
81. 5, 11, 23, ...
82. 10, 22, 46, ...
83. 37, 41, 47, ...
84. 3, 2, 9, 6, 27, ...
85. 3, 6, 10, 15, ...
86. 2, 6, 12, 20, ...
87. 1, 8, 27, 64, ...

88. 125, 64, 27, 8, ...

89. 36, 49, 64, 81, ...

90. 64, 49, 36, 25, ...

91. If 3 + 4 = 25 and 4 + 5 = 41, then 5 + 6 = ?

92. If 2 + 3 = 25 and 3 + 4 = 49, then 4 + 5 = ?

93. If 6 – 4 = 20 and 5 – 3 = 16, then 4 – 3 = ?

94. If 8 – 6 = 4 and 7 – 4 = 9, then 5 – 2 = ?

95. If 7 + 9 = 32 and 3 + 6 = 18, then 5 + 4 = ?

96. If 3 + 2 = 25 and 3 + 4 = 49, then 3 + 5 = ?

97. If 9 – 5 = 2 and 25 – 15 = 5, then 12 – 6 = ?

98. If 2 x 3 = 12 and 3 x 4 = 25, then 4 x 5 = ?

99. If 2 + 3 = 13 and 3 + 4 = 25, then 2 + 5 = ?

100. If 6 – 3 = 9 and 7 – 2 = 25, then 8 – 4 = ?

101. If 5 + 2 = 19 and 2 + 3 = 13, then 3 + 5 = ?

102. If 6 – 3 = 27 and 5 – 4 = 9, then 6 – 4 = ?

103. 4 – 2 = 4 and 6 – 4 = 4, then 5 – 3 = ?

104. If 3 + 5 = 64 and 2 + 3 = 25, then 4 + 6 = ?

105. If 1 + 4 = 10 and 2 + 5 = 14, then 3 + 6 = ?

106. If 3 + 2 = 60 and 3 + 3 = 90, then 3 + 4 = ?

107. If 5 x 3 = 2 and 17 x 6 = 11, then 18 x 5 = ?

108. If 4 x 5 = 60 and 2 x 8 = 48, then 3 x 6 = ?

109. If 9 – 5 = 2 and 25 – 15 = 5, then 12 – 6 = ?

110. If 5 x 8 = 13 and 7 x 9 = 16, then 3 x 7 = ?

111. If $\dfrac{3}{4} + \dfrac{5}{6} = \dfrac{8}{10}$ and $\dfrac{6}{7} + \dfrac{2}{3} = \dfrac{8}{10}$, then $\dfrac{3}{4} + \dfrac{2}{3} = ?$

112. If 4 x 7 = 11 and 11 x 4 = 15, then 7 x 9 = ?

113. If $\dfrac{5}{7} = 12$ and $\dfrac{1}{10} = 11$, then $\dfrac{3}{5} = ?$

114. If 25 + 12 = 13 and 9 x 3 = 6, then 17 x 4 = ?

115. If 5 ÷ 2 = 7 and 11 ÷ 2 = 13, then 8 ÷ 3 = ?

116. BCD, CDE, DEF, ...

117. XYZ, WXY, VWX, ...

118. AZ, BY, CX, DW, ...

119. ACE, BDF, CEG, DFH, ...

120. ZX, YW, XV, WU, ...

121. AE, BF, CG, DH, ...

122. ABD, BCE, CDF, DEG, ...

123. AN, BO, CP, DQ, ...

124. ABZ, BCY, CDX, DEW, ...

125. ZA, YB, XC, WD, ...

126. A, D, G, J, ...

127. Z, W, T, Q, ...

128. AZY, BYX, CXW, ...

129. BA, DC, FE, HG, ...

130. ZYX, WVU, TSR, ...

FINDING THE WRONG OR SUPERFLUOUS NUMBER

Directions: *Below are given some series, each of which has a wrong or superfluous number. Find it out; that is your answer.*

1. 1, 4, 9, 16, 24, 36

2. 11, 12, 22, 24, 32, 36

3. 13, 17, 22, 28, 35, 41

4. 100, 81, 64, 49, 37, 25

5. 101, 110, 119, 125, 137, 146

6. 23, 33, 44, 56, 70

7. 40, 28, 19, 10, 2

8. 24, 21, 18, 15, 10, 9

9. 17, 15, 12, 13, 11, 9

10. 7, 10, 13, 17, 16, 19

11. 1, 3, 9, 25, 81

12. 2, 7, 12, 17, 19, 22

13. 4, 9, 16, 24, 25, 36, 49

14. 5, 11, 17, 23, 26, 29, 35

15. 3, 7, 8, 18, 33, 53

16. 1, 7, 27, 64, 125

17. 20, 10, 15, 11, 6, 0

18. 80, 90, 100, 111, 123, 136

19. 16, 24, 36, 49, 64, 81

20. 100, 93, 86, 76, 66

21. 11, 22, 32, 44, 55, 66

22. 216, 121, 64, 27, 8

23. 4, 9, 16, 25, 35, 49

24. 50, 39, 27, 17, 6

25. 23, 33, 44, 56, 70

26. 80, 71, 62, 52, 44

27. 4, 11, 18, 24, 32

28. 2, 4, 9, 16, 32

29. 1, 4, 8, 12, 19

30. 5, 7, 9, 13, 13, 20

31. 3, 4, 8, 16, 33, 58

32. 6, 13, 21, 27, 34

33. 6, 18, 30, 42, 48

34. 1, 8, 26, 64, 125

35. 6, 18, 28, 42, 54

36. 63, 56, 49, 43, 35

37. 91, 80, 65, 58, 47, 36

38. 2, 5, 18, 17, 26

39. 21, 25, 30, 39, 43, 51

40. 176, 88, 40, 22, 11

41. 8, 21, 34, 45, 60

42. 15, 21, 27, 34, 39

43. 17, 15, 13, 12, 9

44. 100, 90, 81, 71, 64, 52

45. 1, 4, 9, 15, 25, 36

ANALOGY

In analogy questions, three words are given. The first two words to the left of sign : : are related in some way. The same relationship holds between the third word to the right of the sign : : and one of the four responses A, B, C and D given thereunder. You have to choose the correct response, that is your answer.

Here is an example:

Student : Teacher : : Patient : ?

A. Hospital   B. Medicine
C. Doctor   D. Disease

In this case the correct response is C because a Doctor is related to a Patient in the same way as a Teacher is related to a Student.

QUESTIONS FOR PRACTICE

1. Milk : Curd : : Water : ?
A. River   B. Thirst
C. Ice   D. Vapour

2. Girl : Beautiful : : Gold : ?
A. Valuable   B. Bright
C. Ornament   D. Ring

3. Desert : Sand : : Sea : ?
A. Water   B. Tide
C. Fish   D. Crocodile

4. Beautiful : Ugly : : Healthy : ?
A. Sick   B. Weak
C. Strong   D. Fat

5. Cheese : Milk : : Sugar : ?
A. Molasses   B. Palm
C. Sugarcane   D. Syrup

6. Daughter : Mother : : Son : ?
A. Mother   B. Sister
C. Father   D. Brother

7. Book : Paper : : Table : ?
A. School   B. Student
C. Wood   D. Chair

8. Player : Team : : Ship : ?
A. Port   B. Fleet
C. Ocean   D. Captain

9. Kilogram : Weight : : Metre : ?
A. Journey   B. Road
C. Cloth   D. Length

10. Lid : Box : : Cork : ?
A. Seal   B. Bottle
C. Drug   D. Carton

11. Circle : Circumference : : Square : ?
A. Angle   B. Area
C. Diagonal   D. Perimeter

12. Advocate : Law : : Cook : ?
A. Cookery   B. Kitchen
C. Food   D. Dishes

13. Wardrobe : Clothes : : Purse : ?
A. Pocket   B. Zip
C. Money   D. Fare

14. Temperature : Heat : : Humidity : ?
A. Rain   B. Weather
C. Night   D. Moisture

15. Shakespeare : Drama : : Ghalib : ?
A. Urdu   B. Literature
C. Ghazal   D. Stories

16. Grass : Green : : Sky : ?
A. Endless   B. Stars
C. Blue   D. Bright

17. Monday : Week : : January : ?
A. Winter   B. Month
C. Year   D. Season

18. Thermometer : Temperature : : Barometer : ?
A. Atmosphere
B. Wind

C. Atmospheric Pressure
D. Velocity

19. Poverty : Riches : : Glory : ?
A. Penuary   B. Happiness
C. Shame   D. Suffering

20. Table : Chair : : Coat : ?
A. Pajama   B. Shirt
C. Tie   D. Pant

21. Hand : Elbow : : Leg : ?
A. Thigh   B. Knee
C. Ankle   D. Claw

22. Coal : Black : : Snow : ?
A. Water   B. Mountain
C. Cold   D. White

23. Precaution : Accident : : Cleanliness : ?
A. Disease   B. Treatment
C. Filth   D. Garbage

24. January : April : : Sunday : ?
A. Thursday   B. Tuesday
C. Monday   D. Wednesday

25. Soldier : Rifle : : Writer : ?
A. Book   B. Paper
C. Pen   D. Ink

26. Plate : Crockery : : Spoon : ?
A. Knife   B. Fork
C. Chinaware   D. Cultery

27. Night : Evening : : Day : ?
A. Morning   B. Sun
C. Sunlight   D. Daylight

28. Uncle : Aunt : : Father : ?
A. Daughter   B. Mother
C. Brother   D. Sister

29. Lotus : Water : : Fish : ?
A. Creature   B. Food

C. Breath   D. Water

30. Metre : Length : : Litre : ?
A. Weight   B. Number
C. Volume   D. Quantity

31. Heaven : Hell : : Drought : ?
A. Famine   B. Water
C. Flood   D. Crop

32. Sun : Planet : : Earth : ?
A. Satellite   B. Sun
C. Moon   D. Light

33. French : France : : Dutch : ?
A. Hungary   B. Holland
C. Sea   D. Hiroshima

34. Sri Lanka : Colombo : : Japan : ?
A. Island   B. Tokyo
C. Hiroshima   D. Bomb

35. Pen : Write : : Carpenter's Plane : ?
A. Tear   B. Repair
C. Pierce   D. Shave off

36. Thick : Thin : : Inferior : ?
A. Rough   B. Spurious
C. Beautiful   D. Superior

37. Table : Wood : : Book : ?
A. Pages   B. Paper
C. Teach   D. Student

38. Fan : Air : : Bulb : ?
A. Brightness   B. Electricity
C. Switch   D. Light

39. Seven : Number : : Green : ?
A. Colour   B. Forest
C. Field   D. Red

40. Stage : Drama : : Stadium : ?
A. Sports   B. Circus
C. Wedding   D. Convention

41. Fruit : Mango : : Serpent : ?
A. Cobra
B. Poison
C. Creature
D. Hood of a Cobra

42. Rain : Centimeter : : Tempera- ture : ?
A. Celsius   B. Weather
C. Sun   D. Heat

43. Road : Lane : : City : ?
A. Town   B. Metropolis
C. Highway   D. Capital

44. Aspirin : Headache : : Quinine : ?
A. Hepatitis   B. Malaria
C. Influenza   D. Cough

45. Hunger : Food : : Thirst : ?
A. Tap   B. River
C. Water   D. Sweat

46. Cat : Kitten : : Hen : ?
A. Bird   B. Cock
C. Feed   D. Chicken

47. Fruit : Banana : : Mammal : ?
A. Cow   B. Heron
C. Fly   D. Plant

48. Radio : Listener : : Film : ?
A. Camera   B. Actor
C. Viewer   D. Talky

49. Money : Exchange : : Language : ?
A. Write
B. Communication
C. Knowledge
D. Book

50. Friend : Enemy : : Kind : ?
A. Diety   B. Demon
C. Anger   D. Cruel

51. Train : Platform : : Ship : ?
A. Anchor   B. Harbour
C. Ocean   D. Island

52. 1st April : Fool : : 1st May : ?
A. Teacher   B. Doctor
C. Labour   D. Disabled

53. Time : Clock : : Rain : ?
A. Cloud   B. Raingauge
C. Centimeter   D. Barometer

54. Lion : Den : : Horse : ?
A. Stable   B. *Tonga*
C. Chariot   D. Stake

55. Book : Pages : : Flower : ?
A. Bouquet   B. Buds
C. Colour   D. Petals

56. Tea : Leaves : : Coffee : ?
A. Roots   B. Flowers
C. Bark   D. Seeds

57. Horse : Neigh : : Donkey : ?
A. Trumpet   B. Roar
C. Bray   D. Snarl

58. Car : Garage : : Aircraft : ?
A. Sky   B. Hanger
C. Aerodrome   D. Engine

59. Radius : Circle : : Spokes : ?
A. Wheel   B. Table
C. Bus   D. Matchbox

60. Stool : Carpenter : : Shoes : ?
A. Cobbler   B. Foot
C. Leather   D. Polish

61. Bus : Workshop : : Ship : ?
A. Harbour   B. Yard
C. Dockyard   D. Hanger

62. Ring : Finger : : Tie : ?
A. Coat   B. Neck
C. Collar   D. Waist

63. Sew : Needle : : Paint : ?
A. Colour   B. Brush
C. Canvas   D. Landscape

64. Nose : Smell : : Tongue : ?
A. Lick   B. Taste
C. Speak   D. Mouth

65. Pencil : Stationery : : Chair : ?
A. Carpenter   B. Wood
C. Table   D. Furniture

66. Cat : Dog : : Cow : ?
A. Goat   B. Lion
C. Tiger   D. Wolf

67. Snake : Lizard : : Fish : ?
A. Cow   B. Dog
C. Cat   D. Crocodile

68. Honour : Dishonour : : Fame : ?
A. Respected   B. Glorious
C. Infamy   D. Glory

69. Light : Rays : : Sound : ?
A. Ear   B. Wave
C. Velocity   D. Echo

70. Clock : Hand : : Thermometer : ?
A. Temperature   B. Fever
C. Mercury   D. Patient

71. Tractor : Diesel : : Scooter : ?
A. Wheel   B. Petrol
C. Power   D. Engine

72. Cuckoo : Cackle : : Horse : ?
A. Bray   B. Neigh
C. Hiss   D. Roar

73. Pitch : Cricket : : Ring : ?
A. Wrestling   B. Boxing
C. Hockey   D. Badminton

74. Car : Run : : Snake : ?
A. Run   B. Bite
C. Creep   D. Hiss

75. Urge : Deter : : Honest : ?
A. Dishonest   B. *Thug*
C. Robber   D. Cheat

76. Lion : Den : : Bird : ?
A. Tree   B. Chrip
C. Nest   D. Ruins

77. Calf : Cow : : Lamb : ?
A. Wolf   B. Flesh
C. Goat   D. Sheep

78. Obedience : Disobedience : : Life : ?
A. Salvation   B. Death
C. Heaven   D. Universe

79. Tailor : Cloth : : Carpenter : ?
A. Machine   B. Wood
C. Saw   D. Table

80. Cat : Rat : : Tiger : ?
A. Lamb   B. Lizard
C. Crow   D. Fish

81. Bakery : Bread : : Mint : ?
A. Cheque   B. Coin
C. Note   D. Cake

82. Studio : Film : : Shipyard : ?
A. Ship   B. Trawler
C. Boat   D. Net

83. Month : Year : : Hour : ?
A. Day   B. Week
C. Minute   D. Second

84. Food : Hunger : : Water : ?
A. Bath   B. Irrigation
C. Thirst   D. Rain

85. Revolver : Bullet : : Bow : ?
A. Sword   B. Club
C. Arrow   D. Pistol

86. Honey : Bee : : Wool : ?
A. Goat   B. Horse
C. Hare   D. Sheep

FINDING THE ODD ONE OUT

In these questions four pairs of words or four words are given and one of them is odd or does not belong to the class. You have to find out that odd pair/word. Two examples are given below:

Example 1.

A. Wood-Chair
B. Water-Ice
C. Milk-Cheese
D. Teacher-Student

Solution: Chair is made of Wood, Ice is made of Water, Cheese is made of Milk. But Student is never made of Teacher. Therefore, the odd pair is D. That is your answer.

Example 2.

A. Bihar
B. Gujarat
C. West Bengal
D. Calcutta

Solution: A, B and C are names of States. D is the name of a city. Therefore, D is odd. That is your answer.

QUESTIONS FOR PRACTICE

Directions: *In the following questions, find the odd one out.*

1. A. Man-Woman
   B. Brother-Sister
   C. Father-Son
   D. Father-Mother

2. A. Fish-Water
   B. Water-River
   C. Coal-Mine
   D. Bird-Tree

3. A. Hospital-Doctor
   B. Court-Advocate
   C. Thief-Robber
   D. School-Teacher

4. A. Milk-Curd
   B. Brick-House
   C. Paper-Book
   D. Horse-Stable

5. A. Milk-White
   B. Leaf-Green
   C. Sky-Blue
   D. Blood-Red

6. A. Victory-Defeat
   B. Carrot-Radish
   C. North-South
   D. Up-Down

7. A. Mouse-Hole
   B. Bird-Nest
   C. Horse-Stable
   D. Tiger-Forest

8. A. Blue-Sky
   B. Red-Kite
   C. Blue-*Saree*
   D. Black-Horse

9. A. Father-Son
   B. Needle-Thread
   C. Cup-Plate
   D. Chair-Table

10. A. Well-Canal
    B. River-Mountain
    C. Lake-Sea
    D. Gulf-Desert

11. A. Book-Note Book
    B. Rubber-Pencil
    C. Nose-Ear
    D. Leg-Bone
12. A. Friend-Foe
    B. Rich-Poor
    C. Kind-Cruel
    D. Games-Sports
13. A. Fire-Smoke
    B. Sun-Heat
    C. Moonlight-Cool
    D. Paper-White
14. A. Mars   B. Jupiter
    C. Venus   D. Moon
15. A. Grape   B. Raisin
    C. Apple   D. Mango
16. A. Wolf   B. Jackal
    C. Goat   D. Bear
17. A. *Riksha* B. Bus
    C. Car   D. Scooter
18. A. Tiger   B. Horse
    C. Elephant D. Camel
19. A. Monkey
    B. Mongoose
    C. Snake
    D. Cat
20. A. Kanpur   B. Lucknow
    C. Patna   D. Allahabad
21. A. Yen   B. Dollar
    C. Coin   D. Pound
22. A. Diamond   B. Mercury
    C. Iron   D. Copper
23. A. Legs   B. Hands
    C. Ankles   D. Lungs
24. A. Steamer   B. Boat
    C. Ship   D. Harbour
25. A. Rose   B. Lotus
    C. Dahlia   D. Jasmin
26. A. Proteins
    B. Carbohydrates
    C. Copper
    D. Vitamins
27. A. Piano   B. Tabla
    C. Flute   D. Banjo
28. A. Metre
    B. Kilometre
    C. Centimetre
    D. Square Kilometre
29. A. Cat   B. Dog
    C. Monkey   D. Snake
30. A. Snake   B. Lizard
    C. Crocodile D. Frog
31. A. Mercury   B. Earth
    C. Moon   D. Jupiter
32. A. Pencil
    B. Rubber
    C. Ink
    D. Sketch Map
33. A. The Statesman
    B. India Today
    C. The Hindu
    D. The Amrit Bazar Patrika
34. A. Ashoka
    B. Chanakya
    C. Chandra Gupta
    D. Harsh Vardhana
35. A. Tangent
    B. Arc
    C. Radius
    D. Hypotenuse

36.	A.	Delhi	B.	Patna
	C.	Mumbai	D.	Calcutta
37.	A.	Bicycle	B.	Scooter
	C.	Car	D.	Bus
38.	A.	Wheat	B.	Gram
	C.	Ragi	D.	Rice
39.	A.	Iron	B.	Copper
	C.	Steel	D.	Tin
40.	A.	Cancer	B.	Hepatitis
	C.	Bile	D.	Diabetes
41.	A.	Water	B.	Wind
	C.	Gasoline	D.	Soil
42.	A.	Cotton	B.	Rice
	C.	Tea	D.	Jute
43.	A.	Apple	B.	Banana
	C.	Sugarcane	D.	Mango
44.	A.	Dhaka	B.	Colombo
	C.	Karachi	D.	Rangoon
45.	A.	May	B.	March
	C.	April	D.	July
46.	A.	Rouble	B.	Diet
	C.	Dollar	D.	Taka
47.	A.	Libra	B.	Uranus
	C.	Pluto	D.	Neptune
48.	A.	Temple		
	B.	Monastery		
	C.	Mosque		
	D.	Church		
49.	A.	Ounce	B.	Shilling
	C.	Gram	D.	Pound
50.	A.	Shield	B.	Armour
	C.	Sword	D.	Helmet
51.	A.	Ganga	B.	Godavari
	C.	Krishna	D.	Narmada
52.	A.	Cataract	B.	Cornea

	C.	Retina	D.	Iris
53.	A.	Bigger	B.	Greater
	C.	Faster	D.	Larger
54.	A.	Fox	B.	Cow
	C.	Dog	D.	Horse
55.	A.	Jackal	B.	Fox
	C.	Stag	D.	Wolf
56.	A.	Father	B.	Teacher
	C.	Brother	D.	Sister
57.	A.	Shore	B.	Sea
	C.	River	D.	Pond
58.	A.	Moan	B.	Wail
	C.	Weep	D.	Sorrow
59.	A.	Eagle	B.	Crow
	C.	Vulture	D.	Cock
60.	A.	Dwarf	B.	Slender
	C.	Fat	D.	Lame
61.	A.	Mother	B.	Daughter
	C.	Son	D.	Aunt
62.	A.	Eye	B.	Ear
	C.	Neck	D.	Tooth
63.	A.	Tamil Nadu		
	B.	Kerala		
	C.	Karnataka		
	D.	Pondicherry		
64.	A.	Wing Commander		
	B.	Pilot Officer		
	C.	Colonel		
	D.	Flight Lieutenant		
65.	A.	Veena		
	B.	Sitar		
	C.	Sarod		
	D.	Mridangam		
66.	A.	Africa	B.	Asia
	C.	Arabia	D.	America

<table>
<tr><td>67.</td><td>A. Shark</td><td>B. Seal</td></tr>
<tr><td></td><td>C. Whale</td><td>D. Crocodile</td></tr>
</table>

68. A. Square
B. Trapezium
C. Rectangle
D. Diagonal

69. A. Cat B. Dog
C. Fox D. Monkey

71. A. Potatoes
B. Tomatoes
C. Groundnuts
D. Onions

72. A. Influenza
B. Tuberculosis
C. Smallpox
D. Malaria

73. A. Bunglow B. Office
C. Hut D. House

74. A. Fly B. Sweets
C. *Kheer* D. *Gur*

75. A. Root B. Trunk
C. Stem D. Leaves

76. A. Brinjal
B. Potato
C. Beans
D. Lady Finger

77. A. Dog B. Crow
C. Cow D. Goat

78. A. C.V. Raman
B. Meghnad Saha
C. Kalidas
D. Dr. Bhabha

79. A. Pant B. Shirt
C. Shoes D. *Pajama*

80. A. Hydrogen B. Nitrogen
C. Oxygen D. Mercury

QUESTIONS RELATING TO CLOCKS AND CALENDARS

These questions are related to students' knowledge of Clock and days of week. They also involve their knowledge of directions of the hands of the clocks at various times as well as the angle between the two hands of the clock.

CLOCKS

Example: When it is 15 minutes past 12,

(i) What is the angle between the two hands of the clock?

(ii) What is the direction of the hour hand of the clock at that time?

Solution: 15 minutes past 12, is the time when the minute hand is pointing at 3 while the hour hand has just crossed 12. See the illustration below:

Therefore,

(i) The angle between the two hands of the clock is 90°.

(ii) The hour hand is pointed upwards toward 12, *i.e.,* towards north.

Remember:

(i) The sum total of all the angles at the centre of the clock is 360°.

(ii) The dial of the clock is divided into 12 equal parts.

$$\therefore \ \frac{360°}{12} = 30°$$

That the angle formed between each and every two numbers on the dial is always 30°.

(iii) The direction of the hands of the clock is indicated in the following manner:

(a) upside (where 12 is written) is always the north.

(b) down below (where 6 is written) is always the south.

(c) The right side (where 3 is written) is always the east.

(d) The left side (where 9 is written) is always west.

Another Example: When it is 5 o'clock, what is the angle between the two hands of the clock.

Solution: At 5 o'clock:

(i) the hour hand will point at 5

(ii) the minute hand will point at 12.

See the illustration below:

The two hands are 5 numbers apart

$\therefore$ 30° x 5 = 150°

$\therefore$ The angle between the two hands of the clock will be 150°.

Remember that in every hour:

(i) both the hands meet **once**.

(ii) The hands are straight pointing in opposite directions only **once**.

(iii) the hand make right angles **twice**.

(iv) the minute hand moves through an angle of 6° in **one minute**.

CALENDAR

Questions based on calendars are easy to solve.

Example 1: In a particular month, 17th was Friday. Then:

(i) What will be the date on the next Friday?

(ii) What was the date on the previous Friday?

Solution: We know that there are seven days in a week. If 17th of the month was Friday, then the day falling after 7 days (*i.e.,* 17 + 7 = 24), *i.e.,* the 24th will be Friday. Similarly, 17th being Friday, therefore the day falling 7 days before (*i.e.*, 17 – 7 = 10) *i.e.*, 10th should have been Friday.

Example 2: In a particular year, 20th August was Monday. On which day 3rd September will fall in that year?

Solution: August has 31 days. If 20th August was Monday, the next Monday will fall on 27th August. So, 31st August will be on Friday and accordingly, 1st September on Saturday and 3rd September will fall on Monday.

Months which have only 30 days: April, June, September and November

Months which have 31 days: January, March, May, July, August, October and December.

February has only 28 days. Every four years February has 28 + 1 = 29 days. Such a year is called Leap Year.

QUESTIONS FOR PRACTICE

1. If yesterday was Sunday, after how many days the next Sunday will come?

A. 7   B. 6
C. 5   D. 8

2. In a particular month, two days after Monday was the 5th (date), on which day will the 19th (date) of the same month fall?

A. Tuesday   B. Monday
C. Sunday   D. Friday

3. How many times between 4 o'clock afternoon and 10 o'clock night, the two hands of a clock are at right angles?

A. 14   B. 10
C. 12   D. 8

4. If 14th April in a particular year was Thursday. The first Thursday in May of that very year will fall on which date?

A. 3rd May   B. 4th May
C. 5th May   D. 6th May

5. If two days before January 11 was Monday, then the next Monday in the same month will fall on:

A. January 16   B. January 18
C. January 17   D. January 15

6. If February 28 was Tuesday in a particular year, the 5th February in that very year was on:

A. Friday   B. Sunday
C. Saturday   D. Monday

7. If 3 days after Monday was 11th (date) of the month, what day was there on the 22nd (date) of the same month?

A. Friday   B. Monday
C. Sunday   D. Saturday

8. In a particular year the 31st March was Tuesday. On which date was the first Sunday of March in that very year?

A. 1st March   B. 3rd March
C. 2nd March   D. 4th March

9. February 3 was Friday in a particular year. The last Sunday of February in that year will fall on?

A. February 25   B. February 26
C. February 27   D. February 28

10. If July 19 is Tuesday in a particular year, on what day will August 15 fall in that very year?

A. Friday   B. Monday
C. Sunday   D. Saturday

11. At 2 PM, the hands of a clock will make an angle of:

A. 60°   B. 45°
C. 30°   D. 80°

12. During a period of 12 hours, how many times the hands of a clock are at right angles?

A. 22   B. 24
C. 23   D. 25

13. During a day (24 hours), on how many occasions, both the hands of a clock are in a straight line?

A. 23   B. 12
C. 24   D. 22

14. At 4 AM, the hands of the clock will make an angle of:

A. 90°   B. 110°
C. 120°   D. 130°

15. At 25 minutes past 3, the hands of the clock will make an angle of:

A. 90°   B. 60°
C. 30°   D. 45°

16. At 5 minutes past 3, the hands of a clock will make an angle of:

A. 60°   B. 30°
C. 90°   D. 45°

17. At 9 o'clock, the hour hand of the clock will be facing towards:

A. East   B. West
C. North   D. South

18. At 10 minutes past 9, the hands of a clock will make an angle of:

A. 120°   B. 150°
C. 180°   D. 100°

19. A boy looks at the clock and tells the time as 15 minutes past 5. In doing so, he committed the mistake of treating the hour hand as minute hand and vice-versa. What was the correct time in the clock?

A. 15 minutes past 3
B. 20 minutes past 3
C. 25 minutes past 3
D. 10 minutes past 3

20. What will be the time when both the hands of the clock coincide (one over the other) and face towards the west?

A. 9 o'clock
B. 30 minutes past 8
C. 45 minutes past 8
D. 15 minutes past 8

CODING AND DECODING

In a code language the coded letters or numbers are not what they appear but they represent some other pre-determined letter or number. Coding implies use of some letter or number in a systematic way to represent another letter or number.

Decoding means resolving the system involved in a code. In other words decoding means finding out the original letter or number for which coded letters or numbers have been used.

Coding is done on a systematic way. If we are able to discover this system, we can decode.

To explain it further, we shall take some examples.

Suppose MARKET is coded as NBSLFU. In this case, for each alphabet in MARKET, certain other alphabets namely NBSLFU have been used.

Now if you are asked to find out the code for TEAM (on the basis of MARKET coded as NBSLFU), you can do it without much difficulty. You will find that all the letters in TEAM, *i.e.,* T, E, A and M occur in MARKET. To find out the code for TEAM arrange MARKET with its code in the following manner

M A R K E T
N B S L F U

You can find that N is for M, B is for A, S is for R and so on.

You also find that U is for T, F is for E, B is for A and N is for M.

∴ UFBN is for TEAM

∴ Code for TEAM is UFBN.

Similarly, you can find the code for RAT, TEA, MARK, TAKE, EAT, ARM etc. Codes for these will be as under:

RAT = SBU
TEA = UFB
MARK = NBSL
TAKE = UBLF
EAT = FBU
ARM = BSN

Now, we take another example. If EIGHT is coded as CGEFR, then SPOT will be coded as?

For finding out the code for SPOT, we shall follow the following method:

```
        1     3 4 2
A B (C) D (E)(F)(G) H I J K L (M)
              5
(N) O P (Q)(R) S T U V W X Y Z
3 2         1 4
            1 2 3 4 5
```

EIGHT are marked E I G H T, and C G E F R an marked (C)(G)(E)(F)(R)

The pattern above makes clear that one letter has been skipped anti-clockwise at each step while coding.

Therefore, now apply the same formula to find out the code for SPOT.

Mark SPOT as S P O T . Skip one
          1 2 3 4
letter anti-clockwise at each step to find

(Q)(N)(M)(R) or Q N M R

∴ SPOT will be coded as QNMR.

In such questions, mark the expression and its code (as given in the question) in the alphabets (as shown above) to find the clue. Then apply the clue to find the code (as directed in the question).

QUESTIONS FOR PRACTICE

Directions: *In each of the following questions a coded expression is given. Then another expression is given, the code for which is to be found from*

amongst the four choices suggested below.

1. If COME is coded as BNLD, then CARE will be coded as:

A. BBQD B. BZQD
C. BZPD D. BZSD

2. If HIGH is coded as IJHI, then TURN will be coded as:

A. UVQO B. UVTO
C. UVSO D. UVSP

3. If LOAD is coded as MPBE, then PORT will be coded as:

A. QRSU B. QPRU
C. QPUS D. QPSU

4. If GOLD is coded as IQNF, then WIND will be coded as:

A. YKOF B. YLPF
C. YKPE D. YKPF

5. If SHIRT is coded as RGHQS, then ROUND will be coded as:

A. QNTMC B. QNUMC
C. QNTME D. QNTOC

6. If DEAR is coded as FGCT, then READ will be coded as:

A. FGCF B. TGFC
C. TCGF D. TGCF

7. If EASE is coded as HDVH, then SEE will be coded as:

A. DHH B. VHV
C. VHH D. VVH

8. If SERPENT is coded as TNEPRES, then PLAGUE will be coded as:

A. EUAGLP B. EUGLAP
C. EUGALP D. EULAGP

9. If DEFENCE is coded as CDEDMBD, then NEED will be coded as:

A. MCDC B. MCCD
C. MDDC D. DMMC

10. If CHAIR is coded as FKDLU, then RAID will be coded as:

A. ULGD B. ULKG
C. ULDG D. UDLG

11. If CONDEMN is coded as CNODMEN, then TEACHER will be coded as:

A. TAECHER B. TAEECHR
C. TCAEEHR D. TAECEHR

12. In a code language COME is written as 'XLNV' and ABLE as ZYOV, how would you write MOLLY in that code?

A. NLOBO B. NLBOO
C. LNOOB D. NLOOB

13. If CIGARETTE is coded as GICERAETT, then the word DEMONSTRATION is coded as:

A. MEDNSOARTOITN

B. MEDSNOATROITN

C. MEDSNOARTIOTN

D. MEDSNOARTOITN

14. If CENTURION is coded as 325791465, and RANK is coded as 18510, what will the figures 78510 represent?

A. BANK B. SANK
C. TANK D. TALK

15. In a certain code MAHESH is written as NCIGTJ. In that code NEELAM will be written as:

A. OGGNCO B. OGFNBN
C. OGFNBO D. OGHBNO

16. In a certain code FLOWER is written as SEXOMF. How will garden be written in that code?

A. OEERBH B. OFESBH
C. OEESBG D. OEERBG

17. If in a code SCRIPT is written as TCQIQT, how will DIGEST be written in that code?

A. EIGHTT B. TIHETT
C. EIFETT D. EIFERT

18. If RAM is coded as SBN, then FEW will be coded as:

A. GFX B. GHX
C. EFX D. GEX

19. If RUBBER is coded as REBBUR, then DEAD will be coded as:

A. DEAD B. DAED
C. DADE D. DDEA

20. If KANPUR is coded as LBOQVS, then NAGPUR will be coded as:

A. OHBQVS B. HBOQVS
C. OBHQVS D. BOHQVS

21. If DELHI is coded as IDHEL, then TUFAN will be coded as:

A. TNAUF B. NATUF
C. NTUAF D. NTAUF

22. If ANOTHER is coded as 7309521, then THORN will be coded as:

A. 95103 B. 95313
C. 95013 D. 95113

23. If SURENDRA is coded as DHTNPATI, then UNDER will be coded as:

A. PHANT B. HPANT
C. HPNAT D. HNPAT

24. If EFFICIENT is coded as DEEHBHDMS, then FIET will be coded as:

ed as:

A. DHES B. EHSD
C. EHDS D. EDHS

25. If FACE is coded as GBDF, then BADE will be coded as:

A. CBEF B. CEBF
C. CFBE D. CBFE

26. If REST is coded as TGUV, then SETS will be coded as:

A. GUVU B. UVGU
C. UGVU D. VGUV

27. If DECADE is coded as 453145, then DEED will be coded as:

A. 5544 B. 4545
C. 4554 D. 4555

28. If BAD is coded as YZW, then MAD will be coded as:

A. MZW B. NZW
C. OZW D. LZW

29. If DIRT is coded as TDIR, then TRIM will be coded as:

A. MRTI B. MIRT
C. MTRI D. MTIR

30. If PIT is coded as QJU, then HUT will be coded as:

A. KXU B. KVU
C. IVU D. GVU

31. If DECEMBER is coded as ERMBCEDE, then NOVEMBER will be coded as:

A. ERBMVENO
B. REMBVENO
C. ERMBVENO
D. EMRBVENO

32. If ROUGH is coded as ORRJE, how will SMOOTH be coded?

A. PPLLOK B. PPLRQK

C. PJLLOK   D. PPRRKK

33. If MOTHER is coded as PQWJHT, then SISTER will be coded as:
A. VKUVHT   B. VKVVHU
C. VKVVHT   D. VKVWHT

34. If LOFTY is coded as LPFUY, then DWARF will be coded as:
A. DXASF   B. DXBSG
C. DXATF   D. DWBSG

35. If PRICE is coded as SVNIL, then COST will be coded as:
A. FSXY   B. FSWY
C. FTWZ   D. FSXZ

36. If JAILAPPAS is coded as AIJAPLASP, then ECONOMICS will be coded as:
A. COEMONCSI
B. COEOMNCSI
C. OECMONSCI
D. COEMONCSI

37. If in a certain code CLOCK is written as KCOLC, then STEPS will be written as:
A. SPEST   B. SPSET
C. SEPST   D. SPETS

38. If in a certain code SPIDER is written as PSDIRE, then COMMON will be written as:
A. OCMMON   B. OCMOMN
C. OCMMNO   D. OCOMMO

39. In a certain code RECOMMEN-DATION is written as COMMENDA-TIONER, then REMUNERATION will be written as:
A. MUNERATION
B. MUNERATIONRE
C. MUNERATIONER
D. MUNERATIOENR

40. If in a certain code TRIPPLE is written as SQHOOKD, then DISPOSE will be written as:
A. CHRONRD   B. CHROORD
C. CHROMRD   D. CHROMSD

QUESTIONS BASED ON RELATIONSHIP

In these questions, one is required to find out relationship between/among persons such as whose father is A, who is A's father, or what is the relationship between A and B etc. These questions are not very difficult but somewhat involoved.

We shall take some examples to explain how to solve such questions.

Example 1. A is father of both B and C. B is not the brother of C. What relationship exists between B and C?

Solution: When both B and C are children of A, and B is not the brother of C, then only possible relationship between B and C is that one of them is the sister of the other.

Example 2. C is nephew of B. A is husband of B. How is A related to C?

Solution: C is nephew of B. A and B are husband and wife. Therefore, C must be nephew of both A and B.

∴ C is nephew of A too.

And, A is uncle of C.

QUESTIONS FOR PRACTICE

1. Ajit is brother of grandson of Mohan. What is Ajit in relation to Mohan?
A. grandfather   B. grandson
C. son   D. nephew

2. B is A's son. B is my son's uncle. Then A is my:
A. uncle   B. grandfather
C. father   D. brother

3. F is A's brother; C is A's daughter; K is F's sister and G is C's brother. Who is uncle of G?
A. A   B. C
C. K   D. F

4. The brother-in-law of the nephew of my wife will be my:
A. son-in-law   B. nephew
C. cousin   D. brother-in-law

5. Ramesh is Bihari's brother. Indira is Ramesh's wife and her son Devendra is brother of Yogendra. Bihari is Yogendra's:
A. father   B. uncle
C. brother   D. maternal uncle

6. Both A and B are C's children. C is A's father but B is not C's son. Then B is C's:
A. brother   B. sister
C. daughter   D. son

7. My maternal uncle is A and his son is B. C is B's son. Then I am C's:
A. grandfather   B. uncle
C. brother   D. nephew

8. Ram Bihari had three sons—Ram, Pratap and Kripa. Vijai is Ram's son and Veena is Pratap's daughter. Then Vijai is Veena's:
A. uncle   B. cousin brother
C. nephew

9. K is P's sister's daughter. S is K's son. Then P is S's:
A. maternal uncle
B. maternal grandfather
C. father's sister's husband
D. grandfather

10. A is C's father. B is C's wife. Then A is B's:
A. husband's elder brother
B. husband's younger brother
C. father-in-law
D. son

QUESTIONS RELATED TO DIRECTIONS

These questions are related to directions. They are easy for solutions. Students are advised to pin-point on a piece of paper the starting-point. Then they should draw lines as directed (indicated) in the question. Thus, they will have a diagram (figure) of the movement. It will thus be easy to find the direction from the starting-point.

Example. Ramesh starts from his house and goes to the east. After covering 4 km, he turns to right and covers 2 km. Then he turns to right again and covers 4 km. In which direction now Ramesh is from his house?

Solution:

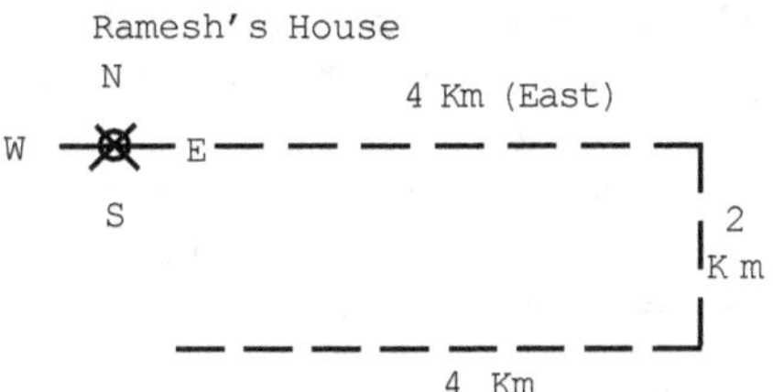

The above diagram indicates that he is now in the south from his house.

QUESTIONS FOR PRACTICE

1. Deepa starts from her house and goes 1 km towards north; then she turns to right and walks 1 km. She turns again to right and walks 1 km to reach her school. In which direction from her house is her school situated?

A. North   B. East
C. South   D. West

2. My house is situated to the east of your house. My friend's house is situated to the south-east of your house. To which direction should I go to reach my friend's house through the shortest route?

A. South   B. South-West
C. South-East   D. West

3. A person starts walking towards north. After sometime he turns to right and after walking some distance he turns to left. Then after walking the distance of 1 km, he turns again to left. To which direction is he walking now?

A. North   B. East
C. South   D. West

4. A person goes 200 m towards west from his house. Then he goes 500 m towards south. To which direction should he now walk for returning to the place from where he started his journey?

A. North-East   B. North
C. South-East   D. North-West

5. A person went towards west from his house and covered a distance of 5 km. Then he turned to left and covered 5 km. He, then, turned to right and covered 9 km. And finally he covered 5 km towards north. In which direction is he now from his starting-point?

A. South-West   B. South
C. West   D. East

6. A police van drove 5 km towards the east. Then it turned to right and travelled 3 km. After that it turned towards the west and covered a distance of 1 km. How many kms away is the van from its starting point?

A. 3 km   B. 4 km
C. 5 km   D. 6 km

7. Standing at the door of a room a policeman saw a wall-clock on the wall facing him, a sofa set near the wall on his right and a TV set near the wall on his left. He also saw rays on his left. He also saw rays of the setting sun falling on the wall-clock. The sofa set was near the:

A. eastern wall

B. western wall

C. northern wall

D. southern wall

8. On a straight road a police van chased a car upto 4 km towards the east. The car turned to right and was chased by the police van for 2 km. The car again turned to right and was caught by the police van after a 2 km chase. In which direction was the police van now from its starting point?

A. North-East   B. North-West
C. South-East   D. South-West

9. Dara is to the east of Vorli at a distance of 10 km. Towards the north is Madu situated at a distance of about 7 km from the above mentioned two places. A police van on patrol duty was proceeding towards Vorli from Dara. While on midway it was instructed to intercept a car that was speeding away from Dara to Madu. To which direction thte patrol van turn to intercept the speeding car?

A. East   B. West
C. North   D. South

10. A person travelled 12 km towards the north. Then he turned to left and travelled 5 km. How many kms is he away from his starting-point?

A. 14 km   B. 13 km

C. 12 km   D. 13.5 km

11. Shyam starts from his house and goes 5 km towards the east. He then turns to right and covers a distance of 5 km. He again turns to right and covers a distance of 5 km. In which direction is he now from his house?

A. East   B. West
C. North   D. South

12. A person started from his house and travelled 1 km towards the north. Then he turned to right and travelled 2 km. He again turned to right and travelled 1 km. How far is he from his house?

A. 1 km   B. 2 km
C. 3 km   D. 4 km

13. Ramesh starts from his house and goes 4 km towards the east. Then he turns to left and goes 3 km. He further turns to right and goes 1 km. He, then turns to left and goes 2 km and again turns to left and goes 5 km. In which direction is he now from his house?

A. East   B. West
C. North   D. South

ARRANGING THE LETTERS TO MAKE MEANINGFUL WORDS

In these questions, some letters are given in a haphazard manner. The students are required to rearrange those letters to make a meaningful word.

Example. Arrange the letters KOBO in such a way as to make a meaningful word.

Solution: These letters may be arranged in various forms such as KOOB, KBOO, OBOK, OKBO, BOKO and BOOK. Of these only BOOK is a meaningful word. Therefore, it is the correct answer.

In some questions, a particular direction may be included, such as arrange the letters in such a way as to make the name of an animal, fruit, vehicle, city, etc.

Example. Arrange the letters EORHS to make the name of an animal.

Solution: When arranged in right order, it will be HORSE.

QUESTIONS FOR PRACTICE

1. Arrange the letters EBUL in such a way as to make the name of a colour.

2. Arrange the letters CINHOC in such a way as to make the name of a city.

3. Arrange the letters UDUR in such a way as to make the name of an Indian language.

4. Arrange the letters NIOR in such a way as to make the name of a metal.

5. Arrange the letters CEAOCPK in such a way as to make the name of a bird.

6. Arrange the letters MANRADA in such a way as to make the name of a river.

7. Arrange the letters RHATE in such a way as to make the name of a planet.

8. Arrange the letters NIPELC in such a way as to make the name of an item of stationery.

9. Arrange the letters IRTEG in such a way as to make the name of a wild animal.

10. Arrange the letters COHYKE in such a way as to make the name of a sport.

11. Arrange the letters RISHT in such a way as to make the name of a wear.

12. Arrange the letters GNMAO in such a way as to make the name of a fruit.

13. Arrange the letters IERC in such a way as to make the name of a foodgrain.

14. Arrange the letters RAGA in such a way as to make the name of a city.

15. Arrange the letters AIRHC in such a way as to make the name of an item of furniture.

16. Arrange the letters NADH in such a way as to make the name of a part of human body.

17. Arrange the letters GIRN in such a way as to make the name of an ornament.

18. Arrange the letters LITMA in such a way as to make the name of the language of a State in India.

19. Arrange the letters MENE in such a way as to make the name of tree.

20. Arrange the letters IRATN in such a way as to make the name of a vehicle (transport).

21. Arrange the letters APUBJN in such a way as to make the name of a State in India.

22. Arrange the letters TCKEICR in such a way as to make the name of a sport.

23. Arrange the letters TERLPO in such a way as to make the name of a fuel.

24. Arrange the letters RIGOUT in such a way as to make the name of a musical instrument.

25. Arrange the letters BYBA in such a way as to make the name of a word representing infants.

26. Arrange the letters DEKYIN in such a way as to make the name of a part of body.

27. Arrange the letters UGOENT in such a way as to make the name of a part of the mouth.

28. Arrange the letters NKODYE in such a way as to make the name of an animal.

29. Arrange the letters ARINHSK in such a way as to make the name of a river.

30. Arrange the letters IDASLAK in such a way as to make the name of a classical Sanskrit poet.

31. Arrange the letters HAIKS in such a way as to make the name of a place of pilgrimage.

32. Arrange the letters RAISP in such a way as to make the name of capital of an European country.

33. Arrange the letters ROPEPC in such a way as to make the name of a metal.

34. Arrange the letters PRAEG in such a way as to make the name of a fruit.

35. Arrange the letters ARNAYMA in such a way as to make the name of an Indian epic.

36. Arrange the letters BRAAK in such a way as to make the name of a Mughal ruler of India.

37. Arrange the letters ABMUR in such a way as to make the name of a neighbour country of India.

38. Arrange the letters TACWH in such a way as to make the name of a machine that tells time.

39. Arrange the letters JNALRIB in such a way as to make the name of a vegetable.

40. Arrange the letters GOEYNX in such a way as to make the name of a gas.

ARRANGING WORDS IN THEIR NATURAL ORDER

In these questions, some words are given. They are to be arranged in their natural order. The arrangement may be, as required in the ascending order, descending order or alphabetical order (as used in dictionary). Sometimes the arrangement has to be made in such order as the things, activities happen in nature or in one's life, *i.e.,* brushing the teeth, breakfast, bath, lunch.

We shall have some examples.

Example 1. Which one of the following words will come in the first place if they are arranged in the manner as in a dictionary.

CAT, CAME, CAR, CAN

A. CAT   B. CAN

C. CAME   D. CAR

Solution: If arranged as required these words (given in the above example) will appear in the following order:

CAME, CAN, CAR, CAT.

Example 2. Which one of the following will come at the end in the natural order:

A. Printing   B. Book
C. Binding   D. Paper

In the natural order these items will appear as: Paper, Printing, Binding and Book.

QUESTIONS FOR PRACTICE

1. Which one is the smallest?
A. Lane   B. Caste
C. Family   D. Town

2. Which one of the followoing came into existence before others?
A. Caste   B. Community
C. Family   D. Clan

3. Which one of the following came into existence first?
A. Wood   B. Chair
C. Seed   D. Tree

4. Which one will come first in the natural order?
A. Shirt   B. Stitching
C. Cloth   D. Cutting

5. Which one will come first in the natural order?
A. Sugar   B. *Khand*
C. Jaggery   D. Sugarcane

6. Which one of the following will come last in the ascending order?
A. Adolscence B. Adulthood
C. Old age   D. Childhood

7. Which will come in the third place from the top?
A. Eyes   B. Waist
C. Knees   D. Legs

8. Which one of the following will come first in the regular order?
A. College   B. University
C. School   D. Nursery

9. Which one of the following is the first vital requirement for life?
A. Food   B. Water
C. Vitamins   D. Air

10. The first thing while crossing the road is:
A. look around B. stop
C. go   D. speed up

MISCELLANEOUS

1. Vipin is taller than Ram Lal. Ram Lal is not as tall as Ahmad. Mahendra is taller than Sheikh, but not as tall as Ram Lal. Ahmad is not as tall as Vipin is. Who is the shortest among them?
A. Vipin   B. Ahmad
C. Ram Lal   D. Sheikh
E. Mahendra

2. School is situated to the west of the hospital which is south to the police post. The court is to the north of the school. If the four places are at the equal distance from each other, the police post is situated to the:

A. East of the court
B. West of the court
C. North of the court
D. South of the court

3. Roads from the north, south, east and west directions meet near a police post. A constable coming on the road from the east finds that the road in front of him leads to a park and the road towards his right leads to the railway station and none of those roads lead to the police post. For reaching the police post, to which direction should the policeman turn?

A. East   B. West
C. North   D. South

4. While standing at the bus stop in the morning I saw a policeman riding a cycle on the other side of the road. With his left hand he was protecting his face from the sun rays and his right hand was towards me. In which direction from the policeman was I standing?

A. East   B. West
C. North   D. South

Directions (Qs. 5-7): *Six students A, B, C, D, E and F are sitting in a park. A and B belong to Nehru House while the rest belong to Gandhi House. D and F are tallish while the others are short-sized. A, C and D put on spectacles but others do not. On the basis of the above information, answer questions 5 to 7.*

5. Two short-sized students who do not put an spectacles are:

A. A and F   B. C and E
C. B and E   D. E and F

6. The tallish Gandhi House student who does not put on spectacles is:

A. B   B. C
C. E   D. F

7. The short-sized Gandhi House student who does not put on spectacles is:

A. B   B. F
C. E   D. A

8. Some boys are standing in a row. Kamal is sixth from the left and Appu is fourth from the right. When Kamal and Appu exchange their places, Appu becomes 17th from the right. What will be the position of Kamal from the left?

A. 20th   B. 19th
C. 21st   D. 4th

9. In the letters of English alphabet from A to Z are written in reverse order, *i.e.,* ZYX.....CBA, the 8th letter to the right of the 10th letter from the left will be:

A. Y   B. I
C. J   D. X

Directions: *Read carefully the following statements and then answer questions 10 to 12.*

Ramesh, Mohan and Edward play cricket.

Mohan, Rahman and Edward play hockey.

Rahman, Ramesh and Mohan play volleyball.

10. Who plays all the three sports?

A. Ramesh   B. Mohan

C. Edward   D. Rahman

11. Who plays cricket and volleyball but does not play hockey?

A. Ramesh   B. Mohan

C. Edward   D. Rahman

12. Who plays hockey and volleyball but does not play cricket?

A. Ramesh   B. Mohan

C. Edward   D. Rahman

Directions: *A cube is painted red on all sides and then it is cut into 64 small cubes of equal sizes.*

Based on the above given information, answer questions 13 and 14.

13. How many small cubes have only one side painted?

A. 4   B. 8

C. 16   D. 24

14. How many small cubes are such as to have none of their sides painted?

A. 8   B. 6

C. 4   D. 1

15. Five boys were climbing a hillock. Hari was ahead of all of them. Ram was ahead of Govind. Krishna was behind Hari and in between Jayant and Ram. All of them were climbing up in a column. Who was in the second position?

A. Jayant   B. Hari

C. Ram   D. Govind

E. Krishna

16. Of the six towns, Dhulia is bigger than Alamner and Sri Rampur is bigger than Nasik; Jalgaon is not equal to Sri Rampur but bigger than Alamner. Alamner is smaller than Nasik but bigger than Manmad. The smallest of them is:

A. Alamner   B. Nasik

C. Jalgaon   D. Manmad

E. Sri Rampur

17. Geeta is more beautiful than Rupa but not as beautiful as Neeta.

Choose the correct statement in the light of the above statements.

A. Rupa is more beautiful than Neeta

B. Neeta is more beautiful than Rupa

C. Neeta is not more beautiful than Geeta

D. None of the above statements is correct

18. All the faces of a cube are painted with different colours. Red and blue colours are on the opposite faces while the blue colour is in between the yellow and green colours. The colour on the face opposite the green colour is:

A. Red   B. Blue

C. Yellow   D. Violet

19. I was alone in the park. After a short while an old man and an old woman came there. They were followed by two couples, each of which was accompanied with a child. Now how many persons were there in the park?

A. 8   B. 9

C. 10   D. 11

20. Sitting on a bench are Girija, Ishan, Francis and Hema. Hema is to the left of Francis. Ishan is flanked by Francis and Girija. Who is at the extreme right?

A. Girija   B. Hema

C. Ishan   D. Francis

21. Shyam is elder than Pradip. Pravin is of same age as Anjan. Amrit is younger than Suresh and Suresh is of the same age as Anjan. Pradip is elder than Pravin. Who among them is the eldest?

A. Pradip   B. Pravin

C. Suresh   D. Shyam

Directions: *A toy cube has pictures of different fruits on its six faces. The top face has the picture of orange. Banana is adjacent to melon and orange. Apple is not at the bottom of the cube and melon is opposite the peace.*

Answer questions 22, 23 and 24 on the basis of the above information.

22. The neighbouring faces of the sixth fruit mango, do not have the picture of:

A. Apple   B. Orange

C. Peach   D. Banana

23. Which fruit is opposite the face having the picture of apple?

A. Banana   B. Peach

C. Orange   D. Mango

24. Which one of the following does not represent the correct pair of fruits on the opposite faces?

A. Orange-Mango

B. Apple-Banana

C. Apple-Mango

D. All the above

25. Manisha is the 11th from either end of the row of girls. How many girls are there in that row?

A. 19   B. 10

C. 21   D. 22

E. 23

26. Is it possible to make a meaningful word with the second, fourth, sixth, seventh, eighth and ninth letters of the word 'LEUTENANT'. If so, write the first letter of the word thus formed.

A. T   B. E

C. N   D. A

E. X

27. A is 3 years elder than B and 3 years younger than C; B and D are twins. How many years elder is C than D?

A. 3   B. 6

C. 2   D. equal in age

E. 12

DETAILED ANSWERS

SERIES

1. B: Multiply the number by 2 and add one to the product to obtain the subsequent number.

2. A: The numbers are 2^2, 3^2, 4^2 and 5^2 respectively. Therefore, the next number will be $6^2 = 36$.

3. C: Add 12 to each number to obtain the subsequent number.

4. C: The numbers are divided by 2 to obtain the subsequent number.

5. C: Two letters are skipped from the beginning (A, D, G) of the alphabets in the first units and two letters are skipped from the end (Z, W, T) of the alphabet in the second units respectively.

6. D: Skip two letters respectively from the beginning of the alphabets.

7. A: The letters in the series are first letter of the alphabet from the end, first letter of the alphabet from the beginning, the second letter of the alphabet from the end and the second letter of alphabet from the beginning respectively. Proceed further on the same pattern.

8. C: $3 + 2 = 5$; $5^2 = 25$ and $3 + 4 = 7$; $7^2 = 49$. Similarly $2 + 3 = 5$; $5^2 = 25$.

9. C: Subsequent numbers are obtained by doubling the number.

10. D: Subsequent numbers are obtained by subtracting 5, 4, 3, etc. from the numbers respectively.

11. 24: Subsequent numbers have been obtained by subtracting 13 from the numbers.

$76 - 13 = 63$; $63 - 13 = 50$; $50 - 13 = 37$.

$\therefore$ Next number $= 37 - 13 = 24$.

12. 37: The numbers in the series are $2^1 + 1$, $3^2 + 1$, $4^2 + 1$ and $5^2 + 1$. Therefore, the next number will be $6^2 + 1 = 37$.

13. 30: The numbers in the series are $2^2 - 2$, $3^2 - 3$, $4^2 - 4$, $5^2 - 5$. Therefore, the next number will be $6^2 - 6 = 30$.

14. 15: The numbers in the series increase by 3 at each step. $3 + 3 = 6$; $6 + 3 = 9$; $9 + 3 = 12$. Therefore, the next number will be $12 + 3 = 15$.

15. 17: The numbers in the series are consecutive prime numbers 3, 7, 11 and 13. Therefore, the next prime number will be 17.

16. 25: The numbers in the series are 1^2, 2^2, 3^2, 4^2. Therefore, the next number will be $5^2 = 25$.

17. 24: The numbers in the series are $1^2 - 1$; $2^2 - 1$; $3^2 - 1$ and $4^2 - 1$. Therefore, the next number will be $5^2 - 1 = 24$.

18. 48: Multiply each number by 2 to find the next number. Therefore, the next number in the series will be $24 \times 2 = 48$.

19. 19: 3, 4 and 5 have been added respectively to find the next numbers in the series. Therefore, $13 + 6 = 19$ will be the next number.

20. 15: 2, 3 and 4 have been added respectively to find the next numbers in the series. Therefore, $10 + 5 = 15$ will be the next number.

21. 161: Multiply the number by 3 and then add 2 to the product to find the next number. Therefore, $53 \times 3 + 2 = 161$ will be the next number in the series.

22. 35: The numbers in the series are $2^2 - 1$, $3^2 - 1$, $4^2 - 1$ and $5^2 - 1$. Therefore, the next number will be $6^2 - 1 = 35$.

23. 7: The numbers in the series are reduced by 6, 5, 4 respectively to find the next numbers. Therefore, the next number will be $10 - 3 = 7$.

24. 63: The numbers in the series are doubled and then 1 is added to the product to obtain the next numbers. Therefore, the next number will be $31 \times 2 = 62 + 1 = 63$.

25. 5: The numbers are reduced to half to get the next numbers. Therefore, the next number will be $10 \div 2 = 5$.

26. 21: Add 5 to each number to find the subsequent number. Therefore, $16 + 5 = 21$.

27. 31: Subtract 7 from each number to find the subsequent number. Therefore, $38 - 7 = 31$.

28. 47: Double the number and then add 1 to the product to obtain the next number. Therefore, $23 \times 2 + 1 = 47$.

29. 29: The numbers in the series are consecutive prime numbers. The next prime number will be 29.

30. 53: Add 10 to obtain each subsequent number. Therefore, the next number will be $43 + 10 = 53$.

31. 46: Multiply the number by 2 and then add 2 to the product to obtain the next number. Therefore, the required number will be $22 \times 2 + 2 = 46$.

32. 25: The number in the series are 1^2, 2^2, 3^2 and 4^2.
$\therefore$ The next number will be $5^2 = 25$.

33. 6: The numbers in the series have been divided by 2 to obtain the next number. Therefore, the next number will be $12 \div 2 = 6$.

34. 11: Alternate numbers are reduced by 1.
For example 14, 13, 12   ...(i)
and 10, 9, 8   ...(ii)
The next number will be in series (i) above.
$\therefore$ The required number will be $12 - 1 = 11$.

35. 74: In this question, the relationship among the numbers of the series is as under:

   (i) add 3 to get the second number.

  (ii) double the second number to get the third number.

 (iii) again add 3 to get the 4th number.

 (iv) again double the 4th number to get the 5th number.

  (v) again add 3 to get the 6th number.

$\therefore$ Double the 6th number (37) to get the 7th number, $37 \times 2 = 74$.

36. 7: In this series, divide the first number by 2 to get the second number; now add 4 to the second number to get the third number. This pattern is repeated.

∴ $32 \div 2 = 16$; $16 + 4 = 20$; $20 \div 2 = 10$; $10 + 4 = 14$;

Now divide 14 by 2. You get 7. This is your answer.

37. 5: There are two series:

(i) 2, 3, 4

(ii) 3, 5, 7

In series *(i)* numbers increase by 1 at each step.

In series *(ii)* numbers increase by 2 at each step.

The next number will be in series *(i)* add 1 to 4 to get 5. This is the required number.

38. 26: Subsequent numbers have been obtained by adding 1, 2, 3, 4 and 5 respectively to the numbers.

∴ The next number will be $20 + 6 = 26$.

39. 126: The numbers in the series have been obtained by adding 1 to the cubes of 1, 2, 3 and 4 respectively such as $(1^3 + 1) = 2$; $(2^3 + 1) = 9$; $(3^3 + 1) = 28$; $(4^3 + 1) = 65$.

∴ The next number will be $5^3 + 1 = 126$.

40. 30: The numbers in the series are obtained as under:

$(1^2 - 1) = 0$; $(2^2 - 2) = 2$; $(3^2 - 3) = 6$; $(4^2 - 4) = 12$ and $(5^2 - 5) = 20$.

∴ The next number will be $(6^2 - 6) = 30$.

41. 37: Subsequent numbers in the series have been obtained by adding 3, 5, 6 and 9 to the given numbers. The numbers added, *i.e.*, 3, 5, 7, 9 are consecutive odd numbers. The next odd number will be 11. Therefore, the next number in the series will be obtained by adding 11 to 26. $26 + 11 = 37$.

42. 41: Subsequent numbers in the series have been obtained by adding 4, 6, 8 and 10 to the given numbers. The numbers added, *i.e.*, 4, 6, 8 and 10 are consecutive even numbers. The next even number is 12. Therefore, the next number in the series will be $29 + 12 = 41$.

43. $\dfrac{7}{8}$: The numerators and denominators of each fraction in the series have been reduced by 1 to obtain the numerators and denominators of the subsequent fractions in the series. For example, the numerators when reduced by 1 become $11 - 1 = 10$, $10 - 1 = 9$ and $9 - 1 = 8$, and the denominators 11, 10 and 9 when reduced by 1. Now to obtain the next unknown fraction in the series, take the last fraction *i.e.* $\dfrac{8}{9}$ and reduce both the numerator and the denominator by 1.

$$\therefore \frac{8-1}{9-1} = \frac{7}{8}.$$

44. 37: In this series the third number, *i.e.*, 9 has been obtained by adding the first number (4) to the second number (5), *i.e.*, $4 + 5 = 9$. The fourth number, *i.e.*, 14 has been obtained by adding the second and the third number *i.e.*, $5 + 9 = 14$, and so on. Therefore the sixth number in the series may be obtained by adding together the fourth and the fifth numbers, *i.e.*, $14 + 23 = 37$.

45. 65: In this question also the method is the same as applied in Q. No. 44. First number + second number = third number; second number + third number = fourth number; and third number + fourth number = fifth number. To obtain subsequent number, apply same method.

∴ Sixth number will be = fourth number (25) + fifth number (40).

∴ $25 + 40 = 65$.

46. 3: In this series, subsequent numbers have been obtained by dividing the numbers by 2, 3 and 4 respectively. Therefore, to obtain the next number, divide the fifth number by 5.

∴ $15 \div 5 = 3$.

47. 49: The numbers in the series are squares of 2, 3, 4, 5 and 6. Therefore the next number will be square of $7 = 49$.

48. 1: There are two series. *(i)* 4, 3, 2 and

(ii) 8, 6, 4

The numbers in *(i)* are reduced by 1 at each step.

Similarly, the numbers in *(ii)* are reduced by 2 at each step.

On the same analogy the next number in *(i)* will be $2 - 1 = 1$.

49. 125: The numbers in the series are cubes of 1, 2, 3 and 4 respectively.

∴ The next number in the series will be cube of $5 = 125$.

50. 44: In this series, the numbers increase by 4, 8 and 12 respectively.

∴ Add 16 to obtain the next number: $28 + 16 = 44$.

51. 26: Subsequent numbers have been obtained by adding 1, 3, 5 and 7 to the numbers. These numbers, *i.e.*, 1, 3, 5 and 7 are consecutive odd numbers. The next odd number is 9.

∴ Add 9 to 17 to obtain the next number in the series.

∴ $17 + 9 = 26$.

52. 2: The numbers in the series have been divided by 6, 5 and 4 respectively to obtain the subsequent numbers.

∴ Divide the last number in the series, *i.e.*, 6 by 3 to obtain the next number. ∴ $6 \div 3 = 2$.

53. 32: Each subsequent number is double of the previous number, as 1 x 2 = 2; 2 x 2 = 4; 4 x 2 = 8 and 8 x 2 = 16.
Now multiply 16 by 2 to obtain the next number in the series.
$\therefore$ 16 x 2 = 32.

54. 21: Subsequent numbers in the series increase by 2, 3, 4 and 5. On the same analogy add 6 to the last number to find the next number in the series.
$\therefore$ 15 + 6 = 21.

55. 25: The numbers in the series are squares of 0, 1, 2, 3 and 4.
$\therefore$ The next number will be $5^2 = 25$.

56. 10: Subsequent numbers have been obtained by dividing the numbers by 3.
$\therefore$ The next number will be 30 ÷ 3 = 10.

57. 49: The numbers in the series are 3^2, 4^2, 5^2 and 6^2 respectively. Therefore, the next number will be $7^2 = 49$.

58. 18: The subsequent numbers have been obtained by adding 3 to each number. Therefore, the next number will be 15 + 3 = 18.

59. 26: The subsequent numbers are obtained by adding 4, 5, 6. Therefore, the next number will be 19 + 7 = 26.

60. 63: Double the number and add 1 to obtain the next number. Therefore, the next number will be 31 x 2 + 1 = 63.

61. 65: The numbers are reduced by 10, 9, 8 etc. respectively. Therefore, the next number will be 72 – 7 = 65.

62. 12: There are two series—*(i)* 2, 4, 8 and *(ii)* 3, 6, 12. In both the series the numbers are doubled to obtain the subsequent numbers. Therefore, the next number will be 6 x 2 = 12.

63. 64: There are two series—*(i)* 3, 9, 27 and *(ii)* 4, 16, ... In series *(i)* the numbers are multiplied by 3. In series *(ii)* the numbers are multiplied by 4. Therefore, the next number will be 16 x 4 = 64.

64. 11: The numbers in the series are reduced by 10, 9, 8 to obtain the next numbers. Therefore, the next number will be 18 – 7 = 11.

65. 30: Add 7 to each number to obtain subsequent numbers. Therefore, the next number will be 23 + 7 = 30.

66. 20: The numbers have been reduced by 8, 6, 4 respectively. Hence the next number will be 22 – 2 = 20.

67. 15: Add 2, 3 and 4 to the numbers respectively to obtain the next number. The next number will be 10 + 5 = 15.

68. 9: Reduce each number by 19 to get the subsequent number. The next number will be 28 – 19 = 9.

69. 35: The subsequent numbers have been obtained by adding 2, 4, 8 respectively. Therefore, the next number will be 19 + 16 = 35.

70. $\frac{3}{4}$: The subsequent numbers have been obtained by dividing the number by 2. $1\frac{1}{2} \div 2 = \frac{3}{4}$.

71. 8: There are two series—*(i)* 2, 4, 6 and *(ii)* 3, 6, 9. In series *(i)* the next number will be 8.

72. 9: There are two series—*(i)* 5, 10, 20 and *(ii)* 36, 18, ... In series *(ii)* the next number will be 9.

73. 17: The numbers in the series are prime numbers. The prime number after 13 will be 17.

74. 32: Each number has been doubled to obtain the next number 16 x 2 = 32.

75. 18: Subtract 9 to obtain the next number 27 – 9 = 18.

76. 25: Add 6 to obtain the next number 19 + 6 = 25.

77. 25: The numbers in the series are $1^2, 2^2, 3^2$ and 4^2. The next number will be $5^2 = 25$.

78. 81: Add 9 to obtain the next number. The next number will be 72 + 9 = 81.

79. 80: The numbers in the series have been increased by 11, 10 and 9 respectively to obtain the next numbers. Therefore, the next number will be 72 + 8 = 80.

80. 2: There are two series—*(i)* 20, 10, 5 and *(ii)* 8, 4, ... The next number in series *(ii)* will be 2.

81. 47: Double the number and add 1 to the product to obtain the next number. Therefore, the next number will be 23 x 2 + 1 = 47.

82. 94: Double the number and add 2 to the product to obtain the next number. Therefore, the next number will be 46 x 2 + 2 = 94.

83. 53: The numbers in the series are prime numbers. The next prime number after 37 will be 53.

84. 18: There are two series—*(i)* 3, 9, 27 and *(ii)* 2, 6, ... In series *(ii)*, the next number will be 18.

85. 21: The next numbers in the series have been obtained by adding 3, 4, 5 etc. Therefore, the next number in the series will be 15 + 6 = 21.

86. 30: The numbers in the series are $2^2 – 2$; $3^2 – 3$; $4^2 – 4$ and $5^2 – 5$. Therefore, the next number will be $6^2 – 6 = 30$.

87. 125: The numbers in the series are $1^3, 2^3, 3^3, 4^3$. Therefore, the next number will be $5^3 = 125$.

88. 1: The numbers in the series are $5^3, 4^3, 3^3, 2^3$. Therefore, the next number will be $1^3 = 1$.

89. 100: The numbers in the series are $6^2, 7^2, 8^2$ and 9^2. Therefore, the next number will be $10^2 = 100$.

90. 16: The numbers in the series are 8^2, 7^2, 6^2 and 5^2. Therefore, the next number will be $4^2 = 16$.

91. 61: $3^2 + 4^2 = 25$ and $4^2 + 5^2 = 41$. Therefore, $5^2 + 6^2 = 61$.

92. 81: $2 + 3 = 5$; $5^2 = 25$ and $3 + 4 = 7$; $7^2 = 49$. Therefore, $4 + 5 = 9$; $9^2 = 81$.

93. 7: $6^2 - 4^2 = 20$ and $5^2 - 3^2 = 16$. Therefore, $4^2 - 3^2 = 7$.

94. 9: $8 - 6 = 2$; $2^2 = 4$ and $7 - 4 = 3$; $3^2 = 9$. Therefore, $5 - 2 = 3$; $3^2 = 9$.

95. 18: $7 + 9 = 16$; $16 \times 2 = 32$ and $3 + 6 = 9$; $9 \times 2 = 18$. Therefore, $5 + 4 = 9$; $9 \times 2 = 18$.

96. 64: $(3 + 2)^2 = 25$ and $(3 + 4)^2 = 49$. Therefore, $(3 + 5)^2 = 64$.

97. 3: $\dfrac{9 - 5}{2} = 2$ and $\dfrac{25 - 15}{2} = 5$. Therefore, $\dfrac{12 - 6}{2} = 3$.

98. 41: $2^2 + 3^2 = 13$ and $3^2 + 4^2 = 25$. Therefore, $4^2 + 5^2 = 41$.

99. 29: $2^2 + 3^2 = 13$ and $3^2 + 4^2 = 25$. Therefore, $2^2 + 5^2 = 29$.

100. 16: $6 - 3 = 3$; $3^2 = 9$ and $7 - 2 = 5$; $5^2 = 25$. Therefore, $8 - 4 = 4$; $4^2 = 16$.

101. 34: $5^2 + 2^2 = 29$ and $2^2 + 3^2 = 13$. Therefore, $3^2 + 5^2 = 34$.

102. 20: $6^2 - 3^2 = 27$ and $5^2 - 4^2 = 9$. Therefore, $6^2 - 4^2 = 20$.

103. 4: $4 - 2 = 2$; $2^2 = 4$ and $6 - 4 = 2$; $2^2 = 4$. Therefore $5 - 3 = 2$; $2^2 = 4$.

104. 100: $3 + 5 = 8$; $8^2 = 64$ and $2 + 3 = 5$; $5^2 = 25$. Therefore $4 + 6 = 10$; $10^2 = 100$.

105. 18: $1 + 4 = 5$; $5 \times 2 = 10$ and $2 + 5 = 7$; $7 \times 2 = 14$. Therefore, $3 + 6 = 9$; $9 \times 2 = 18$.

106. 120: $3 \times 2 = 60$ and $3 \times 3 = 90$. Therefore, $3 \times 4 = 120$.

107. 13: $5 - 3 = 2$ and $17 - 6 = 11$. Therefore, $18 - 5 = 13$.

108. 54: $4 \times 5 = 20$; $20 \times 3 = 60$ and $2 \times 8 = 16$; $16 \times 3 = 48$. Therefore, $3 \times 6 = 18$; $18 \times 3 = 54$.

109. 3: $9 - 5 = 4$; $\dfrac{4}{2} = 2$ and $25 - 15 = 10$; $\dfrac{10}{2} = 5$. Therefore, $12 - 6 = 6$; $\dfrac{6}{2} = 3$.

110. 10: $5 + 8 = 13$ and $7 + 9 = 16$. Therefore, $3 + 7 = 10$.

111. $\dfrac{5}{7}$: Add the numerator and denominators:

$$\dfrac{3}{4} + \dfrac{5}{6} = \dfrac{8}{10} \text{ and } \dfrac{6}{7} + \dfrac{2}{3} = \dfrac{8}{10}$$

$$\therefore \dfrac{3}{4} + \dfrac{2}{3} = \dfrac{5}{7}$$

112. 16: Add the two numbers: $4 + 7 = 11$ and $11 + 4 = 15$. Therefore, $7 + 9 = 16$.

113. 8: Add the numerator to the denominator: $5 + 7 = 12$; and $1 + 10 = 11$. Therefore, $3 + 5 = 8$.

114. 13: Subtract $25 - 12 = 13$ and $9 - 3 = 6$. Therefore, $17 - 4 = 13$.

115. 11: Add the two numbers. $5 + 2 = 7$ and $11 + 2 = 13$. Therefore, $8 + 3 = 11$.

116. EFG: These are two successive letters.

117. UVW: U after X, W, V; V after Y, X, W and W after Z, Y, X.

118. EV: One letter from the beginning and one letter from the end in the same order.

119. EGI: Next successive letters are taken.

120. VT: From the end, the letter just before the letter W, *i.e.,* the letter V, and the letter just before the letter U, *i.e.,* the letter T.

121. EI: Skip three continuous letters in the same order.

122. EFH: One letter is skipped after two letters in their natural sequence.

123. ER: The letters are the first letter and 14th letter; the second letter and the 15th letter; the third letter and 16th letter and so on.

124. EFV: From the beginning, the first two successive letters and one letter from the end.

125. VE: The last letter of the alphabet and the first letter of the alphabet are taken. It is repeated.

126. M: Two letters have been skipped at each step.

127. N: From the end, two letters have been skipped at each step.

128. DWV: One letter from the beginning and two letters from the end have been taken. The same process is repeated.

129. JI: Two successive letters have been transposed. Their order is second-first, fourth-third, sixth-fifth.

130. QPO: From the end, three letters in the reverse order.

FINDING THE WRONG OR SUPERFLUOUS NUMBER

1. 24: It should be 25 as the numbers in the series are $1^2, 2^2, 3^2, 4^2, 5^2$ and 6^2.

2. 32: It should be 33 because there are two series—*(i)* 11, 22, 33 and *(ii)* 12, 24, 36.

3. 41: It should be 43 as the numbers increase by 4, 5, 6, 7 and 8 respectively.

4. 37: It should be 36 as the numbers in the series are $10^2, 9^2, 8^2, 7^2, 6^2$ and 5^2.

5. 125: It should be 128 as the numbers increase by 9 at each step.

6. 70: It should be 69 as the subsequent numbers are obtained by adding 10, 11, 12 and 13 respectively.

7. 28: It should be 29 as the subsequent numbers are obtained by subtracting 11, 10, 9 and 8 respectively.

8. 10: It should be 12 as the subsequent numbers are obtained by subtracting 3 successively.

9. 12: 12 is superfluous as the numbers are reduced by 2 successively.

10. 17: 17 is superfluous as the numbers increase by 3 successively.

11. 25: 25 is wrong; it should be 27. The numbers are multiplied by 3 to obtain the subsequent number.

12. 19: 19 is superfluous. 5 is added to each number to obtain subsequent number.

13. 24: 24 is superfluous. The numbers in the series are 2^2, 3^2, 4^2, 5^2, 6^2 and 7^2 respectively.

14. 26: 26 is superfluous. The numbers increase by 6 at each step.

15. 7: 7 is superfluous. The numbers increase by 5, 10, 15 and 20 at each step.

16. 7: It should be 8 as the numbers are 1^3, 2^3, 3^3, 4^3 and 5^3.

17. 10: It should be 18 as the numbers decrease by 2, 3, 4, 5 and 6 at each step.

18. 80: It should be 81 as the numbers increase by 9, 10, 11, 12 and 13 respectively.

19. 24: It should be 25 as the numbers are 4^2, 5^2, 6^2, 7^2, 8^2 and 9^2 respectively.

20. 86: It should be 85 as the numbers decrease by 7, 8, 9 and 10 respectively.

21. 32: It should be 33 as the numbers increase by 11 at each step.

22. 121: It should be 125 as the numbers are 6^3, 5^3, 4^3, 3^3 and 2^3 respectively.

23. 35: It should be 36 as the numbers are 2^2, 3^2, 4^2, 5^2, 6^2 and 7^2 respectively.

24. 27: It should be 28 as the subsequent numbers are obtained by subtracting 11 at each step.

25. 70: It should be 69 as the subsequent numbers are obtained by adding 10, 11, 12 and 13 respectively.

26. 52: It should be 53 as the subsequent numbers are obtained by subtracting 9 at each step.

27. 24: It should be 25 as the subsequent numbers are obtained by adding 7 at each step.

28. 9: It should be 8 as the numbers are doubled at each step.

29. 12: It should be 13 as the subsequent numbers increase by 3, 4, 5 and 6 respectively.

30. 20: It should be 19 as there are two series—*(i)* 5, 9, 13 and *(ii)* 7, 13, 20. In series *(ii)*, the numbers increase by 6 at each step.

31. 16: It should be 17 as the subsequent numbers are obtained by adding 1^2, 2^2, 3^2, 4^2 and 5^2 respectively to them.

32. 21: It should be 20 as the numbers are increased by 7 at each step.

33. 48: It should be 54 as the numbers are increased by 12 at each step.

34. 26: It should be 27 as the numbers are 1^3, 2^3, 3^3, 4^3, 5^3 respectively.

35. 28: It should be 30 as the numbers are 6 x 1; 6 x 3; 6 x 5; 6 x 7; 6 x 9 respectively.

36. 43: It should be 42 as the subsequent numbers are obtained by subtracting 7 at each step.

37. 65: It should be 69 as the numbers decrease by 11 at each step.

38. 18: It should be 10 as the numbers are $1 + 1^2$; $1 + 2^2$; $1 + 3^2$; $1 + 4^2$ and $1 + 5^2$ respectively.

39. 39: It should be 36 as the number increase by 4, 5, 6, 7 and 8 respectively.

40. 40: It should be 44 as the numbers are reduced by half at each step.

41. 45: It should be 47 as the numbers are increased by 13 at each step.

42. 34: It should be 33 as the numbers are increased by 6 at each step.

43. 12: It should be 11 as the numbers are reduced by 2 at each step.

44. 64: It should be 62 as the numbers are reduced by 10 and 9, 10 and 9 and 10 and 9 respectively.

45. 15: It should be 16 as the numbers increase by 3, 5, 7, 9 and 11 respectively.

ANALOGY

1. C: We get curd from milk: similarly we get ice from water.

2. B: Girl is beautiful (quality): similarly gold is bright.

3. A: In desert we find sand: similarly in sea we find water.

4. A: Beautiful is to ugly (opposite): similarly healthy is to sick (opposite).

5. C: Cheese is made from milk. Similarly sugar is made from sugarcane.

6. C: Daughter is to mother as son is to father.

7. C: Book is made of paper: similarly table is made of wood.

8. B: A group of players is a team: similarly a group of ships is a fleet.

9. D: Kilogram is to weight as metre is to length.

10. B: Lid is to box as cork is to bottle.

11. D: Circle has a circumference as square has a perimeter.

12. A: Advocate knows law as cook knows cookery.

13. C: Wardrobe is meant for clothes: similarly purse is meant for money.

14. D: Temperature indicates level of heat: similarly humidity indicates level of moisture.

15. C: Shakespeare is known for his dramas: similarly Ghalib is known for his *ghazals*.

16. C: Grass is green (colour): similarly sky is blue.

17. C: Monday is a day in a week: similarly January is a month in a year.

18. C: Thermometer measures temperature: similarly barometer measures atmospheric pressure.

19. C: Poverty is to riches (opposite): similarly glory is to shame (opposite).

20. D: Table is to chair (pair): similarly coat is to pant (pair).

21. B: Hand is to elbow (relation): similarly leg is to knee (relation).

22. D: Coal is to black (colour): similarly snow is to white (colour).

23. A: Precaution prevents accident: similarly cleanliness prevents disease.

24. D: January is to April (4th month): similarly Sunday is to Wednesday (4th day).

25. C: Soldier is associated with rifle: similarly writer is associated with pen.

26. D: Plate is an item of crockery: similarly spoon is an item of cultery.

27. A: Night comes after evening: similarly day comes after morning.

28. B: Uncle is to aunt: similarly father is to mother.

29. D: Lotus grows in water: similarly fish lives in water.

30. C: Metre is to length (measure): similarly litre is to volume.

31. C: Heaven is to hell (opposite): similarly drought is to flood.

32. C: Planet revolves round the sun as moon revolves round the earth.

33. B: French is the language of the people of France: similarly Dutch is the language of the people of Holland.

34. B: Colombo is capital of Sri Lanka: similarly Tokyo is capital of Japan.

35. D: Pen writes: similarly carpenters' plane shaves off.

36. D: Thick is to thin (opposite): similarly inferior is to superior.

37. B: Table is made of wood: similarly book is made of paper.

38. D: Fan gives air: similarly bulb gives light.

39. A: Seven is a number (class): similarly green is a colour (class).

40. A: Stage is associated to drama as stadium is associated to sports.

41. A: Mango is a variety of fruit: similarly cobra is a variety of serpent.

42. A: Rain is measured in centimeter: similarly temperature is measured in celsius.

43. A: Lane is a smaller road: similarly town is a smaller city.

44. B: Aspirin cures headache: similarly quinine cures malaria.

45. C: Food satisfies hunger: similarly water satisfies thirst.

46. D: Young one of a cat is kitten: similarly young one of a hen is chicken.

47. A: Banana is one of the fruits: similarly cow is one of the mammals.

48. C: One listens to radio: similarly one views film.

49. B: Money, a medium of exchange: similarly language, a medium of communication.

50. D: Friend is to enemy (opposite): similarly kind is to cruel.

51. B: Train stops at platform: similarly ship stops at harbour.

52. C: 1st April is called Fools Day: similarly 1st May is called Labour Day.

53. B: Clock measures time: similarly rainguage measures rain.

54. A: Lion lives in den: similarly horse lives in stable.

55. D: Book is made up of pages: similarly flower is made up of petals.

56. D: Tea is made from leaves: similarly coffee is made from seeds.

57. C: Horse neighs: similarly donkey brays.

58. B: Garage is the place where car is kept when not in use: similarly hanger is the place where aircraft is kept when not in use.

59. A: Radius is to a circle as spoke is to a wheel.

60. A: Carpenters mends stool: similarly cobbler mends shoes.

61. C: Bus is repaired in the workshop: similarly ship is repaired in the dockyard.

62. B: Ring is put on the finger: similarly tie is put on the neck.

63. B: Needle is used for sewing: similarly brush is used for painting.

64. B: We smell through nose: similarly we taste through tongue.

65. D: Pencil is an item of stationery: similarly chair is an item of furniture.

66. A: Both cat and dog are carnivorous: similarly both cow and goat are harbivorous.

67. D: Both snake and lizard are reptile: similarly both fish and crocodile live in water.

68. C: Honour is to dishonour (opposite) as fame is to infamy.

69. B: Light travels through rays: similarly sound travels through waves.

70. C: In a clock hands tell time: similarly in a thermometer mercury indicates temperature.

71. B: Tractor runs on diesel: similarly scooter runs on petrol.

72. B: Cuckoo cackles: similarly horse neighs.

73. B: Pitch is a term associated with cricket: similarly ring is a term associated with boxing.

74. C: Car runs: similarly snake creeps.

75. A: Urge is to deter (opposite): similarly honest is to dishonest.

76. C: Lion lives in den: similarly bird lives in nest.

77. D: Calf is young one of a cow: similarly lamb is young one of a sheep.

78. B: Obedience is to disobedience (opposite): similarly life is to death.

79. B: Tailor uses cloth to make garments: similarly carpenter uses wood to make furniture.

80. A: Cat kills rat: similarly tiger kills lamb.

81. B: Bakery is the place where bread is prepared: similarly mint is the place where coins are produced.

82. A: Studio is associated with film: similarly shipyard is associated with ship.

83. A: Months make a year: similarly hours make a day.

84. C: Food satisfies hunger: similarly water satisfies thirst.

85. C: Revolver is associated with bullet: similarly bow is associated with arrow.

86. D: Bees give honey: similarly sheep give wool.

FINDING ODD ONE OUT

1. C: In this pair both the items are males while in other pairs one item is male and the other item is female.

2. D: Bird and tree are not related in the same way as coal and mine, water and river and fishes and water.

3. C: Thief and robber are not related to each other as hospital and doctor, court and advocate, and school and teacher are.

4. D: Curd is made from milk, house is made from brick, book is made from paper, but stable is not made from horses.

5. B: Milk is always white, sky is always blue and blood is always red, but leaf may be brown and yellow as well.

6. B: Carrot and radish are not opposite to each other whereas victory and defeat, north and south, and up and down are opposite to each other.

7. D: Tiger lives in den.

8. A: Sky is always blue whereas kite, saree and horse may be of different colours.

9. A: Items in pair A are living beings, whereas items in other pairs are non-living beings.

10. A: Items in pair A are man-made whereas items in all other pairs are nature-made (natural).

11. D: It is not a pair. Others are pairs.

12. D: The two items in the pair are not opposites whereas the two items in other pairs are opposite to each other.

13. **D:** Paper may be of other colours than white, whereas smoke, heat and cool are essential elements of fire, sun and moonlight respectively.

14. **D:** Moon is a satellite while others are planets.

15. **B:** Raisin is a dryfruit while others are fresh fruits.

16. **C:** Goat is a domestic cattle while others are wild animals.

17. **A:** Riksha is man driven while others are power driven.

18. **A:** Tiger is a wild animal while others are draught animals.

19. **C:** Snake does not have legs while all others have legs.

20. **C:** Patna is in Bihar while all others are in UP.

21. **C:** Coin is a general name while all others are names of currencies of various countries.

22. **A:** Diamond is not a metal while all others are names of metals (minerals).

23. **D:** Legs, Hands and Ankles are external parts of body, while Lungs are inside the body.

24. **D:** Steamer, Boat and Ship are means of transport, while Harbour is a place of shelter for ship.

25. **B:** Lotus is a flower that grows in water. Rose, Dahlia and Jasmin grow on land.

26. **C:** Protein, Carbohydrates and Vitamins are needed by human body as parts of balanced diet, while copper is not needed.

27. **C:** Piano, Tabla and Banjo are musical instruments that require the help of hands and fingers in playing, whereas Flute is a wind instrument.

28. **D:** Metre, Kilometre and Centimetre are units of linear distances whereas Square Kilometre is a unit of area.

29. **D:** Snake is a reptile, while others are not.

30. **D:** Snake, Lizard and Crocodile are reptile, whereas Frog is not a reptile.

31. **C:** Moon is a satellite, whereas others are planets.

32. **D:** Sketch Map is not an item of stationery. Others are items of stationery.

33. **B:** India Today is a forgnightly magazine whereas all others are daily newspapers.

34. **B:** Chanakya was a statesman and not a ruler or king whereas others were kings or rulers.

35. **D:** Tangent, Arc and Radius are associated with circle. Hypotenuse is related to right-angled triangle.

36. **A:** Delhi is capital of Delhi (of a country) whereas Patna (Bihar), Mumbai (Maharashtra) and Calcutta (West Bengal) are state capitals.

37. **A:** Scooter, Car and Bus are engine driven vehicles whereas bicycle is pedal driven.

38. B: Wheat, Ragi and Rice are cereals where Gram is a pulse.

39. C: Iron, Copper and Tin are not alloys whereas steel is an alloy.

40. C: Bile is a fluid secreted by liver and helps in the digestion, whereas Cancer, Hepatitis and Diabetes are names of diseases.

41. D: Soil cannot be used as a source of energy whereas all others can be used as a source of energy.

42. B: All other except B are commercial or cash crops.

43. C: Sugarcane is not a fruit whereas all others are fruits.

44. C: Karachi is not a capital town. All others are capital towns.

45. C: April has 30 days whereas May, March and July have 31 days each.

46. B: Diet is the name of the Japanese Parliament whereas Rouble, Dollar and Taka are currencies of different countries.

47. A: Libra is a constellation, whereas Uranus, Pluto and Neptune are planets.

48. B: Monastery is a building where monks live whereas Temple, Mosque and Church are places of worship.

49. B: Shilling is a currency whereas others are units of measurements.

50. C: Sword is a weapon of offence whereas others are defensive coverings.

51. D: Ganga, Godavari and Krishna, all flow from west to east whereas Narmada flows from east to west.

52. A: Cataract is a disease of eye whereas others are parts of eye.

53. C: Faster indicates speed, whereas all the other three words Bigger, Greater and Larger indicate size.

54. A: Cow, Dog and Horse are domesticated but not the Fox.

55. C: Jackal, Fox and Wolf, all are flesh eaters, but stag does not eat flesh.

56. B: Father, Brother and Sister are blood relations whereas Teacher is not.

57. A: Shore is the land that skirts any large body of water, whereas Sea, River and Pond are large body of water.

58. D: Sorrow is a state of sadness. Other words Moan, Wail and Weep are results of state of sadness.

59. D: Cock is a domestic or farmyard fowl, whereas others are not.

60. D: Lameness is the result of some or other accident or disease whereas Dwarfness, Slenderness and Fatness need not be associated with any accident or disease.

61. C: It is different because son is the only male member among females.

62. C: The word Neck has only one vowel, all other words have two vowels each.

63. D: Pondicherry is a Union Territory whereas others are states of Indian Union.

64. C: Colonel is a rank in the Army whereas the other three are ranks in the Air Force.

65. D: Mridangam is a percussion instrument whereas the other three are string instruments.

66. C: Arabia is the name of a country whereas others are names of continents.

67. D: Crocodile is not a fish, whereas others are names of fish.

68. D: Diagonal is a line that connects one angle to the opposite one, whereas Square, Trapezium and Rectangle are quadrilaterals.

69. D: Monkey does not eat flesh whereas Cat, Dog and Fox eat flesh.

70. D: Penicillin is an antibiotic drug whereas the other three are analgesic (pain reliever).

71. B: The other three grow under the earth.

72. D: Malaria is not an infectious disease, whereas the other three are infectious diseases.

73. B: Office is not a place for living, whereas Bunglow, Hut and House are places for living.

74. A: Fly is an insect, all others are non-living things.

75. A: Root is not visible because it is underground; other parts of a tree are visible.

76. B: Potato grows underground; other vegetables grow under land.

77. B: Crow is a bird; all others are animals.

78. C: Kalidas was a poet; all others are scientists.

79. C: All others except shoes are items of garments.

80. D: Except Mercury all others are gases.

QUESTIONS RELATING TO CLOCKS AND CALENDARS

1	2	3	4	5	6	7	8	9	10
B	B	C	C	A	B	D	A	B	B

11	12	13	14	15	16	17	18	19	20
A	A	A	C	B	A	B	B	C	C

CODING AND DECODING

1. B: The letters just preceding the letters C, O, M and E are B, N, L and D. On the same pattern, the letters just preceding the letters C, A, R and E will be B, Z, Q and D.
Hence CARE will be coded as BZQD.

2. C: The letters succeeding H, I, G and H are I, J, H and I. On the same pattern the letters succeeding T, U, R and N will be U, V, S and O. Therefore, TURN will be coded as UVSO.

3. D: The letters just succeeding L, O, A and D are letters M, P, B and E. On the same pattern, the letter just succeeding P, O, R and T will be Q, P, S and U. Therefore, PORT will be coded as QPSU.

4. D: Skip one letter clockwise at each step to find the coded letters for G, O, L and D. These letters are I, Q, N and F. On the same pattern skip one letter at each step to find the codes for W, I, N and D. You will find such letters Y, K, P and F.
Hence, the code for WIND will be YKPF.

5. A: SHIRT has been coded as RGHQS. You will find that just preceding letters have been used as codes, *i.e.,* R for S, G for S, H for I; Q for R and S for T. On the same pattern, the just preceding letters R, O, U, N and D will make the code. These letters are Q, N, T, M and C.
Therefore, code for ROUND is QNTMC.

6. D: DEAR is coded as FGCT. It means one letter has been skipped at each step to find the code letters, *i.e.,* F for D, G for E, C for A and T for R. On the same pattern, skip one letter at each step to find the code for R, E, A and D. These letters will be T, G, C and F.
Therefore, code for READ will be TGCF.

7. C: You will find that two letters have been skipped to find the codes for E, A, S and E. The coded letters are H, D, V and H. On the same pattern skip two letters at each step to find the codes for S, E and E. Code for S will be V, and code for E will be H.
Therefore, code for SEE will be VHH.

8. C: The letters have been written in reverse order as is evident from SERPENT and TNEPRES. On the same pattern, letters of PLAGUE will be written in reverse order to find the code. PLAGUE written in reverse order will be EUGALP.

9. C: The letters just preceding the letters D, E, F, E, N, C and E are C, D, E, F, M, B and D. On the same pattern, the letters just preceding the letters N, E, E and D will be M, D, D and C.
Therefore, code for NEED will be MDDC.

10. D: CHAIR has been coded as FKDLU. It shows that two letters have been skipped clockwise at each step to find the code letters F for C, K for H, D for A, L for I and U for R. On the same pattern, skip two letters to find the code for R, A, I and D. These letters will be U, D, L and G.
Therefore, code for RAID will be UDLG.

11. D: A close look will reveal that letters have exchanged their places to make the coded expression. Your will find that the second and the third letters have exchanged their places; similarly the fifth and the sixth letters have exchanged their places. On the same pattern, in finding out the code for TEACHER, exchange the position of the second and the third letters, *i.e.,* make them AE instead of EA; also exchange the position of the fifth and the sixth letters, *i.e.,* make them EH instead of HE.

Thus the code for TEACHER will be TAECEHR.

12. D: COME = XLNV

$\begin{bmatrix} C = 3rd \text{ alphabet from the beginning} \\ X = 3rd \text{ alphabet from the end} \end{bmatrix}$

$\begin{bmatrix} O = 15th \text{ alphabet from the beginning} \\ L = 15th \text{ alphabet from the end} \end{bmatrix}$

$\begin{bmatrix} M = 13th \text{ alphabet from the beginning} \\ N = 13th \text{ alphabet from the end} \end{bmatrix}$

$\begin{bmatrix} E = 5th \text{ alphabet from the beginning} \\ V = 5th \text{ alphabet from the end} \end{bmatrix}$

Similarly, A, B, L and E are 1st, 2nd, 12th and 5th alphabets from the beginning and Z, Y, O and V are the 1st, 2nd, 12th and 15th alphabets from the end.

Therefore, on the same pattern M, O, L, L, Y will be coded as NLOOB.

13. D: CIG ARE TTE. Make groups of three alphabets each from the left. Write letters in each group in reverse order, and you will get GIC ERA ETT. On the same pattern, make groups of three alphabets each in DEM ONS TRA TION.

Write letters in each group in reverse order as under MED SNO ART OIT N.

14. C:

		8		3		2				4		10
A	B	C	D	E	F	G	H	I	J	K	L	M

5, 5	5	6	5		1, 1		7	9				
N	O	P	Q	R	S	T	U	V	W	X	Y	Z

CENTURION = 325791465
RANK = 18510

Mark the position assigned in the alphabets above.

It means 7 = T
8 = A
5 = N
10 = K, $\therefore$ 78510 = TANK

15. C: The first, third and fifth letters, *i.e.,* M, H and S are replaced by letters just following them, *i.e.,* N, I and T. Similarly, the second, fourth and sixth letters, *i.e.,* A, E and H are replaced by letters obtained by skipping one letter at each step, *i.e.,* C, G and J.

Therefore NEELAM, the first, third and fifth letters, *i.e.,* N, E and A will be replaced by letters just following them, *i.e.,* O, F and B; while the 2nd, 4th and 6th letters, *i.e.,* E, L and M will be replaced by letters obtained by skipping one letter at each step, *i.e.,* G, N and O.

Thus NEELAM will be OGFNBO.

16. D: In FLOWER and SEXOMF, you will find that the second, fourth and sixth letters in F L O W E R are replaced by letters just following these letters, *i.e.,* M, X and S written in reverse order that is S, X and M. The order of the other three letters, *i.e.,* F, O and E is also reversed to make it E, O and F.

Now in G A R D E N, the 2nd, 4th and 6th letters will be placed by letters just following these letters, *i.e.,* B, E and O, but in reverse order, *i.e.,* O, E and B. The other three letters, *i.e.,* G, R and E will also be written in the reverse order.

Thus GARDEN will be OEERBG.

17. C: Compare SCRIPT and TCQIQT. You will find that the 2nd, 4th and 6th letters remain unchanged. The other three letters, *i.e.,* 1st, 3rd and 5th (S, R and P) have changed to T, Q and Q. Here you will notice that T is the letter just following letter S in the alphabet, Q is the letter just preceding letter R in the alphabet and Q is the letter just following letter P in the alphabet.

Now in DIGEST, the 2nd, 4th and 6th letters, *i.e.,* I, E and T will remain unchanged. The first, third and fifth letters, *i.e.,* D, G and S will change to the just following letter E, just preceding letter F and just following letter T.

Thus DIGEST will be coded as EIFETT.

18. A: Compare RAM and SBN. You will find that letter just following in the alphabet have been taken in code. S for R, B for A and N for M are just on the above pattern.

Now for FEW, take the letters just following these letters in the alphabets, *i.e.,* G for F, F for E and X for W.

∴ FEW will be coded as GFX.

19. B: Compare RUBBER and REBBUR. You will find that the letters in RUBBER have been written in just reverse order as REBBUR.

On the same pattern, to find the code for DEAD, write these letters in reverse order as DAED.

20. C: You will find that the letters as coded (LBOQVS) are the letters just following the letters KANPUR.

On the same pattern, the letters just following the letters N, A, G, P, U and R will be O, B, H, Q, V and S.

Therefore NAGPUR = OBHQVS.

21. D: Compare DELHI with IDHEL. You will find that the same letters have been arranged in a different order. The order is last, first, last but one, second and then the third letter at the end.

On the same pattern, change the order of the letters in TUFAN. It will become NTAUF.

22. C: ANOTHER is coded as 7309521

$$7 \quad 3 \quad 0 \quad 9 \quad 5 \quad 2 \quad 1$$
$$\therefore \quad A \quad N \quad O \quad T \quad H \quad E \quad R$$

∴ THORN = 95013.

23. B: Surendra is coded as DHTNPATI

$$\uparrow \quad \uparrow \quad \uparrow \quad \uparrow \quad \uparrow$$
$$S \quad U \quad R \quad E \quad N \quad D \quad R \quad A$$
$$\overline{D \quad H \quad T \quad N \quad P \quad A \quad T \quad I}$$

∴ UNDER = HPANT

24. C: Compare EFFICIENT with DEEHBHDMS.

$$\overline{E \quad F \quad F \quad I \quad C \quad I \quad E \quad N \quad T}$$
$$\overline{D \quad E \quad E \quad H \quad B \quad H \quad D \quad M \quad S}$$

∴ FIET = EHDS.

25. A: G, B, D and F are letters just following the letters FACE. On the same pattern, B, A, D, E will be coded as (just the following letters *i.e.*) C, B, E, F. Therefore, BADE will be coded as CBEF.

26. C: All the letters of SETS are contained in REST

REST = TGUV

∴ SETS = UGVU

27. D: DECADE = 453145

$$D \quad E \quad C \quad A \quad D \quad E$$
$$4 \quad 5 \quad 3 \quad 1 \quad 4 \quad 5$$

∴ DEED = 4554.

28. B: AD is common to BAD and MAD. So it will be coded as ZW. Now B is the 2nd alphabet from the beginning and Y is the 2nd alphabet from the end. On the same pattern, M in MAD is the 13th alphabet from the beginning; it will be coded by the 13th alphabet from the end, *i.e.*, N.

∴ MAD will be coded as NZW.

29. C: DIRT is coded as TDIR. You will find that the same alphabets appear

in the coded expression but the order of the alphabets is changed. The pattern of change in the order of the alphabets is:
The first becomes the second,
The second becomes the third,
The third becomes the fourth, and
The fourth becomes the first.
Now, change the order of alphabets in TRIM as shown above.
Thus TRIM will be MTRI.

30. C: PIT is coded as QJU. You will find that the letters just following PIT are QJU. On the same pattern the letters just following HUT will be IVU.

31. C: D E   C E   M B   E R = E R   M B   C E   D E

∴   N O   V E   M B   E R = E R   M B   V E   N O

32. B: ROUGH is coded as ORRJE. You will find that alternately 2 letters are skipped backward and forward to find the letters in the code.
R = O (2 letters skipped backward)
O = R (2 letters skipped forward)
U = R (2 letters skipped backward)
G = J (2 letters skipped forward)
H = E (2 letters skipped backward)
On the same pattern, the code for SMOOTH will be PPLRQK.

33. C: MOTHER is coded as PQWJHT. You will find that alternately 2, 1, 2, 1, 2 letters are skipped forward in writing the coded letters, as:
M = P (2 letters NO skipped)
O = Q (1 letter P skipped)
T = W (2 letters UV skipped)
H = J (1 letter I skipped), and so on.
On the same pattern
S = V (2 letters TU skipped)
I = K (1 letter J skipped)
S = V (2 letters TU skipped)
T = V (1 letter U skipped)
E = H (2 letters FG skipped)
R = T (1 letter S skipped)
SISTER = VKVVHT

34. A: LOFTY = LPFUY. You will find that the first, third and fifth letters remain unchanged, while the second and the fourth letters are replacd by the next letters in the alphabets, *i.e.,* P for O and U for T.
On the same pattern in DWARF, the first, third and fifth letters will

remain unchanged. The second and the fourth letters, *i.e.,* W and R will be replacd by the just following letters, *i.e.,* X and S.

Thus   D W A R F
        – X – S –

∴ DXASF.

35. D: PRICE = SVNIL.

You will find that 2, 3, 4, 5 and 6 letters are skipped in writing the code.

P = S (2 letters, *i.e.,* QR are skipped)
R = V (3 letters, *i.e.,* STU are skipped)
I = N (4 letters, *i.e.,* JKLM are skipped)
C = I (5 letters, *i.e.,* DEFGH are skipped)
E = L (6 letters, *i.e.,* FGHIJK are skipped)

On the same pattern, to find the code for COST, skip 2, 3, 4 and 5 letters.

C = F (2 letters DE skipped)
O = S (3 letters PQR skipped)
S = X (4 letters TUVWskipped)
T = Z (5 letters UVWXY skipped)

∴ COST = FSXZ

36. B: The letters in JAILAPPAS are divided into groups of three letters each as JAI, LAP and PAS. In each group the first letter is made the third letter as JAI becomes AIJ, LAP becomes APL and PAS becomes ASP. Thus JAILAPPAS becomes AIJALASP.

On the same pattern divide the expression ECONOMICS into groups of three letters each as ECO, NOM and ICS. Now, in each group make the first letter as third letter. They will becme COE, OMN and CSI.

∴ ECONOMICS will be coded as COEOMNCSI.

37. D: CLOCK is written as KCOLC. You will see that the letters have been written in reverse order beginning from the last letter

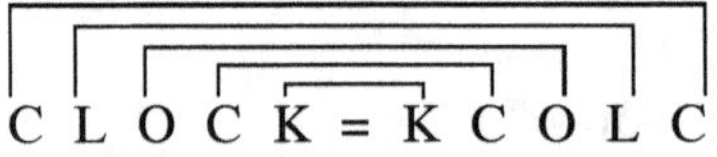

On the same pattern STEPS will be SPETS.

38. C: SPIDER is written as PSDIRE. The expression SPIDER is divided into groups of two letters each as SP, ID, ER. You will find the letters in each group exchange their place, *i.e.,* SP becomes PS, ID becomes DI and RE becomes ER. Thus SPIDER is written as PSDIRE.

On the same pattern divide the expression COMMON into groups of two letters each, *i.e.,* CO, MM and ON. When letters in each group exchange their places, the group will become OC, MM and NO.

Thus COMMON will become OCMMNO.

39. C: Compare RECOMMENDATION and COMNENDATIONER

RE COMMENDATION

COMMENDATION ER

You will find that the first two letters RE exchange their position and occupy the last, position in the expression.

On the same pattern, when RENUMERATION will be written in the code, the first two letters, *i.e.,* RE will exchange their position to become ER and will occupy the last position. Thus the coded expression will become—MUNERATIONER.

40. A: TRIPPLE is coded as SQHOOKD. You will find that the coded letters are just the preceding letters of the letters in the expression. For example, S for T, Q for R, H for I, O for P again O for P, K for L and D for E.

On the same pattern use the just preceding letters to obtain the code for DISPOSE.

D = C

I = H

S = R

P = O

O = N

S = R

E = D

∴ DISPOSE will be coded as CHRONRD.

QUESTIONS BASED ON RELATIONSHIP

1. B: Ajit is brother of Mohan's son. Therefore, Mohan is father of Ajit and his brother. Therefore, Ajit is Mohan's grandson.

2. C: B is A's son.

B is my son's uncle.

∴ A is my father.

3. D: G's uncle is A's brother.

4. A: son-in-law.

5. B: Bihari is Yogendra's uncle.

6. C: C has two children A and B. A is his son while B is his daughter.

7. B: The son of my maternal uncle's son will be my nephew and I will be his uncle.

8. B: Children of Ram, Pratap and Kripa will be cousins.

9. B: The son of the daughter of P's sister will address P as maternal grandfather.

10. C: B is C's wife and A is C's father.

∴ A is father-in-law of B.

QUESTIONS RELATED TO DIRECTIONS

1	2	3	4	5	6	7	8	9	10
B	B	D	A	C	C	D	C	C	B

11	12	13
D	B	C

ARRANGING THE LETTERS TO MAKE MEANINGFUL WORDS

1. BLUE	**11.** SHIRT	**21.** PUNJAB	**31.** KASHI
2. COCHIN	**12.** MANGO	**22.** CRICKET	**32.** PARIS
3. URDU	**13.** RICE	**23.** PETROL	**33.** COPPER
4. IRON	**14.** AGRA	**24.** GUITAR	**34.** GRAPE
5. PEACOCK	**15.** CHAIR	**25.** BABY	**35.** RAMAYAN
6. NARMADA	**16.** HAND	**26.** KIDNEY	**36.** AKBAR
7. EARTH	**17.** RING	**27.** TONGUE	**37.** BURMA
8. PENCIL	**18.** TAMIL	**28.** DONKEY	**38.** WATCH
9. TIGER	**19.** NEEM	**29.** KRISHNA	**39.** BRIJNJAL
10. HOCKEY	**20.** TRAIN	**30.** KALIDAS	**40.** OXYGEN

ARRANGING WORDS IN THEIR NATURAL ORDER

1	2	3	4	5	6	7	8	9	10
C	C	D	C	D	C	C	D	D	B

MISCELLANEOUS

1. D.

2. A: School is to the west of hospital. Police post is to the north of the hospital. Court is to the north of the school. Therefore, the police post is to the each of court.

Court	→ E	Police Post
N		N
↑		↑
School		Hospital

3. D.

4. B.

5. C: B and E are the two short-sized students without spectacles.

6. D: The tallish Gandhi House student without spectacles is F.

7. C:

S. sized	S. sized	S. sized	Tallish	S. sized	Tallish
A	B	C	D	E	F
Nehru	House		Gandhi	House	
↓		↓	↓		
Spectacles	X	Spectacles	Spectacles	X	X

The Gandhi House short sized student without spectacles is E.

8. B: After exchanging positions with Kamal, Appu becomes sixth from the left and seventh from the right which means that there are twenty two children in the row. After exchanging position with Appu, Kamal will be fourth from the right and nineteenth from the left.

9. B: The eighteenth letter from the left will be I.

10. B.

11. A.

12. D.

13. D.

14. C.

15. A: The position of the five boys from the top was as under—Hari, Jayant, Krishna, Ram and Govind.

16. D: Dhulia > Amalner; Sri Rampur > Nasik; Jalgaon < Sri Rampur; Jalgaon > Amalner; Amalner < Nasik; Amalner > Manmad.

Dhulia, Nasik, Sri Rampur and Jalgaon are bigger than Amalner; Manmad is smaller than Amalner.

17. B.

18. C.

19. B: I + old man + old woman + wife + husband + child + wife + husband + child = 9 persons.

20. A.

21. D.

22. B.

23. A.

24. C: Apple is not at the bottom, so it cannot be opposite orange which is at the top. Melon and peach are opposite each other. So none of these will be opposite orange. Also, banana is one of its neighbours. So, the sixth fruit mango must be opposite the orange, and at the bottom.

25. C: 10 + Manisha + 10 = 21.

26. A: The second letter is E, the fourth is T, the sixth is N, the seventh is A, the eighth is N and the ninth letter is T. The meaningful word made from these letters is TENANT.

27. B: Since B and D are twins, therefore, D is also 3 years younger to A, and A is 3 years younger to C. Therefore, C is older than D by 3 + 3, *i.e.,* 6 years.

PLACE ARRANGEMENT

Place arrangement generally refers to the positioning of persons or objects in a manner indicated by set of information given. One has to understand the order of placement and then attempt questions following the given information.

EXERCISE

Directions : *In the following questions, under-stand the arrangement pattern and then select the right answer from the given options :*

1. Five boys are sitting in a row. Raghu is not adjacent to Shyam or Amit. Ajay is not adjacent to Shyam. Raghu is adjacent to Mayank. If Mayank is at the middle in the row, then Ajay is adjacent to whom out of the following?
   A. Amit   B. Raghu
   C. Mayank   D. Shyam
   E. Data Inadequate

2. Mini is to the right of Rajni but to the left of Ananta. Saya is to the right of Mini but to the left of Jaya. Who is on the extreme left if all the girls are facing North?
   A. Jaya   B. Mini
   C. Rajni   D. Saya
   E. Ananta

3. O, P, Q, R, S and T are standing on a bench according to their height. P is taller than O but shorter than S. Only S is taller than T. R is shorter than P but taller than Q. Who is the shortest?
   A. O
   B. Q
   C. P
   D. Cannot be said
   E. None of these

4. Five personalities are living in a multistoried building. Mr. Effortless lives in a flat above Mr. Active, Mr. Charge lives in a flat below Mr. Diligent, Mr. Active lives in a flat above Mr. Diligent and Mr. Behaved lives in a flat below Mr. Charge. Who lives in the topmost flat?
   A. Mr. Charge
   B. Mr. Diligent
   C. Mr. Effortless
   D. Mr. Behaved
   E. Cannot be said

5. In a pile of 10 books there are 3 of History, 3 of Hindi, 2 of Maths, and 2 of English. Taking from above there is an English book between a History and Maths book, a History book between a Maths and an English book, a Hindi book between an English and a Maths book, a Maths book between two Hindi books, and two Hindi books between a Maths and a History book. Book of which subject is at the sixth position from the top?
   A. English   B. Hindi
   C. History   D. Maths
   E. Data Inadequate

6. Five persons P, Q, R, S and T are sitting in a row facing you such that S is on the left of R and Q is

on the right of T. P is on the right of R and Q is on the left of S. If T occupies a corner position, then who is sitting in the centre?

A. P   B. Q
C. R   D. S
E. Data Inadequate

Directions (Qs. 7 to 11) : *Read the following statements and answer the questions given below :*

Nine family members are sitting in a theatre in one row. They are J, K, L, M, N, O, P, Q and R. L is at the right of M and at third place at the right of N. K is at one end of the row. Q is immediately next to O and P. O is at third place at the left of K. J is right next to the left of O.

7. Which of the following statement is true?
   A. There is one person between L and O
   B. R and P are neighbours
   C. M is at one extreme end
   D. N is at two seats away from J.
   E. None of the above

8. The family members sitting on the right of O are :
   A. RML   B. JQP
   C. QPK   D. KPR
   E. Cannot be determined

9. Who is sitting in the centre of the row?
   A. L   B. J
   C. O   D. Q
   E. None of the above

10. Who are sitting next to L?
    A. A and O   B. M and J
    C. M and O   D. P and J
    E. Data Inadequate

11. Who is at the other end of the row?
    A. R   B. J
    C. P   D. N
    E. Q

Directions (Qs. 12 to 14) : (P) There are five friends; (Q) They are standing in a row facing south; (R) Jayesh is to the immediate right of Alok; (S) Pramod is between Babir and Subodh; (T) Subodh is between Jayesh and Pramod.

12. Who is at the extreme left end?
    A. Alok
    B. Babir
    C. Subodh
    D. Data inadequate
    E. None of these

13. Who is in the middle?
    A. Babir
    B. Pramod
    C. Subodh
    D. Jayesh
    E. Alok

14. To find answers to the above two questions, which of the given statements can be dispensed with?
    A. None   B. P only
    C. Q only   D. R only
    E. S only

Directions (Qs. 15 to 17) : *Read the following information and answer the questions given below:*

   (i) P, Q, R, S and T reside in a five-storey building.
   (ii) Q and T do not reside on the ground floor.
   (iii) S resides one storey above P and one storey below R.
   (iv) T does not reside on the top floor.

15. On which floor does S reside?
   A. Second   B. Fourth
   C. Fifth   D. First
   E. Data inadequate

16. How many of them do reside above R?
   A. 3   B. 2
   C. 4   D. 1
   E. Data inadequate

17. To find out the answers to the above two questions, which of the four given statements can be dispensed with ?
   A. Only *(iv)*
   B. Only *(ii)* and *(iii)*
   C. None
   D. Only *(i)*
   E. Only *(ii)* and *(iv)*

Directions (Qs. 18 to 20) : *Read the following information and answer the questions given below :*

(i) Six friends are playing a card game facing at the centre.

(ii) Subodh is to the right of Prabodh.

(iii) There is one person between Uma and Sudha.

(iv) Prabir is between Subodh and Uma and second to the left of Aloke.

18. Who is to the right of Sudha?
   A. Prabodh   B. Uma
   C. Aloke   D. Prabir
   E. Data inadequate

19. If Aloke and Subodh interchange their positions, who will be second to the right of Prabir?
   A. Prabodh
   B. Subodh
   C. Uma
   D. Sudha
   E. None of these

20. To answer the above two questions, which of the following statements can be dispensed with?
   A. (iii) only   B. (iv) only
   C. (iii) or (iv) only   D. None
   E. (ii) only

EXPLANATORY ANSWERS

1. B. : The order of sitting is :
Amit, Shyam, Mayank, Ajay, Raghu

or

Ajay, Raghu, Mayank, Amit, Shyam

2. C. : The order in which the girls are positioned is :
Rajni, Mini, Ananta, Saya, Jaya

or

Saya, Jaya, Ananta

or

Saya, Ananta, Jaya

3. D. : In descending order of height, the standing positions are :

S		S
T		T
P	*or*	P
R		R
O		Q
Q		O

Either O or Q is the shortest. The informa-tion given is not enough to clarify the answer.

4. C. : The personalities living in flats in multi-storied building are in order given below :

    Mr. Effortless
    Mr. Active
    Mr. Diligent
    Mr. Charge
    Mr. Behaved

5. B. : The pile of books is in the order :

1st —	History
	English
	Maths
	History
	English
6th —	Hindi
	Maths
	Hindi
	Hind
10th —	History

6. D. : Sitting order while facing us is :
P, R, S, Q, T

7. A. : Order of sitting for questions 23 to 27 is : N, R, M, L, J, O, Q, P, K.

8. C.

9. B.

10. B.

11. D.

12. A. : For questions 28 to 30 five friends are standing in this order :
Alok, Jayesh, Subodh, Pramod, Babir

13. C.

14. B.

15. D. : For answers 31 to 33 the manner of residing in a five-storey building is :

    Q
    T
    R
    S
Ground floor - P

16. B.

17. C.

18. A. : The manner of sitting is :

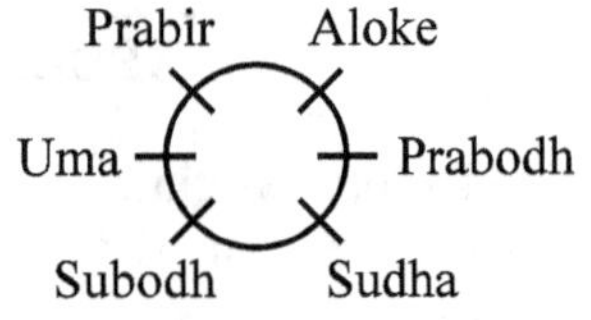

19. B. : After interchanging positions the order will be :

Prabir   Aloke
Uma   Prabodh
Subodh   Sudha

20. A.

DIAGRAMMATIC PUZZLES

In these problems one has to count the geometrical figures in a given complex figure. A little bit of systematic approach is needed to get the correct number of the asked figure. The shapes of all geometrical figures must be clear in mind.

EXERCISE

1. How many triangles are there in the figure given below?

A. 24　　　　　B. 27
C. 25　　　　　D. 26

2. How many parallelograms are there in this figure?

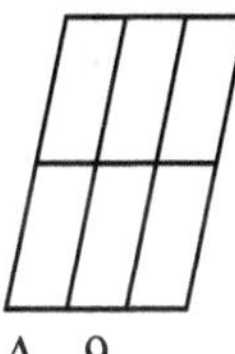

A. 9　　　　　B. 13
C. 15　　　　　D. 18

3. How many triangles are there in this figure?

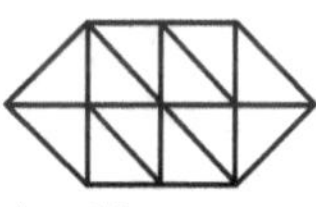

A. 16　　　　　B. 17
C. 18　　　　　D. 19

4. The number of rectangles in this figure are.

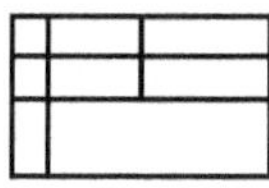

A. 21　　　　　B. 24
C. 23　　　　　D. 25

5. How many squares are hidden in this figure?

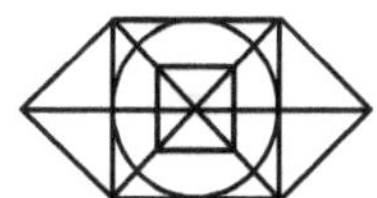

A. 7　　　　　B. 8
C. 9　　　　　D. 10

6. The number of triangles in this figure are.

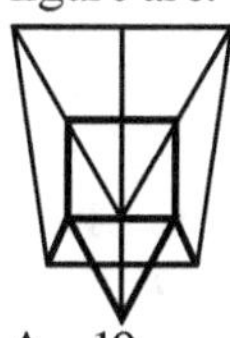

A. 19　　　　　B. 16
C. 21　　　　　D. 15

7. How many squares are there in the figure given below?

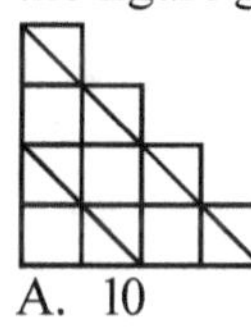

A. 10　　　　　B. 11
C. 13　　　　　D. 14

8. The number of circles in this figure is

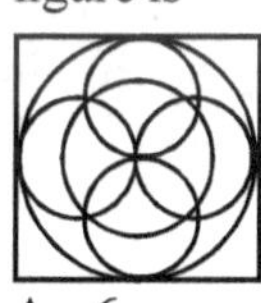

A. 6　　　　　B. 5
C. 2　　　　　D. 3

9. How many triangles are there in the figure given below?

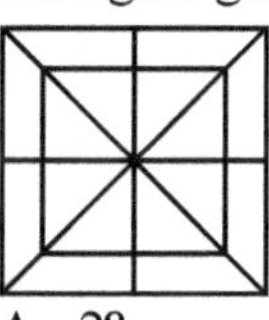

A. 28　　　　　B. 36
C. 24　　　　　D. 32

10. How many straight lines are needed to draw the figure in question 9?

A. 10   B. 12
C. 11   D. 13

11. How many squares are there in this figure?

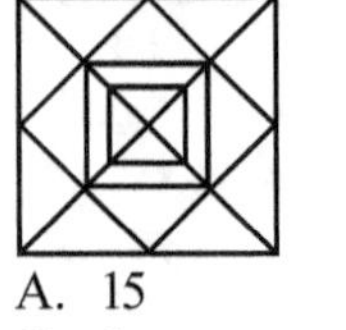

A. 15   B. 11
C. 8   D. 3

12. The number of squares in the figure below is

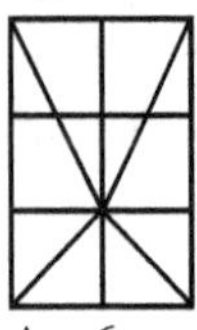

A. 6   B. 10
C. 8   D. 12

13. The number of triangles in the figure given in earlier question is

A. 15   B. 16
C. 17   D. 18

14. How many hexagons are there in the figure given below?

A. 1   B. 2
C. 4   D. 5

15. The number of parallelograms in this figure is

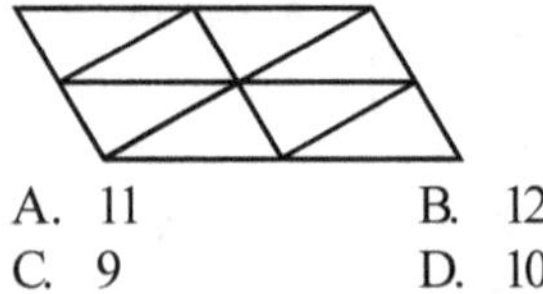

A. 11   B. 12
C. 9   D. 10

16. The number of squares in the figure given below is

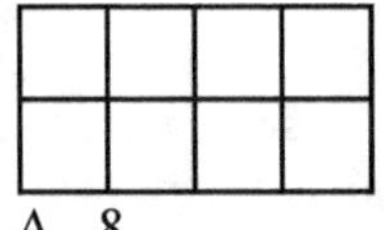

A. 8   B. 10
C. 11   D. 12

17. How many circles are there in the figure given below?

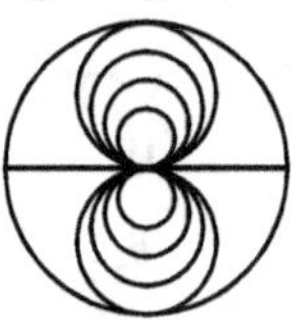

A. 5   B. 6
C. 8   D. 9

18. How many triangles are there in the figure?

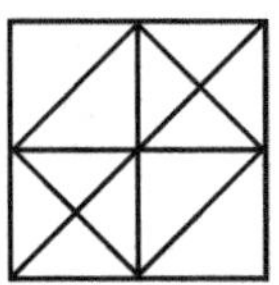

A. 26   B. 25
C. 28   D. 27

19. How many straight lines are used to make this figure?

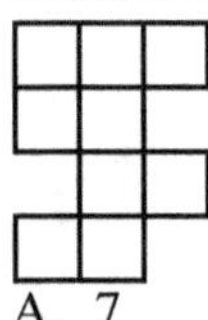

A. 7   B. 11
C. 8   D. 10

20. How many rectangles are there in the figure?

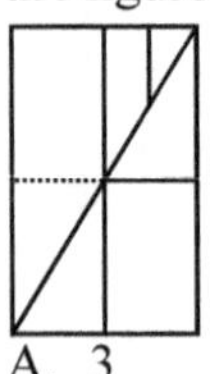

A. 3   B. 5
C. 6   D. 4

EXPLANATORY ANSWERS

1. B **2. D** **3. A** **4. C**
5. D **6. B**

7. C :

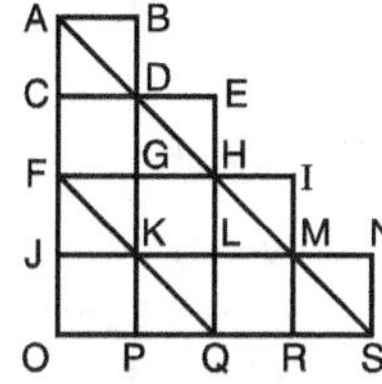

The simplest squares are : ABCD, CDFG, DEGH, FGJK, GHKL, HILM, JKOP, KLPQ, LMQR and MNRS *i.e.* – 10 squares.

Other squares are : CEJL, FHOQ and GIPR *i.e.* – 3 squares

So, the total number of squares is $10 + 3 = 13$

8. A :

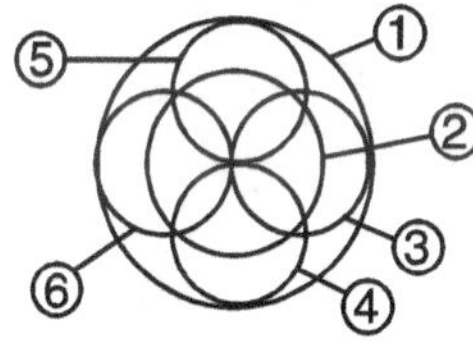

There are two main circles and four smaller circles intersecting each other.

So, the total number of circles is $2 + 4 = 6$

9. D **10. B**

11. C :

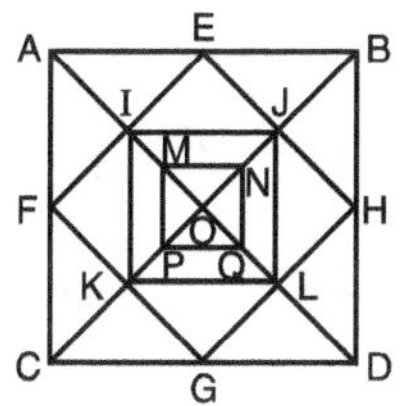

The main squares are : ABCD,

IJKL, MNPQ and EFHG *i.e.* – 4 squares.

Other squares are. EIJO, IFKO, JOLH and OKGL *i.e.* – 4 squares

So, the total number of squares is $4 + 4 = 8$

12. C :

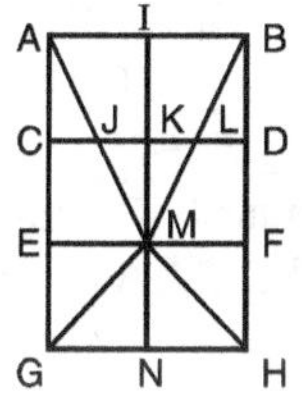

The simplest squares are : AICK, CKEM, EMGN, IBKD, KDMF ad MFNH *i.e.* – 6 squares

Other squares are ABEF and CDGH *i.e.* – 2 squares.

So, the total number of squares is $6 + 2 = 8$

13. B

14. C :

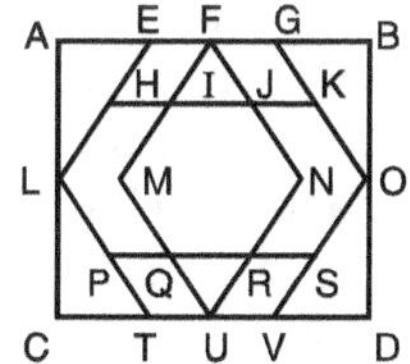

The larger hexagon is : EG – GO – GV – VT – TL – LE *i.e.* – 1 hexagon.

The smaller hexagons are : IJ – JN – NR – RQ – QM – MT, HJ – JN – NR – RP – PL – LH and IK – KO – OS – SQ – QM – MI, *i.e.*, –3, hexagons. So, the total number of hexagons is $1 + 3 = 4$

(Hexagon is a figure having six side of equal length.)

15. A :

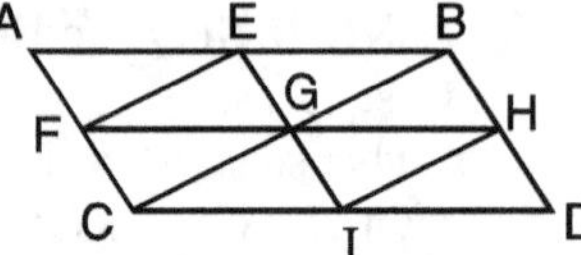

The main parallelogram in ABCD – *i.e.* – 1 parallelogram
The simplest parallelogram are : AEFG, FGCI, EBGH, GHID, FECG and GBIH *i.e.* – 6 parallelograms
Other parallelograms are : ABFH, FHCD, AECI and EBID *i.e.* – 4 parallelograms
So, the total number of parallelograms is
1 + 6 + 4 = 11

16. C

17. D :

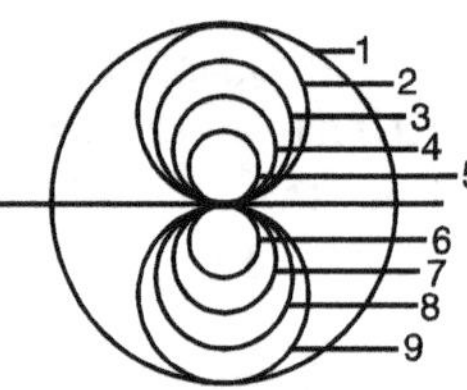

There is 1 main circle, 4 circles on the top of the horizontal lines and 4 circles below it.
So, the total number of circles is 1 + 4 + 4 = 9

18. A

19. B :

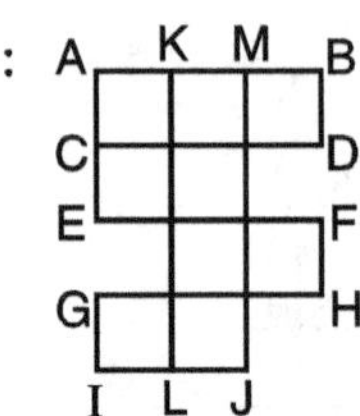

The horizontal lines are AB, CD, EF, GH and IJ *i.e.* – 5 lines
The vertical lines are AC, KL MJ, BD, FH and GI *i.e.* – 6 lines
So, the total number of lines used to draw this figure is 5 + 6 = 11

20. B :

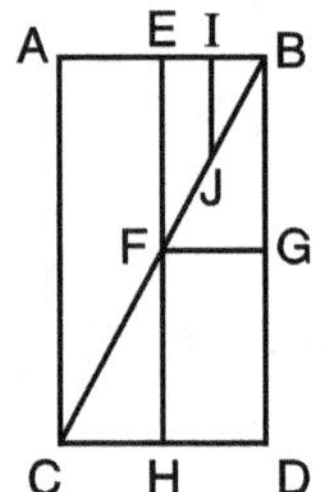

The main rectangle is ABCD *i.e.* – 1 rectangle
The simplest rectangles are AECH, EBFG and FGHD *i.e.* – 3 rectangles

CUBES AND DICES

The questions related to problems on cubes and dices are aimed to check the imaginative power of the candidate. The candidate must have the ability to visualise quickly in three-dimensional object for what is asked of it. To attempt such questions some basic facts should be kept in mind and the visualisation ability should be combined with fast and accurate calculations.

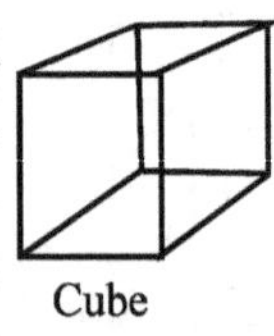

Cube

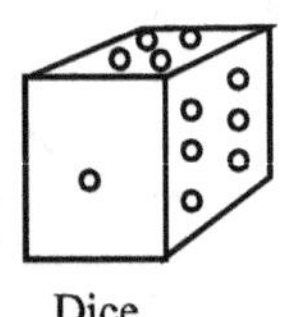

Dice

- Cube has six faces/sides and eight corners.
- Dice has six faces/sides.
- Problems are based on the same or different coloured faces.
- Problems are based only on the value occurring on the six faces.
- Problems are based on cutting the squares into specified number of smaller equal parts.

a	b	a
b	c	b
a	b	a

Diagrammatically, the explanation of a cube which is painted green on all sides can be understood easily taking one side of the cube.

This cube is divided into $3 \times 3 \times 3 = 27$ equal small cubes.

There are four corner pieces 'a'. so 4×2 *i.e.*, **8** pieces will be painted on 3 sides.

There are four middle pieces 'b', so 4×3 *i.e.,* **12** pieces will be painted on 2 sides

There is one middle piece 'c', so 1×6 *i.e.,* **6** pieces will be painted only on 1 side.

There will be one piece right in the centre of this cube *i.e.,* piece will not have paint at all.

So this cube has $8 + 12 + 6 + 1$ *i.e.,* 27 smaller cubes.

EXERCISE

1. Two positions of a dice are shown below. When there are two circles at the bottom, the number of circles at the top will be :

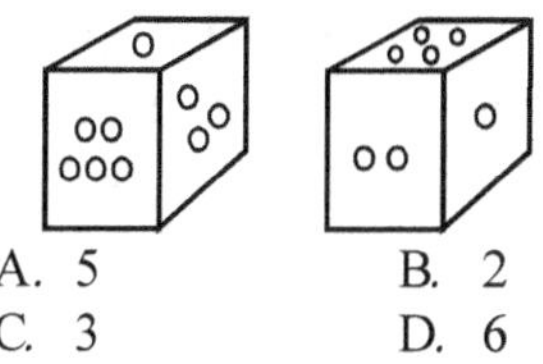

  A. 5   B. 2
  C. 3   D. 6

2. Two positions of a dice are shown below. When 4 is at the bottom, what number will be on the top?

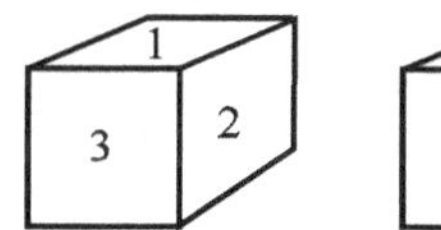 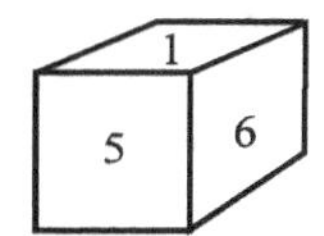

  A. 1   B. 2
  C. 5   D. 6

3. A cube is painted red on two adjacent faces and on one opposite face, yellow on two adjacent faces and green on the remaining face. It is then cut into 64 equal cubes. How many cubes have only one red and one green face?

  A. 4   B. 8
  C. 12   D. 16

4. Two positions of a dice with 1 to 6 dots on its sides are shown below. If the dice is resting on the side with three dots, what will be the number of dots on the side at the top?

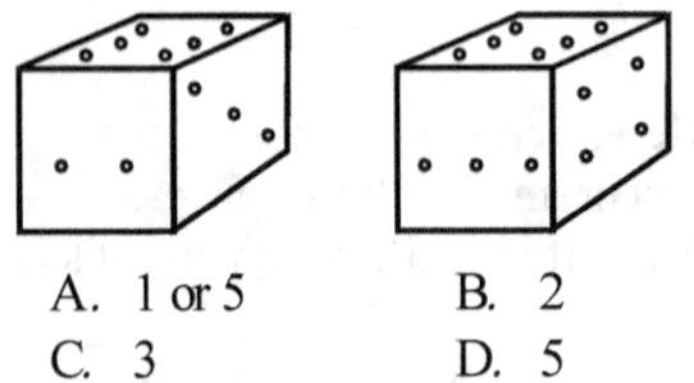

A. 1 or 5   B. 2
C. 3   D. 5

5. A cube, on whose sides letters have been written, is shown below in different positions as can be seen from different directions. Find the missing letter?

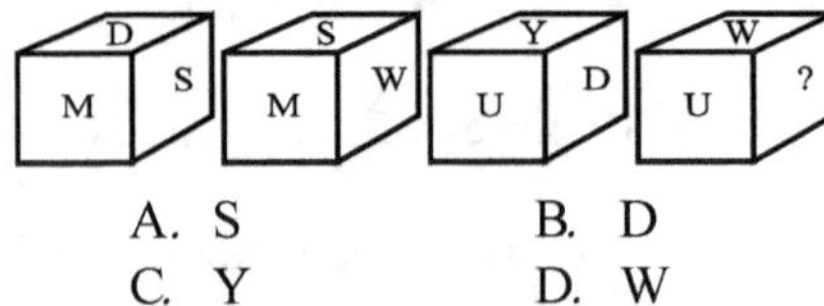

A. S   B. D
C. Y   D. W

6. If the total number of dots on opposite faces of a cubical block is always 7, find the figure which is correct?

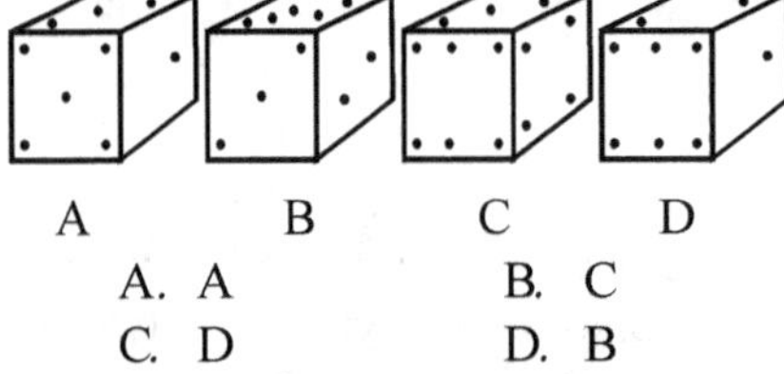

A   B   C   D

A. A   B. C
C. D   D. B

7. The minimum number of colours required to paint all the sides of a cube so that no two adjacent faces may have the same colour, is :

A. 6   B. 4
C. 3   D. 2

8. In a dice a, b, c and d, are written on the adjacent faces, in a clockwise order and e and f at the top and bottom. When c is at the top, what will be at the bottom?

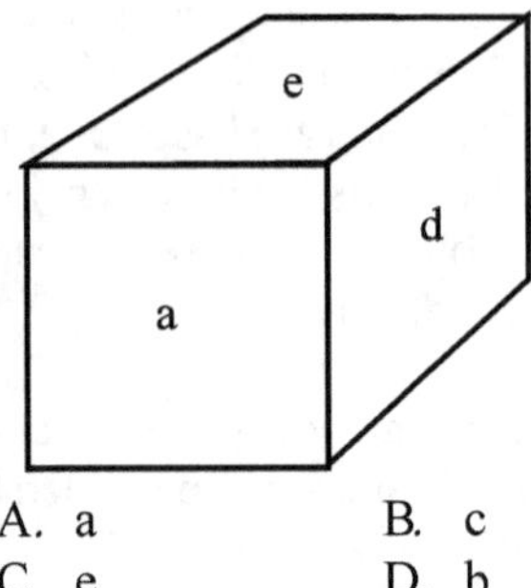

A. a   B. c
C. e   D. b

9. The number of cubes arranged one over the other in this figure will be :

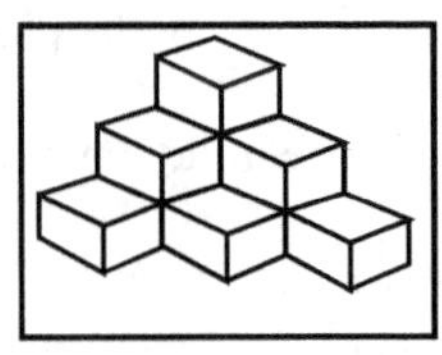

A. 8   B. 6
C. 5   D. 10

10. Two positions of a block are shown below. 5 and 6 are on opposite faces.

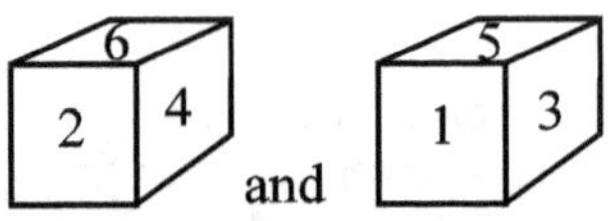 and

When 2 is at the bottom, what number will be at the top?

A. 1   B. 3
C. 4   D. 5

11. Two positions of a dice are given below. When 1 is at the top, which number will be at the bottom?

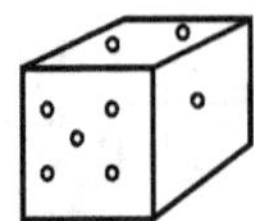 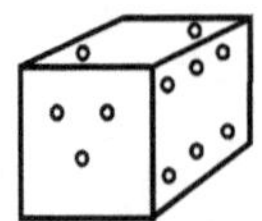

A. 3   B. 6
C. 2   D. 1

12. Two positions of a dice are shown below. When 2 is at the bottom, which number will be at the top?

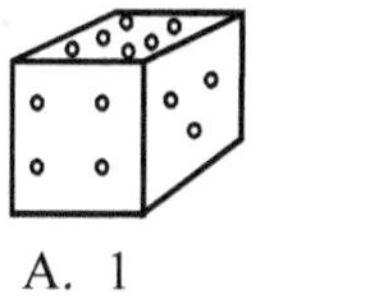

A. 1   B. 2
C. 3   D. 4

13. Study the three dices given below. What number will be opposite to the side bearing number 2?

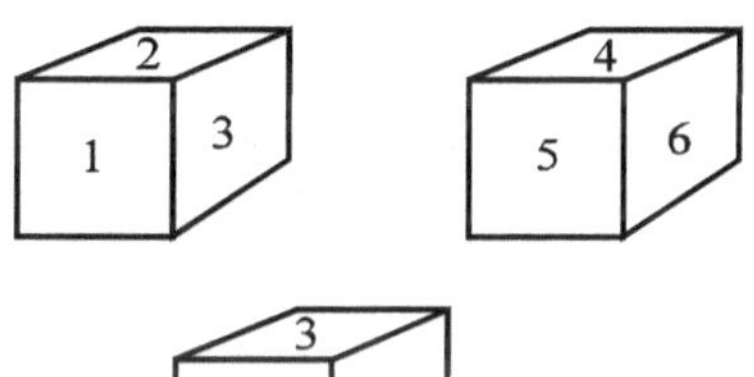

A. 4   B. 3
C. 6   D. 5

14. The sides of a cube are painted in different colours. Black side is opposite to red. White side is between black and red. Green side is adjacent to grey and blue side is adjacent to green. What colour will be on the side opposite to the white side of the cube?

A. Blue
B. Green
C. Grey
D. Data is insufficient

15. A cube is painted black on two adjacent faces and on one opposite face, red on two opposite faces and green on the remaining face. If it is cut into 64 equal cubes, then how many cubes will have only one black coloured face?

A. 32   B. 16
C. 12   D. 8

16. Six sides of a cube are coloured in the following manner

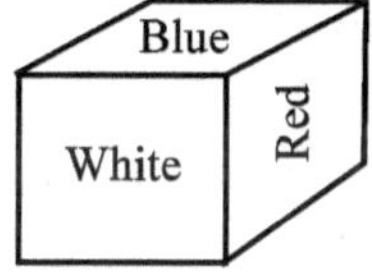
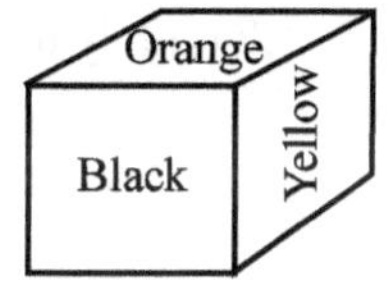

If blue and orange are opposite and red is on the top, which colour will be at the bottom?

A. Orange   B. Purple
C. Black   D. Yellow

17. A toy cube is painted orange on all sides. It is cut into 64 smaller cubes of equal size. How many smaller cubes are not painted at all?

A. 4   B. 8
C. 16   D. 20

18. A six centimetre cube is painted green on all sides. It is cut into two centimetre cubes. How many cubes will be there with two sides painted ?

A. 12   B. 8
C. 24   D. 4

19. What number in the dice, given below, will be on the side opposite to 6?

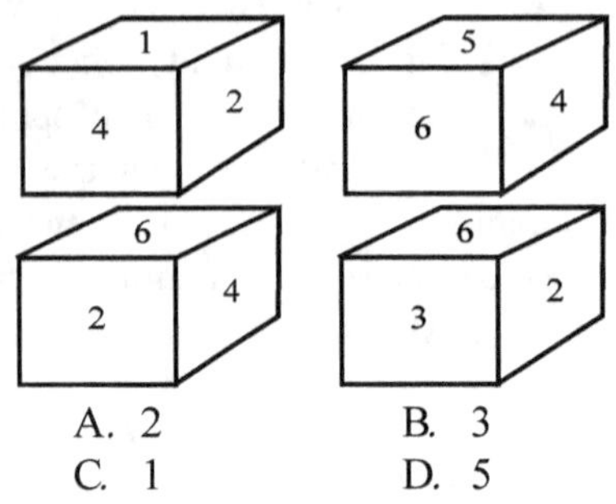

A. 2   B. 3
C. 1   D. 5

20. If the numbers on the opposite sides of the cube total as 7, which one of the following dices is definitely defective?

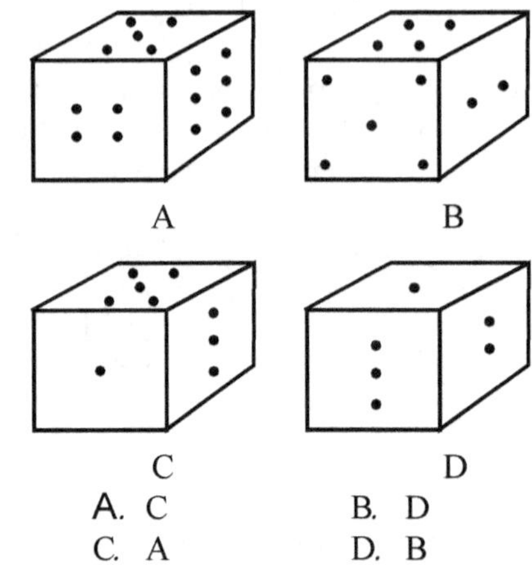

A. C   B. D
C. A   D. B

EXPLANATORY ANSWERS

1. A. : After observing the views of the same dice, the faces that can be clearly understood to be the opposites are :
2 — 5, 4 — 3 and 1— 6.

2. A. : In the given dice, the numbers adjacent to 1 are 3, 2, 5 and 6. So, the numbers on the opposite faces will be 1 and 4.

3. B

4. A. : It is, however, clear that the number on the face opposite 2 dots is the face with 4 dots. But it is not clear if the number 1 or 5 is on face opposite the face 3. The answer is either 1 or 5.

5. C. : The letters on the top and bottom sides are W and D respectively and the letters on the sides are U, Y, M and S clockwise.

6. A. : In this cubical block the number of dots on opposite faces will be 1—6, 3—4 and 5—2.

7. C. : A cube has six sides and two opposite sides can be painted in same colour.

8. A. : The two positions of dice will be :

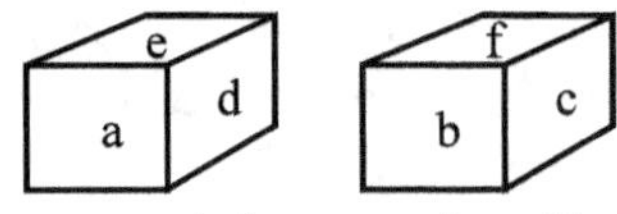

and the opposite sides will be a—c, b—d.

9. D

10. B. : When 5 and 6 are on opposite faces then the numbers on opposite faces will be 4—1 and 2—3. So, if 2 is at the bottom, 3 will be at the top.

11. B. : After observing the two views of the same dice, the faces that can be clearly understood to be the opposites are : 1—6, 2—4 and 3—5. So, when 1 is at the top, 6 will be at the bottom.

12. D. : The sides which are clearly understood to be the opposites are 1—3, 2—4 and 5—6. So, when 2 is at the bottom, 4 will be at the top.

13. D. : The numbers on the sides opposite to each other are 1 and 4; 2 and 5; 3 and 6.

14. B   15. C   16. D   17. B   18. A

19. C. : According to the given figures of the same dice, the numbers adjacent to 6 are 5, 4, 2 and 3. So, the number opposite to the side 6 will be 1.

20. D. : 5 and 2 are on adjacent sides instead of being on the opposite side.

ROWS AND RANKS

These type of problems need easy calculations to find out the number of objects in a row, lane or queue or to find a person's rank in a class of certain number of students; or to find the total number of students.

EXERCISE

1. In a row of trees, one tree is fifth from either end of the row. How many trees are in the row?
   A. 11   B. 8
   C. 10   D. 9
   E. None of these

2. Jaya ranks 5th in a class of 53. What is her rank from the bottom in the class?
   A. 49th   B. 48th
   C. 47th   D. 50th
   E. None of these

3. Mohan ranks twenty-first in a class of sixty-five students. What will be his (Mohan's) rank if the lowest candidate is assigned rank 1?
   A. 44th
   B. 45th
   C. 46th
   D. Data inadequate
   E. None of these

4. If Rahul finds that he is 12th from the right in a line of boys and 4th from the left, how many boys should be added to the line such that there are 28 boys in the line?
   A. 12   B. 14
   C. 20   D. 13
   E. None of these

5. In a row of boys, Rajan is tenth from the right and Suraj is tenth from the left. When Rajan and Suraj interchange their positions, Suraj will be twenty-seventh from the left. Which of the following will be Rajan's position from the right?
   A. Tenth
   B. Twenty-sixth

C. Twenty-ninth
D. Twenty-fifth
E. None of these

6. Mahesh and Suresh are ranked 11th and 12th respectively from the top in a class of 41 students. What will be their respective ranks from the bottom?
A. 32nd and 33rd
B. 29th and 30th
C. 30th and 31st
D. 31st and 30th
E. None of these

7. Uma ranked 8th from the top and 37th from bottom in a class. How many students are there in the class?
A. 47   B. 46
C. 45   D. 48
E. None of these

8. In a queue, Sadiq is 14th from the front and Joseph is 17th from the end, while Jane is in between Sadiq and Joseph. If Sadiq be ahead of Joseph and there be 48 persons in the queue, how many persons are there between Sadiq and Jane?
A. 5   B. 6
C. 7   D. 8
E. None of these

9. Rohan ranked eleventh from the top and twenty-seventh from the bottom among the students who passed the annual examination in a class. If the number of students who failed in the examination was 12, how many students appeared for the examination?
A. 48

B. 49
C. 50
D. Cannot be determined
E. None of these

10. Some boys are sitting in a row. P is sitting fourteenth from the left and Q is seventh from the right. If there are four boys between P and Q, how many boys are there in the row?
A. 19   B. 21
C. 25   D. 23
E. None of these

11. There are five different houses, P to T, in a row. P is to the right of Q and T is to the left of R and right of P, and Q is to the right of S. Which of the houses is in the middle?
A. Q   B. P
C. S   D. T
E. None of these

12. Madhav ranks seventeenth in a class of thirtyone. What is his rank from the last?
A. 13   B. 14
C. 15   D. 16
E. 17

13. Veena ranks 73rd from the top in a class of 182. What is her rank from the bottom if 22 students have failed the examination?
A. 88   B. 108
C. 110   D. 90
E. 93

14. Rakesh ranked 9th from the top and 38th from the bottom in a class. How many students are there in the class?
A. 47   B. 45

C. 46   D. 48
  E. None of these
15. John ranks 19th in class and is
    36th from the last. How many

students are there in the class?
  A. 53   B. 54
  C. 51   D. 50
  E. None of these

EXPLANATORY ANSWERS

1. D.:

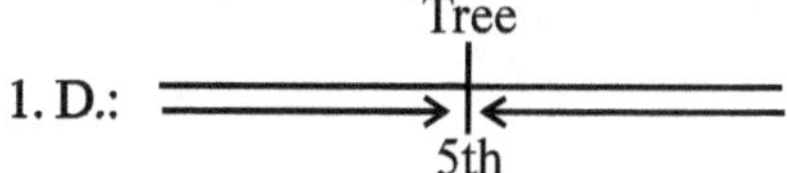

Total number of trees in the row are :
$(5 + 5) - 1 = 9$

2. A.:

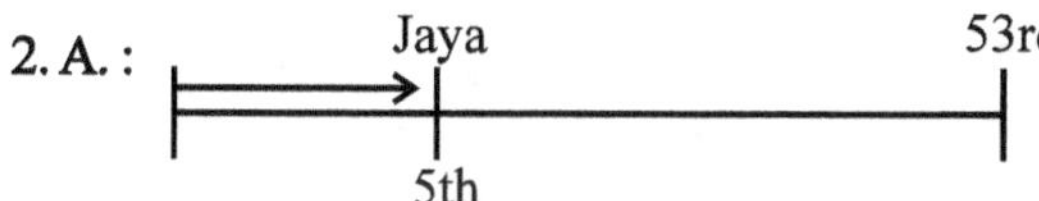

Jaya's rank from the bottom is :
$(53 - 5) + 1 = 49$th.

3. B.:

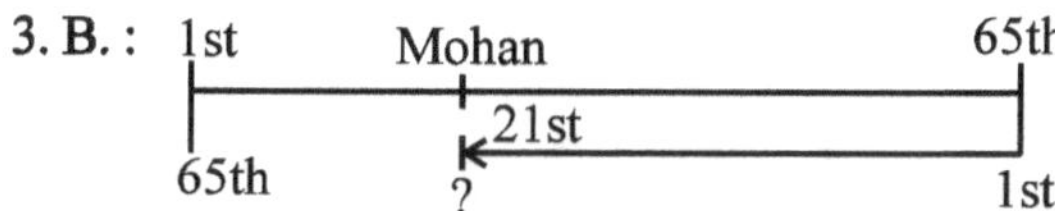

Note : Mohan's rank from the last or the question asked means the same.
Mohan's rank is $(65 - 21) + 1 = 45$th

4. D.:

The number of boys in the line are :
$(4 + 12) - 1 = 15$
To make a line of 28 boys, $(28 - 15)$ *i.e.* 13 more boys are needed.

5. E   **6. D**

7. E.:

Total number of students in the class are :
$(8 + 37) - 1 = 44$

8. C   **9. B**

10. C.:

The number of boys in the row are : $(14 + 4 + 7) = 25$

11. B. : The houses in the row are :
DBAEC

12. C. :

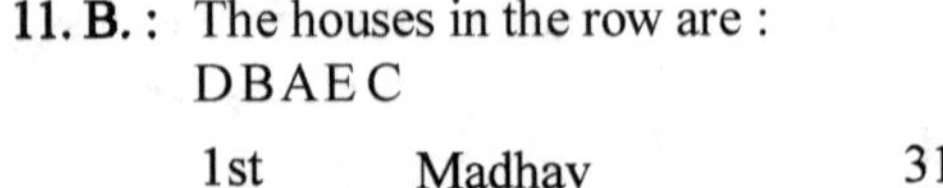
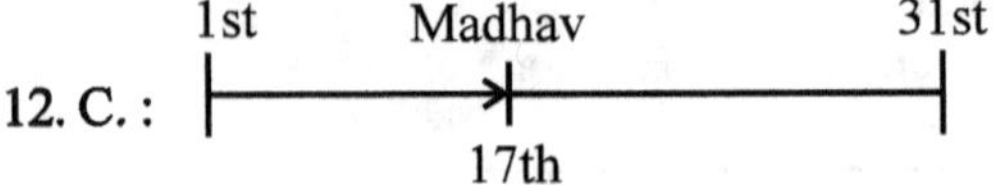

Madhav's rank from the last is :
$(31 - 17) + 1 = 15$th

13. A

14. C. :

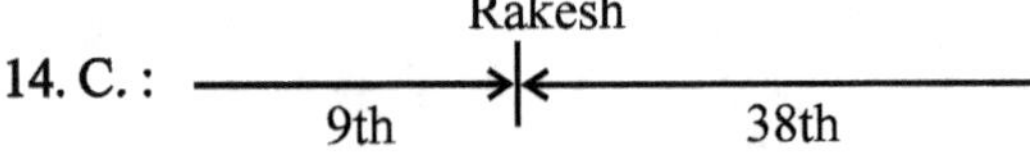

Number of students in the class is :
$(9 + 38) - 1 = 46$

15. B. :

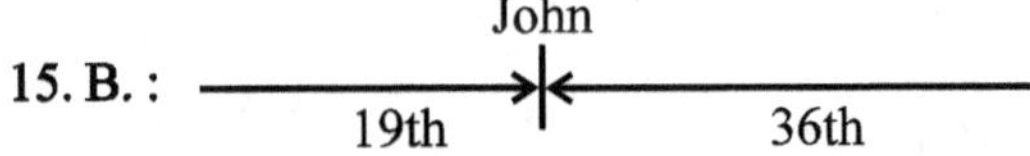

Number of students in the class is :
$(19 + 36) - 1 = 54$

TEST OF ENGLISH LANGUAGE

Test of English Language

What does this test measure

The test of English language measures your knowledge of English language through questions/items of functional grammar, reading comprehension, context based vocabulary, etc. There will be no question on English literature, or on poetic expressions.

The different types of questions which are used in this test can be classified as :

(A) Spotting the Error
(B) Sentence Completion or Fill in the blanks
(C) Reading Comprehension
(D) Sentence Structure
(E) Rearrangement of sentences.

Each of which measures one or more areas of language abilities.

(A) Spotting the Error

Candidate's familiarity with the conventions and grammatical rules of standard written English is tested in this type of question. Emphasis here will be on assessing knowledge of correct expression. A correct sentence should be grammatically and structurally correct.

Each question in this section, is divided into four parts and each part is numbered. You have to decide whether there is any error in the sentence and find out in which of the parts the error exists, if there is any. If the sentence is correct, your answer is 'E' *i.e.* "No error". Study the example given below :

(1) (A) Last week/(B) Arun and Kuldeep/(C) do the work/(D) which was pending./(E) No error.

Note that the sentence has been divided into four parts and each part is numbered. The sentence is about the completion of pending work two persons did the previous week. The error is in the verb used. The verb should denote an act that is already completed. The verb should read as "did" and the correct sentence should be "Last week/Arun and Kuldeep/did the work/which was pending". Since the error is in the third part, the correct answer is "C". Now try the example given below:

(2) (A) Before they left/(B) the office/(C) they switched off/(D) all the lights./(E) No error.

In the above sentence you will note that there is no grammatical error. It is also meaningful. Therefore, this question has no error and your answer should be "E" which is "No error".

(B) Sentence Completion or Fill-in-the Blanks

This type of questions measure your ability to recognise words and phrases that both logically and grammatically complete the meaning of the sentence. A sentence is given with a word missing in it. The missing word will be indicated by a blank. You have to find the most appropriate word/phrase from the given alternatives. In deciding which of the five words best fills the blank space, you must consider the context provided by the sentence.

Given below are two items for practice :

(3) We were so late, we .... had time to catch the train.

(A) nearly	(B) almost	(C) simply
(D) not	(E) hardly	

"So late" sets the tone of the sentence. Because the people were late they just managed to get into the train and only "E", *i.e.,* "hardly" conveys this meaning. "Nearly" and "simply" could have been the right choices if the sentence were to read as "missed the train" after the blank. "Almost" and "not" are not correct grammatically.

(4) Ratesh's shirt has a pattern of boats all .... it.

(A) on	(B) over	(C) down
(D) round	(E) with	

In the above example, the only word which grammatically fits is "over". So "B" is the answer.

You may also be given a passage like the one given below :

Instructions : In the following there are blanks, each of which has been numbered. These numbers are given below the passage and against each, five words are suggested, one of which fills the blank appropriately in the context of the whole passage. Find out the appropriate words.

My father waved me goodbye and the bus **(5)**, The person sitting **(6)** to me was a Government Engineer **(7)** to Hyderabad, **(8)** inspect the roads.

(5)	(A) going	(B) started	(C) arrived	
	(D) stopped	(E) travelling		
(6)	(A) next	(B) besides	(C) near	
	(D) side	(E) neighbour		
(7)	(A) coming	(B) arriving	(C) going	
	(D) visiting	(E) flying		

(8) (A) to (B) for (C) was
(D) so (E) then

In the above passage you have to fill up the blanks in such a way that the whole passage becomes meaningful in the context of the entire passage. It is not sufficient that the sentence alone is meaningful and grammatically correct.

In the first blank the word which would fit in the blank (5) is "started". Even though "arrived" or "stopped", "going" and "travelling" are not grammatically correct and also not meaningful.

In the next blank (6) only "next" fits properly. This is decided by the preposition "to" which comes after the blank. It is unidiomatic to use "near" or "besides" with the preposition "to". To use the words "side" and "neighbour" one has to change the sentence and therefore they are not correct answers.

The blank (7) has to be filled by keeping the entire passage in view. Since the passage is about a bus journey "flying" is a wrong answer. The description of the bus journey is of someone travelling to Hyderabad and therefore "coming" is a wrong alternative. "Arriving" and "visiting" are grammatically incorrect. Therefore, the correct answer is "going".

For the blank (8) "to" is the correct answer. To use "was" and "then" is ungrammatical. The other words "so" and "then" are meaningless.

(C) Structuring Sentences

The questions of this type assess the ability to comprehend, organise and structure sentences. The question consists of a set of five words. These five words have to be arranged to make a meaningful sentence. Note that all the five words should be used and each word should be used only once.

The alphabet in the bracket preceding the word is the code given to the word. Each choice given represents a certain way in which the words can be arranged. You have to find which of the arrangements forms a sentence which is meaningful and grammatically correct.

See the following illustration and try to solve it :

(9) (A) NOW (B) REPLACE (C) THE
(D) PLEASE (E) BOOK

(A) DBAEC (B) BDCEA (C) DBCEA
(D) DEACB (E) DECAB

You should rearrange mentally the words so that a meaningful sentence is formed. You may take one word as a starting point and rearrange various other words to see whether they will form a sentence *e.g.* you may try starting with the word "book" as the first word and rearrange the other words. By referring to the alternatives given you may also be able to decide which of the words to use first as a reference point to arrive at the correct answer. Needless to say, you should be able to do this rearrangement in your mind itself. In the above illustration, the correct answer will be "Please replace the book now". The correct order of letters therefore would be "DBCEA". The correct answer therefore will be "C".

(D) Reading Comprehension

Questions on reading comprehension measure the ability to understand, analyse and apply information and concepts presented in the written form. All questions are to be answered on the basis of what is stated or implied in the given passage. Reading comprehension, therefore, evaluates your ability to :

- understand words and statements in the given passage.
- understand the logical relationships between points and concepts in the given passage.
- draw inference from facts and statements in the given passage.

Guidelines for Answering the Reading Comprehension Test

Given below are some guidelines which would be of use to you in answering satisfactorily the questions set on the passage.

(1) Answer all questions on the basis of what is stated or implied in the passage itself. Even when you do not agree with what the author of the passage is saying, do not let your opinions or knowledge and information influence your judgement of what the author is saying.

(2) Read the questions carefully, making sure that you understand what is being asked. If need be refer back to the passage for finding the answer.

(3) Read all the alternatives carefully. Never assume that you have selected the best answer without first reading all the alternatives.

(4) Remember that understanding is the critical factor in reading comprehension.

(Q. 10-14) Read the following passage carefully and answer the questions given below it. Certain words in the passage have been *italicised* to help you locate them while answering some of the questions:

Malaria is always associated with damp and marshy land. This is not because the land is damp but because still water is the breeding place of the mosquito, which begins its life as a larva living in water. Malaria does not frequently occur in dry desert countries. We should destroy mosquitoes to prevent their breeding in still water. This can be done by *draining* all ponds and pools, and by keeping them covered in breeding season with a film of kerosene oil, which kills the larve.

(10) Where is malaria not very common?
  (A) In cold countries.
  (B) In dry countries.
  (C) In countries having a lot of rain.
  (D) In hot countries.
  (E) Not mentioned in the passage.

In the above illustration alternative "B" is correct. It is stated in the passage that mosquitoes carry malaria and mosquitoes breed in swamps or in a damp condition. Dry countries are the place where damp and marshy conditions are absent. A country is called a "dry country" because the country is not only hot but also without rains. An alternative that comes closest to this is "In hot countries". However, this cannot be selected because it does not mean that it does not rain in hot countries and consequently there is no dampness. The chances of damp conditions prevailing in countries having lot of rains is very high, so alternative "C" also cannot be a right choice. Same thing is true about alternative "cold countries". The fifth alternative cannot be the right choice because in the passage the conditions under which mosquitoes breed and do not breed is mentioned. So the right answer is "B".

(11) What is the breeding place of the mosquito?
  (A) Flowing water   (B) Shallow water   (C) Dirty water
  (D) Deep water   (E) Still water

For the above question you should refer back to the passage. You will find the second sentence in the passage says "________ because still water is the breeding place of the mosquito". Therefore, the correct answer to the above question is "still water", *i.e.*, "E" is the answer.

(12) What is the use of kerosene oil in preventing Malaria ?
  (A) It kills the fully grown mosquitoes.
  (B) It cleanses the pools and ponds.
  (C) It kills the developing mosquitoes.
  (D) It helps in burning the things around the ponds.
  (E) It purifies the air.

Referring to the passage you will find the correct answer given in the last sentence of the passage where it says "________ by keeping them covered in breeding season with a film of kerosene oil which kills the larve". A larve as you know is a developing mosquito and therefore among the given alternatives "C" is correct.

You may have questions like this also.

(13) Which of the following words is most SIMILAR in meaning of the word *Draining* as used in the passage?

      (A) Depleting   (B) Discharging   (C) Emptying

      (D) Straining   (E) Clearing

"Draining" means letting water off. So "Emptying" is the right choice, as the one with similar meaning of "draining".

(14) Which of the following words is most OPPOSITE in meaning of the word *Still* as used in the passage ?

      (A) Noisy   (B) Flowing   (C) Living

      (D) Yet   (E) Steady

"Still" here means without movement or motion. So the choice "Flowing" is appropriate, as the one opposite in meaning of "still".

(E) Rearrangement of Sentences

Another set of questions, in which ability to understand what is read and to extract information is assessed is discussed below. These questions test your ability to organise your thoughts and ideas in a suitable sequence.

Questions of this type requires the candidates to rearrange the given sentences in the proper sequence so as to form a meaningful paragraph.

(Q. 15-19) Rearrange the following five sentences A, B, C, D and E in the proper sequence so as to form a meaningful paragraph; then answer the questions given below them:

A. When he reached home, he found his father hale and hearty.

B. He decided to rush home after finishing some urgent work.

C. Suresh received a telegram saying that his father was sick.

D. He realised that it was a trick played by someone.

E. In a few hours, he boarded the train for his home-town.

(15) Which sentence should come FIRST in the paragraph?

      (A) A   (B) B   (C) C   (D) D   (E) E

(16) Which sentence should come SECOND in the paragraph?

      (A) A   (B) B   (C) C   (D) D   (E) E

(17) Which sentence should come THIRD in the paragraph?

      (A) A   (B) B   (C) C   (D) D   (E) E

(18) Which sentence should come FOURTH in the paragraph?
  (A) A   (B) B   (C) C   (D) D   (E) E

(19) Which sentence should come LAST in the paragraph?
  (A) A   (B) B   (C) C   (D) D   (E) E

The correct form of meaningful paragraph will be as under:

A.   Suresh received a telegram saying that his father was sick.
B.   He decided to rush home after finishing some urgent work.
C.   In a few hours, he boarded the train for his home-town.
D.   When he reached home, he found his father hale and hearty.
E.   He realised that it was a trick played by someone.

Accordingly, the answer to Question Nos. 15-19 will be as under:

  15 (C)   16 (B)   17 (E)   18 (A)   19 (D)

––––––––––

SPOTTING THE ERRORS

All kinds of errors are possible in using English as a tool of communication. Errors may be due to grammatical mistakes or due to slips in idiomatic uses. A sentence may be defined as a group of words that make a complete sense. A sentence consists of a noun phrase and a verb phrase. When we look at a sentence we have to ensure first that the subject agrees with the verb in number, the correct tense is used, appropriate propositions are used and correct article is used.

Directions (1-100) : *Read each sentence to find out whether there is any error in it. The error, if any, will be in one part of the sentence. The number of that part is the answer. If there is no error, the answer is 'E'. (Ignore the errors of punctuations, if any.)*

1. (A) In spite of working/(B) very neat and careful/(C) he could not win/(D) even third prize./(E) No error.

2. (A) He has been working on/(B) the problem a long time/(C) but is not still/(D) able to solve it./(E) No error.

3. (A) Although the policemen/(B) ran after the thieves/(C) only one of them were/(D) caught by them./(E) No error.

4. (A) Between June to August/(B) the rain fall in/(C) this part of the/(D) country is always low./(E) No error.

5. (A) When I reached his office/(B) I found that/(C) he had almost ready/(D) to leave for home./(E) No error.

6. (A) The teacher said/(B) that Vishal was/(C) capable of doing/(D) more better work./(E) No error.

7. (A) The boy asked/(B) his father why/(C) he cutting/(D) down the tree./(E) No error.

8. (A) One of the issues/(B) which was discussed/(C) in the meeting/(D) was raised by me./(E) No error.

9. (A) The thirsty/(B) children drank/(C) up all/(D) the water./(E) No error.

10. (A) Rohan was fastest than/(B) Somesh, but was not/(C) fast enough to defeat/(D) Shiny in the race./(E) No error.

11. (A) It was decided not/(B) to be included him in/(C) the team for the/(D) world-cup competition./(E) No error.

12. (A) He has been trying to/(B) develop a medicine for/(C) this disease for/(D) the last ten years./(E) No error.

13. (A) No sooner did she/(B) receive the award, there/(C) was a loud applause/(D) from the audience./(E) No error.

14. (A) As sooner did the/(B) actress stepped out/(C) of her car, people/(D) gathered around her./(E) No error.

15. (A) Ten new members/(B) have got enrolled/(C) and seven have/(D) resigned./(E) No error.

16. (A) From thirty and/(B) forty percent of the/(C) people of this village/(D) suffer from malaria./(E) No error.

17. (A) Edison has not only invented/(B) the electric bulb but/(C) also the film projector/(D) used in cinema theatres./(E) No error.

18. (A) Hardly had the/(B) sad news reacher her/(C) ears when she/(D) broke into tears./(E) No error.

19. (A) He is smarter/(B) enough to get/(C) selected for this/(D) prestigious post./(E) No error.

20. (A) No sooner the plane landed/(B) at the airport than/(C) a group of armed/(D) commandos surrounded it./(E) No error.

21. (A) Manindar has not only opened/(B) a restaurant, but also/(C) a grocery shop in the/(D) village where we live./(E) No error.

22. (A) I was to about/(B) go out of my house/(C) when it suddenly/(D) started raining./(E) No error.

23. (A) We are trying/(B) to locate the/(C) historical city for/(D) the past two years./(E) No error.

24. (A) One of the party/(B) members were dismissed/(C) for speaking against/(D) the leader./(E) No error.

25. (A) After listening to/(B) his advice I/(C) decided to not/(D) go abroad for studies./(E) No error.

26. (A) The daily wages that/(B) the worker of this/(C) factory receive range/(D) between twenty to thirty rupees./(E) No error.

27. (A) As soon did he/(B) open the old/(C) wooden box than a rat/(D) jumped out of it./(E) No error.

28. (A) The robbers were/(B) caught just as they/(C) were about to/(D) escape from the jail./(E) No error.

29. (A) No body believed him/(B) when he said that/(C) his son was gone/(D) out of the country./(E) No error.

30. (A) Hardly did she went/(B) out of her house/(C) when the postman came/(D) with the telegram./(E) No error.

31. (A) Nihal's father advised/(B) him not to/(C) ride the motorcycle/(D) lately at night./(E) No error.

32. (A) The faster he completes/(B) the work given to/(C) him, the largest/(D) will be his profit./(E) No error.

33. (A) Rashmi's performance in the/(B) film was better than/(C) Nidhi's but not/(D) so better as Ranjna's./(E) No error.

34. (A) The boys are playing/(B) outside the house whereas/(C) the girls are sitting/(D) inside and talked loudly./(E) No error.

35. (A) They usually comes/(B) to our house/(C) whenever they pass/(D) through our home-town./(E) No error.

36. (A) She must had/(B) completed her work/(C) by now because/(D) she is very punctual./(E) No error.

37. (A) The money-lender told/(B) that he would/(C) like help us/(D) in our efforts./(E) No error.

38. (A) Tarun told me/(B) that I am/(C) ready to do/(D) any work./(E) No error.

39. (A) Ashish possesses/(B) all those good qualities/(C) which every ideal/(D) student should possesses./(E) No error.

40. (A) An immediate action/(B) has awaited/(C) in order to complete/(D) our work in time./(E) No error.

41. (A) The children observed silent/(B) just for a while/(C) before they ran/(D) to greet their leader./(E) No error.

42. (A) Some people get/(B) used to changes/(C) very easily than/(D) others do./(E) No error.

43. (A) Vijay is more studious/(B) than any other/(C) student of/(D) his age./(E) No error.

44. (A) The policemen fired all the/(B) students when/(C) they were attacked/(D) by some of them./(E) No error.

45. (A) The train was/(B) moving so fast/(C) that we could not see/(D) the places properly./(E) No error.

46. (A) Although the patient/(B) was rude with the/(C) nurses, he behaved/(D) nice with the doctor./(E) No error.

47. (A) He interrupted me when/(B) I was to about/(C) tell the truth/(D) to his father./(E) No error.

48. (A) Sanjay and Satish used/(B) to work for almost twelve/(C) hours in the factory/(D) they are working earlier./(E) No error.

49. (A) Whenever they go out/(B) for shopping, they/(C) take their/(D) pet dog with them./(E) No error.

50. (A) Although he is usually/(B) rude with everyone/(C) he behaved nice with/(D) all of us today./(E) No error.

51. (A) He ran so fastly/(B) that he reached/(C) the destination in/(D) just two minutes./(E) No error.

52. (A) The policemen started/(B) firing the crowd/(C) when the striking/(D) workers became violent./(E) No error.

53. (A) The firemen could not/(B) succeed in rescue the/(C) child although they/(D) could put out the fire./(E) No error.

54. (A) Kitti used to/(B) work for almost ten/(C) hours in the organisation/(D) where she has employed./(E) No error.

55. (A) Neeraj is so best/(B) a player that/(C) he would be certainly/(D) included in the team./(E) No error.

56. (A) The driver could not/(B) prevent the car from hit/(C) the child although he/(D) applied the brakes suddenly./(E) No error.

57. (A) He has not only built/(B) this big theatre but/(C) he also built a few/(D) bungalows in this city./(E) No error.

58. (A) There has not been/(B) any rainfall in this/(C) part of the country/(D) since the last two years./(E) No error.

59. (A) Amar thought that he/(B) would pass the examination/(C) although he did not answer/(D) most of the question correct./(E) No error.

60. (A) All the people/(B) living in the house/(C) including the servant/(D) was invited there./(E) No error.

61. (A) His father promised to/(B) give him anything what he/(C) wants if he/(D) passes in the examination./(E) No error.

62. (A) They have agreed/(B) to give him/(C) anything whatever/(D) he asks for./(E) No error.

63. (A) He is about to/(B) open the gate of/(C) the house when the/(D) dog started barking./(E) No error.

64. (A) Hardly had we/(B) all stepped out of/(C) the house when it/(D) suddenly started raining./(E) No error.

65. (A) I advised him/(B) to do not go/(C) abroad for/(D) further studies./(E) No error.

66. (A) We were about to/(B) hire a taxi when/(C) Babu stopped his car/(D) and gave us a lift./(E) No error.

67. (A) Ashu exercise/(B) everyday so/(C) that he may/(D) keep himself healthy./(E) No error.

68. (A) Amit is as/(B) fast as or/(C) perhaps faster/(D) than Arun./(E) No error.

69. (A) He walked/(B) quick so that/(C) he would not/(D) be late./(E) No error.

70. (A) The little children was/(B) quite indifferent towards/(C) the teacher who was/(D) accompanying them./(E) No error.

71. (A) After the allotted/(B) time was over/(C) they torn off all/(D) the papers which they had used./(E) No error.

72. (A) Dr. Ramesh has not only started/(B) a pathology laboratory but/(C) also a maternity/(D) clinic in our town./(E) No error.

73. (A) Ravindar has run/(B) fastest enough to/(C) get selected for the/(D) international sports competition./(E) No error.

74. (A) He has a scheme/(B) of his own which/(C) he thinks perferable/(D) than that of any other person./(E) No error.

75. (A) No sooner did/(B) the lights went/(C) off than some/(D) boys started shouting./(E) No error.

76. (A) For the past several/(B) years, he has been/(C) trying to develop a/(D) medicine for cancer./(E) No error.

77. (A) The Government decided/(B) to sanction any money/(C) that was required for/(D) completing the project./(E) No error.

78. (A) The higher we/(B) climb up the/(C) mountain the cool/(D) we feel./(E) No error.

79. (A) One of his many/(B) good traits that/(C) come to my mind/(D) is his modesty./(E) No error.

80. (A) The chairman was force/(B) to resign as/(C) the opposition members/(D) were in majority./(E) No error.

81. (A) Did you see/(B) any of the child/(C) when you were/(D) in the garden?/(E) No error.

82. (A) Anamika's parents told/(B) her to not/(C) go to her friends,/(D) houses at night./(E) No error.

83. (A) Yesterday the thief/(B) was caught just as/(C) he is about to/(D) break open the door./(E) No error.

84. (A) Hardly had he/(B) went out of the/(C) room when people/(D) started criticising him./(E) No error.

85. (A) Jyotsna passed the/(B) examination although/(C) she did not/(D) work very hardly./(E) No error.

86. (A) The fast he finishes/(B) the construction work/(C) the larger will be/(D) his profit margin./(E) No error.

87. (A) Anjna has written no only/(B) this popular song but has/(C) also composed the/(D) music for the same./(E) No error.

88. (A) No sooner did I/(B) took the doll from/(C) the baby girl/(D) than she started crying./(E) No error.

89. (A) It being a rainy/(B) day, Rinki decided/(C) to stay indoors and/(D) do some writing./(E) No error.

90. (A) All the players of/(B) the football club, except/(C) one, was selected/(D) for the competition./(E) No error.

91. (A) Since the last several/(B) days, there has been/(C) heavy snowfall in this/(D) part of the country./(E) No error.

92. (A) The leader advised the people/(B) not to be carried away by/(C) the rumours spread/(D) in the city./(E) No error.

93. (A) He overcame with sorrow/(B) when he heard/(C) the sad news/(D) of his failure./(E) No error.

94. (A) They have requested me/(B) not take any action/(C) unless and until/(D) I don't see all the documents./(E) No error.

95. (A) He has gone/(B) to his native place/(C) with the intention/(D) of staying there./(E) No error.

96. (A) He had/(B) taken off his shirt and threw/(C) it on the floor/(D) before entering the house./(E) No error.

97. (A) Yesterday while/(B) crossing the road,/(C) he was/(D) run out by a truck./(E) No error.

98. (A) The applicant/(B) being a householder/(C) he is/(D) entitled to vote./(E) No error.

99. (A) The captain was/(B) so excited that/(C) the team members failed/(D) to held him in his seat./(E) No error.

100. (A) Every customer is/(B) entitled to pick-up/(C) a bag which is/(D) as small like this one./(E) No error.

15

ANSWERS

1. B : The words 'neatly and carefully' should be used in place of 'neat and careful', as 'neat and careful' are Adjectives and 'neatly and carefully' are Adverbs and in the given sentence, Adverbs should be used with Verb. For example :

(*i*) Asha **runs** very fast.
↓ ↓ ↓
Verb Adv. Adv.

(*ii*) Jitendar **speaks** very **fluently.**
↓ ↓ ↓
Verb Adv. Adv.

2. B : The word 'for' should be used in place of 'from' because the sentence is in 'Present Perfect Continous Tense' and 'a long time' indicates 'Period of Time' *Remember*, 'for' is used for 'Period of Time' and 'Since' is used for 'Point of Time', in Present Perfect, Present Perfect Continuous, Past Perfect Continuous, etc. For example :

(*i*) *Rohini has lived here for a month/since November.*
↓
Present Perfect

(*ii*) *Rohini has been living here for a month/since November.*
↓
Present Perfect Continuous

(*iii*) *Rohini had been living here for a month/since November.*
↓
Past Perfect Continuous

3. C : 'Was' should be used in place of 'were', because in this clause, 'only one' is the Subject and it is Singular. For example :

Only one of them **is** here.

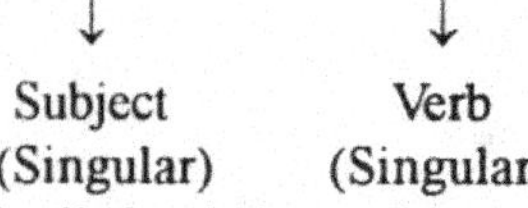

Subject Verb
(Singular) (Singular)

4. A : 'And' should be used in place of 'to', because after the use of 'Between', the conjunction 'and' should be used to make the sentence meaningful and correct; For example :

Between April and June.

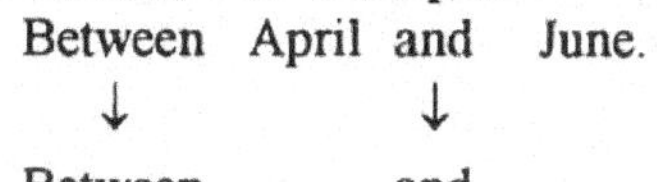

Between and

Note : The sentence can also be corrected by replacing the word 'Between' by 'From'. For example :

From April **to** June.

From   to

5. C : The word 'was' should be used in place of 'had' or 'had' should be followed by the word 'been', because 'was + Complement' or 'had been + Complement'. For example :

(*i*) Mrs. Indira Gandhi was the Prime Minister of India.

Or

(*ii*) Mrs. Indira Gandhi had been the Prime Minister of India for many years.

Remember, when 'had' is used as 'helping verb', V_3 is used instead of had + complement.

6. D : Delete the word 'more', as Double Comparative Degree (more better is not used in the sentence. For example :

She is better these days. (and not *more better*)

7. C : Insert the word 'was' before 'cutting', as the sentence is in 'Indirect Narration' and one 'helping verb' should be used before the verb 'cutting', and in the given sentence 'was' should be the helping verb.

8. B : 'Were' should be used in place of 'was', because 'who/which/that', etc., are relative Pronouns and the Verb should be used according to Noun/ Pronouns (which is called Antecedent of Relative Pronouns). For example :

One of the **boys** **who** **are** rich **has** not come.

Subject	Noun	Relative	Verb	Verb
(Singular)	(Plural)	Pronoun	Plural	(Singular)
		(Antecedent)		

9. E : The sentence is correct.

10. A : The word 'fastest' should be replaced by 'faster', because use of 'than' indicates that construction of the sentence is comprising of 'Comparative Degree'.

11. B : Instead of 'to be included him', the words 'to include him' should be used, because 'decide to do something' is used. For example :

It was decided **to transfer** him.

to V_1

12. E : The sentence is correct.

13. B : Insert 'than' before 'there', because 'No sooner ...... than' is used together. For example :

No   sooner did Monika leave the room than the rain

    ↓   ↓

No sooner   than

started

14. A : Substitute 'As sooner did' with 'As soon as', because after 'As soon as' no Conjuction is used with the Main Clause and keeping this in view no conjuction has been used before 'people'. For example :

As soon as Anjana came, **the children started clapping.**

                                 ↓

Main Clause

Note : No Counjuction has been used before 'Children'.

15. E : The sentence is correct.

16. A : Replace the word 'and' by 'to', because 'to' is used after 'from'. For example :

From twenty **to** thirty students have come.

    ↓   ↓

From   to

17. A : 'Invented not only' should be used in place of the words 'not only invented', because in this sentence effort has been made to join two 'nouns' with the use of 'Not only ...... but also'.

18. D : Replace the word 'broke' with 'burst', because 'burst into tears' is 'Idiomatic'.

19. A : Replace the word 'smarter' with 'smart', because 'Positive Degree Adjective + enough' is used.

She is **good**   **enough** to help Asha.

        ↓   ↓

    Positive   enough

    Degree

    Adjective

20. A : Replace the word 'landed' with 'land', because first form of verb (V_1) is used with 'do/does/did'. For example :

  (*i*) Ajay **did/does/**not write.

  (*ii*) The children **do** not **play.**

           ↓   ↓

    did/does/do V_1

Note : Alternately, the sentence can also be corrected by replacing 'did' with 'had', because third form of Verb (V_3) is used with had/has/have. For example :

(*i*) Swati **has finished** her work.

$\quad\quad\quad \downarrow \quad\quad \downarrow$

$\quad\quad\quad$ has $\quad$ V_3

(*ii*) They **have gone** for lunch.

$\quad\quad\quad \downarrow \quad\quad \downarrow$

$\quad\quad\quad$ has $\quad$ V_3

21. A : 'Not only opened' should be replaced with 'opened not only', because effort has been made to join two Nouns, by the use of 'Not only ...... but also'.

22. A : Replace the words 'to about' to read as 'about to', because to + V_1 is used together.

23. A : 'Are' should be replaced with 'have been/had been OR 'are trying' should be replaced with 'have tried', because 'for the past two years' has been used.

24. B : Were should be replaced with 'was', because 'one of' is followed by Plural Noun/Pronoun but Singular Verb. For example :

$\quad\quad$ **One** of the **students** $\quad$ **was** sleeping in the class.

$\quad\quad\quad \downarrow \quad\quad\quad\quad\quad \downarrow \quad\quad\quad \downarrow$

$\quad\quad$ Subject $\quad\quad\quad$ Noun $\quad\quad$ Verb

$\quad\quad$ (Singular) $\quad\quad$ (Plural) (Singular)

25. C : 'Not' should be used before 'to' because 'not' is used before 'Infinitive' (to +V_1). For example :

Prince is **not** **to** **purchase** this typewriter.

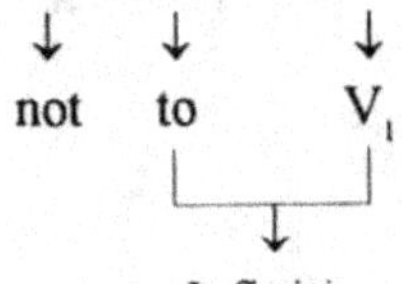

26. D : 'To' should be replaced with 'and', because Conjuction 'and' is used after 'between', For example :

(*i*) You may come **between** 2 p.m. **and** 5 p.m.

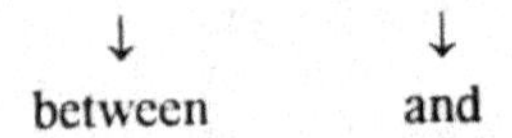

27. A : 'As soon' should be replaced with 'No sooner' because 'No sooner + did/had + Subject' is used and in part A of the sentence, did + Subject' has been used. Again in Part C, 'than' has been used, which confirms that this sentence is based on 'No sooner did ...... than'.

28. D : Delete the word 'the', because 'escape from jail' is used.

29. C : 'Was' should be replaced with 'had', because in 'Active Voice', 'to be' (is/are/am/was/were) is not used before third form of Verb (V_3). Instead 'have/has/had' is used. As 'he said' indicates Past Tense, Reported Clause should also be in Past Tense. For example :

    (*i*) Pushpa said that she **was done** some work. (Incorrect)

    (*ii*) Pushpa said that she **had done** some work. (Correct)

Note : The sentence can also be corrected by replacing 'gone' with 'going'.

30. A : 'Hardly did she went' should be replaced with 'Hardly had she gone'. *Remember*, first form of Verb (V_1) is used with do/does/did.

31. D : 'Lately' should be replaced with 'late', because 'lately' means 'recently' and 'late' means 'after the usual time'.

32. C : 'Largest' should be replaced with 'larger', because in both parts of the sentence 'Comparative Degree' is used if the construction of the sentence is parallel. For example :

The **more** he gets, **more** he wants.

    ↓   ↓

Comparative Comparative

Degree   Degree

33. D : 'Better' should be replaced with 'good', because when two persons/things are compared in Positive Degree, 'so/as + Positive Degree + as' is used. For example :

Anu is not **so/as** **good** **as** Neetu.

    ↓   ↓   ↓

    so/as Positive as

          Degree

34. D : 'Talked' should be replaced with 'talking', because when two Principal Verbs are used with an Auxiliary Verb both Principal Verbs should be in the same form. For example :

The girls **are** **sitting** and **talking** loudly.

    ↓   ↓   ↓

  Aux. V_4 V_4

35. A : 'Comes' should be replaced with 'come', because Subject of the sentence 'They' is Plural.

36. A : Replace the word 'had' with 'have', because first form of Verb (V_1) is used after the word 'must'. For example :

She **must**   **go**   now.

↓   ↓

must + V_1

37. C : Insert the word 'to' before 'help', because 'like + to + V_1 is used. For example :

(*i*) Rohan **likes**   **to help** me. (Temporary Action)

↓   ↓   ↓

Verb + to + V^1

(*ii*) Moreover, 'Like + Gerund' is also used. For example :

(*iii*) Nisha likes **swimming** (Permanent Action)

↓

Gerund

38. B : Replace the word 'am' with 'was', because when Past Tense is used in the 'Reporting Verb' : it should also be used in the 'Reported Speech' (Except Universal Truth). For example :

Shalu   **told**   me that I   **was**   ready.

↓   ↓

Past Tense   Past Tense

39. D : Replace the word 'possesses' with 'possess', because 'should + V_1' is used. For example :

The students **should come** regularly.

↓   ↓

should + V_1

40. B : As the sentence is in the 'Passive Voice', the word 'has' should be replaced by 'is' (or was). The sentence is also correct if 'been' is used after 'has', because 'has + been + V_3' is also Passive Construction.

(*i*) The result **is** awaited.

(*ii*) The result **was** awaited.

(*iii*) The result **has been** awaited.

41. A : Replace the word 'silent' by 'silence', because 'observed' has been used as 'Transitive Verb' and it should be followed by 'Object'. *Remember*, 'Noun' of 'Noun Equivalent' word is used as 'Object' and 'Adjective' or 'Adverb' should not be used in its place.

For example :
    (*i*) Isha likes **smartness**. (and not **smart**)
    (*ii*) Prince likes **friendship**. (and not **friendly**)

42. C : The word 'more' should be used in place of 'very', because 'than' has been used after the word 'easily', which indicates that the sentence is in Comparative Degree. For example :
    (*i*) Rajiv can read **more** repidly **than** other
                ↓   ↓
              more   than

43. E : The sentence is correct.

44. A : 'At' should be inserted after 'fired', because 'fire + at + somebody/ something' is used. For example :
    (*i*) Sonu **fired at** his enemy.
          ↓ ↓
       fired at

45. E : The sentence is correct.

46. D : 'Nicely' should be used in place of 'nice', because 'behaved' is 'Intransitive Verb' which should be followed by 'Adverb' and not 'Adjective'. For example :
    She **behaved nicely** with me.
       ↓   ↓
     behaved Adverb

47. B : 'To about' should be replaced with 'about to' because in the construction of the sentence :
Subject + to be (is/are/am/was/were) + to + V_1 is used.

48. D : 'Were' should be used in place of 'are', because Past Tense has been used in the beginning of the Sentence 'Sanjay and Satish used to work' and for maintaining the sequence of the sentence, it is necessary to use Past Tense in Part D also.

49. D : The sentence is correct.

50. C : 'Nicely' should be used in place of 'nice', because 'behaved' is 'Instransitive Verb' which should be followed by 'Adverb' and not 'Adjective'. For example :
    Kamlesh **behaves nicely** with me.
       ↓   ↓
     behaved Adverb

51. A : 'Fast' should be used in place of 'fastly', because there is no such word

as 'fastly'. The word 'fast' is used as 'Adjective' and 'Adverb' both.
For example :

(*i*) Anju and Sangeeta are **fast runners**.

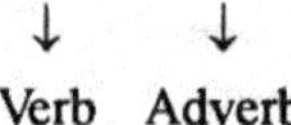

Adj.   Noun

(*ii*) Geeta is **running fast**.

Verb   Adverb

52. B : 'Firing' should be followed by 'at', because 'fire + at + somebody/ something' is used. For example :

(*i*) Sunil **fired at** the tiger.

(*ii*) The police started **firing at** the crowd.

53. B : 'Rescue' should be replaced with 'rescuing', because V_4, *i.e.*, Verb + Gerund (ing) is used after the Prepositions 'by/before/after/in/at/on', etc. For example :

She aims **at achieving** the success.

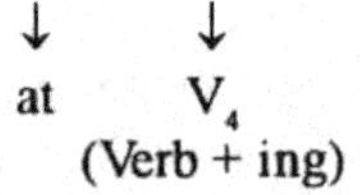

at V_4
(Verb + ing)

54. D : 'Has' should be replaced with 'was', because Past Tense has been used in the beginning of the sentence 'Kitti used to work' and for maintaining the sequence of the sentence, it is necessary to use Past Tense in Part D also.

55. A : 'Best' should be replaced with 'good', because when two persons/things are compared in Positive Degree, 'so/as + Positive Degree + as' is used. For example :

Ashish is so/as **good** a player as ....

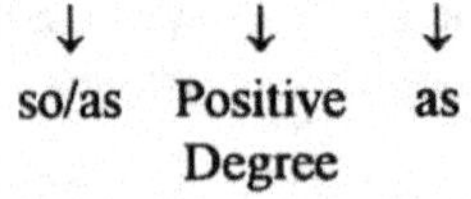

so/as   Positive   as
Degree

56. B : 'Hitting' should be used in place of 'hit' because Verb + Gerund (ing) is used after the Prepositions 'by/at/in/on/after/before, etc.

57. C : Insert 'has' after 'he' because both parts of the sentence indicate the construction of the sentence as Present Perfect Tense.

58. D : 'Since' should be replaced with 'for' because 'since' is used with 'Point of Time', while as 'for' is used with 'Period of Time'.

For example:
   (*i*) Anil has been working here **for two years.**

              ↓   ↓

              for   Period of Time

   (*ii*) Anil has been working here **since January.**

             ↓   ↓

           Since   point of time

59. D : 'Correct' should be replaced with 'correctly', because 'correct' is an Adjective, while an Adverb should be used with the Verb.

For example :
   (*i*) She gave **correct answers** to all the questions.

            ↓   ↓

         Adjective Noun

   (*ii*) She **answered** all the questions **correctly.**

       ↓   ↓

     Verb   Adverb

60. D : 'Was' should be replaced with 'were' because Subject of this sentence 'All the people' is Plural.

61. B : Delete the word 'anything' or replace the word 'what' with 'that', because no 'Antecedent' is used before 'what'. Similarly, 'Relative Pronoun' 'that' is used with 'anything'. For example :
   (*i*) I will give you what you like. (and not 'anything what you like)

                    Or

   (*ii*) I will give you anything that you like. (and not 'what you like')

62. C : The use of 'anything' is superfluous, as the meaning of 'whatever' is also 'anything'. For example :
   (*i*) Take, whatever you like.
   (*ii*) Take anything that you like.

63. A : 'Was' should be used in place of 'is' because Part D of the sentence 'dog started barking' indicates that the incident relates to the **Past**.

64. D : The use of the word 'suddenly' is superfluous.

65. B : Instead of the words 'to do not go', 'not to go' should be used because 'advise somebody to do something' is used. For example :
   The teacher advised me to work hard.

        ↓   ↓ ↓

    advised somebody   to V_1

Similarly, 'advise somebody not to do something' is used. For example :

My mother advised me not to play with fire.

advised   not to play

66. **E :** The sentence is correct.

67. **A :** The word 'exercise' should be replaced by 'exercises', as the Subject 'Ashu' is Singular.

68. **E :** The sentence is correct.

69. **B :** The word 'quickly' should be used in place of 'quick', Adverb should be used with the Verb 'walked' and not the Adjective, to make the sentence meaningful.

70. **A :** 'Were' should be used in place of 'was', as the Subject of the sentence 'The children' is 'Plural Noun', which should be followed by Plural Verb.

71. **C :** The word 'tore' should be used in place of 'torn', as V_2 of tear (V_1) is tore and not 'torn' (V_3).

72. **A :** 'Started not only' should be used in place of 'not only started', because with the use of 'not only .... but also', effort has been made to join two 'Nouns'.

73. **B :** The word 'fast' should be used in place of 'fastest', as 'Positive Degree + enough' is used. For example :

(*i*) He is **kind enough** to help me.

Positive enough
Degree

(*ii*) He is **intelligent enough** to understand your tricks.

Positive   enough
Degree

74. **D :** Replace the word 'than' by 'to'. the word 'prefer' is followed by the Preposition 'to'. For example :
She prefers **to** take milk.

75. **B :** The word, 'went' (V_2) should be replaced by 'go' (V_1), because V_1

is used after the words, 'do/does/did', etc. For example :

   (*i*) **Did** she not **write** to you ?

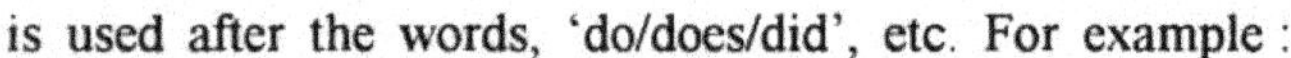

     Did V^1

   (*ii*) **Do** they **finish** their work in time ?

     Do V_1

76. E : The sentence is correct.

77. B : Replace the word 'any' with 'the' because 'money' has become **definite** with the use of 'that was required'. For example :

   The dog that barked at Swati did not bite her.

78. C : The word 'cool' should be replaced with 'cooler', because The + Comparative Degree is used on both parts of parallel construction. For example :

   The higher he climbs, **the cooler** he feels.

   the Comparative   the Comparative
      Degree   Degree

79. E : The sentence is correct.

80. A : The word 'force' should be replaced with 'forced' as the sentence is in Passive Voice and in Passive Voice, V_3 is used with the words 'is/are/am/was/were'. For example :

   She **was forced** to resign.

     was V^3

81. B : 'Child' should be replaced with the word 'children', because if the word 'any of' is followed by 'countable Noun', it is used as 'Plural'. For example :

   Any of the **boys/girls/students/chairs/toys.**

    Any of   Plural Nouns

82. B : 'To not' should be replaced with the word 'not to', because to + not + V_1 is used. For example :

   (*i*) The teacher asked the students **not to make** a noise

                  not to V_1

   (*ii*) I advised her **not to be** careless.

           not to V_1

83. C : The word 'was' should be used in place of 'is', as the sentence is in Past Tense.

84. B : The word 'gone' (V_3) should be used in place of 'went' (V_2) because V_3 is used with have/had/having. For example :

(*i*) Anjna **has forgotten** to bring the books.

↓ ↓

has + V^3

(*ii*) Ashish **had** hardly **gone** to the village ....

↓ ↓

had V^3

85. D : Replace the word 'hardly' by 'hard', because 'hard' means 'laborious' and 'hardly' means 'rarely' or 'with difficulty'.

86. A : The word 'faster' should be used in place of 'fast' as Comparative Degree has been used in both parts of the sentence.

The **faster** they run, the **better** they do.

↓ ↓

Comparative   Comparative
Degree   Degree

87. A : 'Not only written' should be used in place of 'written not only', as the Verb 'composed' has been used after the word 'also', *e.g.* : not only **written** .... but .... also **composed**

↓ ↓

Verb   Verb

88. B : The word 'take' (V_1) should be used in place of 'took' (V_2). Do/does/did are followed by V_1. For example :

(*i*) Hardly **does** she **come** here.

↓ ↓

does V^1

(ii) No sooner **did** he **go** there ....

↓ ↓

did V^1

89. E : The sentence is correct.

90. C : 'Were' should be used in place of 'was' as the Principal Subject of the sentence 'All the players' is Plural.

91. A : 'Since' should be replaced with the word 'For' as 'Since' is used with 'Point of time' and 'For' is used with 'Period of Time'. For example :

(*i*) Since **November, 1994,** etc.

↓

Point of Time

(*ii*) For **many years/months**.

↓

Period of Time

92. C : Replace the word 'spread' by 'spreading'. The use of Gerund (ing) with 'spread' makes the sentence clear and meaningful.

93. A : Replace the word 'overcame' by 'was overcome' because the sentence has 'Passive Construction'. For example :
    (*i*) Rahul cheated me. (Active)
    (*ii*) I was cheated by Rahul. (Passive)

94. C : Delete the word 'don't. The words 'until, unless, till, refuse, deny, lest, forbid', etc., and not followed by negative sentence. For example :
    (*i*) You should wait until I **don't** come back. (*Incorrect*)
    You should wait until I come back. (*Correct*)
    (*ii*) You will not succeed, unless and until you **don't** work hard.
    (*Incorrect*)
    You will not succeed, unless and until you work hard.
    (*Correct*)
    (*iii*) You will not do well, unless you **don't** work hard. (*Incorrect*)
    You will not do well, unless you work hard. (*Correct*)

95. E : The sentence is correct.

96. B : The word 'threw' should be replaced by 'thrown', because have/has/had + V_3 is used. For example :
    (*i*) Sunil **has met** me and **talked** to me.
    ↓ ↓ ↓
    Has V_3 V_3

97. D : The word 'run out' should be replaced by 'run over'. Because 'run out' to come to an end' and 'run over' means 'to knock down a person in riding or driving'.

98. C : The use of word 'he' is superfluous, as the Subject in the sentence is 'The applicant'.

99. D : 'Hold' should be used in place of 'held', because 'to' + V_1 is used. 'held' is the 2nd form of the Verb 'hold'.

100. D : Substitute the word 'like' with 'as', because Conjuction 'as is used after 'as'. For example :
    She is as good as you. (and not **'like'** you)

SOME FUNDAMENTAL RULES FOR CORRECTION

RULE 1 :

The words each, every, everyone, someone, somebody, everybody, anybody, nobody, anyone, are always used in Singular. In the following examples, the *italicised* words are incorrect and the words shown within the brackets are correct. For example :

1. Everybody *like* to praise his own work. (likes)
2. Every student *are* to be given free medical aid in this college. (is)
3. Each of the six boys *are* taking interest in their work. (is)

RULE 2 :

In the case of 'as well as' 'together with' alongwith, 'and not' 'in addition to', 'besides', etc., Verb relates to the first Subject instead of the second Subject.

1. Hari alongwith his father *are* going to Ambala, for purchasing some books for his studies. (is)
2. Captain along with his soldiers *were* killed in the Second World War.
   (was)
3. She besides her friends *have* decided to visit Delhi this time. (has)
4. Savita as well as her sister *are* making their programme to see the film.
   (is)
5. He and not his friends *are* expected to qualify the test. (is)

RULE 3 :

In the case of 'neither nor' 'either or', 'not only, but also', etc., the Verb relates to the second Subject *i.e.* the nearest word.

1. Not only he but also his brother *are* trying best to qualify the test. (is)
2. Either her friends or she *have* made the loss good. (has)
3. Neither the Prime Minister nor the Members of the Parliament *is* to do anything in this respect. (are)
4. Neither the principal nor the teacher *is* expected to attend the function.
   (are)

RULE 4 :

Some words : unless, till, until, refuse, deny, lest, forbid, are not followed by negative sentence.

1. He will not join the Army until he is *not* premitted by the parents.
   (Delete not)
2. Wait here till I *do not* come back. (Delete 'do not')

3. She will not be happy unless her friends *does not* help her.
(Delete 'does not')

4. He forbade me *not to* appear for the test. (Delete 'not')
5. Walk fast lest you should *not* miss the train. (Delete 'not')

RULE 5 :

Double future should not be used in one sentence, in case the conditional word is found in the sentence (*i.e.* if, as and when, in case, when, provided, until, unless, till before, etc.).

1. If she *will go* to Delhi, she will bring some gift for you. (goes)
2. It will be better for you if you *will* study carefully. (Delete 'will')
3. He will not have a sign of relief unless he *will qualify* the written test.
(qualifies)

4. Please ensure that you will not waste your time on one question in case you *will* find it difficult. (Delete will)
5. She will have left the college before you *will* reach there. (Delete will)

RULE 6 :

'Neither' can be used without 'Nor' but 'neither' is used for two persons or two things whereas 'none' is used for more than two persons or two things 'neither' and 'none' are always used in singular on the basis of 3rd person, when there is no counting of persons or things, in that case, any of the two words. (*i.e.* 'neither' and 'none') can be used *e.g.*

1. None of the boys *want* to be arrested in the presence of their parents.
(wants)

2. None of the assets of the company *have been* revalued so far. (has been)
3. *Neither* of my seven friends helped me during my illness. (None)
4. *None* of the two sisters loves each other due to some misunderstandings.
(Neither)

5. Neither of them *have* anything to say on this point. (has)

RULE 7 :

'Either' is used for two persons or two things whereas 'any' is used for more than two *e.g.*

1. Here are none balls, you can choose *either*. (any)
2. Have you read *either* of the three novels written by Mr. Vijay Magon ?
(any)

3. Do you like *any* of the two methods suggested by the principal ? (either)

RULE 8 :

Some words : insist, persist, abstain, refrain, fond, keen, succeed, prohibit and confident are used in Gerund along with Prepositions *e.g.*

1. She is confident *to speak* English even in the presence of her officers.
   (of speaking)
2. Though he was advised not to drive heavy vehicle yet he insisted *to do* so. (in doing)
3. I prohibited her *to park* her car near the police station. (from parking)
4. Everybody in this country should abstain *to speak* ill. (from speaking)
5. He acted upon my advice and succeeded *to secure* first division in Mathematics. (in securing)

RULE 9 :

In special cases, we use 'that' in place of 'who, which, where' the words—all, any, none, only, nothing, the few, the little are found in the sentence. *e.g.*
1. She spent the little money *which* she had in her pocket. (that)
2. In the meeting there was none *who* did not praise his own work. (that)
3. All *which* glitters is not gold. (that)
4. She was the only student *who* could attempt all the problem figures in the exam. (that)
5. Is there any *who* does not love her country ? (that)

RULE 10 :

Use of that of, those of e.g.
1. The goats of Tibet are more beautiful than *that of* Nepal. (those of)
2. My teaching is better *than* Jawahar. (than that of)
3. The climate of Kulu is better *than* Manali. (than that of)
4. The apples of Kashmir are better *than* Shimla. (than that of)

RULE 11 :

The words 'last', 'yesterday', 'a few days ago', are used in Past Indefinite Tense.
1. He *has sold* all his goods a few day ago. (sold)
2. She *has passed* M.A. (Final) in 1986. (passed)
3. Her mother *has come* back from tour, yesterday. (came)

RULE 12 :

Some words : stop, help, remember, avoid, reach, resemble, dislike, enjoys (is followed by first form of Verb) are used in Gerund but are not followed by any Preposition *e.g.*
1. Many girls avoid *to see* the picture with their parents. (seeing)
2. He enjoys *to play* football in the evening daily. (playing)
3. Nobody should dislike *to buy* the old books from her friends. (buying)
4. Stop *to count* the money as the time is over. (counting)
5. 'Special Book' will help *to increase* your day-to-day knowledge. (increasing)

RULE 13 :

Junior, senior inferior, superior, prior, interior, prefer are followed by 'to'. But My senior officer, My junior officer, His prior approval, etc. are used without 'to'. These words are also not followed by any comparison word e.g.

1. Character is preferable *than* wealth. (to)
2. He is more *senior than* me not only in service but also in age. (senior to)
3. Ashok is junior *from* me by four years in service. (to)
4. My senior officer is proposing to proceed on leave next week. (No error)
5. Ram is poorer than Mahesh. (No error)
6. He is more careful than his brother. (No error)

Note : Comparative Degree is always followed by 'than' Superlative Degree :

1. Vikas is the best boy in the class. (No error)
2. Vivekanand was one of the most popular saints in India. (No error)
3. India is one of the greatest countries. (No error)

RULE 14 :

The words : need, dare, better, rather are not followed by 'to'. *e.g.*

1. Nobody can dare *to* challenge my authority. (Delete to)
2. You need not *to* worry about your health. (Delete to)
3. Something is better than nothing. (No error)

RULE 15 :

If the Principal Clause (sentence on the left hand) is given in the Past Tense, then the Subordinate Clause must be in the Past Tense. *e.g.*

1. The doctor asked the patient if he *can* walk on feet. (could)
2. He worked hard so that he *may* qualify the test with distinction. (must)
3. It was decided by the Bank that the company *will be* granted cash credit limit of Rs. 50 lakhs. (would be)
4. In the meeting, it was discussed that the poor children *are* to be given free medical aid. (were)

RULE 16 :

Use 'that' in place of 'who' and 'which' after 'Superlative Degree' (means word followed by 'est' or 'most'). *e.g.*

1. Ashoka was the greatest king *who* ruled over many countries. (that)
2. Rahul is one of the best players *who* have been-awarded certificates. (that)
3. He is the most intelligent student *who* has got first division in Mathematics.
(that)
4. 'Geeta' is regarded as one of the best movies *which* have been produced so far by the Film Industry. (that)
5. It is one of the most popular books *which* have been written by Tagore.
(that)

RULE 17 :

The word 'that' is not used with the words how, who, whether, what, where, when, whom, whose, which, why, etc. *e.g.*
1. She could not explain *that* why she did not take interest in the studies. (Delete 'that')
2. He does not know *that* how to speak Hindi with his friends. (Delete 'that')
3. It is difficult to say *that* whether she will get the job without experience. (Delete 'that')
4. Nothing can be said *that* when he is expected to return from his tour. (Delete 'that')
5. He asked me *that* why I should go there. (Delete 'that')

RULE 18 :

The word 'one of' is followed by the Plural word but is used in Singular. *e.g.*
1. One of the *proposal* made by the students is still to be viewed. (proposals)
2. One of the schemes made by the bank *are* to be launched. (is)
3. One of my friends *have* made up his mind to start his private business. (has)
4. Sanjay who *have* qualified the written test is one of my friends. (has)
5. Shekhar is one of those who *is* ready to die for country. (are)

Note : Serial No. 5 'one of' is not Subject. Therefore, it has not been used in Singular.

RULE 19 :

The words scenery, machinery, work, business, poor, rich, furniture, news, luggage, bread, hair, poetry, issue, fruit and fleet are used in Singular only. *e.g.*
1. The owner of the shop is going to sell all his *furnitures*. (furniture)
2. Many manufacturers use imported *machineries* just to increase the quality of their products. (machinery)
3. The *informations were* broadcast from Television. (information was)
4. The *sceneries* of Shimla *are* very charming. (scenery is)
5. Sarla has no *issues*. (issue)
6. She had gone to but *fruits*. (fruit)
7. Her *hairs are* jet black. (hair is)
8. The mother feeds the *poors*. (poor)
9. I told *these* news to my father. (this)
10. The fleet *were* destroyed by the enemy. (was)

RULE 20 :

The words : advice, mischief, abuse, alphabet, etc., are used in Singular only. *e.g.*
1. The teacher gave us many advices. (wrong)
    (a) The teacher gave us advice or piece of advice. (right)

2. My younger brother did many mischiefs. (wrong)
   (*a*) My younger brother did many acts of mischief. (right)
3. The boys were shouting abuses. (wrong)
   (*a*) The boys were shouting words of abuse. (right)
4. I have learnt the alphabets. (wrong)
   (*a*) I have learnt the letters of alphabets. (right)

RULE 21 :

The words : rupee, dozen, mile, year, food are used in Signular when used after numerical and followed by their noun. *e.g.*
1. I have a five *rupees* note. (rupee)
2. He bought two *dozens* pencils. (dozen)
3. He ran in a two *miles* race. (mile)
4. Abida is a ten *years* old girl. (year)
5. The distance is of 2 miles/kms. (no error)
6. A five *years* plan is going to be started. (year)

RULE 22 :

The words : vegetables, spectacles, trousers, Himalayas, people, orders, repairs, scissors (noun) are always used in plural. *e.g.*
1. I had gone to buy *vegetable*. (vegetables)
2. The road is closed for *repair*. (repairs)
3. The judge passed *order* for his release. (orders)
4. Very few *peoples* are hard working. (people)
5. His *spectacle is* blunt. (s) (are)
6. The *scissor is* blunt. (s) (are)
7. Your *trouser is* not loose. (s) (are)
8. The *Himalaya is* the highest mountain(s). (s) (are)

RULE 23 :

The words : fish, deer, sheep, cattle are used always in Singular for Singular and Plural purposes. *e.g.*
1. The fisherman catches many *fishes* in the pond. (fish)
2. I saw many *sheeps* and *deers* in the forest. (sheep, deer)
3. The cattle *are* returning to the village. (cattle is)

RULE 24 :

When two persons or two things are compared, use Comparative Degree. *e.g.*
1. She is braver than her sister. (No error)
2. He is taller than I by 3 inches. (No error)
3. Anup is *intelligent* than Amrik at least in English. (more intelligent)

Note : In Comparative Degree, Object will be in Subjective Case *i.e.* 'I' for me, 'He' for him 'She' for her, etc.

RULE 25 :

When two qualities of the same person are compared (Instead of comparison of two persons or two things). Use the word 'more' in place of comparative word. *e.g.*

1. She is *wiser* than honest. (more wiser)
2. He who is an officer of the Railway is *honest* than wise. (more honest)

RULE 26 :

Generally the relative words 'who' and 'which' are placed after the word for which these are used :

1. The woman/died of cholera/who lived in this cottage. (1 + 3 + 2)
2. None of the students/could qualify the test/who was intelligent.

$$(1 + 3 + 2)$$

3. It is I who *is* responsible for your bright career. (am)

RULE 27 :

The word 'call at' is used for place whereas 'call upon' or 'call on' is used for persons. *e.g.*

1. All of us *called upon* her office. (called at)
2. They *called at* us yesterday to discuss the cash credit account. (called upon)
3. I found them playing hockey when I called *on* his house. (at)
4. When I called *on* 'Subhash' residence, he had left his house. (at)

RULE 28 :

'Each other' is used for two persons and things whereas 'one another' is used for more than two. *e.g.*

1. All the five brothers were quarrelling with *each other* over their father's property. (one another)
2. They were discussing the point with each other. (No error)
3. Ambika and Sonia are fast friends and they love *one another* very much.

(each other)

RULE 29 :

The word 'who' is used for Subject whereas 'whom' is used for Object. *e.g.*

1. *Whom* do you think, will be our teacher. (who)
2. Please provide us efficient worker *who* you think honest. (whom)

RULE 30 :

We used the word 'the' before the names of oceans, rivers, mountains, sacred books, newpapers, magazines, ships, buildings, provinces, nation and communities and with the Superlative Degree *e.g.*

1. *Hindus* should not hate the Bengalis. (The Hindus)
2. Jawahar Lal was *greatest* man of the world. (the greatest)
3. *Tribune* gives us day-to-day knowledge. (The Tribune)

Note : We do not use the word 'the' before the names the of disease, persons, country and metal.

1. *The Gold* is a precious metal. (Gold)
2. He with his friend lives in *the Russia.* (Russia)
3. *The small pox* has broken out in the village. (small pox)

RULE 31 :

'Both' and 'As well as' cannot be used together in a sentence. If 'Both' is to be used, Verb will be used in Plural. If 'As well as' is to be used, Verb will be according to the 1st Subject. 'Both' is followed by 'And'. *e.g.*

1. *Both* Sanjay as well as his friends is proposing to launch a new scheme for his country. (Delete both)
2. Both Ravi *or* Shankar are going to see off their uncle. (and)
3. Both she *as well as* her sister are going to see the picture. (and)

RULE 32 :

One of the two words 'in my opinion' and 'I think' is used. *e.g.*

1. *(In my opinion)* (*I think*) he might have qualified the test. (use any one)

RULE 33 :

'Different' and 'separation' are followed by 'from' instead of other words. *e.g.*

1. Under these circumstances, I cannot bear *my sister's separation.*

(separation from my sister)

2. It is quite different *to* this. (from)

RULE 34 :

The words 'worth' and 'for' cannot be used together. *e.g.*

1. He has sold his scooter *for worth* seven thousand rupees. (for or worth)

RULE 35 :

The words 'exceed' and 'more than' are not used together. One of the two is used. *e.g.*

1. In the examination, your essay should not *exceed more than* fifteen lines.

(exceed or more than)

RULE 36 :

'It' is used for lifeless things and 'He' is used for living things. *e.g.*

1. *Being* a blind, I told him the way of his house. (he, being)
2. *Being* a cloudy day, we did not go out for a walk. (It being)
3. *It* being weak in Math, I told him this sum. (He)

RULE 37 :

'Let' and 'between' are followed by objective Clause. *e.g.*

1. Do not disclose the secret as this is between you and *I.* (me)

2. Let *she* study for the test which is to be held shortly. (her)

RULE 38 :

It two nouns denote the same meaning, both the Nouns are treated as Singular.
1. The manager and clerk of this office *are* one leave today. (is)
2. The manager and secretary of the firm *have* got the books of account audited.

(has)

3. Both the students are going to school. (No error)
4. The secretary and treasurer was absent. (No error)
5. The secretary and the treasurer was absent. (were)

RULE 39 :

'A majority of the students' is treated as one group. 'The majority of the students' is treated as Plural *i.e.* more than one group. *e.g.*
1. The majority of the students *agrees* with the teacher on this point. (agree)
2. I large number of students *has* got through the written test. (have)

Note : 'A large number of the students' mean Plural on account of the word 'large'.

RULE 40 :

When one Noun denotes to a person and other denotes to an animal, we use 'that' in place of 'who' or 'which'. *e.g.*
1. He and his sheep *which* fell into the well, were injured. (that)
2. She and her dog *which* I saw on the road, meet with an accident. (that)

Note : 'who' is used for living person(s) and 'which' is used for animals, birds and lifeless things.

RULE 41 :

We do not use double Comparative Degree in a sentence.
1. In hockey, he is *more* better than I. (delete more)
2. She is *more* cleverer than her brother. (delete more)

RULE 42 :

'Between' is followed by 'and' whereas 'from' is following by 'to'. *e.g.*
1. The company will be granted cash credit limit between Rs. 3 lace *to e.g.* Rs. 5 lacs. (and)
2. We are proposing to hold a meeting today from 4.20 pm *by* 6.30 pm.

RULE 43 :

In one sentence double negative should not be used. *e.g.*
1. He has not done *nothing* wrong in this case. (anything)
2. Ramesh did not like to help *nobody*. (anybody)

RULE 44 :

The following Conjunction are used in pairs :

though	yet	hardly	when
scarcely	before or when	such	as
neither	nor	either	or
not only	but also	one	one's
whether	or	no sooner	than
lest	should		

1. Though Ram played well *still* he lost the match. (yet)
2. Hardly had he gone out *than* it started raining. (when)
3. No sooner did he *reached* the station, when *the* train whistled off.

(reach, than the)

4. Walk fast lest you should miss the train. (No error)

FILL IN THE BLANKS

This type of test is given to examine the ability of the Candidates in the use of nouns, pronouns, adjectives, adverbs, articles, prepositions, verbs and tense, etc.

In this type of test, the sentences are given with a blank and four or five alternatives are suggested. The candidates are required to choose a correct alternative from the five alternatives given below each sentence.

Directions (1-75) : *Pick out the most effective word/phrase from the given words/phrases to fill in the blank to make the sentence meaningfully correct.*

1. The union leader put the ...... of the workers before the management.
A. difficulties   B. problems
C. demands   D. feelings
E. desires

2. The prisoner escaped from the police custody ...... is bound to cause the dismissal of many policemen.
A. that   B. it
C. which   D. as
E. who

3. The prescribed medicine provided him ...... a little relief.
A. with   B. for
C. by   D. to
E. indeed

4. The elections were held peacefully barring the ...... incidents.
A. widespread   B. anticipated
C. sporadic   D. major
E. expected

5. Madhur was ...... how to use a dictionary.
A. informed   B. taught
C. learn   D. told
E. suggested

6. Ashok aims ...... starting some new work.
A. in   B. to
C. at   D. for
E. by

7. Mohit was determined ...... compromise with you.
A. for   B. to
C. by   D. in
E. at

8. Although people are doubtful, it is ...... that he would win the election.
A. certain   B. confident
C. unsure   D. infinite
E. unnecessary

9. Rashmi and her family intend to accompany us on ...... trip to Kanyakumari.
A. our   B. her
C. their   D. our's
E. its

10. The minister flew ...... the flooded areas in a helicopter.

A. along   B. over

C. in   D. at

E. about

11. Rajesh is ...... us for a ride by not keeping his promise.

A. took   B. takes

C. taking   D. taken

E. take

12. Some of the trains got delayed as a ...... of heavy rains.

A. matter   B. result

C. condition   D. fall

E. cause

13. They ...... no notice of what people say about them.

A. mind   B. keep

C. listen   D. make

E. take

14. Neelu could ...... a lot of experience by working in that organisation.

A. perform   B. know

C. maintain   D. gain

E. learn

15. A river has to be ...... to reach the temple.

A. flowed   B. cut

C. swam   D. rowed

E. crossed

16. Mr. Vijay Magon tried his best to ...... the condition of the blind.

A. improve   B. repair

C. correct   D. develop

E. raise

17. Ranjana strongly feels that she should ...... me a camera on my birthday.

A. photograph   B. give

C. sell   D. borrow

E. can

18. You must obtain first class in order to be ...... to apply for this post.

A. illegible   B. elected

C. forced   D. eligible

E. legible

19. Man ...... be happy if his basic needs are not satisfied.

A. must   B. doesn't

C. can't   D. will

E. can

20. As there was ...... all round, he could not read the book with concentration.

A. disturb   B. peace

C. troublesome   D. weather

E. noise

21. If you honestly ...... your fault, others do not take it seriously.

A. refuse   B. neglect

C. correct   D. warn

E. admit

22. Only bad people like to give ill-treatment ...... their subordinates.

A. to   B. for

C. about   D. with

E. of

23. ...... her child was not well, she did not go to office.

A. Although   B. In spite of

C. Since   D. However

E. Even if

24. We have so nicely practised that we are now confident ...... winning the match.

A. for   B. into

C. of   D. with

E. in

25. The old man has become ...... weak that he can hardly walk.

A. too   B. so

C. very   D. as
E. much

26. Satish did not work ...... so his master asked him to leave.
A. proper   B. rightly
C. properly   D. straight
E. neat

27. How much did it ...... you to reach Bombay by car ?
A. estimate   B. cost
C. price   D. pay
E. charge

28. Dinesh is unhappy with me ...... my carelessness.
A. because   B. for
C. regard   D. as
E. since

29. The waiter took the plates ...... after we had finished eating.
A. out   B. up
C. of   D. away
E. across

30. Do you know the person ...... owns that house ?
A. that   B. whom
C. which   D. who
E. to

31. Unless we go ...... once we shall miss the train.
A. now   B. so
C. for   D. that
E. at

32. I feel ill because I had been working too hard ...... months.
A. for   B. at
C. since   D. those
E. these

33. Being a sportsman is one and being a coach is ....
A. another   B. different

C. second   D. same
E. separate

34. Neeru is not happy with her present job ...... the salary is very low.
A. although   B. even if
C. in spite of   D. their
E. as

35. Saveta got scared when the beggar stared ...... her.
A. over   B. on
C. about   D. at
E. to

36. Rakesh was planning to go on leave ...... he was planning to get married.
A. and   B. so
C. but   D. hence
E. as

37. In spite of her own difficulties Bhavna ...... to be helpful to her neighbours as much as possible.
A. decides   B. tries
C. agrees   D. allows
E. attempts

38. The cat was ...... by a speeding truck.
A. run over   B. crossed over
C. killed over   D. moved over
E. moved over

39. Although I was doubtful, my mother was ...... that I would pass.
A. from   B. uncertain
C. decided   D. sure
E. believed

40. When I saw him in old clothes, I was ...... by surprise.
A. taken   B. took
C. takes   D. taking
E. take

41. Monika has been suffering ...... fever for the last three days.
A. in
B. from
C. with
D. for
E. against

42. Dheeraj had ...... wanted to be an engineer in his life.
A. altogether
B. almost
C. always
D. although
E. absolutely

43. The meeting was ...... and he had to stay back for a day more.
A. allowed
B. prolonged
C. waived
D. sluggish
E. stopped

44. Milan and Mahu are twins who ...... each other very much.
A. look alike
B. resemble
C. alike
D. match
E. identify

45. Much against her wishes, Veena's father ...... her to give up studies.
A. talked
B. encouraged
C. requested
D. compelled
E. advices

46. We will be ...... her on Friday at Ramesh's house.
A. talking
B. taking
C. seeing
D. meet
E. passing

47. There are ...... people living in this street.
A. many
B. much
C. lot
D. plenty
E. sufficient

48. Kaveri promised me that he would come ...... did not turn up.
A. though
B. still
C. but
D. so
E. and

49. These medicines are ...... for curing cold.
A. effective
B. powerful
C. real
D. capable
E. proper

50. Vineeta came ...... me to see the circus.
A. across
B. along
C. towards
D. together
E. after

51. The shopkeeper ...... the customer all types of toys in his shop.
A. showed
B. placed
C. called
D. saw
E. allotted

52. He ...... asleep while he was driving.
A. falls
B. fell
C. fallen
D. goes
E. went

53. We will be late if we ...... not leave now.
A. will
B. shall
C. did
D. do
E. does

54. The bus stand is directly ...... the police station.
A. around
B. about
C. towards
D. nearly
E. behind

55. The ...... has expressed his love for nature in his poem.
A. writer
B. producer
C. author
D. poet
E. journalist

56. It was a pleasant morning and we went ...... for a walk.
A. in
B. out
C. to
D. on
E. away

57. It is good that you are ...... of your faults.
A. known   B. short
C. aware   D. removing
E. approving

58. The girls complained ...... malpractice of the warden.
A. to   B. on
C. about   D. for
E. against

59. I fail to comprehend why he has developed a tendency to look down ..... his juniors.
A. at   B. on
C. upon   D. with
E. from

60. Even after his best efforts, he could not make her yield ...... his allurement.
A. before   B. for
C. in   D. to
E. by

61. You should not ...... lunch at this time because you are too late.
A. hope   B. expect
C. hope for   D. demand
E. ask for

62. We have remembered you ...... the time you parted with us.
A. till   B. since
C. for   D. up to the time
E. as

63. The bomb ...... and killed no fewer than forty people.
A. erupted   B. exploded
C. cracked   D. volleyed
E. roared

64. Since we wanted to get an experience, we have ...... such a tiring journey.
A. travelled   B. gone
C. fulfilled   D. curtailed
E. undertaken

65. The little boy ...... frightened and ran away.
A. got   B. get
C. became   D. had
E. show

66. Kapil plays tennis ...... often than Sachin does.
A. more   B. as
C. so   D. far
E. nearly

67. The crop has been ...... well after the rains.
A. grown   B. growing
C. grow   D. grows
E. grew

68. Keerti is intending to accompay them on ...... next visit abroad.
A. her   B. theirs
C. our   D. their
E. its

69. They ...... no attention to what people say about them.
A. keep   B. listen
C. pay   D. take
E. mind

70. Apparently, the disease is ...... by some mosquitoes.
A. concealed   B. conveyed
C. spread   D. speeded
E. taken

71. The train started from the station ...... and picked up speed afterwards.
A. suddenly   B. abruptly
C. feebly   D. brokenly
E. slowly

72. We became so ...... in the game that we did not notice a passenger who had got into our compartment.
A. skillful   B. absorbed
C. neglected   D. inattentive
E. meticulous

73. The exercise should not be done...... after taking food.
A. as soon as   B. much
C. as far as   D. seriously
E. immediately

74. A ...... fear of doctors persists among children.
A. universal   B. recognised
C. introduction   D. threatening
E. polite

75. If I receive a ...... encouragement, it will help me.
A. few   B. least
C. some   D. most
E. little

ANSWERS

1	2	3	4	5	6	7	8	9	10
C	C	A	C	B	C	B	A	A	B

11	12	13	14	15	16	17	18	19	20
C	B	E	D	E	A	B	D	C	E

21	22	23	24	25	26	27	28	29	30
E	A	C	C	B	C	B	B	D	D

31	32	33	34	35	36	37	38	39	40
E	A	A	E	D	E	B	A	D	A

41	42	43	44	45	46	47	48	49	50
B	C	B	B	D	C	A	C	A	B

51	52	53	54	55	56	57	58	59	60
A	B	D	E	D	B	C	C	C	D

61	62	63	64	65	66	67	68	69	70
B	B	B	E	A	A	B	D	C	C

71	72	73	74	75
E	D	E	A	E

COMPREHENSION

A. Objectives

Comprehension test ascertain candidate's ability to understand the ideas contained in the prose passage. For solving the comprehension questions, the condidates should bear in mind that the various comprehension questions are set with the following objectives in view :

(a) To test his capability to understand the implicit as well as the explicit ideas of the passage writer.

(b) To test his richness and accuracy of vocabulary.

(c) To judge his capability to pick out the various arguments advanced by the writer for or against a certain topic.

(d) To test the candidate's ability to comprehend and interpret the given passage.

(e) To test his ability to detect the central ideas or the focal point in the passage.

(f) To test, though not very often, his power of appreciating critically the views contained in the passage.

B. The best way to answer the Comprehension Questions

For answering the comprehension questions correctly, constant practice is of utmost importance and is quite necessary. However, the following method will be helpful to the candidates in tackling these questions.

(a) First of all, the entire passage should be read carefully and quickly. This speed reading will help you to understand the gist of the passage and to remember the important details.

(b) Then read the passage for the second time, this time a bit slowly and steadily, concentrating your attention on the questions set below it. This second reading of the passage, with an eye of the questions, will help you to find out the correct answer to the given question.

(c) In third stage, make your answer in the answer sheet, as directed.

C. Few important points to remember

(a) Utmost care should be taken to ensure that the comprehension questions are answered within the time allotted.

(b) As all the questions carry equal marks, do not waste time over difficult questions. Put a cross on the serial number of the un-answered question, so as to easily identify them later on.

(c) If the time permits, do revision and carry out the necessary corrections.

PASSAGE 1

Directions : *Read the following passage carefully and answer the questions given below it. Certain words/ phrases have been italicised to help locate them, while answering some of the questions.*

Once upon a time there lived a merchant named Madhav who was very rich. However, as time went on, he lost all his money and became very poor. Madhav then decided to leave the city to try his luck elsewhere. He sold all he owned in order to *clear* his debts. The only item he kept was an *antique* iron beam weighing about half a ton, Madhav asked his friend Lakhan to keep the beam with him while he was away. Lakhan gladly accepted *charge* of the beam.

Years passed. Madhav travelled widely and made a lot of money. He returned to his native place as a rich man. A few days after settling down, Madhav remembered the beam. He went to see Lakhan to ask for its return. But Lakhan had no *intention* of returning the beam. "Oh, Madhav, what will I tell you !" he said in excuse. "While you were away, I kept the beam in my godown and the mice ate it. Please do foregive me for this." Madhav did not comment. When he rose to leave, he said, "Lakhan, my friend, you have been so kind in keeping the beam for me ! So I have brought you a present. Please send your son, Ramu, to *collect* it. Lakhan felt guilty. But he sent Ramu with Madhav. On reaching home,

Madhav got Ramu locked up in a room. When Ramu did not return home by evening, his father came in search of him. "Oh, I'm terribly sorry! Madhav apologised to Lakhan". "While we were coming here, a hawk flew down and carried Ramu away. I could not do anything. Please forgive me." Lakhan got *wild* on hearing this. He started quarrelling with Madhav.

The matter was finally taken to the court. The judge observed that it was not possible for a hawk to fly off with a grown-up-boy. "Yes sir, it is just as possible for a hawk to fly off with a grown-up-boy, as it is for mice to eat an iron beam weighing half a ton" explained Madhav. The judge asked what he meant and Madhav told his story. The judge ordered Lakhan to return the beam in exchange of the boy and the matter was settled.

1. What did Madhav do to pay off his debts ?
A. He sold the iron beam to Lakhan.
B. He borrowed some money from Lakhan.
C. He sought the help of his friend Lakhan.
D. He kept the iron beam with Lakhan.
E. None of these.

2. Why did Madhav go to Lakhan's house after returning to the city ?
A. He wanted to give a present to Lakhan.
B. He wanted to take Ramu to his house.
C. He wanted to keep an iron beam with Lakhan.

D. He wanted to collect a present from Lakhan.

E. He wanted to take back the iron beam from Lakhan.

3. What did Madhav do to Ramu ?

A. Madhav told Ramu to lock up the room.

B. Madhav sent him to his house.

C. Madhav took him as a present from Lakhan.

D. Madhav allowed him to be carried away by a hawk.

E. Madhav forcibly kept him in his house.

4. Lakhan went to Madhav's house to ...

A. enquire about Ramu.

B. apologise to him.

C. release Ramu from the room.

D. accept the present brought by him.

E. give back the iron beam.

5. When Lakhan went to Madhav's house, he was told that ...

A. Ramu was locked up in a room.

B. the mice had eaten up the beam.

C. Ramu had returned to his house.

D. a hawk had taken Ramu away.

E. a present has been brought for him.

6. Madhav decided to leave the city so that...

A. he could keep the iron beam with Lakhan.

B. he could pay off the debts.

C. he could try his fortune in some other place.

D. he could travel widely.

E. None of these.

7. Which of the following statements is *True* in the context of the passage ?

A. The judge ordered Lakhan to keep the iron beam with him.

B. The iron beam was not actually eaten up by mice.

C. Madhav kept the iron beam with Lakhan after coming back to his native place.

D. Lakhan did not return the iron beam because Madhav did not pay his debts.

E. None of these.

8. Which of the following statements is *Not True* in the context of the passage ?

A. Madhav brought a present for Lakhan when he returned as a rich man.

B. Lakhan was not at all interested in returning the iron beam.

C. Ramu was not at all carried away by a hawk.

D. Madhav did not quarrel with Lakhan when the iron beam was not returned to him.

E. Madhav told a lie in order to regain his iron beam.

9. When Madhav asked for the beam, Lakhan said that ...

A. he wanted to keep the beam for himself.

B. the beam was eaten up by mice.

C. he would send the beam along with Ramu.

D. the beam was lying safely in the godown.

E. a hawk flew down and carried away the iron beam.

Directions (10-13) : *Choose the word which is **most nearly the same** in meaning as the word or group of words in Capital Letters, as used in the passage.*

10. INTENTION
A. willingness   B. hope
C. ambition   D. determination
E. choice

11. CHARGE
A. duty   B. responsibility
C. care   D. receipt
E. safety

12. CLEAR
A. receive   B. sell
C. finish   D. pay
E. buy

13. WILD
A. abnormal   B. emotional
C. angry   D. impatient
E. disturbed

Directions (14-15) : *Choose the word which is **most opposite** in meaning of the words in Capital Letters, as used in the passage.*

14. COLLECT
A. gather   B. give
C. throw   D. distribute
E. take

15. ANTIQUE
A. ancient   B. pure
C. beautiful   D. clean
E. new

PASSAGE 2

Directions (1-15): *Read the following passage carefully and answer the questions given below it. Certain words in the passage have been **italicised** to help you locate them while answering some of the questions.*

Sultan Nasiruddin was a wise and *just* ruler. Everydody sang his praises. He was kind to the poor. He used to distribute money to the poor and the needy. His treasury was full of wealth. In spite of having so much wealth, he did not spend anything on himself. He earned his living by copying the holy book of the Muslims. Though a king, he felt that he must earn his own livelihood. He led a simple life. His wife was forced to do all the household chores. She had to cook her food, sweep the floor, make cothes and do many other household duties. At night, she complained of *severe* pain in her body. She *muttered* to herself, "My life is so miserable. I am tired of working from morning to evening."

One day, while cooking food, she burnt her fingers. She started weeping. On seeing her weeping, Sultan Nasiruddin asked her, "Begum, what is the matter ?" The queen started grumbling. "See, I have burnt my fingers. In spite of my being a queen, I have to work like other poor women. Why don't you employ some maid-servant ?" Sultan Nasiruddin replied, "No Begum, I earn my livelihood by copying the Koran. My income does not permit me to spend *lavishly*." The queen was annoyed. She said, "Sultan, for whom is this treasury full ? As a King, you must spend on yourself and your family. Sultan Nasiruddin disagreed. He replied, "Begum you are mistaken. I cannot touch the treasury. It is people's wealth. I am answerable to God. I must earn my livelihood." The Begum was *quiet*. She was convinced by the Sultan's argument and accepted it willingly.

1. The queen got annoyed because...
A. she had burnt her fingers.
B. of the Sultan's statement about his own income.
C. the Sultan was busy copying the holy book.
D. of the Sultan's undue concern for her.
E. the Sultan forced her to work with other poor women.

2. Why did Sultan Nasiruddin not use the money in the treasury for himself ?
A. He was afraid that his subjects would accuse him of theft.
B. He had already distributed the money to the poor.
C. He wanted to annoy his Begum.
D. He was convinced that the money belonged to the people.
E. None of these.

3. The demand of the queen was that the ......
A. Sultan should earn his own livelihood.
B. Money in the treasury should not be distributed to the poor.
C. Sultan should employ a maid servant.
D. Sultan should help her in her household duties.
E. Sultan should stop copying the holy book.

4. Why was Sultan Nasiruddin popular among his people ?
A. He was devoted to the holy Koran.
B. He was fair to all and was full of wisdom.
C. He had kept the treasury full of wealth.
D. He made his wife work like an ordinary woman.
E. None of these.

5. Which of the following statements is *true* in the context of the passage ?
A. Nobody used to praise the Sultan.
B. The wife of Nasiruddin never got tired of doing household duties.
C. The queen used to do all domestic chores.
D. The wife of Nasiruddin was from a poor family.
E. The Sultan was never God-fearing.

6. What forced the queen to do all the household chores ?
A. The simple life style of the Sultan.
B. The lack of money in the treasury.
C. The poor working of the maid servant.
D. The Sultan's greed for money.
E. None of these.

7. Why did Sultan Nasiruddin use to copy the Koran ?
A. It was the holy book of the Muslims.
B. He wanted to prove that he was religious minded King.
C. He wanted to teach his wife a lesson.
D. He wanted to learn Koran by copying it.
E. None of these.

8. What made the queen weep ?
A. The Sultan's unwillingness to use the wealth in the treasury.
B. The Sultan's lack of attention towards her.

C. The severe pain in her body.
D. The burning of her fingers.
E. None of these.

9. Which of the following statements is *Not True* in the context of the passage ?

A. The income of the Sultan did not permit him to be extravagant.
B. The queen wanted the King to spend the money in the treasury on themselves.
C. The Sultan was sympathetic to the poor and the needy.
D. The queen made the Sultan employ some servants for her.
E. The Sultan and the queen led the life of ordinary people.

10. What was the cause of the severe pain in the queen's body ?

A. The daily washing of the floor by her.
B. The burning of her body while cooking.
C. The pain was a trick to avoid domestic duties.
D. Not mentioned in the passage.
E. None of these.

Directions (11-13) : *Choose the word which is **most nearly the same** in meaning as the words in Capital Letters, as used in the passage.*

11. SEVERE

A. sad   B. serious
C. deep   D. bad
E. intense

12. QUIET

A. sorry   B. kind
C. grim   D. peaceful
E. silent

13. MUTTERED

A. apologised   B. grumbled
C. thought   D. addressed
E. reminded

Directions (14-15) : *Choose the word which is **most opposite in meaning** of the words in Capital Letters, as used in the passage.*

14. JUST

A. unbiased   B. only
C. cruel   D. unfair
E. foolish

15. LAVISHLY

A. miserly   B. minutely
C. extravagantly   D. financially
E. doubtfully

PASSAGE 3

Directions : *Read the following passage carefully and answer the questions given below it. Certain words/ phrases have been **italicised** to help you to locate them while answering some of the questions.*

This happened not so long ago in a remote village in South India. There lived in this village, a middle aged woman named Thangamma, who earned her living by selling vegetables in the market. She had a small farm near her house, where she cultivated different types of vegetables. Near her house, lived a woman named Mangamma, who owned a farm *adjacent* to Thangamma's farm. Mangamma, who was not as old as Thangamma, did not cultivate anything in her farm, but spent most of her time dreaming of getting some hidden wealth in her farm. In fact, an astrologer had once told her that she would become rich overnight. She had then gone around saying this to everyone in the village. Mangamma often *made fun of* Thangamma saying that only fool would toil so much.

One day while Mangamma was wandering over her farm, a storm *broke out* and she took shelter under a tree. As she stood there, her eyes fell upon an ordinary-looking earthen pot lying at her feet, half buried in the ground. Her curiosity aroused. She dug out the pot and with trembling fingers brushed off the mud from the lid. To her amazement, it was filled with glittering ornaments. She looked around and after ensuring that nobody was watching her, quietly took the pot home. After reaching home, she hid the pot inside a wooden box in her house. Being overjoyed at her dream coming true, she started celebrating by buying *expensive* clothes and other things for herself. In a few days she spent all the money she had. She then took out the pot and went straight to the shop of the village goldsmith to sell all the ornaments. The goldsmith after examining them carefully, threw them back to her. Mangamma asked him what he meant. The goldsmith scornfully declared that the ornaments were fake.

The fake gold ornaments were in fact the ones worn by stage actors while *portraying* mythical characters. It was none other than Thangamma who kept the pot of fake ornaments in Mangamma's farm. She did this to teach Mangamma a good lesson.

On hearing the goldsmith's words, Mangamma stood dumb-founded. She soon understood her folly and left the shop realising the merit of the old proverb. "All that glitters is not gold."

1. How did Thangamma earn her living ?
A. She worked in the farms of the villages.
B. She sold grains in the market.
C. She bought vegetables from Mangamma and sold them in the market.
D. She sold the vegetables she cultivated.
E. None of these.

2. What can be inferred from the passage regarding the age of Thangamma ?
A. She was an aged woman.
B. She was not as old as Mangamma.
C. She was of the same age as Mangamma.
D. She was older than Mangamma.
E. She was a young woman.

3. Once an astrologer had told Mangamma that she would
A. become rich at night.
B. loss all her money.
C. get a pot of ornaments in her farm.
D. become wealthy all of a sudden.
E. get some fake ornaments in her farm.

4. What did the jeweller say after examining the ornaments ?
A. He said that they were worn by stage actors.

B. He said that they were not real gold ornaments.

C. He said that he would give a few rupees for the ornaments.

D. He said that the ornaments were not shiny.

E. He said that he does not buy old ornaments.

5. Which of the following is *True* in the context of the passage ?

A. Mangamma decided to sell the ornaments although she had some money with her.

B. Mangamma wanted to cheat the goldsmith by selling the fake ornaments.

C. The astrologer did not keep the pot of ornaments in Mangamma's farm.

D. The goldsmith was responsible for teaching Mangamma a good lesson.

E. The pot of ornaments was kept in Mangamma's farm by the stage actors.

6. The ornaments kept in the pot were actually the ones

A. Worn by Thangamma when she acted in dramas.

B. Used by actors who played the role of characters from mythology.

C. Made by the goldsmith to teach Mangamma a lesson.

D. Worn by the ancient stage actors.

E. One of these.

7. What did Mangamma do with the pot of ornaments after taking it home ?

A. She took it to the goldsmith.

B. She hid it under the ground.

C. She kept it in a box.

D. She sold it to buy expensive clothes.

E. She hid it under a tree.

8. Which of the following is *Not True* in the context of the passage ?

A. Mangamma did not cultivate vegetables in her farm.

B. Mangamma tried to sell the pot of ornaments to the village goldsmith.

C. Mangamma did not tell Thangamma about the pot of ornaments.

D. Mangamma, in her dream, saw the pot of ornaments lying under the tree.

E. Mangamma often made fun of Thangamma.

9. Where did Mangamma find the pot of ornaments ?

A. Under a tree in the forest.

B. In Thangamma's farm.

C. In her own farm.

D. Near Thangamma's house.

E. Inside a wooden box in the farm.

Directions (10-12) : *Choose the word which is **most nearly the same** in meaning as the word or group of words in Capital Letters,, as used in the passage.*

10. CULTIVATED

A. marketed   B. ploughed

C. grew   D. collected

E. made

11. MADE FUN OF

A. ridiculed   B. requested

C. praised   D. advised

E. cursed

12. PORTRAYING

A. dressing   B. depicting

C. pretending   D. decorating

E. exposing

Directions (13-15) : *Choose the word which is **most nearly the opposite** in meaning as the word or group of words in Capital Letters, as used in the passage.*

13. ADJACENT
A. joining   B. distant
C. unequal   D. near
E. unrelated

14. BROKE OUT
A. started   B. gathered
C. vanished   D. exploded
E. thundered

15. EXPENSIVE
A. attractive   B. costly
C. dull   D. dirty
E. cheap

PASSAGE 4

Directions : *Read the following passage carefully and answer the questions given below it. Certain words/ groups of words have been italicised to help you to locate them easily while answering some of the questions.*

King Vikramaditya was renowned for his impartial judgement. His brother-in-law, Rishiketu was very ambitious. He considered himself to be very wise; much wiser than he really was. He *used* to be *present* in the court while Vikramaditya conducted trials. Rishiketu developed a feeling that he could also give judgements like the king. Sometimes he *made* his comments *privately* to some of the courtiers who were friendly to him but his boasting reached Vikramaditya's ear. One day Vikramaditya asked Rishiketu to disguise as an old man wearing a false beard and a royal robe and to sit in his judgement seat. He announced to the courtiers, "Here is our old friend, the famous chief judge of our neighbouring kingdom. He will dispose of today's cases while I attend to some other important things. "Vikramaditya left the court but hid himself behind the screen just *close* to Rishiketu's Chair.

Rishiketu heard the first case of a thief who had stolen a hen. He ordered the thief to go and steal another hen and ordered the soldiers to follow him and arrest him immediately after his stealing the second hen. He further added that he would give his judgement only after that.

While everyone sat amazed with this *funny* trial, Vikramaditya came out and *led* Rishiketu into his private room. There he asked Rishiketu why he wanted the thief to steal one more hen. Rishiketu explained thoughtfully, "Your Majesty, a few days ago, you had fined a gold coin to a thief who had stolen two hens. In our kigndom there is no half gold coin. How can I fine half gold coin for stealing one hen ? Therefore I asked him to steal one more hen, so that I could fine him one gold coin."

1. Which of the following statements is *True* in the context of the passage ?
A. Rishiketu was not at all deserving to be a judge.
B. Rishiketu had never praised himself for his wisdom.
C. The thief had stolen another hen as per Rishiketu's order.

D. After Rishiketu heard the case, Vikramaditya fined a gold coin to the thief.

E. Rishiketu had decided to fine half gold coin to the thief.

2. Which of the following is the meaning of 'after that' as used in the last sentence of the third paragraph ?

A. After the soldiers follow the thief.

B. After carefully listening to the case of theft.

C. After Vikramaditya takes over from Rishiketu.

D. After the thief had stolen another hen.

E. After the thief was released for repeating the crime.

3. What surprised the people in the king's court ?

A. Vikramaditya's act of asking an outsider to sit in his seat.

B. Rishiketu's act of asking the thief to steal another hen.

C. Rishiketu's ordering the guards to follow and arrest the thief.

D. Rishiketu's explanation for postponement of the judgement.

E. Vikramaditya's act of giving more importance to other things than to the trials.

4. Rishiketu used to tell his courtier friends :

A. To be present in the court while he conducted trials.

B. That Vikramaditya could conduct trials very impartially.

C. Not to tell Vikramaditya his privately made comments.

D. That he was a capable of judging cases as the king.

E. None of these.

5. What did Vikramaditya do after placing Rishiketu in his judgement seat ?

A. He went out to attend to some other important things.

B. He appeared before Rishiketu in the disguise of a thief.

C. He wore a false beared and a royal robe.

D. He hid Rishiketu behind the screen, very close to the judge's seat.

E. He remained in the court without being noticed by others.

6. Vikramaditya introduced Rishiketu to his courtiers as :

A. his brother-in-law.

B. a thief who had stolen a hen.

C. the chief judge of the neighbouring kingdom.

D. a fake judge wearing a beard and a royal robe.

E. None of these.

7. After listening to Rishiketu's explanation for his judgement in the thief's case, Vikramaditya most probably would have :

A. asked him to continue in his judgement seat.

B. been pleased with his intelligence and rewarded him.

C. shown him his right place.

D. admired his ability as a judge.

E. appointed him as chief judge of his own kingdom.

Directions : (*8-12*) *Which of the following is **most nearly the same** in meaning as the words in Capital Letters, as used in the context of the passage.*

8. ADDED

A. summed   B. deposited

C. mixed   D. said
E. judged

9. LED
A. carried   B. forced
C. persuaded   D. left
E. followed

10. USED
A. utilised   B. continued
C. applied   D. liked
E. consumed

11. MADE
A. prepared   B. decided
C. expressed   D. felt
E. considered

12. FUNNY
A. happy   B. annoying
C. pleasant   D. exciting
E. ridiculous

Directions (13-15) : *Which of the following is **most opposite in meaning** of the words in capital letters, as used in the passage :*

13. PRESENT
A. absent   B. past
C. return   D. withdraw
E. disappear

14. CLOSE
A. open   B. away
C. disclose   D. near
E. long

15. PRIVATELY
A. lonely   B. officially
C. secretly   D. decisively
E. openly

PASSAGE 5

Directions : *Read the following passage carefully and answer the questions given below it. Certain words have been italicised to help you to locate them while answering some of the questions.*

Long ago, there lived a poor slave. One day, tired of heavy work and of the little food, he decided to run away but was caught. His master became furious and decided to punish him. He condemned the slave to a most horrible death; to be torn alive and eaten by a lion. He did this to amuse himself and his friends.

So, on the fixed day, the poor slave was dragged to the circus area and a big lion was brought in. The beast had been kept fasting for two days and so on seeing the poor man, came running towards him. But to everyone's surprise, as he drew near, he stopped and began to lick the slave's hand. It was *evident* that the beast was happy. He was wagging his tail like a dog.

The slave now started patting the lion and whispered something in his ear. Everyone was taken by surprise at the *strange* behaviour of the lion. They wondered why the beast did not *devour* the man. The master then asked the slave to give an explanation.

"It is not the first time that I attempted to run away", began the poor slave. "Once when I was the slave to another master, I had run away and had hidden myself in a cave for some days. One day this lion entered the cave limping. A big thorn had got into his right paw and caused him a lot of pain. I pulled out the thorn from his paw. From that moment, he became my friend. One day both of us were caught and *separated* by a gang of hunters. We have now come together."

The story of the poor slave *touched* everyone present there. The slave and the lion were immediately set free by the master.

1. The slave tried to run away from his present master because :
A. he wanted to meet his friend, the lion.
B. his master became furious one day.
C. he wanted to teach his master a lesson.
D. he was condemned to a horrible death.
E. he was badly treated by the master.

2. The lion did not harm the slave in the arena because :
A. the slave was the friend of the lion.
B. the slave whispered something in the lion's ear.
C. the lion had a thorn in its paw.
D. the slave started patting the lion.
E. None of these.

3. The poor slave was condemned to be eaten by a lion because :
A. he was tired of heavy work.
B. he had tried to escape.
C. there was very little food for him to eat.
D. the lion was kept fasting for two days.
E. the master wanted to test the slave's strength.

4. The poor slave hid himself in a cave after :
A. running away from the lion.
B. escaping from his present master.
C. seeing the lion in the circus arena.
D. running away from his former master.
E. removing the thorn from the lion's paw.

5. What did the slave do when the lion entered the cave ?
A. He ran away and hid himself in another cave.
B. He told something in the lion's ear.
C. He removed the thorn from the lion's paw.
D. He decided to kill it.
E. None of these.

6. Why were the spectators in the arena taken by surprise ?
A. The slave did not try to run away.
B. The lion was limping.
C. The lion came running towards the slave.
D. The lion did not harm to the slave.
E. The slave removed the thorn from the lion's paw.

7. The slave and the lion were set free by the master soon after :
A. seeing the lion limping.
B. listening to the tale of their friendship.
C. they were touched by everyone present there.
D. keeping them together in the arena.
E. the slave pulled out a thorn from the lion's paw.

8. Which of the following statements is *Not True* in the context of the passage ?
A. The slave and the lion were once caught by a group of hunters.
B. The spectators did not believe in the story narrated by the slave.
C. In the arena, the lion recognised the slave as his old friend.
D. The lion was not given food for two days before bringing it to the arena.
E. After seeing the slave in the arena, the lion started wagging its tail like a dog.

9. Which of the following statement is *True* in the context of the passage ?
A. The lion licked the slave's hand in the arena.
B. Before meeting the slave in the cave, the lion was kept fasting from two days.
C. It was the first time that the lion met the slave in the arena.
D. The lion was in pain because it was injured by a hunter.
E. The slave patted the lion as soon as it entered the cave.

Directions (10-13) : *Choose the word which is **most nearly the same** in meaning as the words in Capital Letters, as used in the passage.*

10. TOUCHED
A. contracted   B. affected
C. surprised   D. related
E. cautioned

11. STRANGE
A. unnecessary   B. kind
C. unusual   D. silly
E. mild

12. DEVOUR
A. eat   B. throw
C. punish   D. save
E. catch

13. AMUSE
A. watch   B. laugh
C. treat   D. show
E. entertain

Directions (14-15) : *Choose the word which is **most opposite in meaning** of the words Capital Letters, as used in the passage.*

14. SEPARATED
A. removed   B. added
C. invited   D. united
E. collected

15. EVIDENT
A. doubtful   B. unimportant
C. clear   D. understood
E. disagreed.

ANSWERS

Passage 1

1	2	3	4	5	6	7	8	9	10
E	E	E	A	D	C	B	A	B	A

11	12	13	14	15
B	D	C	B	E

Passage 2

1	2	3	4	5	6	7	8	9	10
B	D	C	B	C	A	E	D	D	E

11	12	13	14	15
B	E	B	D	A

Passage 3

1	2	3	4	5	6	7	8	9	10
D	D	D	B	C	B	C	D	A	C

11	12	13	14	15
A	B	B	C	E

Passage 4

1	2	3	4	5	6	7	8	9	10
A	D	B	D	E	C	C	D	A	B

11	12	13	14	15
C	E	A	B	E

Passage 5

1	2	3	4	5	6	7	8	9	10
E	A	B	D	C	D	B	B	A	B

11	12	13	14	15
C	A	E	D	A

———

ARRANGEMENT OF PARTS
OF SENTENCES

Now various recruits bodies have included the questions of this type with a view to test your knowledge of English Language. The sentence is broken in six parts. The first and last parts of each sentence are numbered as 1 and 6. The rest of the sentence is split into four parts and named P, Q, R and S. These four parts of the sentence are jumbled *i.e.* not given in the proper order. To recreate the original sentence from its parts, read the sentence carefully and find out which of the four combinations, given in the suggested answers, is correct.

Example 1 :
1. One of the aims
P. build character,
Q. of education is to
R. to impart some sort of moral instruction
S. and to inculcate certain traits,
6. which help a person in leading a responsible life.
A. PQRS   B. QPRS   C. RQPS   D. QRPS

The correct sentence which can be recreated from the above jumbled words is 'One of the aims of education is to build character, to impart some sort of moral instruction and to inculcate certain traits, which help a person in leading a responsible life'. Hence, the answer is QPRS which is given at (B).

Example 2 :
1. What was necessary
P. and so promises
Q. not so necessary today
R. to an individual yesterday,
S. is some how
6. are broken and forgotten.
A. SRQP   B. PQSR   C. RSQP   D. PQRS

The correct answer is 'What was necesary to an individual yesterday, is some how not so necessary today and so promises are broken and forgotten'. Hence RSQP given at answer 'C' is correct.

Directions : *In the following questions, the first and the last part of the sentence are in their proper orders. The rest of the sentence named PQR and S are not given in their proper order. Read the sentences and find out which of the four combinations is correct.*

1. 1. Voice is one
   P. which can be
   Q. controlled
   R. phycical attributes,
   S. among the
   6. cultivated and trained
   A. PRQS   B. SRQP
   C. SRPQ   D. QPRS

2. 1. The syllabus notified
   P. or, specialised study
   Q. is in broad general terms
   R. for the proper general knowledge
   S. and does not require advanced
   6. of the subject concerned.
   A. PQSR   B. RQPS
   C. QSPR   D. QRSP

3. 1. Handball is a game
   P. or, board by the players,
   Q. or, against a single wall
   R. with their hands
   S. played in a walled court
   6. to strike the ball.
   A. PQRS   B. SQPR
   C. RSQP   D. QSPR

4. 1. So still was
   P. dried autumn leaves fell
   Q. the air and
   R. that the
   S. such calm was there,
   6. straight from the tree.
   A. PSQR   B. RSPQ
   C. SPRQ   D. QSRP

5. 1. It is no secret
   P. is growing impatient
   Q. that the United States
   R. over the reluctance
   S. with Iraq
   A. RQPS   B. PQRS
   C. SRQP   D. RPQS

6. 1. A rich uncle
   P. that you spend this sum
   Q. in somewhat peculiar way
   R. has given you two hundred rupees
   S. on condition
   6. within twenty-four hours.
   A. SRPQ   B. PSRQ
   C. QRPS   D. RSPQ

7. 1. When he was a boy, Rahul,
   P. a distinguished statesman and philosopher,
   Q. in the printing office of his brother,
   R. learned his trade
   S. who afterward became
   6. who published a paper in Bombay.
   A. RPSQ   B. SPRQ
   C. PSQR   D. QPRS

8. 1. Gandhiji's elder brother had thought
   P. Gandhiji would have roaring legal practice in India
   Q. that after his return from England

R. and would become a rich and famous barrister,
S. as a qualified barrister,
6. in no time.
A. QSPR   B. SPRQ
C. RPSQ   D. PQSR

9. 1. In his whole life,
P. with an optimism,
Q. he continued
R. he had never received a letter
S. born of hope and faith, but
6. and was always the first to arrive at the post office.
A. QPRS   B. RPSQ
C. QPSR   D. PQSR

10. 1. Her two elder sisters
P. and now the youngest daughter lay,
Q. with the usual difficulties
R. in finding husbands and providing dowries
S. had been married
6. like a silent weight upon the heart of her parents.
A. RPSQ   B. SPQR
C. SQRP   D. RSPQ

11. 1. Efforts must be
P. schools in such
Q. no child may have to walk
R. made to open primary
S. a large number that
6. more than a mile.
A. PQRS   B. RQSP
C. SPQR   D. RPSQ

12. 1. The passengers
P. that there was
Q. assured them
R. were afraid
S. but the captain
6. no danger.
A. QRSP   B. SRQP
C. RSQP   D. PRQS

13. 1. It gives me
P. to this Extraordinary General Meeting,
Q. great pleasure
R. to welcome you
S. which has been convened
6. to change the name of your company.
A. QRPS   B. RPSQ
C. PSQR   D. SRPQ

14. 1. After toiling very hard,
P. period of time,
Q. he had made
R. over a long
S. he found that
6. no profit at all.
A. SRPQ   B. RPSQ
C. QSRP   D. PRSQ

15. 1. We regret to inform you
P. is left uncleared
Q. that some account
R. for a long time,
S. by you
6. despite a reminder.
A. PQRS   B. RSQP
C. QPRS   D. RPSQ

16. 1. Even today, in many countries,
P. neglected and there are far
Q. women continue to be
R. who have had the benefit of
S. fewer women than men
6. education and vocational training.
A. PRQS   B. QPSR
C. RQSP   D. SQRP

17.
1. Hobbies can fill our spare
P. physical fatigue, and
Q. moments with enjoyment
R. and pleasure, they also relieve
S. mental tiredness and
6. corporate hinder our regular work.

A. QRPS   B. QRSP
C. SQPR   D. PQSR

18.
1. Certainly,
P. who always
Q. happy is the man,
R. the company
S. keeps
6. of good books.

A. RSQP   B. QPSR
C. QRSP   D. SQRP

19.
1. Law should be
P. making it compulsory
Q. made by the parliament
R. to undergo sterilisation
S. for every couple
6. after three children.

A. RPQS   B. SRPQ
C. QPSR   D. PSRQ

20.
1. I am also happy
P. in the backward district of Hisar
Q. upon a large industrialisation programme
R. to inform you
S. that your company is the first to embark
6. with an investment of Rs. 3 crores.

A. PRSQ   B. PQRS
C. SQPR   D. RSQP

EXPLANATORY ANSWERS

1. C : Voice is one among the physical attributes, which can be controlled, cultivated and trained.

2. C : The syllabus notified is in broad general terms and does not require advanced or, specialised study for the proper general knowledge of the subject concerned.

3. B : Handball is a game played in a walled court or against a single wall or, board by the players, with their hands to strike the ball.

4. D : So still was the air and such calm was there, that the dried autumn leaves fell straight from the tree.

5. A : It is no secret over the reluctance that the United States is growing impatient with Iraq.

6. D : A rich uncle has given you two hundred rupees on condition that you spend this sum in somewhat peculiar way.

7. B : When he was a boy, Rahul, who afterward became a distinguished statesman and philosopher, learned his trade in the printing office of his brother, who published a paper in Bombay.

8. A : Gandhiji's elder brother had thought that after his return from England as a qualified barrister, Gandhiji would have roaring legal practice in India and would become a rich and famous barrister, in no time.

9. **C :** In his whole life, he continued with an optimism, born hope and faith, but he had never received a letter and was always the first to arrive at the post office.

10. **C :** Her two elder sisters had been married with the usual difficulties in finding husbands and providing dowries and now the youngest daughter lay, like a silent weight upon the heart of her parents.

11. **D :** Efforts must be made to open primary schools in such a large number that no child may have to walk more than a mile.

12. **C :** The passengers were afraid but the captain assured them that there was no danger.

13. **A :** It gives me great pleasure to welcome you to this Extraordinary General Meeting, which has been convened to change the name of your company.

14. **B :** After toiling very hard, over a long period of time, he found that he had made no profit at all.

15. **C :** We regret to inform you that some account is left uncleared by you for a long time, despite a reminder.

16. **B :** Even today, in many countries, women continue to be neglected and there are far fewer women than men who have had the benefit of education and vocational training.

17. **B :** Hobbies can fill our spare moments with enjoyment and pleasure, they also relieve mental tiredness and physical fatigue and do not hinder our regular work.

18. **B :** Certainly, happy is the man, who always keeps the company of good books.

19. **C :** Law should be made by the parliament making it compulsory for every couple to undergo sterilisation after three children.

20. **D :** I am also happy to inform you that your company is the first to embark upon a large industrialisation programme in the backward district of Hisar with an investment of Rs. 3 crores.

SYNONYMS AND ANTONYMS WORDS

IMPORTANT POINTS FOR SYNONYMS AND ANTONYMS

1. Wherever possible, the question and answer words must be of the same Part of Speech. For example, if the question word is in the Passive the answer should also be in Passive. Similarly, if the question word is in the Past Tense, the answer should also be in the Past Tense and so on.
2. A favourite trick of the examiner is to include an antonym in the answer choices for a synonym question or a synonym in the answer choices for an antonym question. Be very careful about what is asked before answering a question.
3. Don't be nervous if you don't get the dictionary meaning. You are only expected to choose the best possible answer.
4. Don't ponder over a question for too long. It is better to answer those questions you know first. Then come back to those that you don't know.
5. It may be possible to choose the correct answer by rejecting those words that simply cannot be the proper choice. This is done by a process of reasoning and elimination. However, you are advised to use this process only when you are not certain of the answer, but this process is time consuming and should be used only when you are not able to choose the best possible answer.

SYNONYMS WORDS

Directions (1-100) : *Choose the word nearest in meaning to the given words.*

1. ABORTIVE
A. ineffective
B. fruitful
C. silly
D. premature
E. none

2. ABSOLVE
A. spoil
B. agree
C. acquit
D. mix
E. none

3. ABSORB
A. rub
B. remove
C. soak
D. starve
E. none

4. ACKNOWLEDGE
A. enter
B. receive
C. approve
D. admit
E. none

5. ACCUMULATE
A. buy
B. add

C. store D. approve
E. none

6. ADHERE
A. accept B. stick
C. fight D. oppose
E. none

7. ADJOURN
A. postpone B. increase
C. drop D. record
E. none

8. ADMONISH
A. admire B. abolish
C. warn D. harm
E. none

9. AFFECTION
A. attraction B. interest
C. fondness D. attachment
E. none

10. AGILE
A. girlish B. poor
C. dull D. active
E. none

11. AKIN
A. cousin B. friendly
C. foreign D. related
E. none

12. ALLURE
A. attract B. agitate
C. entrap D. deceive
E. none

13. ANALOGY
A. comparison B. linking
C. psychology D. attitude
E. none

14. APPLAUD
A. suspend B. agree
C. graise D. condemn
E. none

15. ASSAIL
A. sell B. depart
C. attack D. invite
E. none

16. ATTEMPT
A. try B. answer
C. explain D. solve
E. none

17. AWE
A. dream B. fear
C. ghost D. lie
E. none

18. BAFFLE
A. sink B. puzzle
C. postpone D. mix
E. none

19. BALMY
A. irritating B. dirty
C. soothing D. stormy
E. none

20. BARGAIN
A. account B. deal
C. sale D. profit
E. none

21. BEHEST
A. battery B. command
C. nest D. business
E. none

22. BEHOLD
A. see B. catch
C. chase D. examine
E. none

23. BENEFICENT
A. kindly B. useful
C. cheap D. poisonous
E. none

24. BENEVOLENT
A. charitable B. gentle

C. wealthy   D. helpful
E. none

25. BETRAY
A. tear   B. beat
C. puzzle   D. deceive
E. none

26. BID
A. command   B. befool
C. obey   D. answer
E. none

27. BITTER
A. unfriendly   B. mannerless
C. sweet   D. harsh
E. none

28. BLAST
A. storm   B. fire
C. explosion   D. furnace
E. none

29. BLEND
A. polish   B. grind
C. mix   D. dissolve
E. none

30. BLUNDER
A. foolishness   B. fall
C. accident   D. error
E. none

31. BONDAGE
A. slavery   B. bravery
C. agreement   D. hardship
E. none

32. BOOTY
A. gain   B. loss
C. footwear   D. dirty
E. none

33. BRAWL
A. noise   B. tip.
C. agitation   D. fight
E. none

34. BREACH
A. disagreement   B. violation
C. rift   D. divorce
E. none

35. BRITTLE
A. breakable   B. little
C. glassy   D. bitter
E. none

36. CALLOUS
A. unlovable   B. careless
C. hard   D. legal
E. none

37. CARESS
A. ignore   B. watch
C. inspect   D. embrace
E. none

38. CATALOGUE
A. dictionary   B. encyclopaedia
C. directory   D. list
E. none

39. CAUSTIC
A. impure   B. severe
C. bitter   D. costly
E. none

40. CELEBRATED
A. famous   B. holy
C. joyful   D. big
E. none

41. COMPENSATE
A. reward   B. compel
C. punish   D. to make up for
E. none

42. COMPREHENSIVE
A. extensive   B. annual
C. complete   D. successful
E. none

43. CONFOUND
A. comment   B. confuse

C. recover   D. discover
E. none

44. CONQUEST
A. control   B. attack
C. defence   D. victory
E. none

45. CONSPIRACY
A. enmity   B. murder
C. plot   D. mischief
E. none

46. CONVICT
A. companion   B. guard
C. supervisor   D. criminal
E. none

47. CORDIAL
A. difficult   B. neighbourly
C. sleepy   D. friendly
E. none

48. CORPORAL
A. physical   B. fat
C. concrete   D. true
E. none

49. COUNTERFEIT
A. false   B. rival
C. natural   D. opposite
E. none

50. COURTESY
A. honesty   B. simplicity
C. politeness   D. sweetness
E. none

51. CREDITABLE
A. reasonable   B. honourable
C. believable   D. desirable
E. none

52. DEARTH
A. delicacy   B. scarcity
C. want   D. necessity
E. none

53. DEBAR
A. imprison   B. prevent
C. dismiss   D. detain
E. none

54. DEFINE
A. summarise   B. expand
C. explain   D. clarify
E. none

55. DEFORMITY
A. disturbance   B. indiscipline
C. irregularity   D. ugliness
E. none

56. DELICACY
A. softness   B. freshness
C. grace   D. nicely
E. none

57. DENOUNCE
A. announce   B. decrease
C. condemn   D. auction
E. none

58. DESCEND
A. depart   B. slip
C. direct   D. fall
E. none

59. DICTATE
A. overpower   B. rule
C. direct   D. suppress
E. none

60. DISCIPLE
A. follower   B. worshipper
C. believer   D. client
E. none

61. DISGUISE
A. distort   B. spoil
C. conceal   D. deface
E. none

62. DIVERSE
A. complex   B. many

C. strange   D. various
E. none

63. DOWNRIGHT
A. straight   B. sincere
C. slippery   D. slow
E. none

64. DRENCH
A. shrink   B. trench
C. drown   D. wet
E. none

65. DROWSY
A. weak   B. stale
C. ugly   D. sleepy
E. none

66. DWELL
A. disappear   B. swell
C. stay   D. compel
E. none

67. EBB
A. fly   B. vanish
C. decline   D. rise
E. none

68. ECONOMY
A. business   B. ceapness
C. saving   D. bargain
E. none

69. EGOTISTIC
A. orthodox   B. obstinate
C. stupid   D. self-centred
E. none

70. ELAPSE
A. spend   B. cancel
C. pass   D. decrease
E. none

71. ELIGIBLE
A. qualified   B. readable
C. necessity   D. educated
E. none

72. EMERGENCY
A. importance   B. necessity
C. readable   D. educated
E. none

73. EMOLUMENT
A. gift   B. employment
C. salary   D. allowance
E. none

74. ENDORSE
A. recommend   B. approve
C. simplify   D. repeat
E. none

75. ENORMOUS
A. big   B. savage
C. multisided   D. devilish
E. none

76. ENTANGLE
A. enlarge   B. involve
C. enclose   D. rectangle
E. none

77. ENVOY
A. messenger   B. judge
C. journalist   D. writer
E. none

78. ENVY
A. neighbourer   B. rivalry
C. conspiracy   D. competition
E. none

79. EPIDEMIC
A. physical   B. circular
C. external   D. general
E. none

80. ETERNAL
A. adventurous   B. internal
C. quiet   D. everlasting
E. none

81. EVIDENT
A. clear   B. trustworthy
C. deep   D. fair
E. none

82. EXCEL
A. progress   B. rise
C. surpass   D. compete
E. none

83. EXCEPTIONAL
A. unhappy   B. signincant
C. unusual   D. critical
E. none

84. EXPEDITE
A. hasten   B. expel
C. improve   D. repeat
E. none

85. EXPENSIVE
A. latest   B. vast
C. costly   D. pretty
E. none

86. EXTRAVAGANT
A. unimportant   B. irrelevant
C. heavy   D. excessive
E. none

87. FACULTY
A. power   B. success
C. talent   D. achievement
E. none

88. FANTASTIC
A. dearest   B. high
C. whimsical   D. false
E. none

89. FATAL
A. rash   B. lucky
C. quick   D. deadly
E. none

90. FICTITIOUS
A. borrowed   B. harrow
C. invisible   D. false
E. none

91. FLUCTUATE
A. punctuate   B. flourish
C. control   D. to rise and fall
E. none

92. FLUENT
A. sudden   B. smooth
C. fast   D. flexible
E. none

93. FRAGILE
A. personal   B. weak
C. strange   D. unseen
E. none

94. FUTILE
A. fruitful   B. delicate
C. useless   D. lenient
E. none

95. GAIETY
A. joyousness   B. variety
C. honesty   D. speed
E. none

96. GIDDY
A. light   B. greedy
C. dizzy   D. speedy
E. none

97. GLOOM
A. sunset   B. darkness
C. bloom   D. glory
E. none

98. GRACE
A. addition   B. beauty
C. bonus   D. birthday
E. none

99. GUILD
A. association   B. crime
C. boom   D. gold
E. none

100. GUILTY
A. corrupt   B. mischievous
C. sinful   D. honest
E. none

ANSWERS

1	2	3	4	5	6	7	8	9	10
D	C	C	C	D	B	D	C	D	D

11	12	13	14	15	16	17	18	19	20
A	C	C	A	C	A	B	B	C	B

21	22	23	24	25	26	27	28	29	30
D	A	C	D	D	B	A	B	A	D

31	32	33	34	35	36	37	38	39	40
B	A	A	C	A	C	C	D	D	D

41	42	43	44	45	46	47	48	49	50
A	B	A	D	C	D	C	D	A	A

51	52	53	54	55	56	57	58	59	60
C	C	A	A	D	B	D	D	D	C

61	62	63	64	65	66	67	68	69	70
D	B	C	B	D	C	A	C	D	C

71	72	73	74	75	76	77	78	79	80
B	A	B	A	C	B	B	C	C	A

81	82	83	84	85	86	87	88	89	90
A	C	C	A	D	D	D	C	C	D

91	92	93	94	95	96	97	98	99	100
D	B	B	C	B	B	A	C	A	C

ANTONYMS WORDS

Directions (1-100) : *Each of the following words is followed by five or four words one of which is its most opposite in meaning. Mark that word which you find most opposite in meaning.*

1. ABANDON
A. to yield   B. keep
C. to leave   D. ensure

2. ABHOR
A. love   B. have
C. to regard   D. generous
E. vulgar

3. ABRUPT
A. sharp   B. hurried
C. lacking   D. gradual
E. come

4. ACCUSE
A. impeach   B. exanerate
C. to blame   D. to call
E. renounce

5. ACUTE
A. extremely   B. dull
C. sharp   D. critical
E. profound

6. ADHERE
A. to stick fast   B. to be devoted
C. locate   D. loosen
E. equip

7. ADMIRE
A. to regard   B. venerate
C. celebrate   D. display
E. despise

8. ADVERSARY
A. an opponent   B. antagonist
C. tangible   D. ally
E. unsuccessful

9. ADVERSITY
A. affliction   B. adverse fortune
C. catastrophe   D. dropping
E. prosperity

10. AFFECTION
A. simplicity
B. conspicuous
C. strenuous pursuit
D. friendliness
E. dislike

11. AFFIRM
A. to state   B. deny
C. aver   D. assert
E. mystify

12. AGILE
A. brisk   B. ready
C. dim   D. disarming
E. sluggish

13. AGREE
A. consent   B. accede
C. differ   D. coincide
E. conform

14. ALLEVIATE
A. endure   B. worsen

C. enlighten   D. manoeuvre
E. humiliate

15. ALOOF
A. at a distance   B. impartial
C. reserved   D. careless
E. involved

16. AMALGAMATE
A. equip   B. separate
C. generate   D. materialise
E. repress

17. AMASS
A. concentrate   B. rotate
C. concern   D. separate
E. recollect

18. AMBIGUITY
A. uncertainty   B. explicitness
C. equivocation   D. obscurity
E. secular

19. AMENABLE
A. obedient   B. liable
C. stubborn   D. docile
E. abnormal

20. AMICABLE
A. penetrating   B. compensating
C. unfriendly   D. zig-zag
E. unescapable

21. AMPLIFY
A. distract   B. infer
C. publicise   D. contact
E. pioneer

22. ANALYSE
A. to examine critically
B. explicate
C. synthesise
D. dissect
E. quicken

23. ANGULAR
A. unbending   B. having corners
C. inflamed   D. round
E. puzzling

24. ANIMATE
A. deceive   B. to give life
C. fortify   D. encourage
E. kill

25. ANXIOUS
A. concerned   B. confident
C. eager   D. worried
E. troubled in mind

26. APATHETIC
A. not interested B. indifferent
C. emotional   D. thorough
E. indignant

27. APPARENT
A. discernible   B. visible
C. manifest   D. ostensible
E. obscure

28. APPEASE
A. to satisfy   B. enrage
C. to concede   D. shorten
E. urge

29. APPREHEND
A. obviate   B. set free
C. shiver   D. understand
E. contrast

30. ARROGANT
A. proud   B. insolent
C. meek   D. profound
E. angry

31. ARTLESS
A. unsophisticated
B. free from deceit
C. uncontrived
D. simple
E. cunning

32. ASCETIC
A. good-natured
B. puritan
C. one who wages
D. self-indulgent
E. one who leads simple life

33. ASSERT
A. deny
B. to state with confidence
C. predicate
D. asseverate
E. inverse

34. ASSOCIATE
A. one who shares in an enterprise
B. link
C. colleague
D. accompany
E. adversary

35. ATTAIN
A. gain   B. secure
C. miss   D. accomplish
E. reach

36. BAFFLE
A. make way   B. thwart
C. confuse   D. check
E. substitute

37. BARREN
A. unprolific   B. sterile
C. ineffective D. fertile
E. dull

38. BENEVOLENT
A. expressing goodwill
B. cruel
C. low-necked
D. altruistic
E. humanitarian

39. BENIGN
A. gracious   B. modern
C. sinister   D. humane
E. novel

40. BIAS
A. in a diagonal manner
B. preconception C. prejudice
D. impartiality   E. loss of mobility

41. BLATANT
A. loud   B. tasteless
C. vociferous   D. quiet
E. quick

42. BLEND
A. to mix together
B. clear
C. separate
D. harmonise
E. visualise

43. BLISS
A. heaven
B. complete happiness
C. classic
D. paradise
E. misery

44. BLEMISH
A. to accuse   B. purify
C. to destroy   D. defect
E. futile

45. BLUFF
A. heartily outspoken
B. to mislead someone
C. rough
D. subtle
E. discourteous

46. BREVITY
A. shortness of time
B. length
C. forceful
D. honesty
E. dropping

47. BRUTAL
A. unreasoning   B. cruel
C. vulgar   D. inhuman
E. human

48. CALM
A. without rough motion
B. peaceful
C. excitement
D. self-possessed
E. superior

49. CANDID
A. vague   B. secretive
C. experienced   D. anxious
E. clear

50. CAPTIVATE
A. seize   B. repel
C. to enthrall   D. subjugate
E. dangerous

51. CEREMONIAL
A. informal   B. conventional
C. formal   D. delectable
E. polished

52. COMPLEX
A. difficult
B. simple
C. perplaxing
D. interconnected parts
E. fragile

53. CONCEAL
A. withdraw from observaticn
B. prevent from divulging
C. yield
D. reveal
E. deny

54. CONFESS
A. grant   B. conceal
C. concede   D. acknowledge
E. desist

55. CRYPTIC
A. tomb-like   B. secret
C. famous   D. candid
E. coded

56. DISMAL
A. cheerless   B. puzzling
C. bankrupt   D. reserved
E. gay

57. DORMANT
A. latent
B. eternal
C. awake
D. immoral
E. headless

58. DROWSY
A. active
B. lethargic
C. sleepy
D. famous
E. incapable

59. EMOLUMENT
A. loss
B. output
C. capital
D. penalty
E. honararium

60. ETERNAL
A. permanent
B. perpetual
C. transitory
D. active
E. binding

61. EXPUNGE
A. investigate
B. perpetuate
C. cleanse
D. purge
E. delete

62. FEASIBLE
A. theoretical
B. impatient
C. constant
D. present
E. impracticable

63. FICTION
A. fabrication
B. fantasy
C. conducive
D. something feigned
E. fact

64. FLEXIBLE
A. unable
B. rigid
C. rational
D. easy
E. likeable

65. FRAGRANT
A. scented
B. aromatic
C. indecisive
D. helpless
E. foul-smelling

66. GENIOUS
A. adept
B. proficient
C. idiot
D. desperate
E. enlightened

67. GLOOMY
A. depressing
B. cheerless
C. exhilarating
D. dark
E. dim

68. GRACEFUL
A. comely
B. clumsy
C. polished
D. lovely
E. novel

69. GRAVE
A. significant
B. realistic
C. mean
D. insignificant
E. momentous

70. GREAT
A. global
B. spiritual
C. critical
D. august
E. small

71. HAPPINESS
A. contentment
B. joyous
C. gloom
D. obedience
E. renunciation

72. HARSH
A. humiliate
B. definite
C. strong
D. gentle
E. stringent

73. HATE
A. abhor
B. admire
C. concern
D. display
E. loathe

74. HIDE
A. disguise
B. suppress
C. modest
D. reveal
E. automatic

75. HUMBLE
A. soft
B. lowly

C. beautiful
D. accommodating
E. proud

76. HUMOUR
A. temperament B. whim
C. fun D. waggery
E. seriousness

77. HYPOCRISY
A. deceit B. truth
C. falsehood D. illegitimacy
E. determination

78. IDEAL
A. fancied B. imperfect
C. beautiful D. useful
E. visionary

79. IDENTICAL
A. similar B. sincere
C. equivalent D. unlike
E. alike

80. ILLUSION
A. dream B. equivalent
C. obvious D. farsight
E. actuality

81. IMITATE
A. impersonate B. simulate
C. modify D. copy
E. lacking logic

82. IMPARTIAL
A. fair B. shrewd
C. absured D. equitable
E. biased

83. LAWFUL
A. legal B. illegal
C. authorised D. errant
E. shameless

84. LAZY
A. calm B. polished
C. transformed D. slow
E. industrious

85. LIABLE
A. immune B. amenable
C. frivolous D. mean
E. responsible

86. LIFT
A. lower B. elevate
C. inflammable D. constructed
E. changing

87. MAD
A. sane B. exasperated
C. demented D. healthy
E. coward

88. MILD
A. placid B. harsh
C. soft D. dented
E. temperate

89. MISERABLE
A. forlorn B. disconsolate
C. eloping D. happy
E. fearsome

90. NEGLECT
A. care B. oversight
C. renovate D. quantify
E. inspire

91. NOISY
A. giant B. interpreter
C. quiet D. loud
E. clamorous

92. OBEDIENT
A. tractable B. dishonourable
C. inspired D. recalcitrant
E. complaint

93. OPPONENT
A. rival B. enemy
C. mischievous D. supporter
E. trusted

94. PANIC
A. alarm B. calm

C. apprehension D. cautious
E. indifferent

95. PLENTY
A. vastness B. dearth
C. mass D. regiment
E. number

96. REBUKE
A. rebuff B. reprimand
C. censure D. apprehend
E. raise

97. SHREWD
A. sly B. surreptitious
C. substantial D. dull

E. discriminating

98. VULGAR
A. rebald B. insensible
C. refined D. timid
E. indifferent

99. WOE
A. affiction B. anguish
C. joy D. conspiracy
E. difficulty

100. YIELD
A. abandon B. resist
C. bend D. bestow
E. understand

ANSWERS

1	2	3	4	5	6	7	8	9	10
A	D	B	B	B	E	D	D	E	E

11	12	13	14	15	16	17	18	19	20
B	E	C	B	E	C	D	B	D	B

21	22	23	24	25	26	27	28	29	30
C	C	D	E	B	C	E	B	B	C

31	32	33	34	35	36	37	38	39	40
E	D	A	E	C	A	D	B	C	B

41	42	43	44	45	46	47	48	49	50
D	C	E	B	E	D	D	A	C	B

51	52	53	54	55	56	57	58	59	60
B	B	D	B	D	E	C	A	D	B

61	62	63	64	65	66	67	68	69	70
B	E	E	E	B	C	C	B	D	E

71	72	73	74	75	76	77	78	79	80
C	D	B	E	D	E	B	E	C	E

81	82	83	84	85	86	87	88	89	90
B	D	E	B	A	A	D	A	B	A

91	92	93	94	95	96	97	98	99	100
C	D	D	B	B	E	D	C	C	B

CLOSE TEST

PASSAGE 1

Interviews are very important for all of us. We must face interviews with confindence. There is ..(1).. any person who at one time or the other has not ..(2).. an interview situation. While ..(3).. are a day to day ..(4).. for people who ..(5).. with others in their daily chores, we are here ..(6).. with interview situation when one is a ..(7).. aspiring for an ..(8).. Such situations are not very ..(9).. In one's life, there are happy ..(10).. when the candidate likes to come on top of the situation. This calls for careful study and preparation.

1. A. possibly   B. probably
   C. perhaps   D. hardly
2. A. measured   B. seen
   C. faced   D. known
3. A. meeting   B. discussions
   C. interviews   D. seminars
4. A. happening   B. feeling
   C. possibility   D. experience
5. A. react   B. concern
   C. speak   D. interact

6. A. interested   B. involved
   C. concerned   D. meeting
7. A. student   B. person
   C. beggar   D. candidate
8. A. establishment
   B. elevation
   C. estimation
   D. employment
9. A. important   B. consequent
   C. frequent   D. happy
10. A. occasions   B. hours
   C. minutes   D. times

PASSAGE 2

Some ..(1).. at the door. A lady opened it. A stranger was standing at the ..(2).. He said, "Madam, please excuse me for ..(3).. you. May I ask you something ? ..(4).. by your house everyday on my ..(5).. to work, I have ..(6).. that everyday you hit your son on ..(7).. head with a loaf of bread." The lady replied "Yes, that's" ..(8).. The stranger asked. "This, morning I saw you ..(9).. him with a chocolate. Why ..(10).. The lady replied, "Today is his birthday. Therefore I hit him with a sweet thing."

1. A. pointed   B. knocked
   C. looked   D. moved
   E. stood
2. A. fence   B. gate
   C. compound   D. door
   E. step

3. A. disturbing   B. harassing
    C. asking   D. enquiring
    E. worrying

4. A. waiting   B. watching
    C. standing   D. passing
    E. connecting

5. A. office   B. steps
    C. legs   D. journey
    E. way

6. A. decided   B. felt
    C. noticed   D. remembered
    E. surprised

7. A. your   B. his
    C. my   D. our
    E. fore

8. A. right   B. obvious
    C. surprising   D. clear
    E. clean

9. A. feeding   B. bestowing
    C. giving   D. hitting
    E. offering

10. A. bread   B. then
     C. so   D. change
     E. thus

2. A. distractions
    B. hardships
    C. predicaments
    D. stresses

3. A. steep   B. slow
    C. moderate   D. low

4. A. active   B. limited
    C. drastic   D. substantial

5. A. delivery   B. storage
    C. procurement   D. supply

6. A. additionally
    B. notwithstanding
    C. nevertheless
    D. besides

7. A. methods   B. modes
    C. measures   D. manners

8. A. resolution
    B. regulations
    C. determination
    D. requirement

9. A. redirection   B. distribution
    C. division   D. supply

10. A. slump   B. jump
     C. decline   D. grow

PASSAGE 3

The common people of India, whose condition always had been ..(1).. suffered great ..(2).. during world wars. There was a ..(3).. rise in the prices of all goods. There was a ..(4).. reduction in the ..(5).. of essential commodities ..(6).. all ..(7).. of control ..(8).. of price, government procurement and ..(9).. of essential supplies continued to ..(10)..

1. A. deplorable   B. neglected
    C. delectable   D. melancholy

PASSAGE 4

The human mind seems to have built in ..(1).. against original thought : for instance, we ..(2).. equipped with a wonderful ..(3).. for accepting evidence which agrees with our ..(4).. almost unconsciously allow our thinking to be ..(5).. on what we first thought, or were ..(6).. when we approached the subject. If ..(7).. man could be freed from the yoke ..(8).. this age old assumptions, prejudices, traditional imagery and ..(9).. about what is right and what is wrong ..(10).. might wake up one day to find that even the greatest and gentlest of his aspirations was possible.

1. A. interests B. safeguards
   C. prejudices D. ideas
2. A. have B. had
   C. may have D. having been
3. A. capacity B. sense
   C. sensibility D. capability
4. A. views
   B. thoughts
   C. conceptions
   D. pre-conceptions
5. A. based B. biased
   C. rooted D. fixed
6. A. spoke B. told
   C. expressed D. said
7. A. sometimes B. only
   C. frequently D. when
8. A. on B. in
   C. under D. of
9. A. negativeness B. certainly
   C. positiveness D. negation
10. A. he B. man
    C. men D. they

PASSAGE 5

There is an old story told ..(1).. a man who ..(2).. into a drunken sleep. His friend stayed by him as long as he ..(3).. but being compelled to go and fearing that he might be in want, the friend hid a ..(4).. in the drunken man's garment. When the drunken man ..(5).. not knowing that his friend had ..(6).. a jewel in his garment, he wandered about ..(7).. hungry. A long time afterward the two men met again and the friend told the poorman about the jewel and advised him to look

..(8).. it. Like the drunken man of the story, people ..(9).. about suffering in this life of birth and death ..(10).. what is hidden way in their ..(11).. nature. Pure and untarnished, the priceless treasure of God.

1. A. of B. to
   C. with D. by
   E. that
2. A. left B. felt
   C. fail D. fell
   E. gone
3. A. might B. can
   C. would D. had
   E. could
4. A. garment B. drink
   C. jewel D. treasure
   E. sleep
5. A. slept B. recovered
   C. discovered D. drinking
   E. realised
6. A. taken B. presented
   C. substituted D. replaced
   E. hidden
7. A. vain B. search
   C. sleep D. poverty
   E. pursuit
8. A. for B. to
   C. at D. in
   E. with
9. A. search B. wonder
   C. wander D. trouble
   E. unknown
10. A. conscious B. unconscious
    C. unknowingly D. unexpected
    E. useless
11. A. hidden B. inner
    C. obvious D. given
    E. covered

ANSWERS

Passage 1

1	2	3	4	5	6	7	8	9	10
D	C	C	D	D	C	D	D	C	A

Passage 2

1	2	3	4	5	6	7	8	9	10
B	B	A	D	E	C	B	B	D	C

Passage 3

1	2	3	4	5	6	7	8	9	10
A	B	A	C	D	B	C	B	B	C

Passage 4

1	2	3	4	5	6	7	8	9	10
C	D	A	D	A	B	B	D	A	A

Passage 5

1	2	3	4	5	6	7	8	9	10
A	D	E	C	B	E	A	A	C	B

11
B

PRACTICE PAPER

1. (1) We play/(2) tennis together/(3) every morning/(4) since last June/(5) No error.

2. (1) I personally feel that/(2) cleanliness in the city/(3) is one proof of the/(4) efficiently civic administration/(5) No error.

3. (1) When I/(2) last see him/(3) he was/(4) in Calcutta/(5) No error.

4. (1) During last days/(2) I was continuously trying/(3) to contact you/(4) but you were not available/(5) No error.

5. (1) The historian/(2) has been working/(3) on the project/(4) from last 12 years/(5) No error.

6. (1) A detailed inquiry/(2) in the incident/(3) has been initiated/(4) by the Central Government/(5) No error.

7. (1) The last year proved/(2) quite bad/(3) as major inustries/(4) witness lots of problems/(5) No error.

8. (1) I see you/(2) in Kanpur/(3) during my next visit/(4) in the month of May/(5) No error.

9. (1) A lot of money/(2) is wasted in/(3) the duplication of work/(4) in any organisation/(5) No error.

10. (1) According to me/(2) the Indians in general is/(3) not a vigilant/(4) and security conscious people/(5) No error.

Directions (11-17) : *Pick out the most effective word from the given words to fill-in-the-blank, to make the sentence meaningfully complete.*

11. Last year the performance of this production unit was . . . .

1. tall
2. staggard
3. fantastic
4. below
5. upwards

12. The blood donation camp was organised . . . . . the Naval Youth Club.

1. to
2. by
3. from
4. with
5. along

13. Vinayak is the . . . . . head of the family and commands a lot of respect from the family members.

1. solely
2. strongest
3. undisputed
4. full
5. controversial

14. I am going to Bhopal today and plan to . . . . . by tomorrow evening.

1. returning
2. returned

3. have returned   4. be returning
5. return

15. We all must . . . . . that people are the most important assets of any organisation.

1. find   2. look
3. realise   4. involve
5. dispel

16. After a recent mild paralytic attack his movements are . . . . . restricted; otherwise he is still very active.

1. not   2. entirely
3. slightly   4. nowhere
5. frequently

17. . . . . . he woke up, he saw that his bag was stolen.

1. if   2. when
3. where   4. so
5. neither

Directions (18-25) : *In the following passage there are blanks, each of which has been numbered. These numbers are given below the passage and against each, five words are suggested, one of which fits the blank appropriately. Find out the appropriate word.*

Whatermelons.. (18).. to India by the 4th century AD. Sushruta, the great Indian physician,.. (19).. wrote Sushruta Samhita, mentions that watermelons were grown.. (20).. the banks of the river Indus.. (21).. are also mentioned in ancient books. Sushruta calls it as Kalinda (hence Kalingad in Marathi). It was.. (22).. to China in the 10th or 11th century and.. (23).. it is grown throughout the tropics.

Wild watermelons are.. (24).. compared to huge cultivated ones; some of which weigh up to 25 kg. The heaviest fruit weighing 118 Kg. was produced at Hope, Arkansas, USA, the State to which President Clinton.. (25)..

18. 1. came   2. go
      3. arrived   4. started
      5. grew

19. 1. did   2. when
      3. certainly   4. who
      5. whom

20. 1. above   2. outside
      3. from   4. ahead
      5. along

21. 1. It   2. They
      3. Some   4. That
      5. Those

22. 1. took   2. gave
      3. taken   4. take
      5. taking

23. 1. also   2. though
      3. now   4. tomorrow
      5. soon

24. 1. heavier   2. small
      3. thinner   4. smaller
      5. shorter

25. 1. rules   2. belongs
      3. grew   4. elects
      5. elected

Directions (26-30) : *Rearrange the following five sentences A, B, C, D and E in the proper sequence so as to form a meaningful paragraph and then answer the questions given below them.*

A. Kiran received a call to attend the interview.

B. He applied for a new job.

C. Kiran was an ambitious boy.

D. But, he was not happy there.

E. His father had put him in a clerical job.

26. Which sentence should come LAST in the paragraph ?

1. A   2. B
3. C   4. D
5. E

27. Which sentence should come FIRST in the paragraph ?

1. A   2. B
3. C   4. D
5. E

28. Which sentence should come FOURTH in the paragraph ?

1. A   2. B
3. C   4. D
5. E

29. Which sentence should come SECOND in the paragraph ?

1. A   2. B
3. C   4. D
5. E

30. Which sentence should come THIRD in the paragraph ?

1. A   2. B
3. C   4. D
5. E

Directions (31-35) : *In each of the following questions, some words are given which are denoted by the letters A, B, C, D and E. By using each of these words only once, you have to frame a meaningful and grammatically correct sentence. The correct order of the words is your answer. Choose from the five alternatives the one having the correct order of words.*

31. A. not   B. hotel
C. comfortable   D. was
E. the
1. CDEBA   2. ECDAB
3. CDAEB   4. AEBDC
5. EBDAC

32. A. was   B. and
C. Satish   D. kind
E. loving
1. CADBE   2. EBDAC
3. CDBEA   4. AEBDC
5. ABCDE

33. A. not   B. Hari
C. away   D. run
E. did
1. ACEDB   2. CEDAB
3. EBDCA   4. BEADC
5. BACDE

34. A. left   B. the
C. house   D. he
E. suddenly
1. ADBCE   2. BACED
3. DEABC   4. EBCDA
5. BDACE

35. A. I   B. immediately
C. salary   D. my
E. want
1. DCAEB   2. AEDCB
3. BEADC   4. DBCEA
5. DEACB

Directions (36-50) : *Read the following passage carefully and answer the questions given below it.*

Yeshwant Patil—a poor farmer used to live in a village named Narasopur. He was hard-working and sincere. His father, Bhagirath, mother, Dhirubai, and younger brother, Dadu, lived with him. They were gentle and affectionate. However, Yeshwant's wife—Sonabai was a loud mouthed woman. On each and every issue she would quarrel. Yeshwant was a peace loving man. He was not much ambitious. On the other hand, Sonabai was very cunning and would not get satisfied easily. She wanted to have all luxuries of life and all household articles. Regular quarrels was a part of their family.

Sonabai in spare time used to visit neighbouring families. She would provoke other women. She would ask them to demand such things from their husbands. A lot of women started following her advice.

The farmer had a few animals including a mule. The mule would draw the small cart. The farmer used to love and take care of his animals as he knew their importance in farming. Sonabai, however, did not like this. Particularly she did not like the mule. Whenever she was required to feed the animals she would ignore the animal as far as possible. She also did not give adequate food to these animals. The animals also did not like her.

Once, Yeshwant was to go to visit his friend Kashinath. He left the house in the morning. He was to stay in that village for two-three days. Before leaving his house he patted all his animals. He instructed Sonabai to take proper care of the animals. Sonabai as usual did not pay attention to the animals. The feeding time of the animals was over but they were not fed. The mule was standing on the ground and Sonabai with great force hit him with a burning stick. The mule turned its back and kicked her furiously. Alas ! She collapsed and in a few minutes died. Messages were sent and Yeshwant returned to his village. The news of the death of Sonabai spread and people gathered in large numbers. A passing by traveller asked Devram, the elder brother of Yeshwant, "Oh, was she so popular ! Why is there so much rush ?" Someone said, "No, We are here to purchase the mule, high price is being quoted". People have not come to pay their respect for this lady. She was terrible ! She had spoiled other ladies also.

36. Why did Yeshwant love his animals ?

1. He knew that animals were partners in his progress.
2. He knew that if animals are loved people will offer more value.
3. Bhagirath had asked him to love the animals.
4. He had nothing else to offer to the animals.
5. None of these.

37. Why did people offer high price for the mule ?

1. It was very strong.
2. The cost of feeding this mule was negligible.

3. It was capable of protecting the house.
4. It was considered to be very lucky.
5. None of these.

38. People turned in large numbers to meet Yeshwant . . . . . .
1. as this was a normal practice of the villagers.
2. as they were shocked and in grief.
3. to purchase the mule.
4. to console the parents of Kashinath.
5. to take care of the mule and other animals.

39. What activity Sonabai used to do in her free time ?
1. Look after the animals.
2. Visit Kashinath's house.
3. Help the neighbours.
4. Not given in the passage.
5. None of these.

40. Who among the following does not belong to Patil's family ?
1. Dadu
2. Bhagirath
3. Dhirubai
4. Kashinath
5. Devram

41. Why did Sonabai not give sufficient food to the animals ?
1. As per instructions of Yeshwant.
2. There was shortage of animal fodder.
3. The animals were lazy.
4. Not given in the passage.
5. Dhirubai did not like the animals.

42. Sonabai had succeeded in . . . . .
1. creating a group of followers. selling the mule.

3. taking care of the animals.
4. commanding love and respect of the villagers.
5. controlling her behaviour.

43. Why did the mule attack Sonabai ?
1. She had beaten all the animals on that day.
2. Sonabai did not allow the mule to pull the cart.
3. Sonabai used to harass the family members.
4. It would not allow anyone to touch except Yeshwant.
5. None of these.

44. Which of the following correctly describes the behaviour of Sonabai ?
1. She would quarrel only occasionally.
2. She was ambitious and strong willed.
   1. Only 'a'
   2. Only 'b'
   3. Either 'a' or 'b'
   4. Neither 'a' nor 'b'
   5. Both 'a' and 'b'.

Directions (45-47) : *Choose the word which is most nearly the SAME in meaning as the word in Capital Letters, as used in the passage.*

45. DRAW
1. ride 2. push
3. run 4. pull
5. sketch

46. REGULAR
1. big 2. large
3. frequent 4. systematic
5. disciplined

47. PART
1. piece   2. feature
3. sign   4. whole
5. separate

Directions (48-50) : *Choose the word which is most OPPOSITE in meaning of the word in Capital Letters, as used in the passage.*

48. GREAT
1. short   2. unknown
3. weak   4. powerful
5. ordinary

49. LIKE
1. similar   2. hate
3. differ   4. calm
5. refuse

50. FOLLOWING
1. ignoring   2. leading
3. beginning   4. closing
5. observing

EXPLANATORY ANSWERS

1. (1) Replace the words, 'We play' by 'We have been playing' to make it meaningfully correct.
   In 'Present Perfect Continunous Tense', the construction of the sentence should be as follows :
   Subject + have/has + been + V_4 (Verb + ing) + for/since + time
   She   has been   playing   cricket   since January 95

2. (4) Replace 'efficiently' by 'efficiency of the' or 'efficient'.
   The word 'efficiently' should not be used as it is an Adverb, which does not express the quality of Noun, while as 'efficient' is an Adjective, which makes the sentence meaningful.

3. (2) Replace 'see' by 'saw', as the incident has happened in the past.

4. (1) Replace 'last days' by 'the last few days'

5. (4) Replace 'from last' by 'for' the last', because the sentence is in 'Present Perfect Continuous Tense' and 'last 12 years' indicates 'Period of Time'.
   Remember : 'for' is used for 'Period of Time' and 'since' is used for 'Point of Time', in 'Present Perfect', 'Present Perfect Continuous', 'Past Perfect Continuous', etc. For example :
   (*i*) Saveta has lived here for a month / since January.
   Present Perfect   for Period since Point of
          of Time   Time

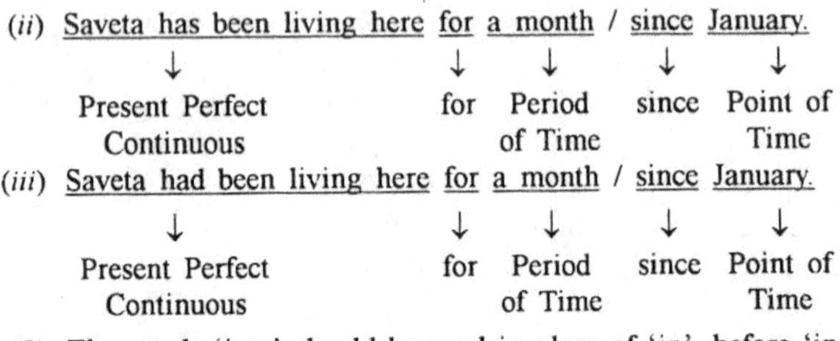

6. (2) The words 'into' should be used in place of 'in', before 'inquiry' is followed by 'into'.

7. (4) The word 'wintnessed' should be used in place of 'witness', as the sentence indicates 'Past Tense'.

8. (1) The words 'I will see you' should be used in place of 'I see you', as the sentence indicates 'Future Tense'.

9. (2) The Preposition 'on' should be used in place of 'in' 'waste' is followed by 'on'.

10. (2) The Verb 'are' should be used in place of 'is', as the Subject 'the Indians' is Plural.

For example :

(i)   He   is playing in the field.
       Subject   Verb
       (Singular) (Singular)

(ii)   They   are playing in the field.
       Subject   Verb
       (Plural)   (Plural)

11	12	13	14	15	16	17	18	19	20
(3)	(2)	(3)	(5)	(3)	(3)	(2)	(1)	(4)	(5)
21	22	23	24	25	26	27	28	29	30
(2)	(3)	(3)	(4)	(2)	(1)	(3)	(2)	(5)	(4)
31	32	33	34	35	36	37	38	39	40
(5)	(1)	(4)	(3)	(2)	(1)	(5)	(3)	(5)	(4)
41	42	43	44	45	46	47	48	49	50
(4)	(1)	(5)	(2)	(4)	(3)	(2)	(3)	(2)	(1)

PREVIOUS TEST PAPERS
(Based on Memory)

ENGLISH LANGUAGE

PAPER - 1

Directions (1-5) : *Read each sentence to find out whether there is any grammatical/idiomatic error in it. The error, if any, will be in one part of the sentence. The letter of that part is the answer. If there is no error, the answer is 'E'. (Ingnore the errors of punctuation, if any).*

1. (A) In spite of the difficulties/(B) on the way/(C) they enjoyed their/(D) trip to Gangothri/(E) No error.

2. (A) We decided not tell to/(B) the patient about/(C) the discease he was/(D) suffering from/E. No error.

3. (A) No sooner did he/(B) got up from bed/(C) than he was sent/(D) to the diary/(E) No error.

4. (A) Even after being requested/(B) he did not/(C) tell us that how/(D) he solved the problem/(E) No error.

5. A. We never thought/(B) that Mahesh is/(C) oldest than the other/(D) players in the team/(E) No error.

Directions (6-10) : *Pick out the most effective word from the given words to fill in the blank to make the sentence meaningfully complete.*

6. The lights .... just as we sat down to watch the movie on television.
A. went off   B. shut out
C. put out   D. blew down
E. gone off

7. The villagers have not .... over the shock of losing everything in the earthquake.
A. got   B. made
C. forgotten   D. freed
E. felt

8. Since Vivek stays far away from our place, we do not meet each other ....
A. rarely   B. shortly
C. timely   D. frequently
E. momentarily

9. Since the priest did not arrive in time, the ceremony was .... late.
A. beings   B. begun
C. began   D. beginning
E. begin

10. He succeeded in getting possession .... his land after a long court case.
A. to   B. against
C. of   D. with
E. for

Directions (11-20) : *Read the following passage carefully and answer the questions given below it. Certain words/phrases are printed in italic to help you locate them while answering some of the questions.*

Morning and afternoon, all the young girls and maidens used to *gather* around the village well with their water pots. There they exchanged pleasantries, chatted and discussed. Lakshmi was the prettiest girl at the well. But, she was an orphan.

One day, a well built man came to Lakshmi's house. He brought with him the richest clothes and jewels as presents for her. "I am your dead father's brother", he told the astonished girl. "You have not seen me before because I have been staying abroad. You must come and live with me now." Lakshmi believed his sweet words and in a short time, locked up her little house and set out with the man.

But a terrible surprise was in store for poor Lakshmi when she got to her new found uncle's home. The man locked her in a room. "I am not your uncle, but a robber. And I am going to marry you," he told her, Lakshmi howled and wept when she heard this. Saying he would be back in a day or two after making arrangements for the wedding, the man went away. Lakshmi continued sobbing for a while and then stopped. "I must think of a plan to escape," she told herself. Lakshmi guessed that the robber would try to enter her room. So she kept near her bed a sharp krife which she could find in the room.

One night the robber did enter her room but Lakshmi did not make any sound. She just kept a tight hold of the knife and pretended to be sound asleep. When the robber was near her bed, she stood up suddenly, brandishing the knife. The robber was taken aback and with a loud cry, he ranout. Lakshmi *gave chase* and he climbed up the nearest tall tree. Lakshmi then gathered some dry twigs and sticks around the foot of the tree and set them on fire. On seeing the rising flames, the robber gave a mighty yell and jumped down. But it was such a long way to the ground that he broke a couple of bones and was unable to move away from the place he fell.

In the meantime, the police was informed by someone about the robber. Very soon they reached the spot and arrested the robber. The people who had gathered at the spot were all praise for Lakshmi's courage and presence of mind.

11. Which of the following is most nearly the SAME in meaning as the phrase, *gave chase* as used in the passage ?

A. escaped   B. continued
C. followed   D. prevented
E. raced

12. The reason given by the man for his inability to meet Lakshmi earlier was that :

A. he was not knowing where she lived.

B. he was not in friendly terms with her father.

C.   he was living in a foreign country.
D.   he was not sure whether she would recognise him.
E.   he was staying in another village, for away from her place.

13. Why did Lakshmi go with the man ?
A.   She was convinced that the man was her uncle.
B.   She wanted to accompany him and then get him arrested by the police
C.   She intended to teach him a good lesson.
D.   She wanted the man to marry her.
E.   She felt it necessary to verify his claim by accompanying him.

14. How was the robber injured ?
A.   Lakshmi stabbed him with the sharp knife.
B.   He fell down accidentally while climbing the tree.
C.   He was beaten by Lakshmi and his bones were broken.
D.   He jumped down from the tree to save his life.
E.   He got burnt in the rising flames.

15. Why did the robber run out of the room ?
A.   He was stabbed by Lakshmi.
B.   He got scared of the rising flames.
C.   Lakshmi told him to go out as fast as possible.
D.   He was afraid that Lakshmi would strike him with the knife.
E.   He ran out to catch hold of Lakshmi and bring her back.

16. Which of the following is *True* in the context of the passage ?
A.   Lakshmi told the robber to climb up the tall tree.

B.   At night, the robber entered Lakshmi's room with a knife.
C.   Lakshmi had no near relatives and she stayed alone.
D.   The robber started running after jumping from the tree.
E.   The people who had gathereed at the spot set fire to the tree.

17. Which of the following is most OPPOSITE in meaning of the word 'gather' as used in the passage ?
A. collect   B. reduce
C. distribute   D. break
E. disperse

18. Which of the following statements is *Not True* in the context of the passage ?
A.   The police was summoned by Lakshmi herself.
B.   The well built man was not the real brother of Lakshmi's father.
C.   When the robber entered the room at night, Lakshmi was awake.
D.   Lakshmi used to go to the village well to collect water.
E.   Lakshmi's guess regarding the robber turned out to be correct.

19. "But a terrible surprise was in store _______ uncle's home". What is the "terrible surprise" that is being referred to ?
A.   The man told her that her father was dead.
B.   The man refused to marry her.
C.   The man took away her ornaments and locked her in a room.
D.   The man told her that he was her real uncle.

E. The man turned out to be a robber interested in marrying her.

20. Where did the robber apparently go after locking up Lakshmi ?

A. He went to her house to loot all the things.

B. He went out to bring a sharp knife.

C. He went away to bring clothes and jewels for her.

D. He went away to make preparations for his marriage.

E. He went out to bring the priest for performing the wedding ceremony.

Directions (21-25) : *Rearrange the following six sentences a, b, c, d, e and f in the proper sequence so as to form a meaningful paragraph; then answer the questions given below them :*

a. A taxi was summoned and Venu was taken to Lifeline Hospital.

b. While hurrying home from school, Venu was hit by a car.

c. Since they did not succeed, they decided to take him to a hospital.

d. When Venu opened his eyes, he found himself surrounded by doctors and nurses.

e. Some people rushed towards him and tried to bring him to his senses.

f. He was thrown a couple of feet away and lost consciousness.

21. Which sentence should come LAST (*i.e.* sixth) in the paragraph ?

A. b   B. c   C. a
D. d   E. e

22. Which sentence should come FIRST in the paragraph ?

A. d   B. f   C. b
D. e   E. c

23. Which sentence should come SECOND in the paragraph ?

A. e   B. a   C. d
D. c   E. f

24. Which sentence should come THIRD in the paragraph ?

A. f   B. b   C. e
D. a   E. d

25. Which sentence should come FOURTH in the paragraph ?

A. c   B. e   C. f
D. b   E. a

Directions (26-30) : *In each of the following questions, six words are given which are denoted by a, b, c, d, e and f. By using all the six words, each only once, you have to frame a meaningful and grammatically correct sentence. The correct order of the words is your answer. Choose from the five alternatives the one having the correct order of words.*

26. a. the   b. near
     c. theatre   d. met
     e. they   f. him

A. edafbc   B. bacfed
C. fbaced   D. bedacdf
E. edfbac

27. a. there   b. while
     c. he   d. sick
     e. fell   f. staying

A. cfabed   B. bfaced
C. caebfd   D. bcfaed
E. afbced

28. a. on   b. keep
     c. table   d. the
     e. things   f. those

A. afcbde   B. bdeafc
C. dcbafe   D. bfcadc
E. debafc

29.	a. playing	b. students		30.	a. seen	b. to
	c. many	d. seen			c. talking	d. he
	e. were	f. football			e. somebody	f. was
	A. cebdaf	B. bedacf			A. efadcb	B. dfcbea
	C. cbedaf	D. bafedc			C. dafcbe	D. dfacbe
	E. beadcf				E. efacbd	

EXPLANATORY ANSWERS

1. **E** : The answer is correct.
2. **A** : 'not to tell' to appears in place of 'not tell to'.
3. **B** : 'get up' to come in place of 'got up' because after 'did' usually the 1st form of Verb is applicable.
4. **C** : Remove 'that' before 'how'.
5. **C** : 'Oldest of all the other' should come in place of Oldest than the other.

6	7	8	9	10	11	12	13	14	15
A	A	D	B	C	C	C	A	D	D
16	17	18	19	20	21	22	23	24	25
C	E	A	E	D	D	C	E	C	A
26	27	28	29	30					
E	B	D	C	D					

PAPER - 2

Directions (1-10) : *In each of the questions you will find a word followed by four alternative words. You will have to find out alternatives, the word which means the same as the first word.*

1. DESTRUCTION
A. restoration   B. ruin
C. renovation   D. replacement

2. LENIENT
A. cruel   B. rough
C. kind   D. harsh

3. ROBUST
A. weak   B. useless
C. able   D. stupid

4. GENUINE
A. correction   B. germinate
C. separate   D. proper

5. IRRELEVANT
A. irregular   B. illegible
C. not connected   D. immature

6. GENERATE
A. prefer   B. pace
C. command   D. produce

7. LATENT
A. hand   B. concealed
C. visible   D. display

8. ACUTE
A. rice   B. accidental
C. sever   D. curious

9. PLEASURE
A. happiness
B. disappointment
C. grief
D. anxiety

10. RIVAL
A. friend   B. partner
C. associate   D. opponent

Directions (11-20) : *In the sentences given below the italicised words are grammatically incorrect. You will have to correct them. Following each sentence, there are four possible corrections, only one of which will correctly replace the incorrect part of the sentence. For each incorrect sentence choose the correct word.*

11. I have full confidence *on* you.
A. over   B. with
C. in   D. towards

12. There is no alternative *of* the plan.
A. to   B. for
C. towards   D. against

13. She is very much fond *for* music
A. of   B. towards
C. at   D. with

14. Ram could not go to school *for* fever
A. on account of   B. for
C. on   D. because

15. He should not have told this *at* his face.
A. in   B. on
C. to   D. before

16. A man who does not stick *at* his principles can never prosper.
A. in   B. with
C. to   D. into

92

17. I have no interest *of* cinema.
A. at   B. about
C. for   D. in

18. He has no faith *on* you.
A. over   B. at
C. towards   D. in

19. He has no ambition *of* learning.
A. about   B. for
C. towards   D. to

20. He has a passion *of* music
A. with   B. for
C. to   D. on

Directions (21-30) : *In each question here five words (marked as A, B, C, D and E) are given. Of these five words only one has been wrongly spelt. Find out correct word.*

21. A. Regiment   B. Enunciate
     C. Envelope   D. Marvell
     E. Materialism

22. A. Allmighty
     B. Ballot
     C. Desend
     D. Compartment
     E. Allocate

23. A. Gallon   B. Idiom
     C. Interfere   D. Sovereign
     E. Fillament

24. A. Ballon   B. Obsolete
     C. Stumble   D. Deliberate
     E. Forestall

25. A. Begining   B. Inject
     C. Gleaming   D. Optimism
     E. National

26. A. Mechanic   B. Shackel
     C. Pneumonia   D. Rumble
     E. Synthesis

27. A. Unwholesome
     B. Erchant
     C. Memoir
     D. Galary
     E. Unwining

28. A. Pretending
     B. Unpronounceable
     C. Comissionors
     D. Patience
     E. Allure

29. A. Topsyturvy   B. Varsetile
     C. Salvage   D. Segregate
     E. Jealous

30. A. Toothache   B. Spurious
     C. Insuportable   D. Courage
     E. Oppressive

Directions (31-40) : *Here you will have to spot errors in sentences. Read each sentence to find out whether there is any error in any of the under lined parts. If you find that there is an error in an underlined part of the sentence, note the index of the underlined part (i.e., A or B or C or D).*

31. (A)/In the high school girls often do/(B) as good as boys,/(C) if not better/(D) than the boys./(E) No error

32. (A)/The Selection Board will call only/(B) those candidates/(C) whom have the/(D) proper qualifications./(E) No error

33. (A)/Due to the explosion/(B) the walls/(C) bursted apart and the roof/(D) was blown off./(E) No error.

34. (A)/No employee are permitted to/ (B) act on behalf of the company/ (C) in financial/(D) matters./(E) No error

35. (A)/The authorities states that the students/(B) are responsible for the/(C) lack of discipline in/(D) the colleges./(E) No error.

36. (A)/We are fortunate in/(B) being able to visit Puri because there/(C) is many who cannot/(D) go there./ (E) No error.

37. (A)/If a man joins a post and do not work/(B) he is asked/(C) to resign/(D) the post./(E) No error.

38. (A)/There will be increased emphasis /(B) on heavy industry/ (C) in the seventh five year/(D) plan./(E) No error.

39. (A)/Us may/(B) stay in Darjeeling/ (C) until the monsoon/(D) starts./ (E) No error.

40. (A)/After Independence many people have/(B) say many things/ (C) about the/ (D) national language./(E) No error.

Directions (41-45) : *Read the passage carefully and answer the related questions.*

Aldinga reef is a watery paradise, a teeming sea jungle, a happy hunting ground for under-water spear-fisherman like myself. Forty of us each in black rubber suit and flippers, glasswindowed face mask and spear-fishing gun were waiting for the reference's nine O'clock whistle to announce that the annual South Australian skin diving and spear-fishing championship competition has begun. Each of us would have five hours to bring into the judge the biggest bag, reckoned both by total weight and by number of different species of fish. My own chances looked good. I have owned the 1961-62 championship and I had been runner-up the next session. I had promised Kay that this would be my last competition. I meant to clinch to the title and then retire in glory, diving thenceforth only for fun, when Kay and I might both want to.

Lesser sharks—like the Bronze whaler and Grey nurse—are familiar to skin divers and have not proved aggressive. Fortunately the dreaded white hunter or 'white death' sharks, caught by professional fisherman in the open ocean, are rarely seen by the skin divers. But as a precaution two high powered patrol boats criss-crossed our hunting area keeping a wary lookout.

41. To protect the skin divers from the 'white death' the authority :

A. took no measure at all.

B. provided them with the safety measures such as glass mask, black rubber suit and spear-fishing gun.

C. provided patrol boats for searching the place and protecting them.

D. arranged the competition in such an area of the sea where the' white deaths' are rarely seen.

42. The competitors were evaluated in terms of the :

A. amount of time spent under the water.

B. number of sharks killed.
C. total weight and number of different types of fishes.
D. number of fishes caught.

43. The author was so optimistic about his success due to the fact that :
A. he was a good swimmer.
B. he was a good sportsman.
C. he was one of the competitors of South Australian skin diving and spear-fishing championship.
D. he won championship last year and was runner-up for the next session.

44. Aldinga reef is a paradise for those who :
A. love to take bath in the sea.
B. love swimming.
C. like spear-fishing in underground water.
D. like to contest for the skin diving championship.

45. The most suitable title for the passage would be :
A. Dangers under the sea.
B. Shark and the swimmer.
C. Story about spear-fishing championship.
D. None of these.

EXPLANATORY ANSWERS

1	2	3	4	5	6	7	8	9	10
B	C	C	D	C	D	B	C	A	D

11	12	13	14	15	16	17	18	19	20
C	A	A	A	B	C	D	D	B	B

21. D : The correct word is : 'Marvel'

22. A : The correct word is : 'Almighty'

23. E : The correct word is : 'Filament'

24. A : The correct word is : 'Balloon'

25. A : The correct word is : 'Beginning'

26. B : The correct word is : 'Shackle'

27. E : The correct word is : 'Unwinning'

28. C : The correct word is : 'Commissioners'

29. B : The correct word is : 'Versatile'

30. C : The correct word is : 'Insupportable'

31. B : Replace 'as good as' with 'as well as'.

32. C : Replace 'Whom' with 'who'.

33. C : Replace 'bursted' with 'burst'.

34. A : Replace 'are' with 'is' because 'No employee' in Singular.
35. A : Replace 'states' with 'state'.
36. C : Replace 'is' with 'are'.
37. A : Replace 'do not' with 'does not' because 'man' in Singular.
38. A : 'will be' should be followed by 'an'.
39. A : 'us' should be replaced by 'we'.
40. B : 'say' should be replaced by 'said'.

———————